MW00654514

Aspects *of my* Pilgrimage

An Autobiography

James Earl Massey

Published by Anderson University Press
Anderson University, 1100 East Fifth Street
Anderson, Indiana 46012 U.S.A.

Project Editor, Barry L. Callen.
Cover Design by Kerry Shaw.
Interior layout and design by Virginia L. Wachenschwanz
      and Randal Dillinger.

For information, write to the Editor, Dr. Barry L. Callen, c/o Anderson
University, 1100 East Fifth Street, Anderson, Indiana 46012. E-mail:
blcallen@anderson.edu. For additional titles available from Anderson
University Press, consult the web site at www.anderson.edu/aupress.

Inventory and sales are handled through Warner Press, Anderson, Indiana.
To order this or other Anderson University Press books, contact Warner
Press, specifying that you wish to order a product of Anderson University
Press (Warner Press inventory numbers for this and other books are found on
the Anderson University Press web site, www.anderson.edu/aupress). Bulk
orders (ten or more copies) are available at discount. Contact Dr. Callen at
Anderson University (not Warner Press).

Printed in the United States of America.

TABLE OF CONTENTS

FOREWORD

Seldom am I one to mention my personal experiences except when trying to illumine some message in a speech or writing. So I felt a bit awkward at some points while writing this autobiography. I have written it nevertheless, and for good reasons. I have written: To pay tribute to the grand heritage that informed me, and to the good persons who influenced me; To mention some of the individuals, groups, organizations, and institutions whose openness to me allowed, encouraged, and enhanced what I tried to do in response to my times; and To glorify God, who entrusted a life to me, and who granted timely guidance as I sought to honor that trust.

Thus, I offer this autobiography with its sometimes self-conscious treatment of selected aspects of my pilgrimage. I have tried to do justice in this story to the people, the facts, and the happenings in my life as I viewed and understood them at the time. Where the record appeared to require it, I have been unsparing with details.

As will be seen, this is at many points a corporate story because of my long relationship with several institutions. Chief among them is the Metropolitan Church of God in Detroit, Michigan. The charter members of that congregation and I bonded with such affinity and affection that we became life partners in pilgrimage and work. While my telling of our corporate story here focuses mainly on my aims and actions as their founding pastor, the congregational life is always in the background, granting depth and dimension to the account.

These pages report relationships and interactions I have been privileged to have with many other significant persons, groups, and institutions across more than fifty years of service as a minister and educator. In addition to my relations with several agencies of the Church of God (Anderson, Indiana), I have reported my relations with the general religious world and with the educational scene in America, especially with the two

4

educational institutions with which I have been chiefly and proudly associated, Anderson University and Tuskegee University.

I have not written this story from memory alone. I was aided throughout these pages by many records and resources, among them a personal diary whose journal entries date back to my teenage years when I began writing notes to myself as a way to reflect on my experiences. Across the years my journaling has helped me to assess the character and effects of happenings in my life. This book, then, has been informed, coordinated, and shaped in relation to my journals, with help from letters, official records, and other personal papers. All of this makes this auto-biography an admittedly selective accounting, thus I have used the word "aspects" as part of its title.

I am especially indebted to two persons whose help during my preparation of this account was necessary, strategic, and timely. One is my longtime friend Barry L. Callen, University Professor of Christian Studies at Anderson University, who as Editor of Anderson University Press oversaw the process that readied this book for publication. The other is my wife Gwendolyn Inez (Kilpatrick), my devoted partner in this story across more than fifty years. Gwendolyn initially wondered whether I might be writing my story too soon, but she finally agreed that I could tell it now, insisting strongly that I must report not only the sunshine experiences but also the dark, cold days when the icicles of trouble made me shiver—and to con-fess that I did shiver. Her love and trust were warming factors as we lived through all those times, and I am deeply grateful for her companionship.

"The Outback"
Greensboro, Alabama
Summer, 2002
JAMES EARL MASSEY

To my brothers:

George Wilson Massey, Jr.,

Melvin Mavis Massey,

whose pilgrimage began before mine;

and in memory of:

Howard William Massey
(1939-1976),

Raymond Lee Massey,
(1926-2002)

who reached The End first.

ROOTS IN
HOME AND CHURCH

On January 3, 1930, a Friday night, a saintly widow walked hurriedly toward the Massey house. Choir rehearsal had just ended at the Wisconsin Avenue Church of God, four blocks away. While singing, she suddenly felt an urge to see how her friend Elizabeth Massey was doing as she neared the end of a troublesome pregnancy.

The widow's anxieties were partly eased when she neared the house and saw no light at any of the front windows. Assuming that all was well inside the house, she turned and went on home, two blocks further. Her feeling of concern had deepened by morning, however, and at noon on Saturday she obeyed the impulse to go again to look in on her long-time friend and fellow choir member.

Her steps were divinely ordered, because when widow Nettie Brown finished trudging through two blocks of snow and reached the Massey house, Elizabeth Massey was in severe distress. The birth time for the expected child had come, but the child was not rightly positioned for a normal entrance into the world. Nettie Brown's rap at the door was well-timed. George Wilson Massey, Sr., had just left the house, on his way to a nearby grocery store two blocks away to telephone the family doctor about the crisis.

Upon entering the house, Nettie Brown acted with insight and dispatch. Using the skills she had gained as a midwife, she took hold of the one foot she saw protruding, located the other foot, gave a needed turn to the rest of the child's body, and

7

assisted the delivery process. When Doctor Henderson arrived, the birth crisis had been brought under management and the child was breathing on his own.

I was that child, and that is the story my mother related to me years later about my birth on Saturday afternoon, January 4, 1930. A godly widow's timely obedience to a prompting from God became my ticket into life. That obedience put the right person at the needed place at just the right time and with the right skills. Except for the sensitivity and obedience to God of Nettie Brown, there would be none of the story that unfolds in the pages that follow.

I have thought long and often about the details surrounding my birth, but I have done so because I continue to see something more in the story than the mere fact of a birth. The story has sensitized me to the value of ordered steps, to the reality of divine guidance, and to the sobering fact that a person's obedience (or disobedience) to God can sometimes be a death or life issue for someone else. This understanding has never been far from my thought, and across the years it has kept me sensible about private planning for my life. I learned early that so much in life depends upon ordered, obedient steps.

The Arena of Home

My father, George Wilson Massey, Sr., was thirty-three years old when I entered the family circle. Born on December 8, 1897, in Bessemer, Alabama, he was the only child born to Bettie Sue (Wilson) and Sanford Massey. Bettie Sue grew progressively ill after his birth and died three months later. During the brief time of her sickness George was cared for by Bettie Sue's older sister, Amanda Idell Coleman, who, after Bettie's death, adopted and raised him with her own two young children, Emma Australia and John Walter Coleman. Thus it was that my father, a Massey, came to be one of Amanda (Wilson) Coleman's children, and thus it was that we, his children, grew up relating affectionately to her as our Grandmother rather than our Grand Aunt. There was no difference made in the Coleman household between the other children and my father as adopted son. They were all descendants within the Wilson line, grandchildren of Ed and Caroline Wilson, they through Amanda, their bloodmother, and George through Bettie Sue, their blood aunt. My father thus grew up in Bessemer not only as brother to Emma Australia and John Walter Coleman, who were near him in age, but also to Ruth, Philip, Salome, and Naomi, who were born to Amanda during her marriage with George Abernathy after her husband Johnny Ed Coleman died.

My father served in the United States Army. He had enlisted in early 1918. Anticipating that he would be drafted, he joined up "for the duration of the war," which did not last very long after all. He was sent first to Fort Thomas, Kentucky, and thereafter to Fort Huachuca, Arizona, where he completed basic training and was assigned to the famed Tenth Cavalry, Machine Gun Troop, Section 3. There are several pictures in the family photograph album of George Wilson Massey in his uniform, "proud as a peacock." The pride was partly that of a uniform, but was mainly due to his esteemed outfit.

The Tenth Cavalry was a famed unit, one of four black regiments at the time. The all-black regiment had once been led by John J. Pershing. Its officers and soldiers had distinguished themselves by bravery and loyalty despite the paradox of being defenders of a nation that reluctantly used them and even subjected them sometimes to savage prejudices. The Tenth Cavalry had a good record as a fighting outfit, a well-trained defense unit, and my father was proud to be part of these "Black Regulars," as they were called. I remember hearing my father talk to us now and again about his army service period, about serving on patrol along the Mexican border during the time of the exploits of Mexico's Pancho Villa. Villa had supported Venustiano Carranza in his fight to free Mexico from President Huerta's oppressive government, but he finally turned against him when Carranza gained power. When Villa was defeated in a major battle at Celaya, he retreated to nurse his wounds and recoup his losses and blamed his defeat on the help the United States had given his opponents. He promised revenge and raided American territory along the border at New Mexico. The Tenth Cavalry was part of a military force sent to deal with him, and what became a punitive expedition against him was led by Brigadier General John J. Pershing. Many blacks were killed during the routing clashes, but their heroism in battle added to the praise and pride already enjoyed by that regiment. My father was not in any of those battles along the border, nor across the border in Mexico, but he did see service as part of the regular patrols along that border. He delighted in telling us that he had qualified as a marksman with his Colt 45, and held Private First Class rank.

Army service at that stage of my father's life offered a kind of security. Like many black men at that time of change in a South suffering from a mass exodus of blacks and whites to the industrialized North, he considered the army as a good place within which to better his circumstances. His reasons for enlisting were several, including to meet his financial needs as a young man wanting to be on his own, to fulfill a desire to see other parts of the nation, to deal with his anticipation that he was about to be drafted into military service, and because of an agreement with three close friends who wished to remain together. George Wilson Massey and his three close friends had reached that age when opportunities for blacks in the South seemed too few, yet they felt the greater demands upon them to contribute to family upkeep and demonstrate independence. My father viewed army service as a wise choice at the time. He was twenty years old when he enlisted.

The regimented army life braced his spirit and added to the already disciplined approach to life he had gained as one of Amanda's children. Intelligent, literate, and industrious, he sought to excel. He was hailed as one of the best boxers on the army post, boxing being a sport that he considered "clean and wholesome," and he gained honors both in marksmanship and in horseback-riding. It was with considerable pride that I used to look at the medals and ribbons he had been awarded and had preserved from his army service. My father spent most of his brief army service time at Fort Huachuca. He was honorably discharged in 1919 at Hattiesburg, Mississippi, and went from there to Detroit, Michigan, joining with Amanda and other family members who had moved there from Bessemer, Alabama, in June of 1917.

According to my father, he experienced Christian conversion in Detroit, Michigan, in 1920, the year after he was discharged. It happened during a Sunday service of worship at the Church of God of Detroit, located at Chene and Jay Streets. This congregation was associated with the Church of God Reformation Movement that had arisen in the late nineteenth century and was dedicated to Christian holiness and unity. Daniel Felix Oden had preached that day of father's conversion. After pastoring in Bessemer for many years, Oden had answered the call from a growing number of his former parishioners, now living and working in Detroit, to come there and pastor them. Daniel Oden and John Richards baptized my father in the Detroit River, out at a beach on Belle Isle. Sometime later, following a call to ministry, my father would work under both Oden and Richards as a local minister. He would serve as Richards' assistant pastor at the Wisconsin Avenue Church of God, located in the Eight Mile Road Area of northwest Detroit.

In August, 1921, while attending a camp meeting of the National Association of the Church of God at West Middlesex, Pennsylvania, George Wilson Massey, then twenty-four years old, met Elizabeth Shelton, a bright and beautiful eighteen-year-old who was there with her older married sister Mary Shelton Kelem, and with whom she was then living in Fairmount, West Virginia. George and Elizabeth afterward wrote to each other, courting by mail, and they were married two years later on February 14, 1923, in Fairmount. The two had a brief honeymoon in Canada, after which they located in Detroit, where George was employed at a local manufacturing company. Always the steady and indefatigable worker, intent to

11

make things better for himself and his own, for a time he took on another shift, working at a lumber yard, to increase his earnings. Living as they were with William and Artelia Powell, Elizabeth's first cousin, in their house in the Hamtramck section of Detroit, George was projecting and planning for a house of their own.

Through Rufus Dennis, a real estate agent and fellow member of the Church of God of Detroit, George Massey learned about a newly developing area out in Royal Oak Township, just across the Eight Mile Road boundary of North Detroit, in Ferndale, Michigan. After visiting the area he bought a 47 x 102 feet corner lot on Glenlodge Street at Cloverdale. He engaged John Echols, a local black builder, and they made beginning plans for a house. The agreement was that the builder would complete all the outside and first floor work, but that the upstairs should be completed across time, as money would allow—there being no bank loans available to blacks building in that section. Meanwhile, on November 23, 1923, George, Jr., the first addition to the Massey family, was born there in Hamtramck. George and Elizabeth moved with their new son into their new house in Ferndale in late September of 1924. It was a rather modest wood frame building, but the corner lot, which had cost only $825, was a choice spot for raising a family. There was a grade school just across the street from the house on the opposite corner, and the other neighbors had erected their houses with evident pride and care. It was in that house at 312 Glenlodge Street that the other four Massey sons were all born (Raymond, Melvin, James, and Howard), and it was with that house that our lives were steadily involved until we each grew up and moved out. Even after moving out on our own, that residence continued to serve us all as a place for family renewal until my father and mother sold it in their retirement years and moved into an apartment building for senior citizens in downtown Detroit.

Although my father could trace his family line back as far as the grandparents on his mother's side, the Wilsons, my mother had known only her mother and father, Clorie and Zack Shelton. My mother was born to them in 1903 in Greensboro, Alabama, a town just a few miles from Zack's hometown of Newbern. Elizabeth was the second of four children from the Shelton union, with her sister Helen as the first, and Edmond and James being third and fourth. This was Clorie's second set of children. Four others had been born to her earlier while wife of Alexander Williams, Jr., who died. Elizabeth, Helen, Edmond and James Shelton thus grew up with Ezell, Albert, Timothy and John Caesar Williams, their stepbrothers.

Both my father and mother were native Alabamians, as were my mother's parents and my father's mother. My father's father, it is believed, was originally from North Carolina. My father was rather serious in his way of going about things, informed by some deep-seated convictions which he did not mind sharing. After we were older, he mellowed more, probably feeling less pressure due to our apparent growth in understanding and regard for what he considered the best for his children. But all the while we were growing up we knew that his word was to be obeyed and that any deviation from his directives would not go unnoticed or unpunished.

Growing up just across the street from the neighborhood grade school and its much-used playground put us right in the path of a constant coming and going of other youths, some of whom were not viewed by my father as worthy of our company and attention because of how they sometimes disported themselves. Always concerned that his sons not fail their home training and embarrass him as a minister and active community leader, my father was sometimes overly protective of us as far as our friends and daily companions were concerned.

I remember that time when my mother, suffering again from nervous exhaustion, was away from the house, being cared for by Artelia Powell, her cousin, in Hamtramck. My mother's condition demanded a quieter setting than she had at the house with us boys, so the Powells had received her into their home for the time needed for her recovery. Getting ready to drive over from Ferndale one summer afternoon to visit her in Hamtramck, my father called Raymond, Melvin, and me into the family living room and gave us some strongly-put instructions on the behavior he expected on our part until he returned that night. Finally, we were told not to leave the house. We listened, but with the ears and wandering minds of children. Assured that he had made his point with us, Daddy left, driving off in the family car. We three stood at one of the windows and watched him drive away.

It was not long before the summer heat made us uncomfortable inside the house; the air was not circulating sufficiently despite the screened front door and windows. The gaiety in the voices of other children playing on the school lawn just across the street didn't make the discomfort any easier to manage, so we began talking about going outside on the porch. We did, and soon talked ourselves right on across the street to join in play with our other young friends. Unfortunately, Daddy found it necessary to return to the house for something—perhaps he had forgotten to carry with him something my mother had requested and he had come back to get it. Whatever my father's reason, Melvin recognized the car as it was passing near us and he hurriedly called out to warn me. He and I almost froze in panic, but managed to make our legs respond and get us across the street, up the steps of the front porch, and back into the house. But too late! Daddy saw us as we raced in guilty haste. He promptly whipped Melvin and me.

Strangely, Daddy whipped Raymond too, although Raymond had not joined us in going across the street to the playground. He had only gone outside the door to stand on the shaded porch. But Daddy protested to Raymond that the instructions were not to go out of the house! That whipping affected Raymond quite deeply. Taking the afternoon heat into account, Raymond considered both the confining instructions and the whipping unfair. His antagonism lasted for several days. As I have thought back on that event, I am more and more confirmed in my judgment that it was the unfortunate result of

14

our father's overly-protective concern for us, a concern that was sometimes aggravated by my mother's absences from the house during periodic times of illness. Never robust or in full health after I was born, my mother had frequent bouts with nervousness and depression during my young years.

Like many other church-oriented parents of that time, my parents were eager to fulfill Paul's injunction regarding children, to "bring them up in the discipline and instruction of the Lord" (Eph. 6:4b). This concern made them bring into question any and all activities and personages in the community not in line with the behavioral codes of the family church. Most of the youngsters with whom we boys associated at school and in the neighborhood were either taken by their parents or allowed to go alone to see a movie; we Massey boys were not. To be sure, there were some wicked currents of life from which we needed to be protected, but my father's concern to guard us against such influences was sometimes heavy-handed, provoking us to the anger Paul mentioned as a possibility. George, Jr., oldest of the Massey boys, left home for a while after he became fifteen. He blamed his leaving on the anger Daddy stirred within him by his sometimes inflexible rules. George returned home some weeks later, however, chastened by some sad experiences from being hungry!

Once I thought about running away. I prepared a lunch for myself, hid it from view, and was waiting on two of my friends to come that night and join me in leaving home. I was ten at the time, and fed-up with so many restrictions. George, Raymond, and Melvin all had more liberties than I was allowed at my age. But I grew hungry between supper and darkness and, feeling famished, I ate the lunch I had stashed away—and decided, cowardly, to stay put!

My father's strong will not only showed itself in the home life he shaped for his growing sons, but also in the steadiness and strength of his will to be an achiever. While engaged as a foundry worker at Kendrick Manufacturing Company, he learned about a school in Chicago that offered correspondence studies to prepare one to be an electrician. Daddy enrolled in the course and kept up his studies until he felt ready to take the licensing exam administered by the State. He took the exam and passed it. Over time, he gained standing recognition in the city and state as a skilled and trustworthy licensed electrical contractor. He started his own business in the 1940s, "Massey's Electrical Service," and brought additional money home from his steady work schedule. He trained all of his sons in the trade, and he let us work with him. Working with my father kept me supplied with money during all my high school years and my first two years in college. During a lean time in the business, Daddy answered an ad from Ford Motor Company for an electrician; he was hired and held that job at the River Rouge plant until he retired.

My mother, Elizabeth, was also a strong-spirited person. Although her body underwent periodic need for prolonged rest, her mind was quite able and her inner resources were trustworthy. Together, because of a true love for each other, my mother and father developed a strong center of home life and gave a vibrant Christian witness in the community across many years. Between 1924 when they built their house in Ferndale, in the Royal Oak Township, and 1975 when their house was sold, vacated, and demolished under a community renewal project, the Eight Mile Road Community had seen in them the effects of a vital Christian faith and a responsible concern for family and others.

Reared like my father in a Christian home, my mother was like him in having a strong regard for the Scriptures. She and he led us in reading the Scriptures regularly, in studying them deeply, and in regarding them fully. My father had a good working knowledge of many biblical passages and their teachings, but his use of that knowledge was sometimes more dogmatic than necessary. My mother used the Scriptures devotionally, as the context for a conversation with God as she made her pilgrimage through life.

I cannot think about my parents and their teaching of the

Christian Scriptures to us without some emotion. As I was growing up, my father was often engaged as a supply preacher here and there among the congregations of the Church of God. Being with him on many of his preaching engagements allowed me to observe his readiness to interpret and apply the insights of the Bible. His ability to quote Scripture amazed me. But beyond this, I was sensing the charm of the world within the Scriptures and feeling the cutting edge of its truths. At times of Bible-reading in the home, and Bible exposition in Sunday School and Sunday morning worship, and during the mid-week prayer meetings at the church to which our family belonged, I found my imagination challenged by the Bible heroes and heroines in their experiences and exploits. Like the citizens of ancient Athens, who always honored and promoted the gods and heroes of their city-state, always telling stories to their sons to make them hope and work for that time when they too would be mighty ones in the nation's history, my father and mother acquainted us with the stories and statements of the Christian Scriptures, and they steadily encouraged us to accept and regard the meanings found in them.

Early on, the Bible so excited me that I decided to dedicate my life to understanding and spreading the revealing message of hope its books present and preserve. Across the years that many-splendored message has been relevant to my heart, mind, and life. It has given needed comfort when my heart was hurting. Its lifting power has kept me steady when my health was under assault, and its rays of light have calmed me when my path was dim and my mind baffled.

The reassuring encouragement of Scripture was a large part of my mother's stability of mind and life across her years of physical illness. The Scriptures gave her grounds for hope. Across many years her lungs were weak and her resistance to certain barometric pressures was lowered by increasing life circumstance, but she held on to hope, realizing that she did not need to despair. That hope was nurtured at times by certain radio broadcasts to which she regularly listened. I recall

17

her fondness for the sermons of Dr. Merton S. Rice that were broadcast from his Metropolitan Methodist Church there on Woodward Avenue. Dr. Rice was considered one of the nation's greatest preachers, and my mother loved to hear him. I sometimes listened with her when she tuned in on those broadcasts, and there was an openness on her part that deeply impressed me. She was wise enough to know that the Word of God is not a denominational treasure, but a gift given to the entire church. She recognized evidences of God's touch upon a life wherever she found it, and she recognized the touch clearly in those like Dr. Merton S. Rice who spoke for God in a manner and spirit that transcended denominational lines. If there has been an ecumenical flavor in my own life, it is due in some measure to the openness I saw exemplified in my mother's life to the ministry of Christian leaders who were not of our particular church group.

I was never privileged to meet and know my mother's father, Zack Shelton. He died during her childhood years in Greensboro, Alabama, where she was born, but I did get to meet her mother Clorie. It was during a trip our family made to Alabama in 1932. I was only two years old at the time and I cannot remember much about the visit or specific details surrounding the trip. I later met my mother's sister Helen during a visit to West Virginia where she was living with her husband and family of three children. I had occasions to know Uncle Edmond and Uncle James more intimately because they moved north and lived in Detroit for several years. Of my mother's four stepbrothers, I only got to know Uncle Ezell and Uncle John Caesar. Our family sometimes visited Uncle Ezell and his family at their home in Chicago, and I saw Uncle John Caesar regularly after August of 1936 when he came to Detroit to visit my mother during one of her times of illness. He found a job while there and had his wife and family come from Greensboro, Alabama, to join him. I got to know Uncle Johnny quite well because he roomed at the house with us until he relocated in preparation for the coming of his family.

18

My memories of Grandma Amanda, my father's mother, are many, quite vivid, and precious because we had so many occasions for a treasured closeness across my childhood, youth, and adult life. Grandma Amanda had special graces and gifts for relating. Hers was the lofty role of the African-American grandmother, and she fulfilled that role as a focal figure of love, stability, and sharing down to the day of her death at ninety. She was the one around whom all the Wilson descendants gathered in high regard and trust. By the time I got to know Grandma Amanda she was a wife for the fourth time. She had been widowed three times, and after being Mrs. Coleman (mothering two), then Mrs. Abernathy (mothering four more), and Mrs. Noble (with no additional births), she was next Mrs. Townsend, wife of Collins Townsend, a minister who had come to Detroit, Michigan, from Oklahoma. Collins Townsend was the only grandfather I knew, and we children affectionately called him Grandpa Townsend. He had a characteristic way of addressing me whenever we saw each other. He would always ask, "And how are you, little man!" That greeting always made me feel a bit taller and more adult.

Amanda Townsend epitomized the social pattern and spiritual values that gave our larger family group its unity and support base. Her house at 2144 Mullett Street on Detroit's lower East Side was a favorite spot in the life of the Wilson clan. During our visits to her house it was not unusual for my father to meet her other sons and daughters, even if there was nothing special to bring them there, like a birthday occasion or other family-gathering event. I benefited greatly from the attentive way Grandma Amanda related to the younger ones. It was from her that I gained encouragement to start and develop a garden. I was nine years old when I expressed a desire to have a garden after seeing the garden she tended in the backyard of her house. She told me how to get started. She afterward came out to our Ferndale home to inspect the growth in the garden I started in the side yard of our property. Proud of my progress in handling the garden, I briefly thought I should become a farmer!

Grandma Amanda was an even greater help to me after I became seriously open to God and announced my call to the ministry. Her no-nonsense bearing, coupled with a native warmth and openness to others, provided a grand model of how holiness and humanity rightly relate. Grandpa Townsend died in 1947, a year after I had publicly acknowledged my call to the ministry, so he did not live to see me in a ministerial role. Grandma Townsend did. She lived long enough to see me established in ministry, and it was my honored privilege to be her pastor during the last decades of her life. It was always a strengthening sight to see her stepping along as worship was about to begin, rocking as she moved toward her favorite pew. During her last years her worship attendance was infrequent because of the arthritis that so often made it frightfully painful for her to walk. It was an ailment, I was later told, that followed the Wilson family line, and I saw its effects on Uncle John Walter, my aunts Australia and Ruth, and later on my father. Daddy lost the use of his legs just after turning eighty-four and he had to receive daily care in a nursing home. I ministered to my grandmother as she was dying and, despite my bereavement, I gave the eulogy at the funeral service held for her at our church.

The Fellowship of the Church

Although my father and mother and older brother George, Jr., had moved into their Eight Mile Road area home in late 1924, it was not until 1926 that they transferred their church membership from the Church of God of Detroit, usually referred to by its location as "The Chene and Jay Streets Church," to the now-closer sister congregation which met in the Eight Mile Road Community (on the Detroit side of the populous black district). For one thing, my father had been deeply involved in the life of the downtown church, serving on the board of trustees there, and after his call to the preaching ministry in 1925 he was "sitting under" Pastor Oden there, learning from that experienced leader. Another reason they did not transfer their membership right away was that the Chene and Jay Streets church was the mother church of the fellowship and Amanda Townsend was "second lady" in the congregation since she was the wife of Collins Townsend, associate minister to Daniel F. Oden. Grandpa Townsend was a highly regarded minister, and he was so much a part of the leadership scene at the church that he remained the associate pastor there until his death. When he died in 1947, Grandpa Townsend had served as associate pastor at the Church of God of Detroit with Daniel F. Oden, Charles A. White, J. D. Smoot, and Raymond S. Jackson.

There was still another reason my parents did not immediately transfer their church membership when they moved to Ferndale. The Church of God congregation in that area had had no settled leadership since it started in 1921, and my father preferred the setting and guidance available at the downtown church. The members met together in homes, but by 1924 they had erected a building, with support from Daniel F. Oden and John Richards. Within a year, Richards became the group's first pastor. The new building was located on Wisconsin Avenue at Chippewa, on the Detroit side of the Eight Mile Road Community. Our house was just four blocks away, on the Ferndale side of the community area. Since the entire area was known as The Eight Mile Road Community, the sister congregations in the metropolitan area began referring to the Wisconsin Avenue Church as "The Eight Mile Road Church."

In the early 1930s there were five sister congregations of the Church of God (Anderson, Indiana) in the Metropolitan Detroit area. There was The Church of God of Detroit downtown, the "mother church," the Palmerston Avenue Church of God in nearby River Rouge, the Goodrich Street Church of God in the northern section of Ferndale known as "The Nine-and-a Half Mile District" because that was the distance in miles it was from downtown Detroit, the Bethany Church of God located in east Detroit, and the Wisconsin Avenue Church which was the spiritual home I knew in my earliest years.

21

The Church of God of Detroit started in 1916 when black members of the Bethany Church began meeting together on the lower east side of the city to evangelize other blacks living there. The church located in River Rouge began in 1917. Both the Ferndale and Wisconsin Avenue churches began in the 1920s. Several other congregations of our communion were started in the metropolitan area later, but when I was a boy growing up in the Wisconsin Avenue Church all the people in the five congregations knew each other, and they sometimes gathered at the large sanctuary on Chene and Jay for special observances.

I especially remember the regard I saw people show my Grandmother when large meetings were held at the downtown church. I only later came to understand the reason for this: she and Collins Townsend were two of the "pillars" in the downtown Detroit church. They had given the first $100.00 during the building campaign through which the congregation erected its classic brick structure. More importantly, the mid-week services which helped to nurture the life of the congregation during its earliest growth were held in the living room of the Townsend's house. The members of all the churches knew them, and some of those persons, like the Robinsons, the Odens, and the Wilsons (Major and Bessie), had known Amanda and her family in Bessemer, Alabama, and were all fellow-members in the Mortimer Street Church of God there under D. F. Oden. Actually, some of the families in the mother church had come to Detroit not only to find new work opportunities, but to continue their long-term relationship with others who had moved there from Alabama. Further, the fact that their previous pastor was now serving the Detroit congregation gave them even greater incentive to make the move. There has been in my possession for many years a photograph of the congregation of the mother church as it was in July 1928. The photograph was taken by a Mr. Theus, a black photographer with studios located on Hastings Street. It shows hundreds of members standing together in symbolized oneness in front of the distin-

22

guished-looking brick church building at the Chene and Jay location. Although Pastor Oden and many other notables are a part of the congregational scene, I can never look at that photograph without fixing my attention on Grandma and Grandpa Townsend who are positioned, interestingly, right at its center!

The relationship between the Wisconsin Avenue Church and the congregation in River Rouge was especially strong because for many years John Richards served both simultaneously as pastor. As in church circuits in the South, he would give a Sunday morning at the one place and a Sunday afternoon or evening at the other, changing around each week. In Richards' absence, local ministers in the two churches took charge of the worship and preaching. Across several years my father served as John Richards' assistant pastor at the Wisconsin Avenue Church. He assisted with visitation of the sick and shut-ins and alternated with him in preaching more often than the other local ministers there, of whom there were several, both male and female. Our church tradition never made a distinction between the sexes where gifts for ministry are concerned. I became accustomed to seeing women ministers in the pulpit exercising their gifts of ministry with the same freedom as the men.

The opportunity to assist John Richards was part of the reason my father decided to transfer his membership from the Church of God of Detroit to the Eight Mile Road church. As a former member of the downtown church himself, Richards knew my father's family, and he knew that my father was one of the trustees as well as a trusted younger minister. It was a rather natural and expected response on his part when John Richards asked my father to come and serve with him at the Eight Mile Road church.

Having announced his call to preach in 1925, my father began earnest preparation for the task. The apprentice system was the customary method for ministerial training in our churches in those days, so my father "sat under" Pastor Daniel F. Oden to learn the message and methods for ministry. Being chosen later by John Richards as his assistant granted my father a grand opportunity for further involvement and learning. In time, he took several "Training For Service" courses being promoted widely in the Church of God at that time, and in the early 1930s he took classes at the Morehouse Institute of Greater Detroit, a Baptist school for ministers. Paul C. Cooley, a long-time friend and ministerial colleague, was a fellow student there with him. In 1938, while serving as John Richards' assistant, my father received his ordination. The service took place at the National Association Camp Ground of the Church of God at West Middlesex, Pennsylvania, during the annual camp meeting. Gabriel P. Dixon was also ordained in the same service.

The wooden frame church building on Wisconsin and Chippewa was rather small when compared with the downtown Detroit church my parents had known, but it offered adequate space for the group that met there during the earlier years. The membership of this church was less than one hundred until much later. The building was an open sanctuary, oblong in size. Outside, a set of stairs led up from the sidewalk to the front door that opened on Chippewa Street, and just inside the front door was a small vestibule where one could place coats, hats, umbrellas, and galoshes before entering the open sanctuary for seating. Each Sunday morning all the Masseys joined other members at the church for worship, except when my father was scheduled to preach for another congregation. Unless we were already there in the building for Sunday school, which preceded the worship hour, we would all leave home together in the family car, although we boys would sometimes be allowed to walk the short four blocks distance from the house, especially when we thought it too warm a day to be bunched in the family car.

Eleven o'clock on Sunday morning was a sacred hour for us, and all of the church's members and their families would usually be present for the worship service. We all knew when someone was sick, out of town, or had to work on Sunday.

Sunday work was rare for most of the members in those days. The Depression years were upon us, although there were some among us who held jobs as domestic workers and everyone understood when they sometimes had to miss one of the services because of special demands placed upon them. The church did not frown upon Sunday work because the very opportunity to be employed was a treasured blessing.

Several Sunday school classes met in the open sanctuary at 9:30 each Sunday morning. Given the rather small setting within the building, each class was located only a few feet from the others, which was usually problematic when a teacher or respondent became too demonstrative or loud, as it sometimes happened when the lesson was especially engaging. The classes always ended as they began, with a plenary session under the guiding voice of the general superintendent of the Sunday school.

Two of my most precious memories in connection with Sunday school as a boy at Wisconsin Avenue Church of God are of the winsome teaching done by the Rev. Mrs. Nora Harris and the caring attitude Mrs. Lucy Washington always showed as general superintendent in the plenary sessions before and after classes. I especially mention their winsomeness and warmth because, after experiencing the voices of authority across the week at home and at school, I was eager for some relief and difference when Sunday came around. I found that relief and difference in the spirit and manner of Nora Harris and Lucy Washington. Nora Harris was one of the local ministers at the church, which perhaps made me even more appreciative of the warmth she evidenced in dealing with us as growing selves. The Harrises were close friends of our family, and so were Nora's sister Lily Mae Jackson and her husband Charlie Jackson, who was head deacon at the time. The Harrises, Jacksons, and Masseys were often in and out of each other's homes. I took notice and never forgot the regard I felt when in their presence. I always was open to Mrs. Nora Harris when she taught and when she preached, sometimes alternating with my father in handling the worship on a Sunday when Pastor Richards was serving at the River Rouge church or elsewhere.

All of our church gatherings were held in that sanctuary. In addition to Sunday school classes, and Sunday morning and evening services, there was also the weekly Young People's Meeting held each Sunday at 6:00 P.M. The Wednesday night prayer meeting was held there too, as well as church business meetings, funerals, and weddings. That church building was a central arena of group life, and much of what went on there made a deep impression upon me.

Our congregation was a rather intimate circle of members. The adult members and church leaders were to me like parents and the younger members were all like sisters and brothers. Belonging to such a group helped me to sense the meaning of the unity theme that was often treated from the pulpit, and explained as one of the cardinal teachings of the Reformation Movement of which our church was representative. From an early age I was made aware of the Reformation Movement heritage of the God-given call for unity of believers and, because most of the members of our local group were Negroes, I was very aware of Black Church vitality. As for unity, our local group was an interracial fellowship. There were three white families in our church in those days, and the interaction and intimacy seemed natural. I grew up experiencing the impress of the unity ideal that Movement preachers regularly voiced to us, and feeling the vitality that such a vision made possible within those who were open to live by it. Early on, I saw that what is Afro-American can be in essential agreement with what is Anglo-Saxon when both traditions are informed by agape love, and I learned that what is best in both traditions always provides a creative context for spiritual vision and social learning.

My first pastor, John Richards, and his wife Beatrice were a rather contagious couple. Usually seeing them together, I cannot remember him without thinking about her as well. She looked a bit older than he, and only in my adult years did I learn that she was, although this was not a question that I could expect to ask my parents and have answered. Both he and she were of the "old school" in Reformation Movement concerns, which is to say that they were two Church of God ministers who, typical of the others, claimed a direct link between what they were seeking to do and what the first followers of Jesus were sent out to do following the Pentecost event. Their understanding of what the church is and is to do was drawn formally and fully from the first century model about which the Book of Acts reports. This means that, in all their preaching and teaching, John and Beatrice Richards pointed always to the primitive church as the basic reference group for doctrines, procedures, behavior, and traditions.

In hearing them preach I was acquainted with restorationist teachings, but particularly those two qualities considered basic by the earliest community of believers, namely Christian holiness (purity of life) and unity (experiential oneness of believers). The following news item, which appeared in print on page nine in the April 9, 1931, issue of The *Gospel Trumpet* (the weekly journal of the Movement), reflects the zealousness with which Richards sought to school and guide the congregation in the holiness and unity emphases. Written by Lily Mae Jackson, secretary for our local church, the report was as follows:

> We are glad to say in regard to our work, it is going forward in the strength of Christ. Our pastor, Bro. John Richards, of River Rouge, Mich., is giving us some rich messages from time to time. Our Sunday school is increasing some in attendance and is doing well in finance under the present financial depression. Our young people are on the forward move. Our meetings in general are increasing more and more in spirituality. The Lord is adding to the church such as would be saved.

Captioned "Church Work at Eight Mile Road, Detroit, Mich. (Colored)," that report about what was happening under Richards at our church tells us much more than what is stated. The use of the phrase "from time to time" in connection with Richards' preaching must be understood to mean that Richards was not at the Eight Mile Road church every Sunday, since he was actually a circuit pastor serving two area churches. The reference to Sunday school finances being stable despite "the present financial depression" can be understood as saying that the work was being supported despite hard times. The accent on the youth activities, the spirituality of the services, and addition of saved persons to the church reflects a concern to show the vitality of the church in line with the New Testament idealism.

Saved At Six

John Richards was well known throughout the Church of God Reformation Movement, and he sent periodic reports to the group's weekly publication to keep others informed about his ministry and its effects. This was a custom Richards established early in his ministry when he was in Macon, Georgia, where he was reared, and he continued it across the years. Such notices were especially helpful when one was eager to do evangelistic preaching and have camp meeting engagements here and there. The notices kept readers informed about the success of one's ministries and where one could be contacted for ministerial services. With John Richards so prominently known among the churches, what was happening at the congregations he served as pastor also became known, which meant that he was not only engaged to preach and teach elsewhere across the year, but that our church had many visitors and pulpit guests in turn. Many of those guests were noted preachers. I experienced my conversion under the preaching of one of them.

My experience of conversion, of "being saved" as our church group referred to it, happened during a revival meeting conducted at our church by the Reverend Charles Jacob Jones, a guest evangelist from Selma, Alabama. I was six years old at the time, but I understood the call the preacher made to those needing to "come to Christ," and I obeyed the prompting I felt within myself to answer that call affirmatively. So I walked forward toward the kneeling rail that Sunday morning and knelt down to pray. Evangelist Jones walked over to where I had knelt; he then knelt beside me and asked what I was seeking from the Lord. I told him that I had come forward to be forgiven for my sins and be saved. He patted me on my head, smiling as he looked intently into my eyes. Then he moved on to talk with the person kneeling beside me.

After those of us who came forward had prayed and returned to our seats, Jones asked each of us to stand and "testify for the Lord." The rest did, and so I did. Partly echoing what some of the others had said, but with a strong realization that I was voicing my own faith, I said, "I believe that the Lord has saved me!" Evangelist Jones smiled again and loudly commented, "Bless his heart! He was saved when he came here!" Was he suggesting that I might still be too young to really know what sin is? Or did he mean that my testimony, voiced with such surety, was indication that I already knew the Lord before walking forward to that prayer altar? Whatever Evangelist Charles Jacob Jones meant by his statement, I knew what I meant by my testimony. I felt convinced that within I was in harmony with God.

Although converted at the age of six, I was not baptized right away. In our church at that time baptism was a ceremony restricted to adult believers, reserved for that time in one's life when the turn to God was considered so final that a public witness would be more appropriate. I do not remember being anxious over the need to be baptized; I knew that the proper time for it would come. Meanwhile, I sensed that my mind and heart were being conditioned to love God increasingly. I had a steadying consciousness of God's presence with me.

In thinking back on that conversion experience and its effects upon me, I still view that experience as the beginning of a conscious relationship with God. It was more of a commitment to the sensed claim of God upon my life than any dramatic turn away from sins associated with a depth awareness of personal depravity or life-marring failures. Was this what Evangelist Jones had in mind as he made his comment about my testimony? Whatever he meant, I knew sin as a child knows sin, as that deed of failure to honor someone's instructions or trust. I also now knew God in a conscious way. I later knew sin as a teenager because that early consciousness of God's claim upon my life was not honored without interruption as I grew older. But God graciously renewed my joy and dismissed all felt judgment when I prayerfully returned to him, chastened by that divine love that would not let me go.

My reaching out to God became especially active in my life in 1944. I had turned fourteen and was sensing the need to determine the direction my life should take. Several persons at the church had shown increased interest in me and were generous in their praise when I recited poetry or sang or played the piano as part of some program featured during the Sunday evening Young People's Meeting. I was soon asked to take part in adult activities at the church, and was elected secretary for the Sunday school. That was an honor because, as my parents told me, it was the first time that anyone my age had ever held such a responsible post there. Given such indications of evident trust from the people, I gave myself to the new task with a steady zeal.

But I was not to be in office very long. John Richards decided that with advancing age it would be in his best interest, and that of the two churches, to give himself fully to but one. Both churches had been growing under his ministry and, as I later learned, each church had been asking Richards to give all of his time to either one or the other. Richards chose to stay with the Palmerston Avenue Church in River Rouge, a choice influenced to a considerable extent, I believe, by the fact that he had for years been living next door to that church. The pastoral vacancy at the Wisconsin Avenue Church lasted from late 1943 until

June 1944, at which time Charles A. White, whom Richards recommended to the church, became pastor there.

When White's name was first presented to the church in candidacy, my father, among others, raised an objection. Although aware that John Richards had submitted White's name for church consideration, Daddy objected because in his opinion Charles A. White seemed to be lacking in sound judgment at that stage of his life. He reminded the members that it was due to this complaint that White had been asked to resign from the pastorate at the Church of God of Detroit in 1938. When the church business meeting in which this matter was debated took place in early 1944, Charles A. White was serving the Monroe Street Church of God in Ypsilanti, Michigan. Daddy spoke as one of our congregation's leaders, and as one who had strong connections with the downtown mother church. The whole issue greatly interested me. It was my first experience of such a weighty church business discussion.

When the vote was taken and White was chosen, Daddy asked the congregation to understand why he would not wish to remain and be under White's leadership. He stated that, although no final decision had been made as yet, he would probably transfer his membership back to the downtown church. He further stated that, although he would be leaving Wisconsin Avenue, he would not try to persuade anyone else to leave with him. He then tendered his resignation from the staff of church leaders there. My mother decided to leave the church also. I later learned that my father had placed no pressure on her to do so, and that the decision, although painful, was for her own reasons. My mother thus resigned from her work as a member of the choir.

Neither my father nor my mother said anything to me about changing churches, but I was fourteen years old and knew that my place was with them. I thus resigned from my elected post as secretary of the Sunday school. Our family thereafter held membership at the Church of God of Detroit, the mother church located on Jay at Chene Street. The noted Raymond Samuel Jackson was pastor there at the time. He had come to Detroit from a St. Louis, Missouri, church in 1943 to succeed the equally noted preacher J. D. Smoot, who had resigned. The change of churches was for me a providential and fruitful one, just how fruitful only time would reveal.

John Richards' health began to decline and he died in 1947. My father and Richards had been close through many years. Daniel F. Oden and John Richards had endorsed him for ordination, thus honoring his services and growing influence as a minister in the Michigan state area. Richards and Daddy worked together to plant a church in Romulus, Michigan, and a later work in Mount Clemens. When one of the families of the Wisconsin Avenue Church, the Bledsoes, moved from Detroit to Goodells, Michigan, a farming area, John Richards and my father would alternate in going there to assist them in services to spread the Church of God message among the neighbors. After Richards left the Wisconsin Avenue Church, Nora Harris and Daddy alternated in nurturing the Goodells work until Willie Mae Appling, another woman minister in the church, became its regular supply pastor.

Although my father differed with John Richards over his known recommendation of Charles A. White to succeed him as pastor at the Eight Mile Road Church, the two never broke ranks over the disagreement. Daddy still went to River Rouge to see Richards and to preach occasionally in services at his church there.

James Earl Massey

LIFE AND LEARNING IN THE PUBLIC SCHOOLS

The public schools I attended in our district were all named after presidents of the nation. There was Ulysses S. Grant School, just across the street from our house, where I experienced the kindergarten through sixth grade classes. There was William Howard Taft Junior High School, about a mile from our community, where I did seventh grade studies. The area high school was named after Abraham Lincoln. Grant School was predominantly black in student body, but Taft Junior High and Lincoln High were interracial. When the number of younger African Americans in our community sizably increased, the school board decided to add a junior high school curriculum at Grant School, and I remember being transferred back to Grant for the eighth grade after the one year at Taft. A new addition to the Grant School building had also been completed during that time. My second period at Grant ended with graduation from the eighth grade, and I moved on with others to Lincoln High School, which was a walking distance of about two miles from our house.

A Debt To Great Teachers

My grade school years at Grant School brought me under the concerned tutelage and intellectual guidance of some outstandingly effective teachers. Three among them must be named because their ministry to the life of my mind and spirit at that time was special. Those three were Miss Mary O. Doctor, Mrs. Helen Toodle, and Mr. Coit C. Ford. All three were African Americans. Mr. Ford was an industrious, concerned, and dapper figure. I was impressed by how he dressed and how he disported himself in the classroom and during all school functions. He would stand at his classroom door during change of periods, greeting students as we filed into or out of his class. He had the ease of someone at home in his work and he gave us a steadying assurance that we mattered to him.

I shall never forget the walls of Mr. Ford's classroom. Each wall had a wall-length blackboard, and just above the border line he had placed photographs of important African American leaders for our recognition and emulation. At planned times during the semester, he called attention to one or more of those pictured leaders in order to supplement the class lesson. In this way he gave us further insight into American history by treating the life and work of black persons whose stories had not been included in the textbooks we had to use. As I think back on it all, his treatments of black success-stories held us in awe like what we knew when listening to the stories about Bible characters. In this way I first came to know about Colonel Charles Young, who graduated from West Point in 1889, about Benjamin O. Davis, who finished West Point in 1936, and became the first black general. We learned much about W. E. B. DuBois, the scholar, about Marian Anderson, the singer, about educators like Booker T. Washington, Mary McLeod Bethune, and Mordecai Wyatt Johnson. The stories about George Washington Carver and Charles Drew never failed to stir our pride, and those about William Grant Still, Paul Robeson, Langston Hughes, and Joe Louis, among others, never failed to spur our ambition. Mr. Ford, a graduate of Wilberforce University, had known Colonel Young personally. His remarks about that great black military leader were flavored by such a first-hand acquaintance.

Mr. Ford talked quite learnedly about all whose portraits adorned the walls of our classroom, and with each mention the person whose life was being treated usually stood out from the picture frame a little more, life-sized and legendary, each one a hero or heroine with whom we young Negroes (we were not saying "blacks" at that time) could readily identify. I cannot remember a time when I did not have a healthy self-image as a black person, and between home and school there were multitudinous occasions when our self-identity and self-worth were strengthened. As for the role of school life in this process, it was teachers like Mr. Ford, Miss Doctor, and Mrs. Toodle who must be given credit.

Mr. Ford himself became a hero-figure for me after a time. The exact occasion was when he succeeded Howard Kern, Grant School's principal (white). A vacancy in the principalship occurred when Kern was appointed to serve as district superintendent. The entire black community took increased pride in Mr. Ford as the first black principal of Grant School. Although my parents had long been active in the Parent-Teacher Association, they drew even closer and worked still harder in that organization after Mr. Ford became principal over the grade school. Mr. Ford served as principal for about five years, after which he returned to full-time teaching. He was succeeded by a Dr. Stewart, also black, who had recently completed a Ph.D. in education at Wayne University.

Even though he was no longer principal, Mr. Ford still held the community's respect as a senior teacher at Grant School and as an active public figure. His dedication to his work and its setting never wavered, although he lived on Detroit's West Side and had to drive the lengthy distance back and forth between home and school in Ferndale each day. Mr. Ford had a natural dignity and an excellent spirit by which I was captured. I never learned why he gave up administrative work to return to full-time teaching—whether this was by preference or whether he had been superseded by someone with higher academic credentials, but whatever the reasons, his manner and attitude never seemed different after the change, which made him an even greater example as such questions were being asked (and as varying answers were being ventured) within the community circles. Mr. Ford's career at Ferndale's Ullyses S. Grant School spanned thirty-four years of active service, five of which were spent as its first black principal. He retired from teaching in 1960.

Heavily influenced by the philosophy of W. E. B. DuBois and the race betterment culture in which he had been steeped as a student at Wilberforce University, Mr. Ford talked often to Grant School students about the "talented tenth" among our people. I recall those times when he talked privately with me, and with some sternness, when my classroom work and deportment were less than he had expected, less than my tested IQ level promised, and certainly less than he knew my parents would approve!

There were those times when some of us gave less than our best to our studies. I always felt like a heel when he had to speak to me about this, but I also felt some sense of pride when he reminded me about "your mental ability," as he termed it. He even held me over after school a few times to talk further with me about what he thought I could accomplish in life if I would but apply myself more readily. Aware that Mrs. Toodle had double-promoted me during my time in the third grade, Mr. Ford wanted to see me continue to demonstrate that earlier interest and avidity. Reasoning that part of my proneness to mischief and meddling with other students might well be due to a felt lack of challenge, Mr. Ford decided to supplement my regular classwork (which I sometimes hurriedly completed) with additional study tasks; he was seeking to tap that "something more" he thought he saw in me. I received several whippings at home for serious misdemeanors at school. I knew that was in the offing when I did not work well for or with my teachers, because in our community home and school were in agreement on the care and nurture of the young.

I shall never forget that day during my last year at Grant

School when I made an illuminating discovery while out of class during the lunch hour. My mother sent me on an errand to the grocery store, and while returning I spotted a large rock beside the path, probably turned up by the huge street scraper that was sent up and down our streets periodically to clear and smooth the roads, which were not yet paved. With a bit of boyish strength I seized the rock, lifted it above my head, and sent it crashing down on the hardest section of ground near me. The rock split under the impact. I went over, picked up one of the pieces in order to cast it down and split it further. But as I stooped and picked up one piece, I noticed some curiously shaped ridges here and there on the flat side of the split; the ridges were all shell-like in appearance. I looked still closer and realized that I had uncovered some fossils previously hidden within the rock. My find so excited me that I could not wait to return to school and show the discovery to Mr. Ford.

When Mr. Ford saw what I presented to him for class use, he thanked me. He afterward lectured to the class about what that rock meant as an embodied fact from life now extinct after thousands of years. It was an important event for me. Finding that fossil sparked my interest in the scientific investigation of the natural world. There on the split side of that slate lay a concentrated lesson, the first of many by which I was awakened to nature's processes and the impact of abiding forms upon our thought about God's ways with the created order of things. It was all for me an instructive fortune.

Mr. Ford lived to see the late 1980s. He visited church services in which I preached. In 1956, when the congregation I pastored purchased and dedicated our building at 2705 Joy Road, he kindly brought greetings. In 1963 he attended the farewell service the congregation gave us when Gwendolyn and I left for a three-year period of educational service in Kingston, Jamaica, West Indies. Mr. Ford stayed in touch with me across the years. In 1976, during one of his many visits to Metropolitan Church, he brought with him a copy of *The Ferndale Gazette-Times,* dated Thursday, June 17, 1976, which carried a report about the

Royal Oak Township Community Culture Day, part of the nation's Bicentennial Heritage events in the area where I had grown up and where he had taught across so many years. Much of the report quoted from the speech Mr. Ford had given on the program for that day. His speech traced the early days of Grant School life and the contributions its graduates had made across the years. He pointed with pride to the number of graduates who had become physicians, those who had become lawyers, those who had been fighter pilots during World War II, those who had made successful careers in music—namely jazz bassist Ron Carter and musician-professor Anderson White, and, in addition, those five who had become clergymen.

When Mr. Ford handed me that newspaper, the morning worship had just ended and we were standing at the front of the sanctuary where I had chosen to remain to greet the people that day. As he greeted me, he almost casually remarked that there was an important article in that issue that I should read, and that he had come to bring it to me. Knowing that I would soon be taking the post as international radio speaker for our denomination, he said he wanted me to know of his continuing admiration as I moved on "ahead," as he put it. It was a moment of deep feeling and understood regard as we shook hands and parted. Later, examining the newspaper he had given me, I came to that section of his reported speech in which Mr. Ford had listed the five graduates of Grant from his years there who became ministers. He had listed me as the leading one among them. Mr. Ford's assessment aside, no success on my part could have been possible apart from the attentiveness, prodding, and patience he exercised toward me during those crucial adolescent years of mine. What he voiced about a concern for our possibilities he also felt compelled to help us realize. Mr. Coit Cook Ford was one of the landmark persons I have known. To him I am forever indebted.

Enriched At Cass Tech

I spent only one year at Lincoln High School. Desiring to be nearer a certain young lady whom I had met after attending the downtown church, and toward whom I had a strong interest, and to have access to a more extensive music curriculum than I had found available at Lincoln, I transferred to Cass Technical High School in downtown Detroit. As for the young lady I liked, she was a grade ahead of me when I met her. I attended summer school at Highland Park High in 1946 and caught up with her class, intent to graduate along with her.

The concern to transfer to Cass Technical High School placed two demands upon me. The first was to take a qualifying entrance exam. I took the exam and passed it. The second demand was to obtain a Detroit residence so that I would be eligible to study at Cass Tech as a resident of the city. My parents and Grandma Townsend agreed that I could live with her and thus satisfy that requirement, and I thereafter stayed at her house whenever I did not wish to make the trip out to Ferndale. My grandparents' house on Mullett Street, on the East Side, was within walking distance of Cass Tech, which meant a much shorter time in travel than if making the long bus trip from Ferndale to get to an eight o'clock morning class. Furthermore, the girl I liked, and in the pursual of whom I had transferred from Lincoln High School, lived only a short distance from my new Mullett Street address!

The transfer to Cass Tech was not only a convenience to satisfy a love-influenced heart, it was an educationally progressive move, and in more than one way. The move was indeed progressive in that my musical interests could be better served there than at Lincoln High in Ferndale. I was doubly benefited in that I was granted advanced standing in piano performance on the basis of additional examinations administered by the music department to me as a new student. I was both proud and relieved by testing out of some courses which other students who lacked my background would have to take, but this meant that I could move on to many other electives in place of courses about which the tests had certified my knowledge and competence.

During the late 1940s Cass Technical High School was the second largest school of its kind in the world. Along with a similar-type school in Brooklyn, New York, it was considered unique among America's high schools because of its many technical-level programs of study not available elsewhere at the high school level. But Cass not only gave technical-level training in fifteen curricula of rigidly prescribed courses. The school was also readying all its students for college entrance. In order to satisfy both the technical and college prep demands, we had to have five courses each semester while students in standard high schools only had to take four classes each semester. Actually, some of us at Cass were taking course work in our graduation year that first year college students encountered.

Being at Cass gave me all that I have mentioned, but it also gave me daily contact with several other young persons from the Church of God of Detroit who attended that high school. All of them were excellent students and the togetherness we developed benefited us mutually. The church group consisted of Rufus and Arthur Anderson, Jacqueline Cromer, Joyce Tabitha Green, Rosemary Oden (daughter and last child of Daniel F. Oden), Andrew Lomax, and Gwendolyn Inez Kilpatrick—the girl I liked and wanted to be near! During my time at Cass my brother Melvin returned home after service in the Merchant Marine Corps and also joined us as a fellow student at Cass. The young people from our church who attended Cass Tech became and remained a closely-knit group across the years of our lives.

All Cassites could expect a thorough grounding in all of the general studies and in their chosen area of interest. I still remember the general studies teachers I had: H. Gaylord, G. Luros, and J. Takken in chemistry and biology; E. K. Takken in English; Marjorie G. Smith, who introduced me to my first formal course in speech, a recent addition to the English curriculum along with journalism, radio, and dramatics; for mathematics (geometry) I had F. Frey and S. E. McCullagh; for social studies I had Mabel G. Goodfellow, J. Marcotte and J. Wenzel as teachers. In my chosen area of interest, music, I had Clarence Byrn, head of the department, Michael Bistritsky, Laurietta Klink, Grace Molzoff, and Glenn Klepinger. William Stirton was principal at Cass Tech, and during student assemblies he constantly stressed the importance of "good citizenship and good scholarship." The first was expected, the second was demanded, and success in both was rewarded in appropriate ways.

My music teachers at Cass were first-rate in their areas of expertise and they were serious in helping each of their students to learn music theory and develop well in performance skills as instrumentalists and vocal artists. Actually, only those students were admitted into the music department who had been tested for aptitude in music. As previously mentioned, when I applied for entrance, Clarence Byrn, head of the music department, tested my piano keyboard skills. He had to know at what level I was prepared to learn. I played the first movement of Ludwig van Beethoven's piano sonata Number 14 (Opus 27, Number 2), the "Moonlight." Byrn listened intently as I played, watching my hand movements, pedaling, and reacting to my tonal treatment of the notes and phrases. I was somewhat ill at ease as we started into the testing process, but I soon lost myself in the playing, grateful for the opportunity which was now mine to be heard by such a "pro." I knew that so much was at stake, so I had to do well. When I concluded the sonata movement, Bryn voiced a warm compliment. He smiled as he leaned over to tell me that he was admitting me into the music department and that I could register for the advanced music classes. I was thrilled! I sensed that my time at Cass Tech was going to be a fullness of time for me. It was!

While growing up in our modest house in Ferndale there was one piece of furniture that I prized above all the rest. It was an upright piano, a "Player" piano with several music rolls which made my thoughts and feelings soar to great heights when they were played. My mother had taken piano lessons from Ethel Harris, daughter of Turner and Nora Harris, and she took time to play selected music on her own when she did not wish to entertain us by using the built-in player capacity of the piano. Although very young at the time, I found myself deeply moved when my mother's piano teacher came each week to hear the assigned piano music. I stood as close as they both allowed while the lesson was in progress. When I was playing one of the themes on my own, having had no lessons, my mother saw my proneness to music and asked Ethel Harris to begin teaching me to read music. She did, and I have been reading notes and making music on the piano ever since. The beauty of making music so enthralled me that I seldom if ever tired of practicing. I even carried music manuscripts with me to church and read through them during the worship, so familiarizing myself with the musical structure of an assigned piece that I could afterward go to the piano and render it in sound with greater ease.

Among the music by composers for the keyboard, I found the creations of Johann Sebastian Bach, Ludwig van Beethoven, and Wolfgang Amadeus Mozart especially appealing, revealing, and memorable. I never had difficulty memorizing their piano works. The very first piano sonata that I memorized was one by Beethoven. I had heard the first movement theme of his "Moonlight" over the radio during a broadcast of the Longine Symphonette Hour and I was captured. I located a copy of the entire sonata in sheet music form at Grinnell Brothers in downtown Detroit, brought it home, and learned that first movement in one sitting. That was the movement I played years later when being tested for entrance into the music department at Cass Technical High School. I had lived with that piece for a long time and it had become an expression of my own heart and life.

Now at Cass, I plunged wholeheartedly into the multi-phased program of music studies. I was admitted to the concert band as a French horn (Bb) player, one of three persons in that section. I had earlier studied and played the French horn during that year at Lincoln High School, playing in Lincoln's marching band, one of its two black members. I sang in the Cass Chorus under Henrietta Klink and Glenn Klepinger. The theory, composition, and instrument classes exacted time and effort as I sought to move fully into the challenging but inspiring world of music and music-making.

There were many days of great fun as we students worked together in our music classes. I especially remember the fun we had in Michael Bistritsky's classes with the stringed instruments. I recall his words to me at the close of the semester during which I had been assigned to study the stringed bass. There had been class times when I had neglected to bring the instrument with me because of having to rush from some other class on a lower floor, wait on an elevator to reach the fourth floor instrument room, wait in line to sign out a stringed bass, and then lug it into another elevator to reach his sixth floor music room before the class bell would ring. As that semester was about to close, Mr. Bistritsky looked up from his desk and waved a pointed finger at me as I stood in front of him. In his Russian-flavored English, he admonished, "James, you will only get a "B" this time because you didn't bring your bass to class enough times!" He knew that bringing a bass to class under such conditions had often been a real problem. There were hundreds of students at Cass during those years, and gaining a spot on an elevator in the midst of such a press between classes, even without an instrument, was no small feat. So when I sometimes entered the stringed bass class without an instrument I had checked out, I would borrow someone else's bass and play the passages Bistritsky had assigned. When I did that, he would look at me and shake his head in a gesture of mild disapproval.

In 1947, when I was about to graduate from Cass, Mr. Bistritsky informed me that one of the students had told him that I was not going to be continuing in music but would begin studying for the Christian ministry. I shall forever treasure the kind words he spoke in approval and his comment about wanting to be present to hear me preach my first sermon. He also placed that comment in my senior yearbook.

I can remember no time in my life when I did not feel deeply drawn to music. When I was given lessons in making music on the piano I had found a great new world for my spirit. I was about seven years old when I began playing on the family piano. Music scores intrigued me and I always wanted to master them. I attacked some lessons with a vengeance, eager to be done with those works I did not feel as deeply as those of my favorite composers. Playing the piano was for me a time of encounter with the inarticulate; no words were needed in the relationship with music, only notes, only sounds which, rightly interpreted, could lead me to the edge of the infinite. There were times when I would just play a hymn to God, releasing the longings of my soul in structured poetry and sequential tones.

The music students at Cass Tech were always ready to make music, or talk about music and music-making. We all had a deep interest in music, but several were planning to have a career in the field. Many who had settled on a career in music-making were not only music majors in our department but were being tutored by members of the Detroit Symphony Orchestra on a private basis. This fact made the level of music-learning and music-making in class a high level indeed, and it also allowed for some understood name-dropping by students when some musical opinion was being shared. These contacts and conditionings were prophetic of the future some of my classmates were to have. These were the students who outdistanced the others in their skills, insights, and harnessed experienced. A few of them were pedants, and I avoided them, but I admired their prowess nevertheless. There were times when I wished I could match the way some of the Polish students handled the works of Chopin; they had such a grasp of his technical demands. But then I had to remember that they had grown up hearing that composer's works and were readily familiar with his rhythms and constructions. Meanwhile, I felt I had an understanding of Beethoven's musical language that the playing of few of them seemed to make evident. Although not German by background, I felt in my element when interpreting that giant's works. I felt the questing that fills his music, and I could identify with his pain.

Being at Cass also allowed us to see and converse with guest musicians who often came to do recitals and concerts in Detroit. Although guest musicians would sometimes visit our school, we were also privileged to receive passes now and again to go and hear them, both in rehearsal and final performance with the symphony orchestra. Mr. Michael Bistritsky's brother was a string player in the Detroit Symphony at the time, and he saw that a few passes were made available for some of the "teacher's chosen." I loved Cass Tech for all it made possible for us, and I cannot remember missing one day of classes there.

As expected in a high school of that size and importance, there were many extra-curricular activities in which we students could participate, but I found myself interested in only one of them. It was a weekly after-class Bible study activity sponsored by some wealthy Christian businessmen in the Detroit area. The Bible study group was known as "The Miracle Book Club." Our leader was Mrs. R. G. Harris, a personable and thoughtful woman who was the wife of one of the directors of the noted R. G. & G. R. Harris Funeral Homes. Five of the Cassites from our church belonged to the study group and we always attended with regularity: Jacqueline Cromer, Joyce Green, Gwendolyn Inez Kilpatrick, Rosemary Oden, and myself. I served the group as song leader one semester, and sometimes Gwendolyn and I would sing a duet. One of the songs we especially liked and sung was "I'll Go Where He Wants Me to Go." Gwendolyn was elected Club president during the last semester before we graduated.

The Cassites from our church were very involved in extra-curricular activities at our high school. Joyce Green was a member of the school yearbook staff and helped to produce *The*

Triangle. Rufus Anderson was busy with work on the student council, and he was a senior representative of his department (science). Gwendolyn Kilpatrick was also a senior representative from her department (home economics). Both she and Rosemary Oden were members of the Masque and Gavel Club. Jacqueline Cromer, a member with me of the music department, was also on the student council, a member of the National Honor Society, and specializing in voice and violin in the school orchestra. We were an active, close-knit, and rather contagious group, so contagious indeed that many other Cass students admired our Christian spirit and visited our church with us now and again. Joyce Green once confessed that it was the Christian contagion she felt when with the group of students from our church that influenced her to visit and finally leave Bethel A.M.E. Church to join us as a member at the Church of God of Detroit.

I had occasion to join some of my fellow Cassites each week in settings other than our high school classrooms. Some, like Aaron Hicks, my brother Melvin and I, were members of two popular choral groups in the city. The one group was the DuPre Victorian Choir, named after and directed by its founder, the gifted tenor Marvin Dupre. The other choral group was the Hines Chorean Choir, founded and directed by William G. "Billy" Hines, a noted musician and teacher of piano. The decade of the 1940s was, despite the recent war, one of the great cultural periods of musical life in Black Detroit. The Detroit public as a whole seemed more culturally oriented at that time, and there was a burgeoning interest within black musical circles to honor and enhance the musical legacy from the Harlem Renaissance. There was also a serious interest in classical studies needed to break into opera or to have a concert stage career. Robert L. Nolan, head of The Nolan School of Music, had a weekly column as music critic for *The Michigan Chronicle,* and his comments and critiques were "must" reading for all of us who were seriously interested in music and music-making. Mrs. Nellie Watts was also one of the great promoters of serious music among blacks in the city at that time, and she sponsored a noted concert series each year, bringing to the city great black musicians from across the nation, but particularly those who had become known in the New York music scene. The cultural climate in Detroit at the time had a positive impact upon those of us who were serious about musical careers. Having a part in choirs led by such distinguished musical artists as DuPre and Hines kept our hopes high and our sensitivities sharpened.

It was during an engagement of the DuPre Victorian Choir at the historic Metropolitan Baptist Church that I first heard the fabled Dr. Adam Clayton Powell, Sr., preach. We had practiced for that service across two weeks, and the choir sang for that service at a high level of evident but controlled excitement. That contact with one of our great African American preachers stirred many of us at a depth level. I knew of Adam Clayton Powell, Jr., the congressman, of course, but seeing and hearing his legendary preacher-father was like an excursion into the richness of black history. We were making primary contact with a major black event-maker. The impression from that service remains vividly etched in my memory. Dr. Alfred C. Williams, father of Theodore "Ted" Williams who sang bass in the choir, was pastor of Metropolitan Baptist Church at the time. I later learned that Dr. Williams had known Gwendolyn Inez Kilpatrick's father, the Rev. Judson Lyons Kilpatrick, that they had been classmates at Atlanta Baptist College (later renamed Morehouse College), and that they both graduated in the class of 1912.

Stability of Divine Assurance

I had entered Cass Tech with great joy, but my leaving involved a bit of pain. On graduation night in June 1947 I was rushing down the hall toward the room in which the music department graduates were to assemble. Mr. Glenn Klepinger saw me and asked me to wait for a moment because he needed to discuss a problem that had come to his attention while examining my record of courses taken. Mr. Klepinger was now music department head, Clarence Byrn having just retired. I waited with bated breath as Klepinger informed me about a course I had missed. "In screening your college entrance preparation subjects," he said, "I noticed that you had not taken English Composition Four, which all Cass graduates are required to take."

I listened, painfully anxious as he spoke, but an inner assurance soon steadied me and I replied that my advisor had allowed me to substitute a Speech course for the one in English Composition because of my plan to do pre-ministerial studies in college. Department chairman Klepinger looked intently at me, sensed my apparent dismay at being questioned about this at so late a time, then told me that he had discussed the matter with Principal William Stirton. The moment of pause before he gave the outcome of their discussion seemed like an eternity, but Klepinger went on to say that they had thought of letting me walk across the platform with my class, and that I could receive a dummy diploma to spare me embarrassment, and that I could return for a summer course in English Composition and thus complete the requirement. But after another brief pause, he went on to tell me what Principal Stirton had determined. The decision was that I would be graduated that night, as scheduled, and that the college to which I apply could determine how the apparent deficiency should be handled. Klepinger thought it a wise decision. So did I. Remembering that brief moment of pain, I walked across the platform of the auditorium that night very much aware that my life was in the hands of God. Clutching my diploma, I descended the stairs with mingled pride, praise, and humility.

The steadying "inner assurance" to which I refer was rooted in my understanding about the graciousness and guidance of God for all who look trustingly to him, but it was also strengthened by successive experiences I had had of divine assurance and help when faced with some problem or need. One such experience from that very period in my life well illustrates the basis for the assurance I felt as Mr. Klepinger and I talked that night before the graduation ceremony.

During my last year at Cass, with only a few weeks left before the expected June graduation, one afternoon I walked from school to our new church location on Detroit's West Side at Vermont and Hancock. As choir pianist, I wanted to practice my piano part before the choir rehearsal at church later that evening. After choir rehearsal, I stayed for the regular Friday night prayer vigil that most of the local ministers of the church attended. The prayer time ended rather late, so someone volunteered to drop me along the bus route that would get me home without having to change buses, as I always had to do if going out to the house in Ferndale. Once out of the car, standing at the bus stop under the streetlight, I suddenly realized that I had spent too much for lunch and did not have enough money left for my fare home. I felt in my pocket and located only four pennies—but a full fare was ten cents! I began praying. I was praying that God would let someone drive by who might recognize me and offer a ride. Several cars whizzed by, but no one stopped. I continued praying and soon remembered the spare nickel I kept stashed away in a secret pocket of my wallet. I opened the wallet and extracted the nickel—grateful for the memory. But I still had only nine cents when I needed ten. It occurred to me that I could get on the bus and risk asking the driver to let me ride with paying less than the full fare, but I felt too embarrassed and dismissed the thought.

The drama continued. As I prayed aloud, I began walking. In the course of finishing a block I was aware that my foot had kicked a coin. I stopped suddenly, listened intently to the sound of the rolling coin, and went over to where I thought it had stopped. Reaching down, I felt around on the sidewalk, located the coin, and rushed to the nearest streetlight to see what I had found. It was a penny! My heart was pounding anxiously as I reached into my pocket to see if perchance I had dropped (and found) one of the four pennies I knew I had. The four other pennies were still there. When the bus came, I entered, sat down, and continued giving God thanks for answering my prayer. I had needed ten cents to pay my fare, and God had provided the needed penny to complete that amount! That was but one of the many experiences which deepened my sense of assurance about the mindfulness of God toward my life and its needs.

While growing up at home we Masseys were constantly reminded that God is the Source of all that blesses our life. We began every meal with thanksgiving to God for the good gift of food, and we closed every day with thanksgiving for all the other needs which had been met. Life and teaching at church steadily deepened what we heard, read, and said at home. There were many readings from Scripture about God as provider, and we were even encouraged to memorize them. I cannot begin to number the times I heard my father or mother speak so appreciatively about the goodness and mercies of the Lord. They spoke out of our family's experience of accented needs during the struggling Depression years. Even now, many years afterward, the memory of how God provided for us during those years remains fresh in my mind. As Roger Hazelton, one of my teachers at Oberlin Seminary used to say to us, "Prayer is nothing without the living trust that what we need God has to give us."

Jesus encouraged us with this promise: "Ask, and it will be given you; search, and you will find; knock, and the door will be opened for you" (Matt. 7:7). That instruction taught me the importance of prayer for my needs, and it stirs me so to pray. We ask; God grants. I have stated the matter simply here, although it has taken a lifetime of experience to clear away some misunderstandings that blocked my faith and dulled my focus as I sought to correlate my anxious askings with God's multiple and ready provisions.

3

LEARNING TO PREACH AND LEAD

I did not choose the ministry; it was divinely chosen for me, and I was summoned to it through an experience of call that is still as fresh in my memory now as when it first happened. I had not planned to be a minister, but a musician, a classical pianist. All the signs along the path of my planning pointed to a musical career, not being a preacher. But it was not to be so, and for reasons known only to God.

God Is Calling!

My experience of being called to preach happened on a Sunday morning in 1946. I was at church, part of the congregation at worship in the sanctuary of the Church of God of Detroit. The morning worship service was in progress, but my attention was not on God but on a music score I had brought with me that day. It had been my custom to carry a music score with me and use any available time to study it. That day I had with me the score of a waltz by Chopin, and I was deeply engrossed in it, intent to overcome some problem that hindered my memorizing of the piece. But during a brief let-up in my concentration on the score, I found myself being captured by the spirit of the worship occasion. As I honored the meaning of the worship hour and opened myself to God, I felt caught up into an almost transfixed state, and I heard a Voice speaking within my consciousness: "I want you to preach!"

It was a strange but sure happening. The Voice both disturbed me and settled me. The message was so forceful and the meaning was so clear. I knew I would have to say Yes, and I did. Still in the grip of the encounter, I turned to see who was sitting next to me. On my right was Dolores Mathis, one of the more serious young ladies at the church. In the rush of my feeling I interrupted her worship. Intent to announce the news about my new direction, I asked her, "Do you know what I am going to do with my life?" She politely answered, "No, James. What?" "I'm going to be a preacher," I declared. Her reply was almost immediate, and she smiled as she gave it: "Why, James, that is wonderful!"

It was all so graphic to my inner sight, and so gripping upon my mind and spirit. In all the years which have transpired since that holy hour, I have never had any reason to reinterpret what happened to me during that great listening moment of grace. The Voice that called me was so clear, and its bidding, though gentle, bore the unmistakable authority of a higher realm. Since that time of encounter during worship I have known the work to which my head, heart, and hands were to be devoted. I did, however, know a time during that first year after being called when I hungered more for the piano than I was eager for the pulpit. But that hunger was finally disciplined and my interest in the pulpit finally became keener than my retreat into music.

I had new direction, but I also had a problem. Questions soon began to plague me as I wondered how my depth involvement in music was to fit into what I was now called upon to do. For me, music had been like breathing. It was so natural and necessary for my life. Indeed, music was my life, my deepest joy. Some of my closest friendships were with other musicians. I was becoming known in the Detroit area for my music-making. I had played for some of the top musicians in Detroit's black community, and I had accompanied some excellently gifted soloists at weddings, special community gatherings, and ecumenical church functions now and again. The new direction I had been given put me into an identity crisis since I saw myself

53

starting all over. But knowing that I was to obey the Voice, I set myself to do so, and thus began a prolonged and painful process by which I was inwardly sifted.

Through it all I would be helped to learn at a deeper level how to submit my will and planning to what I understood as God's sovereign plan for me. I would come to learn that there was so much that has been of transfer value from my years as a music student. For instance, there is the discipline of memorizing and the ability to focus attention on a given biblical text (like a musical score), looking for the structure and flow of meaning. I soon learned that the joy of music could flow even from my sermonizing. Music and ministry were to be interlocked for me.

It was fortunate for me that I had to be away from Detroit during that eventful summer, working with my father at the National Campground at West Middlesex, Pennsylvania, because being away allowed me needed time and space to process what had happened to me in that encounter and how I would respond to the new demands which that encounter would bring to bear upon my life.

At the request of Joseph Crosswhite, Sr., camp manager at the National Association Campgrounds, my father spent the months of June and July inspecting and updating the electrical system on the grounds. With the enlarging of the tabernacle and the increasing number of cabins and cottages, a system updating had been overdue. In his capacity as electrical contractor, my father was assigned the task and my brother Melvin and I went to Pennsylvania to assist him. While there, I attended the midweek prayer service the Christian workers held each week in one of the camp buildings. During one of the services I "testified," and the contagion of my witness impressed someone who afterward gave my name to a member of the program committee for the Tri-State Youth Convention which was to convene that July in nearby Meadville. I received an invitation to preach during the convention.

I did not give an immediate reply. The challenge made me know that I needed to pray about the matter, and I needed to assess my readiness to preach. I never admitted that until then I had not ever prepared or preached a sermon! I talked with my father about the invitation; he encouraged me to continue praying, and sought to assure me that the Lord would direct me on what to do. I did, and my answer soon came. I felt the challenge deepen as I responded to the invitation with a sensitively spoken "Yes, I will preach at the Convention!"

On the appointed day I was introduced and presented to the convention audience by George Gibbs, another young but more experienced minister who was a member of the church in Sharon, Pennsylvania. Gibbs presented me in such a confident manner that panic almost claimed me before I rose to speak. My stomach tightened, my hands were wet with a cold sweat, and I felt a tremor in my knees. I was sensing the burden I was to bear as a preacher. I was just plain scared. But as Gibbs finished his introductory remarks, an assurance warmed me. I lifted my head, stood up, and although too immature and nervous to linger in any pleasantries to ease myself or the hearers, I found myself voicing an audible prefatory prayer. Across the years I had always seen other preachers audibly pray before preaching, but it took that freighted moment to show me just why they had done so.

I cannot recall how long I spoke, but I do remember how the people were looking up at me and responding in ways that made me know that something meaningful had transpired. I had done my best. My father rose from beside me, extended an invitation for faith and commitment, and many young persons walked forward to present themselves to God. I had spoken on "The Law of Christ" from Galatians 6:2. An offering was received for me. I put a tithe of that offering back into the offering tray, grateful for the goodness and sustaining presence of God. That was the scene and circumstance of my first sermon. Had I not been away that summer, working with my father and brother, I would no doubt have preached my first sermon back in Detroit at the home church where the faces were familiar and where the pastor could observe and afterward instruct me. I did give a full accounting to our pastor upon my return.

Later that year, I was surprised to see that my call had been announced in print in the November 1946 issue of the *Shining Light Survey*. It was mentioned in the "Congregational Report" section of the magazine, part of a report from our Detroit church written by Hattie Lee, one of our youth counselors. The report stated: "Recently, three young men serving in the youth department made known their call to the ministry—James Massey, Clemmie Mays, and John Parker. Brother Massey, just seventeen, is attending one of the public schools here; Brother Mays is one of our university students, and Brother Parker is also in school so as to better prepare himself for his work."

As I surrendered myself to an unfolding awareness of what the new direction for my life meant, I understood and accepted the demand that getting ready for a ministry would have to have my primary attention. Still in high school, with a year remaining before graduation, I began letting my friends there know my plans for the future, and I took an increased interest in those courses that I knew would increase my readiness for what I knew was my calling.

My strong interest to become an effective minister did not involve me immediately in formal classrooms and assigned textbooks. Having grown up in the Black Church tradition, I knew that the expected pattern of preparing for ministry in that setting demanded relating with a responsible pastor, and faithful involvement as a learning-worker under that pastor's steady guidance. "Sitting under" that leader, submitting oneself to supervision, staying open to that leader's example, teaching, and counsel allowed one's growth in grace and readiness for service to be monitored, and occasions for service to be provided. I knew that in time a license to preach would be received and that ordination to ministry would follow at the proper time. At the time I received my call to the ministry, it was the custom in our church group for the local pastor to determine when a person should be ordained to the ministry. Not only did the pastor determine the time, the pastor also did the ordaining, assisted by any others whose ministry within the local churches gave them a reputable standing. In later years, the authority to ordain would be restricted to a state assembly.

To be ordained by a teaching pastor was considered the best recommendation for one's ministry, since that ordination represented recognized standards which one had met, as well as the approbation of a regarded leader. This method of supervising and guiding new ministers was more than a mere means of control; it was obvious testimony to the belief that readiness for ministry was to be gauged by ecclesiastical measurements and not by norms related only to a formal education.

The Church of God of Detroit had long held the honor of being one of the great churches within the Reformation Movement of the Church of God, and its pastors had been some of the "princes of the Church." The congregational life was blessed by the most efficient modes of operation, and every pastor who had served there had enhanced the programming for more effective church life. Each pastor had been a teaching leader, and the church was a known center for Christian learning, growth, and outreach.

The Apprentice Years

In 1946, when I first informed the pastor and announced to the congregation that I had experienced the "call" to preach, the members numbered about 450. In addition to the dozen or so older lay preachers in the church, there were ten of us, newly-called, who looked to Raymond S. Jackson for the traditional guidance expected in preparing ourselves for ministry. It was under his guidance that we processed a deeper understanding of the "call" we had received, and by risking ourselves in various assigned tasks we gained insight into our own giftedness. The many opportunities we were given both to observe and to serve aided us in discerning our deepest interests and in focusing our gifts.

The local ministers at our church also had many opportunities for study through the well-developed Christian education program there. In addition to many leadership courses, our education for ministry was further enhanced through our involvement in the congregational organization known as the "Ministers and Gospel Workers Association." This group met monthly for learning and reflection under the pastor's supervising attention, but with one of the local ministers serving as the chairperson. The group elected the chairperson, who was afterward ratified by the pastor. Once ratified, that chosen leader became one of the pastor's assistants and handled assigned tasks on a part-time basis across the year in office. There were times when the same leader was reelected and thus chaired the ministerial group for more than one year.

Just three years after announcing my call, I was elected chairperson of the ministers. Serving as part-time assistant to Rev. Jackson, eventually I became his choice as his first full-time associate. That apprenticeship with Raymond S. Jackson as my pastoring coach was considerably instrumental in readying me to understand and handle the intricacies of church relations and the sometimes rigorous responsibilities of church management.

The Reverend Raymond Samuel Jackson impressed me deeply. His widely known and contagious ministry challenged me steadily. I sensed my good fortune as I was privileged to live so close to his mind and spirit. My "sitting under" him helped me to gain an understanding of what a solid preaching and pastoral ministry means, involves, and makes possible for people. It was no secret that I was duly impressed by that skillful pastor and pulpiteer. As one year followed another, I added analysis to my admiration of Jackson and I added research to my reflection about him, and began gathering materials and making notes about the story of his life. Aware that his services as leader within the wider church were too relevant and extensive to be overlooked by historians, early in 1949 I decided to begin shaping a biographical treatment about

Jackson. The full fruit of that decision ripened many years later (*Raymond S. Jackson: A Portrait,* 1967), but the decisive seeds for it were first sown in 1949, a particularly important year in my spiritual growth and the widening of my horizons as a believer concerned about effectiveness as a minister.

I was called to the ministry at a time in the life of the church when expectations of the people for the vocation were steadily rising. There were many ministers for our pulpits, but the number of ministers among us who were theologically trained was not impressive. Like many another communion within the free church tradition, the Church of God did not require even a college degree as preparation for entrance into its ordained ministry, while many other church groups required not only an undergraduate degree but a graduate seminary degree, seven years of study in all, as the educational prerequisites for ordination. Some among us viewed such educational demands as but man-made rules; they argued that this was only "book learning" in contrast to the needed anointing of God that makes a truly effective ministry. In our fellowship, candidates for ordination were commonly expected to train under some seasoned pastor, show clear evidence of having been called by serving faithfully at given tasks, obey the supervising leader, and thus gain endorsement as a loyal, able, and trusted person. All this was implied in gaining a letter of reference from some known leader. It was thus a practical necessity to learn from a pastoral leader whose recommendation would be respected, a leader whose known beliefs, knowledge, wisdom, reputation, and ability to train others would make "sitting under" that person a matter of principal importance to one's anticipated future.

Raymond Samuel Jackson was just such a leader for me after I experienced "the call" to prepare for ministry. He was one of the most successful ministers within the Church of God and was pastoring one of the great churches within the Movement. He was noted for his leadership skills and was a widely regarded teaching pastor. His pulpit prowess was so honored that he was in constant demand as a preacher for camp meetings and revivals across the country. Jackson was widely viewed as a model minister within the Church of God Movement, and most blacks within the Movement took pride in the fact that some of our ablest black pastors and several of our most progressive churches had been blessed by his leadership.

As our relationship developed, I was pleased that Raymond Jackson commended my educational ambitions. Now and again he inquired about my studies, and after I graduated from Cass Technical High School he encouraged me when I began my course work at the University of Detroit. He was especially pleased that my interest in church life did not wane as college demands increased.

As it turned out, because I knew that I was going to become a minister I felt a deeper need for some of the Christian education courses being taught at the church than for some of the courses I was taking at the university. At that time, the Detroit church had Leadership Education classes going throughout the year. With a wide range of courses constantly available, the Leadership Education School appealed not only to persons in our congregation who wanted training for leadership, but even to members in other city churches who availed themselves of the opportunity the school offered. Under Jackson's leadership, assisted by his wife Cleopatra, dean of the school, the Church of God of Detroit had an educational program for developing leaders that was second to none.

A commencement service was held each Spring when credit cards were issued to those who had completed specific courses, and a Certificate of Progress was awarded to those who had completed a prescribed number of courses. The credits and certificates were all part of the programming authorized by and related to the departmental work of the Board of Christian Education of the Church of God, with offices in Anderson, Indiana. I was a student in a few such classes while a student in high school, and I continued in them while in college. Dr. T. Franklin Miller, Executive Director of the Board, came to Detroit several times to award certificates to those who had earned them. Like some other members, I received several certificates of progress. I saw all this as a means for my training and growth.

Quite beyond these common benefits, I sensed the favorableness of the opportunity to learn from Jackson. Just beginning in ministry, I wanted a sound footing as I stepped forth to serve. My own father had schooled me well in the Scriptures. Prodded by his example in memorizing texts, I set myself to master chapters and books of the Bible. My father had also let me read some of his books on sermon outlining, and this, aided by the speech course I had at Cass Tech, helped me in preparing my first sermons. Both my father and Raymond Jackson were topical preachers, and my approach to pulpit readiness was strongly influenced by their example when I began preaching. As expected, I always needed and used a text for every sermon. There were even times when I used two texts to treat some sermonic theme by a contrast approach. But as I continued sermonizing, studied audience responses to my preaching, studied books about the art, and carefully observed preachers whose pulpit practices differed from those common to our church tradition, I soon sensed the wisdom of treating one text well. So I began to risk using the expositional method to prepare for the pulpit. I began doing so out of a growing conviction that my preaching should show more of what I was hearing within the text and less of what I, in my ineptness, was bringing to it.

As my reflection on the preaching process continued to deepen, I found myself moving farther from the usual style of sermonizing honored in our church setting. I preached topically less and less, and expositionally more and more. To be sure, I did not neglect the narrative mode so highly favored within the Black Church tradition, nor did I overlook the doctrinal concerns expected from preaching. I rather wanted to treat each text or passage on its own terms and not seek to confine its meaning and thrust as a purely topical use can sometimes do. I backed my expositional approach with fresh study of each text

I used, and sometimes that was costly because there were those times when I drew from some text a different message or accent from the one some other preacher's topical use of that text was remembered to have given. Some within the congregation did not relate well to my approach; they viewed it as foreign to the traditional proof-text method of preaching. Some others, believing that God was working in my life, listened with openness and continued to encourage me. Pastor Jackson was among them. I distinctly remember one of his comments: "Son, that was a rather deep message you delivered."

Jackson encouraged us to work on sermon outlining. We also learned about correlating texts we intended to use. As my own interest in biblical interpretation continued to deepen, he let me read his copy of a book on the subject by Milton S. Terry (*Biblical Hermeneutics,* 1883), a standard in the field at that time. We spent some time discussing the subject. Jackson knew of my love for the Scriptures and he encouraged me in my concern to learn "the whole counsel of God," seeking to understand it aptly in order to preach it with needed conviction. There were two maxims Jackson kept before those of us preparing for ministry: the first was biblical, from First Timothy 5:22b, "Keep thyself pure" (KJV); the second was a common sense caution—"Never preach beyond your own experience." He often elaborated on both.

In explaining what he meant by "preaching beyond your own experience," Jackson insisted that there is a vast difference between the initial experience of having been "called" and the subsequent readiness to be sent. It was a necessary caution because a few of us were consumed by a zeal that lacked disciplining knowledge and specific direction. Jackson warned us against premature exposure, against spiritual unreadiness, against suffering an emotional burn-out. He knew the rigors of the way and wanted us to anticipate and prepare for them.

My apprentice years with Raymond Samuel Jackson proved to be highly productive ones. My interest in learning was not only being rewarded, but I was doubly fortunate in that Jackson chose to contribute increasingly toward my development as a minister. There were times when he let me fill speaking engagements in his stead, with one of the church choirs accompanying me. One such time was in September 1948 when I preached for him in a service at one of our sister churches (white) on Beniteau at Goethe in East Detroit. My subject was "Which Room Are You In?" It was a sermon about Christian holiness, illustrating the change that took place in the spiritual experience of the first disciples between the time in an upper room when they jealously quarreled with each other during the Last Supper and the time they found a new harmony through the Holy Spirit in the upper room mentioned in Acts 1:13. That upper room might well have been the same one in which the group had met for the passover meal, but the group members meeting there were now different—they were now unselfish, compassionate, and focused for mission. They were ready to live on new terms, equipped with a new power and an Enabling Presence. I elaborated on the meaning, effects, and source of that change and its availability to us as well.

J. Willard Chitty, the pastor there, was impressed by the message. He suggested that it should be published for a wider audience. He even volunteered to send it, if I agreed, to the editor of the *Gospel Trumpet,* our national church journal. As it happened, I had prepared the sermon in full manuscript form, so I had a copy prepared for Pastor Chitty and he sent it with a covering letter to Dr. Charles Ewing Brown, the editor. The sermon appeared as an article in the May 28, 1949 issue of the *Gospel Trumpet.* That was my first published article, and I could not know at the time that it was but the first of many which would appear in that church journal across the years under my name. Interestingly, Raymond Jackson had been elected to membership on the publication board for the *Gospel Trumpet* in 1947, the first black so elected, but he knew nothing about the appearance of my article until it was in print. By means of that article my name came to the attention of Dr. Brown, editor-in-chief for our church publishing house, and, in the opinion of many, he was the foremost writing scholar within the church at that time. A prized relationship developed between us in the years which followed, ending only at his death in 1971.

I have reported the occasion of my first sermon at sixteen, and the background details about my first published article when I was eighteen years old. I handled my first revival at eighteen also. It was a youth revival held at First Church of God in Evanston, Illinois, during the pastorate there of the Reverend Frank J. Harper. The call to be the youth revivalist came about as a result of two sermons Pastor Harper and some of his youth leaders had heard me preach. One was a sermon I delivered during a youth hour in the tabernacle at West Middlesex, Pennsylvania, in 1947, and the other was a sermon I preached later that year during the Mid-Year Youth Inspirational Convention held in Kansas City, Kansas. Also, I was very active within the National Youth Fellowship which annually sponsored the youth convention. My first youth revival went well, as we say, and so did the next one for which I was engaged. That second youth revival took place in Detroit, at Sacred Cross Baptist Church where my friend Stacey Williams, another young preacher, was serving as youth minister. My third youth revival took place in December, 1948, at our own Church of God of Detroit. Earlier, in the Spring of that year, the youth of our Michigan churches elected me president of our state organization.

The year 1949 was for me a year of special "openings," both inner and outer "openings." I was nineteen, about to leave the teenage years, and I was being blessed with some grand times of strategic insight and many moments of meaning. I first began to sense the importance of those experiences and that period in my life when I first heard Dr. Howard Thurman preach in Detroit in the Spring of 1949. He had come to preach for three days during the Annual Noon-Day Lenten Services sponsored by the Metropolitan Detroit Council of Churches. The noon-hour services were held at Central Methodist Church downtown, quite a distance from my classes at the University of Detroit, but I decided that I should not miss seeing and hearing that renowned black pulpit master. I persuaded Gwendolyn Kilpatrick to skip her classes at Wayne University one afternoon and meet me at the church to hear Dr. Thurman. As I recall it now, the gathered audience on the first day of Thurman's ministry there was not large, but as he gave himself in exposing the truth within his message the sanctuary seemed strangely full and vibrantly alive. It was a time of depth worship for me.

The contents of the three sermons delivered by Dr. Thurman during those three days at Central Methodist Church are still vivid in my memory. I was moved by his preaching, very deeply moved, partly because what he said was so insightful, partly because hearing it all validated my own spiritual quest and findings in a way that no other preacher's words or pulpit approach had ever done, and partly because of the realization of divine presence I experienced in connection with his witness. As I listened, understood his witness, and experienced God in my spirit, I sensed then and there that Dr. Howard Thurman and I were inwardly kin.

At the close of this series I went forward, waited my turn to greet him, and thanked him for his ministry to my life that day. As I left the sanctuary I knew that I had found a preacher whose insights spoke to the depths of my own spirit and yearning after God. Listening to Dr. Thurman preach across those three days reinforced my thought that preaching must give a hearer access to God. I was privileged to meet with Howard Thurman on many other occasions in the years which followed. By a sure providence, he and I developed a deep and enriching friendship that affected my life and ministry at crucial levels of importance.

Howard Thurman did not preach like most of the African American preachers I had heard. There was no stormy struggle in his manner, no loud blaring of his words; his was a rather softly-spoken, assured and assuring witness, a statement that seemed to me more like an "inside word" about some treasured truth and not an outside attempt to break into the truth. His style seemed so uniquely at one with his subject. Thurman helped me to experience spoken truth more vividly than any preacher I had ever heard before. I took note of this as something other than the effects of a mere pulpit manner or an oratorical prowess. His message and manner made me sense again that wholeness of being which since a child I had come to believe belongs to the experience of hearing the word of God! From early childhood I had known those times when a sense of divine presence so evidenced itself that I knew myself to be involved in more than my own being. I afterward expected such times to happen again, and especially during events associated with God's name. I well remember seeking God's footprints, as it were, at church gatherings, during family devotions, and during worship occasions in particular, but more often than not I was more aware of human activity when someone preached, sang, or prayed than I was of the God in whose honor those actions were supposed to be taking place.

After being disappointed so often by the way human efforts block a vision of God, even my own, I was glad at last to meet someone like Dr. Thurman, whose approach, spiritual tone, and overt witness inspired worship and clearly mediated spiritual meanings in the way that I knew our activities during worship should do. During that spring of 1949, I sensed at a deeper level that a message and its medium should be in strict relation, and I decided that I would seek the best means possible to give a clear, God-honoring, and worship-inspiring witness about the truth entrusted to me as a preacher. I did not know how I would achieve this result, but I knew I had to find a way. This concern to match sermon subject with a proper sermon style has continued to occupy my attention, both personally and professionally, across the years.

Blessed with so many opportunities for service and leadership, I was determined to fulfill them well. In time, this disciplined approach resulted in my name being placed on the ballot for the presidency of the National Youth Fellowship during the annual camp meeting at West Middlesex in 1949. Having been active within the organization for a few years, and having preached at some of the larger meetings, I was becoming well known within the circle of our youth and attending adults. I won the election that year. No doubt it helped my case for being elected that Raymond S. Jackson was my pastor, plus the fact that he was at that time chairman of the General Ministerial Assembly of the National Association of the Church of God, the parent organization under which the youth ministries operated.

My term of office was for two years, but I did not get to serve a full term because I was drafted into military service before my term expired. I was succeeded in office by John Tilden Olds, a graduate of Anderson College and Theological Seminary, who was then pastoring in Omaha, Nebraska. I was followed in the state youth presidency by Emery C. Williams, a recent graduate of the Anderson seminary who had come to minister in Lansing, Michigan. Williams had the opportunity to carry through on planning that some of us had been doing to unify the white youth and the black youth of our Michigan churches and forge one integrated entity with one state convention instead of the two separate meetings. Knowing about his openness to the whole church, both when he was a college student and as a national evangelist afterward, I had given Williams's name to our planning committee after gaining his permission to do so. His coming to Michigan was timely and his ministry among the state youth helped to fulfill the concern many of us had for a racially integrated state youth work.

I was busy learning and laboring as an apprentice preacher. I had become known beyond the local Detroit scene and was called upon now and again to speak in churches and at other religious gatherings. Since 1948 my name was being listed in the Yearbook of the Church of God. I was quite familiar with the fabric of our church group culture and was proud to be a part of its unique weave.

Mid-Century Advance

Pride on my part for the larger church body that was my home had some unexpected occasions to show itself publicly in 1950, and in a national setting. During the first week of January in 1950 I received a letter from Charles V. Weber. The Mid-Year Youth Inspirational Convention, sponsored each December by the National Youth Fellowship, had convened a few days before at the Church of God of Detroit. Weber had attended the meeting and had been strikingly impressed by what had transpired there. He wrote to express his appreciation to me as the convention president. He then added these comments:

> My earnest prayer for you is that God will strengthen and bless your ministry so that it will become church-wide, not only among your race, but interracially.
>
> We are very happy that you have consented to serve on the sponsoring committee of our evangelistic Advance. I will be writing to you about that at a later date.
>
> In the meantime, I hope, Brother Massey, that you will pray earnestly for the spiritual growth of the whole Church of God, for if we really advance we must first receive an inward fortification for the effort we will make. That will come through prayer and a deepening of our spiritual lives. I will appreciate your prayers.
>
> Your brother in Christ,
> Charles V. Weber

Charles Weber was at that time field secretary for the Church of God World Service Commission. Weber had earlier pastored Bethany Church in Detroit, so I was acquainted with his ministry. He had further impressed me the year he addressed the young people at West Middlesex on the devotional life. His theme was "Living Out of the Overflow" and his insights blessed my life. The "sponsoring committee" mentioned in his letter to me was a group of fifty- nine persons, all leaders from various sections of the nation. Together with John T. Olds, John M. Clark, and Cleopatra C. Jackson (wife of Raymond S.), I was on the sponsoring committee to represent the black churches of the North. The black congregations of the Southern region were represented by E. L. Clyburn and W. H. Delaine.

During the month of April several members on the committee were asked to write a brief statement for publication to emphasize across the church the need for an all-out, church-wide evangelistic advance. A concern was deepening to make the message and presence of our church group's witness felt more acutely in the world. The statements were published in successive issues of the *Gospel Trumpet,* together with photographs of those who had written them. My statement and photo appeared in the June 24, 1950, issue. I wrote:

> The Advance must first start in our pulpits. Our concern is advance, spiritual conquest, reform. Well, we all know that all major historical reforms were not accomplished by platitudinous essays but by Bible-centered preaching; preaching that had a purpose behind it; preaching that came from men who were afire with what came forth from God-anointed lips. When we as preachers advance in this respect the congregations will advance, so will the movement; and from the movement will flow the tide that is to change our age.

Admittedly triumphalistic in tone, that statement reflected my growing view of the importance of preaching as a prophetic witness; it also showed the faith and hope deepening within me for a vital preaching ministry.

The sponsoring committee for the Mid-Century Advance was organized as early as 1949, but its members did not meet in official session until January of 1951, a few weeks prior to my leaving to enter military service. We spent two days in

Anderson, Indiana, location of our general church offices, discussing the pattern of our past and planning with concern for our future as a reform movement. William E. Reed, Secretary of Evangelism, reported the results from a survey done to ascertain the state and needs of our many congregations. Among other things, that survey revealed that membership in our churches was growing more rapidly than the population of the nation; that the number of churches among us had exceeded our supply of pastors; that new churches were out-growing those established earlier; that a large number of our congregations had died within the first ten years after beginning; and that too many of our churches were either paralyzed or at a plateau. We spent time facing facts and seeking solutions to some apparent problems in our group life.

During one of the plenary sessions I addressed the problem of those states that endorsed racially separate ministerial associations, a custom that undermined our church witness about Christian unity. After an initial discomfort, finally eased somewhat by the fact that we were gathered to discuss the needed future by facing present facts, our discussion proceeded to the point of agreeing that the urgency of unified endeavor placed a demand upon our many state assemblies to deal forthrightly with that problem. Years later, there would still be some racially separate state organizations among us, but I was glad that the Church of God in Michigan became an integrated assembly during the early 1950s, just shortly after the Mid-Century Advance emphasis. Actually, this was really a return to the inclusive pattern the Church of God in Michigan had known and exemplified in the first decades of its life and work.

During the 1950 International Camp Meeting at Anderson, Indiana, I had the privilege and responsibility of serving in two leadership roles. I preached in a general service of the camp meeting in the old Tabernacle on Saturday morning, June 24th, and I chaired a youth vesper service that night. Rev. Jackson was serving that year as a member of the pulpit and program committee for the camp meeting. Although nominated in many letters from the field, and even requested by other members of the committee to preach that year, Jackson refused to name himself on the ground of being a committee member. He submitted my name instead. When notified that I had been chosen to preach in a general service of that camp meeting, I felt challenged and choked! I was more than relieved when the burden of that hour was removed. Many from the Detroit church were there to support me with their prayers, including Gwendolyn Inez Kilpatrick. I preached on the previously announced subject, "I Am One of Them." That day, June 24, 1950, remains an unforgettable day in my memory.

One of my memories about that day is a sad one. Albert Kenneth Parker, one of my closest ministerial friends at the Detroit church, suffered a serious injury in a highway accident en route to the camp meeting. Intent to reach Anderson, Indiana, in time for the morning service in which I was to preach, Albert left Detroit at a late hour the night before, bringing additional friends in the car with him. During a severe rainstorm his car skidded, ran off the slippery roadway, and crashed into an embankment. My cousin, Graham H. Williams, was trailing Albert in his car, which was providential because he rushed Albert and the other injured to a nearby hospital for treatment. The accident left Albert's right leg permanently injured. Graham arrived in Anderson well before the worship service began, but, fearing that the news of the accident might affect my concentration, he kept the matter from me until the service was over. Upon hearing the story, I felt a deep hurt. Despite all that had happened in a positive vein that day, the fact of the accident overshadowed it all. I grow solemn each time I reflect upon that special Saturday. Albert Parker and I were close friends. I had been Best Man at his wedding, and we were prayer-partners.

Church life continued to attract and involve me. I went to school by day, and by night I was at the church, which often made it necessary that I study well past midnight. There were times when I remained at my study desk from the time I returned home from church until the rays of dawn pierced the darkness outside our house. I should not have been so involved at church while a student in college, but my zeal was now as great for the things of God as it had been earlier for classical music. I had not yet discerned the difference between Christian spirituality and faithfulness to a church program. My mother cautioned me against overwork, but I gave little heed at first. I was in love with God, deeply interested in church life, and eager to learn—not just from my college textbooks but from the books on theology, church history, biography, and preaching that I was also reading. In time, the pressured scheduling began to affect me severely. I began feeling distressed and started missing classes at the university. After excessive absences, I withdrew from a few courses. I did not return to school for the Spring semester of 1950. I used a part of my time out of school to do some writing. Deeply interested in documenting the career of Raymond S. Jackson, I spent time interviewing him and setting down my findings in a preliminary format. My materials piled. By summer I had done a first draft of a projected treatment of his life and work.

It was during that same time that Charles Ewing Brown, editor-in-chief of Gospel Trumpet Company publications, was completing work on his history of the Church of God Reformation Movement. Upon seeing a notice in several issues of the *Gospel Trumpet* about the work that was in progress, and Brown's request for information about some persons, I wrote and shared with him some additional information about Jackson. Brown wrote back and thanked me for replying to his request. Some of what I shared with him was included in his book *When the Trumpet Sounded* (1951).

According to my recollection, I first learned about the Reverend Raymond Samuel Jackson through a conversation I overheard between my parents. We were all in the family car, returning to Detroit from the National Camp Meeting at West Middlesex, Pennsylvania. My parents were still exulting over a sermon Jackson had preached there. I cannot recall the exact year now, but as I think back upon that remembered conversation in the family car I can recall the tenor of their talk. It was clear to me that my parents had sensed the hand of God upon this man's life and had heard a word from God through his vibrant witness.

When Jackson later came to Detroit in 1943 to pastor the Church of God of Detroit, he was fifty-one years old, a seasoned leader and a highly effective preacher. I was a teenager and there was so much about him for a teenager to admire. His open character, attractive bearing, earnestness and audacious leadership were proverbial. I admired the spirit of discipline I sensed when in his company. I was also aware of an austerity and reserve which made me uncomfortable around him at first, but as I watched and learned from his work I found myself in a son's relationship of warmth and regard. Jackson impressed me as a charismatic leader. He was an adroit churchman—the bishop type. His major focus was the group, and he knew how to lead it. His major message was on the church, its doctrines and purpose, and he knew how to preach it with contagious conviction. He was the right one to know and follow as I wrestled with the demands of preparing for ministry. Meeting Raymond S. Jackson at that well-developed stage of his life allowed me, at that most impressionable age, to benefit immediately from his wisdom and steadily gain insight from his example. I grew in grace under his preaching, and I felt privileged as one he finally recommended as a beloved "son in the ministry."

Accustomed as I was to having dialogue-learning sessions with Jackson, I took seriously the opportunities for dialogue with my professors at the University of Detroit while studying there. I was especially interested in the Jesuit rationale about the meaning, character, structure, leadership, and basic functions of the church. I was seeking a theology of balance and I wanted to incorporate into it the major insights and values from every arena then open to my inquiry. By the time I withdrew in the Spring of 1950, in great need of a break from the pressing routine of formal study, I was more alert to the many facets of a biblical ecclesiology and I held a higher view of the importance of tradition in shaping and sustaining an informed church life.

I remember meeting after class one afternoon with Father Arthur Lovejoy. During the class period I heard him say that the potential for holiness is the main concern in the religious quest, not the attainment of it. He went on to state (probably in defense of a sometimes faulty priesthood) that the sacraments lose nothing of their efficacy when the one handling them is unfit to do so. As I heard him say all this, I was thinking about the apostolic insistence upon godliness and about the emphasis our church (the Church of God) placed on matching obedience with God's claim upon our lives. In our dialogue after class, I admitted to Father Lovejoy that while the "holy sacraments" lose nothing of their efficacy when handled by persons whose beliefs or behavior do not match what the sacraments represent (or re-present), my own view was that the person who does not live by the meaning inherent in holy things loses the right to handle them. I was recalling the Old Testament injunction found in Isaiah "… purify yourselves, you who carry the vessels of the Lord" (52:11b). I was also thinking about Psalm 24:3-5 and the insistence stated there about the conditions to be met for worship to be acceptable, namely that one have a pure heart, a truthful tongue, and a love for the things of God. All in all, my time at the University of Detroit sensitized my spirit to appreciate the fact that there is an essential relationship between Scripture and aspects of tradition, between faith and learning, and also between vital fellowship and creative institutional forms.

I mentioned the surprise invitation to preach at the 1950 Anderson Camp Meeting. I experienced another surprise in the December business meeting of the church that year when Jackson announced that he had chosen me to be his pastoral assistant for the coming year and asked the congregation to ratify the appointment by general vote. The assembled members approved his choice, and thus I entered more fully into the inner workings of congregational planning and ministry. Given such an opportunity, I reasoned that I should not lose it, although accepting the post created a problem for me at that time. Having dropped out of the university for a time, I was now laying plans for marriage and had secured employment at Chrysler Motor Corporation during that Fall of 1950. The church post would provide a modest stipend, but I knew that I would finally need more than the amount initially promised. As it turned out, I took the post as pastoral assistant and continued at my job at Chrysler, working the night shift in order to assist Jackson in ministry in the late morning and early afternoon hours. As one would suspect, there were many times when I became wearied and was tempted to give up one job or the other. But so much was at stake I felt constrained to continue in both.

Just after the beginning of the new year on Sunday, January 7, 1951, I was ordained to serve in the Christian ministry. The service of ordination was simply organized but proved to be a rare and unforgettable experience of prophetic statements and heart-strengthening regard. It left an indelible mark upon my spirit that shall never wear away, and no stress or strain I have experienced since then has ever caused the glow from that high moment of meaning to fade or be obscured. Although several ministers were present and laid their hands upon me, following the treasured biblical custom, the noted young evangelist Horace W. Sheppard from Philadelphia being among them, the Certificate of Ordination presented to me afterward bore the signatures of four ministers whose encouragement and example meant much to me: Raymond S. Jackson, Henry Smith, Leonard Steen, and George W. Massey, Sr., my father.

My brother Raymond was deeply impressed by it all, perhaps more acutely because only a few months earlier he had publicly announced to the church that he too felt called into the ministry. By that time, four of "the Massey boys" had confessed the call to preach. In terms of time, I was the first to acknowledge the call, George was the second, Melvin third, and

Raymond fourth. Our youngest brother, Howard, was the only one of the five Massey sons who did not enter the ministry.

An Interruption

So much was going comparatively well in my life. I was deeply in love and working toward financial readiness to get married. I had made peace with my delayed plans to complete college and consoled myself with the awareness that being Jackson's assistant was more than a stop-gap appointment. It was itself the most intensive preparation for ministry within our church fellowship. Everything seemed in good order.

I was therefore shocked when I opened the mail one October morning and read the notice to me from the local draft board. On March 6, 1951, five months hence, I was to report for induction into the army. A growing military crisis in Korea, together with the continuing need for occupation forces in Europe and Japan, had kept the mandatory draft plan necessary. Since registering for the draft when I turned eighteen, I had put the thought of being drafted out of mind because I knew that I should be exempted on the basis of preparing for the ministry. But it was only when the draft notice arrived that I realized I had failed to have my 1-A classification changed when I began pre-ministerial studies at the University of Detroit! The 1-A classification was now improper in my case, but that was the classification still in the file at Local Board 66 there in Oakland County.

Rev. Jackson wrote a petitioning request that I be deferred because of my service at the church. There was hope for a time that the petition would be honored. But the petition was denied on the grounds that I was not serving the church full-time. Despite the church appointment, my outside employment of forty hours weekly forfeited my right to deferment even though being an ordained minister. Thus it was that on March 6, 1951, I answered the call from the local draft board in Ferndale, Michigan, and reported as a draftee for service in the United States Army. The term was expected to be for two years.

On the Sunday before I reported for the draft I preached a farewell sermon to the church. Jackson did not get to hear it because he was sick in bed from a flu virus. Using Isaiah 25:9, I preached on "This Is Our God." I was making a theological statement to the congregation about the faith they had helped to nurture in me, the faith I was confident would sustain me during the time I would be absent from them. The drama of my imminent departure gave a solemnity to our time together that Sunday morning.

My Grandmother Amanda was there that day, as were my parents. Two of my brothers were present, Raymond and Howard. Melvin had been drafted earlier and was serving in Japan. My brother Raymond had received a medical exemption from military service, and Howard, born in 1939, was just approaching the teenage period. George, my oldest brother, was now in ministry on his own, pastoring in Georgia. Gwendolyn Inez Kilpatrick, to whom I was now engaged, was there. Although in the midst of a three-month psychiatric nursing affiliation at the University of Minnesota, she returned to Detroit that weekend for the service. She had one year left to complete the five-year program in nursing at Wayne University.

As I sat in the pulpit area that morning, looking out across that sea of beloved faces, my mind was crowded with memories and my heart was full. I was remembering how Gwendolyn and I first met, and how meeting and knowing her had made such a creative difference in my life. I thought about that Sunday evening in 1944, our family having just moved our membership from the Wisconsin Avenue Church to the Church of God of Detroit, when I first laid my eyes on her. The youth meeting had just ended, and while talking on the sidewalk with a few of the church fellows I noticed her standing near the front door of the church. The light over the door seemed focused on her as she stood talking, dressed in a red topcoat. The scene arrested my attention. She was well-dressed, looked intelligent, had a composed bearing, and, beyond all that, she was beautiful! I felt smitten! I was so shaken by it all that I interrupted the conversation we boys were having and asked Andrew Lomax, who was standing beside me, who the girl was who was talking with his sister Doris. He told me her name, and that she had recently come to Detroit from Alabama. I was still looking intently at her as I said to him, prophetically it turned out, "She's going to be my wife!" Still looking in her direction, I caught her eyes and smiled at her. She did not return the smile. Her face was wreathed in a blush.

We were only fourteen, but from that time onward I lived with a dream in my heart that never failed to include her; another "opening" had occurred by which I sensed a companionship that I just knew would one day be realized! Years later, while reading one of the works of novelist Thomas Mann (*Joseph and His Brothers*), I thought again about that hour of prophetic "opening" when I saw these words: "Part of the game we play with life consists in the relations of human beings one to another. Take two people who have exchanged their first glance—what could be slighter, what could be more unconscious, tenuous, distant, and casual than the bond between them? And yet it may be destined to take on, some unimaginable day, a character of burning intensity, a frightful and breathtaking immediacy" (p. 555). But something more than love for her deepened within me as my acquaintance with Gwendolyn ripened into friendship. Her Christian commitment was so vital that I was challenged to focus my direction more surely. While I was serious about my opening toward the demands and delights of music, I had not been as serious in my openness toward God. Gwendolyn had refused to let me read a music score if I was sitting beside her in church during worship.She became one of God's agents whose presence and influence helped me to become more serious about spiritual things. I cannot know what thoughts were passing through her mind that day when I stood up to preach, but I knew that apart from her spiritual mission in my life I might never have reached such a time and place.

As the choir guided us in song, I could see my mother among the sopranos, and I thought about all the many things she and my father had done to prepare me for life. There was so much for which to be grateful to them. They had been ardent in showing and teaching me about excellence and godliness, about the oneness of humankind and the divinely ordained equality of persons. Because of their help I was at home in my identity and had achieved a balanced sense of selfhood out of which I felt completely natural in racially mixed settings. I knew how to relate and how to help others do so. Seeing the miracle of their strength to love and their balanced self-pride, I learned early to temper the militancy which made some others in our community go to extremes of vengeance and violence.

My parents had encouraged me to take the Scriptures seriously. Their reverent attitude toward the Scriptures was evident in the way they read from them, interpreted them, and obeyed them. My parents had also been wise to let me develop as a believer in keeping with my growth as a person. They did not try to make me fit an adult mold when only a child in life and a babe in Christ. I never had to unlearn what they modeled and taught their children. They taught their sons how to honor the community of faith and the importance of being able to stand alone in convictions and decision-making. Having watched them exemplify all this, I had learned to trust it all as worthy of my use. As parents they had had much to do, and they had done it well. As I stood there preaching that Sunday morning, about to take my leave from them for the first time, I was grateful to God for the special grace I had known while growing up under their steady and loving guidance.

Feeling deeply, I shared my soul as well as my understanding of that text from Isaiah. But the congregation also shared a word, and hearing it spoken gave me an encouraging surprise. As the service was about to close, the Reverend Leonard Steen, an honored minister within the church, stood and suggested that I should be permitted to resume my duties as assistant pastor after returning from military service. The thunderous roar of many saying "Amen!" assured me of their agreement. All through my time of military service I thus had something to which I could look forward and, alas, something for which to be prepared.

4

IN THE SERVICE OF THE COUNTRY

There is a saying among those who are drafted into military service. They never forget the day they enter it, and they always remember the day they leave it. The reason has to do with the sometimes abrupt changes that are experienced as a result of no longer holding full control over the details of one's life, particularly one's movements and work. From my very first day in the army I decided that I would make the most of the experience.

Making the Most of It

Though separated from family and friends, from the church, and from the girl I would later marry, I determined that I would not complain, believing that God would help me to handle the experience wisely. Given the circumstances, however, I did wonder whether Gwendolyn and I would be able to fulfill our plan to get married that year. All during the period of my basic training this question never stopped haunting us both. Although we let our plan for a late summer wedding stand, we were at the mercy of military jurisdiction. The dark cloud of uncertainty about getting back home to Detroit on our planned timetable was over me when I was taken to Fort Custer, Michigan, for processing, then to Fort Jackson, South Carolina, where I received the requisite basic military training.

Interestingly, shortly after arriving at Fort Custer, I was

summoned to a conference which some of the processing officers there arranged after examining the file on me. When asked how it happened that I became drafted, I explained the situation to them. To a man (there were only male officers present) they felt and stated that as a minister I should have been deferred. A short while later I was given a few days of leave time to go to Lansing, Michigan, so that the Michigan State Director of Selective Service could personally review my case and make a judgment about it. I contacted the Director's office in Lansing and arranged for an appointment. I went to Lansing on the appointed day and presented my case to the Director. Despite all explanations, he could not be persuaded to reopen the matter and change my status. It took me some time to accept the fact that I would not receive the desired change of status. I returned to Fort Custer with a cloudy mind and a wounded spirit. The issue now settled, I was sent on to Fort Jackson in South Carolina where I gave myself fully to the training and was made a squad leader.

Drafted in March, 1951, I was still at Fort Custer in April, awaiting orders, when the news broke that President Harry Truman had summarily relieved General Douglas MacArthur of his supreme command over military forces in the Far East. The tumultuous welcome the General received upon arriving back in America galvanized the national will at that time when so many in the free world trembled in fear of Communist aggression here and there. Hearing by radio the speech MacArthur made to a joint session of Congress affected me deeply. I listened patiently as the General gave his assessment of the military situation the free world faced, and I took courage as he restated the need to move beyond prolonged indecision and act with intent to win against aggression. I too had misgivings about the "police action" concept that governed American military forces then fighting in Korea and I strongly agreed when that former commander declared that "In war, indeed, there can be no substitute for victory." His line of argument proceeded reasonably and his stirring rhetoric made me hang on every word. I thought to myself, what a fitting close to his fifty-two years of military service, and what a word for me as I was beginning my time of preparation to serve the country. For days afterward the inductees in our barracks kept echoing the refrain MacArthur used to conclude that moving and memorable statement to Congress: "Old soldiers never die, they just fade away."

Columbia, South Carolina, where Fort Jackson was located, was the state's capitol city. It was an "army town" with all that this implies. It was also a Jim Crow city in which the segregation pattern allowed a large sector of Black life and housing that depressed me whenever I went to town. The overcrowding made me feel choked and the slum section so disturbed my spirit that I only went to town on Sunday, at which time I would attend the local congregation of the Church of God (black) or go to the Baptist church where the Reverend Maxie Gordon was pastor, the church which many of the teachers and students from nearby Allen University and Benedict College attended. I liked Maxie Gordon's preaching. Gordon helped me to think about my religious experience. His preaching reflected scholarship as well as spiritual depth. Gordon was also teaching at Benedict, in the college's department of religion, and his blend of learning and traditional pulpit warmth always gave me a needed lift.

My barrack buddy was Milton Brunson from Chicago, one of the men in the squad I headed. A Baptist by background and choice, Brunson was an ardent Christian, a fact that gave us a better basis for closeness than I found with some of the other trainees. When free on Sunday to go to town, Brunson and I would usually go together. He would sometimes go with me to the local Church of God, but most of the time we went to Maxie Gordon's church. There were times when we went to other churches, but we did so when engaged for some special afternoon service in which he was expected to sing. Brunson was a gifted baritone soloist who could stir an audience. I served as his pianist. He could sing the song "as written" or as traditionally sung, or as he arranged it himself. I adapted to his chosen rendering. He usually sang in a straightforward style. Those were the days before an overpowering syncopation became the prevailing order. The ballads of Thomas Dorsey were in wide use, but they were not as "doctored" then as they would be in a later period. I took great delight in being able to "sample" the church life of so many congregations in that city as Brunson and I visited and served with our gifts. Milton Brunson later became a minister and pastor and developed a large church in Chicago which featured a mass choir and a regular Sunday afternoon radio program.

On one of my days off the post I went over to the campus of Benedict College, a school founded in 1871 during the Reconstruction Period by the American Baptist Home Mission Society. I went there to attend an academic exercise at the college and was among the many who sat enthralled as Dr. Benjamin Elijah Mays delivered an eloquent, soul-stirring address. The afternoon was hot and the college gymnasium in which the service was held was not air-conditioned, but the place was filled and the speaker sustained our interest by his thought-provoking subject matter and characteristically eloquent manner. His rhetoric was exhilarating and refreshing. As I sat listening, looking, and emoting, I took renewed interest in becoming a well-trained leader and to cultivate the highest type of leadership style.

The African-American congregation of the Church of God in Columbia was a very modest group. I still preferred the services and preaching at Maxie Gordon's church because they were more like what I had known and enjoyed back in the Detroit church, but I enjoyed the fellowship of the local church of my group heritage. I enjoyed the company of the Beachums, one of the leading families. William Beachum was a deacon there. It was after a service at that church that I met the Reverend James E. Forrest, one of the leading white ministers of the Church of God group in the South. He was the speaker that day. I had read some of his articles in the *Gospel Trumpet,* knew

83

about his practice of racial openness, and considered it a privilege to meet and converse with him.

Later in the training period I answered a call from the Reverend George Wilson, Sr., to come to Atlanta, Georgia, and preach at the Martin Street Church of God where he was pastor. Rudolph Smith, a young minister there who had become a friend after our contact through the Mid-Year National Youth Fellowship Convention, had encouraged Pastor Wilson to invite me there as a youth-day speaker. Having himself heard me preach at West Middlesex and at the Mid-Year Youth Convention, Wilson agreed that I should be invited. One visit led to another, and I was also invited to preach a sermon during the annual state camp meeting held in Wadley, Georgia. Being in Wadley that weekend allowed me to meet some of the principal black leaders of the Church of God in the Southeast. Not long afterward I was invited to preach in Dublin, Georgia, where I was privileged to have some quality time with the Reverend James S. May, former pastor of Paulson Avenue Church of God in Pittsburgh, Pennsylvania. May was living in retirement there in Dublin, his hometown. May was a dynamic and colorful preacher. I had heard him often in camp meeting services at West Middlesex; he had also been guest evangelist at our Church of God of Detroit one year.

After I preached in the Dublin church, James S. May drove me downtown where we parked in front of a cafe. It was quite hot outside and I was really hungry. I thought we were going inside and get something to eat, but, pointing to the cafe, he said: "Under other circumstances we would be getting some-thing to eat, but we will have to be content for the moment with a cold bottle of pop. I will be right back." He went inside and quickly returned with two bottles of Coca-Cola. We sat and quenched our thirst as my stomach yearned for something more substantial. I felt relieved, however, only when he finally announced that we would be guests in the home of one of the church members. We were to kill time until the announced hour to gather at that member's house. I could hardly wait to get there.

Just before we pulled away from the curb, a man across the street recognized James May and motioned with his hand for us to wait a minute. Once at the waiting car the man reached into his pocket, pulled out his wallet, took a few bills from it, and gave them to May. "Reverend," he confessed, "it's been a while since I've been to church to hear you. Here is an offering. Take it and use it as you see fit." May smiled and thanked the friend. James S. May was well-respected in his hometown.

Back at Fort Jackson, the rigorous training routine continued on schedule. I was doing well. Our company was within two weeks of completing our basic training when I suffered a fracture in my right foot during a forced march and had to be hospitalized. I had to have a cast on my foot and leg. I wondered whether the wedding plans Gwendolyn and I had made could be carried out on schedule. I also feared that being away from my company those last two weeks would mean that I might not ever get to be again with most if not all of the friends I had made in the company during our time in training. With their training completed, I knew they would be receiving their orders for necessary assignments elsewhere. As I lingered in the hospital, I felt so isolated. It happened as I feared, but I was released from the hospital in time to see many of my barrack buddies before the full company was dispersed. In talking with some of them I learned that most of them had been assigned to service in Korea and Japan.

I did not have to make up the two weeks I lost. I was still walking with a leg cast and was given light duties to occupy my time and attention. One assigned duty I appreciated. It was clearing old Sunday bulletins and unnecessary clutter from the hymnal racks in the nearby Chapel and removing dust from the altar and pews. There was a hidden motive wedded to my appreciation of that duty. Being in the Chapel gave me access to its organ once my assigned work was done. It was by hearing me play the organ that our chaplain learned about my musical training. Not long afterward, Chaplain (Major) Bledsoe asked me to substitute for the regular organist who had been granted a leave. I gladly did so. The new opportunity suited me well and the Chapel service ended early enough for me to get to one of the churches in town before the preaching began. With access to the Chapel organ, I filled my evenings with practice. Brunson and I would rehearse there for upcoming engagements, staying up fairly late at times. Our music-making was for me an oasis of comfort and creativity in the sea of pressures brought on by the draft and the uncertainty I felt when thinking about my wedding plans.

The cloud of uncertainty finally lifted in mid-July. The company commander assured me that the leave-time I had requested would be honored. Hoping against hope, Gwendolyn and I had mailed out the wedding invitations early in June. I was still wearing my leg cast and Gwendolyn had a nightmare about me hobbling down the center aisle of the Detroit church weighted down by that cast! Fortunately, the cast was removed three days before I boarded the train headed to Detroit. She and I were joined in holy matrimony before our church family on the day we had planned, Saturday, August 4, 1951. The following Monday morning Gwendolyn flew back to South Carolina to be with me there for two weeks. Following the suggestion of Reverend Jackson, the church bore the expense for our flight. Wanting me to preach before returning, but knowing that I had to be back in camp that Monday, Jackson promised to send us both by plane if I agreed to preach for him that Sunday night. Gwendolyn considered his request unusual and cruel. Having just married on Saturday evening, it was a bit awkward to oblige Jackson, but I did preach that Sunday. Gwendolyn chided me for agreeing to do so, but I was thinking about the timely convenience for travel that his ministerial bargain with me thus allowed.

Something unusual happened during our wedding that Saturday evening. As Pastor Jackson was officiating, he began to sob in the middle of the ceremony. He soon gained his composure, but not before it was evident to most that his emotions were affected. When Gwendolyn later asked him about the experience Jackson answered that he was temporarily overcome with solicitation about my future. Our wedding ceremony did not include the use of a wedding ring. When Jackson became pastor of the church in 1943 he had banned the use of any finger adornments by the members. This was a restriction the previous pastors had not made.

I had a rather lengthy stay at Fort Jackson after my basic training period ended. Interestingly, during the time I was waiting to receive an assignment I was informed that the company commander over my training unit had forwarded a request through channels that I should be discharged. It was his judgment that as a minister I should not have been drafted. I do not know what part Chaplain Bledsoe might have had in the decision to request a discharge for me, but I do remember receiving some leave time to make a trip to the Selective Service Office in Washington, D. C. to seek the concurrence of that office to strengthen my case for being discharged. I went to Washington and met with some Selective Service officials, but their decision only echoed what the Michigan State Director of Selective Service had stated, so I returned to Fort Jackson to await my assignment orders. I had hoped to be released. I was disappointed when this did not happen.

Shortly afterward I received my orders and learned that I had been given an overseas assignment. I felt inwardly numbed. I tremblingly wondered what the turn of affairs would mean for my life. On November 24, 1951, I left Fort Jackson, South Carolina, with a twelve-day delay en route before having to report to Camp Kilmer, New Jersey, for shipment overseas in December. I reached Detroit the next day, just eleven days since I had been in Washington seeking concurrence from the Selective Service Office for a possible discharge. The brief stay in Detroit with my wife, family, and friends was an experience of mingled joy and foreboding. There was one element of relief in the picture. I was being sent on assignment to Europe rather than to the Far East where the conflict with Communistic forces in Korea was still raging.

Assignment: Chaplain's Assistant

Shortly before boarding the ship for my assignment overseas, I decided to keep a diary record of my experiences. I was
at a strangely new place in life and many thoughts and fears
registered themselves in my consciousness, all clamoring to be
heard and all needing to be managed. Separated from the social
forces of family and church life, I knew that the new context of
my life as a soldier overseas demanded an intelligible faith and
a responsible stance on my part. I knew that keeping a diary
record could help me chart my reactions to the new experiences
I would face and aid my thought processes and responses. I
followed my plan. I began my diary on January 1, 1952, and
I made near-regular entries in it across the next fourteen months
of my life, at which time I had returned to the United States and
was honorably released from military service. I have drawn from
that diary for this chapter about the major happenings in my life
while serving with the United States Armed Forces in Austria.

I was sent to Austria with a clerk typist designation, and I
was a member of the Headquarters and Service Company, 70th
Engineer Combat Battalion stationed at Camp Saalfelden, a
post about fifty miles south of Salzburg. Our army camp was
just a mile from the village of Saalfelden, and it was situated in
a valley track bordered by some of the most picturesque
summits of the Austrian Alps. It was a stimulating mental and
spiritual experience to begin, continue, and end each day in
such a setting, with the mountain peaks pointing like fingers to
heaven. Seeing them daily kept me reminded of the greatness
and nearness of God. Each summit was a majestic, suggestive
sight, a mind-opener, a stimulant to prayer and praise.

My service role was Chaplain's Assistant, and I was fortunate in being assigned to work with Chaplain (Capt.) Weldon H.
Barnett. Chaplain Barnett was a native Texan, white, and a
minister of the Church of Christ. My responsibilities included
the daily management of the Chapel Office and supervising the
care of the chapel building and grounds. As Chaplain's
Assistant I also served as the Chaplain's driver, and a car was

assigned to my use and care for the purpose. Not long after I began my work there at the Chapel an additional duty became mine by a special contractual agreement. The organist who had been playing for the Sunday service moved from the Saalfelden area and I was hired as organist for the two Sunday services for which Chaplain Barnett was responsible. The first service was at 9:00 A.M. at our camp chapel; the second service, held at 11:00 A.M., was at the camp chapel in St. Johann (in Pongau), some miles away. On those Sundays when snow was falling heavily or when rain had made the mountain road slick, it was quite a feat to complete safely the trip to St. Johann in our jeep with enough time to spare before the service there had to begin. The contractual agreement for my service as organist for the two services provided me additional pay. The service of an organist was classified as a skilled craft and the precedent for paying an organist had been set long before I arrived.

I enjoyed working with Chaplain Barnett. He was an intelligent and kind man, serious about his faith, and had high standards for himself as a leader. Although he was an ordained minister of that branch of the Church of Christ which did not use musical instruments in their services of worship, Chaplain Barnett did not seem affected by that tradition as he planned the chapel services in which we regularly served. I found him to be one who loved good music, and he was often generous in his praise when the music for which I was responsible had been well done and well received.

Chaplain Barnett and I had a good working relationship that gave me great freedom as I handled my chapel assignments. Despite his Southern background, his approach and response to me as a "person of color" seemed free from the usual influences of racism. As I worked with him day-in and day-out I sensed that he had not only been freed from the constraining tradition within his denomination which disallowed the use of musical instruments in their worship services, but he seemed freed from the expected stereotyped thinking about black people. Throughout the thirteen months of our togetherness, in both work and leisure hours, I never felt isolated by him or critically assessed along lines of racial difference. He was the kind of liberated Southerner around whom I felt comfortable. While it is true that we were serving in a new and racially-integrated army, and that cooperativeness was the expected order, I soon became aware that the chaplain with whom I worked was truly a man of social openness as well as serious faith. I was grateful to God for this as we did our assigned work.

I not only worked in the chapel office and played the organ for the worship services there, I was quartered there. In the rear of the chapel building, just across from the sacristy, a spare room had been equipped to serve as a guestroom. The room was assigned as living quarters for the chaplain's assistant before me, so I inherited it upon my arrival. Having known the boisterous scenes of barrack living while in training and afterward, having my own room in the post chapel provided a place of privacy that I treasured. Across the months of my stay in Austria, that room was my place of retreat and rest. It was a place of much prayer, meditation, solid reading, reflection, and writing.

Our chapel not only had an organ, which we used each Sunday for our service, but there was also an old upright piano in the sanctuary. I spent many evening hours at that piano, sometimes playing late into the night. In addition to a few books by authors with whose thought my spirit resonated, I had brought with me from America some musical scores. On a visit to Salzburg I located some music stores and purchased additional classical albums from which to practice and extend my repertoire as a pianist. An April visit to Vienna, where the very soil is drenched with music, allowed me to increase my store of musical scores still further. When not at the camp library reading, or socializing at the service club on post, no evening of mine was complete until I had spent time at that piano in the sanctuary of our chapel.

There was a day when Chaplain Barnett announced his need to go to Salzburg and visit with the post chaplain at Camp Roeder there. I drove him to Salzburg where we met and conversed with a Chaplain (Maj.) Andrew L. Johnson, a spry, well-groomed, intelligent-looking and quick-minded black man. Chaplain Barnett and I were both treated to afternoon tea, after which he and Chaplain Johnson discussed the business of the trip. While waiting on the two chaplains to complete their business talk, I began talking with the post chaplain's assistant and another lady, an Austrian presumably, who worked in the chapel office. Noticing a grand piano across the floor in an adjoining room, I asked how and when it was used and to whom it belonged. The Austrian lady answered first, rising to move toward the piano as she spoke. She asked if I played the piano. I answered that I did. She raised the lid from the keyboard and in a voiced pride announced, "This is a Boessendorfer!" I also felt some pride as I sat down and drew some marvelous sounds from that magnificent instrument. More conversation followed, which acquainted me with her love for music and where she was presently studying. I listened with rapt attention because for some months I had nursed the thought of finding a teacher in order to do some advanced study while in Austria. I confessed my desire to do further study and she suggested that I should contact her teacher, Heinz Scholz, a noted pianist and pedagogue who taught there in Salzburg at the Mozarteum. I shared this information with Chaplain Barnett as he and I drove back to Saalfelden. He encouraged me to take advantage of the opportunity.

Blessed by an appointment the Austrian lady secured for me with her teacher, I went to Salzburg on Tuesday, April 22, 1952, to meet Professor Heinz Scholz at his studio in the Mozarteum and to audition for him. A few minutes before the agreed hour I walked into the building and found the designated room. But as I neared it I heard the cascading sounds from someone playing that difficult F minor piano sonata by Johannes Brahms. I paused, almost too afraid to rap on the door, thinking that some student was still involved in practice before the teacher. I did not want to interrupt such serious work. There was another reason for my hesitation. I wondered just how long it would take me to achieve the technique necessary to handle works of such technical difficulty. I feared that the teacher I was there to meet might lay a greater burden of demand upon me than I was ready to shoulder. The hour came, and as the piano sounds continued I broke through all hesitation and knocked at the studio door. The piano sounds stopped and a moment later a distinguished looking gentleman in a gray business suit stood before the opened door, his hand extended to greet me. He introduced himself as Heinz Scholz. He was alone. It was his playing I heard while waiting outside his studio door.

The meeting took place in an atmosphere of ease. Heinz Scholz was a cultured person who knew how to ease the tensions of such a time. After some questions from him about my musical background, he had me play for him. I offered my rendering of Beethoven's "Moonlight" and "Appassionata" sonatas, though not all of each, and ended with the "Revolutionary" etude by Frederick Chopin. Scholz listened with apparent interest and watched my hand movements through it all. I was nervous as I played and I am sure that my slips must have offended his seasoned ears. Even so, the professor was kind with his comments. He paused, pointed out a better tempo for one of the passages in the "Moonlight," and afterward announced that he was willing to accept me as a student. We then discussed the course of studies he wanted me to pursue.

I was to begin with a regimen of Johann Sebastian Bach and Ludwig van Beethoven. For my first lesson I was to prepare Beethoven's piano sonata no. 5 (Opus 10, number 1) and Bach's French Suite number 6. Scholz also encouraged me to begin using Hanon's exercises again as warm-up work for the fingers. The Bach assignment was to give me facility in rendering the baroque style and develop expression in the sometimes simple and sometimes complex jigs and other canonical forms of that master's works. The involvement with Beethoven was to help me develop good musical judgment in moving within the wide range of moods and emotions that the creator expressed as he expanded the limits of the previously rigid classical style. Doing Bach well would help me achieve greater musical coherence, while doing Beethoven well would help me deal musically with structure, dynamics, and tonal color.

Grateful for the opportunity I now enjoyed, I bought the best editions of the Bach French Suites and the Beethoven piano sonatas and plunged heartily into my practice sessions back at the chapel. For the Beethoven sonatas I used the Universal-Edition (Vienna)) edited by Heinrich Schenker (and revised by Erwin Ratz). Schenker was a Polish-born Austrian musician whose theories and analyses of Beethoven's musical creations were considered by many as important for the proper understanding and interpretation of that music. Especially interesting to me were the insights he published regarding Beethoven's last five piano sonatas.

Since Chaplain Barnett and I worked on Sunday, we both took a day off during the week. I chose Tuesday for my off-day. At first I sometimes spent it privately in my room doing serious reading, furthering my research for writing projects, and answering mail from my wife, family, and friends. Occasionally I took the train and went into Salzburg for a relaxed day of sight-seeing and good food. But after April 22, when Professor Heinz Scholz accepted me for advanced piano studies. I used my free Tuesdays as lesson days with him at the Mozarteum.

Heinz Scholz was an esteemed professor at the Mozarteum and his double-windowed studio occupied a first floor corner of the building. Some autographed photographs from leading musicians decorated his studio walls, showing both his regard for them and the esteem they held for him. But holding chief place in the room was his Boessendorfer grand piano. Whenever I sat at that piano I felt intimidated, challenged, encouraged, and subdued, aware as I was of the privilege I had but could not fully enjoy—knowing that my future was to be in a pulpit and not at a piano as a world-class artist.

I practiced hard and learned much from Heinz Scholz during our time together in 1952. He was a patient, careful, learned and caring teacher. I prized our time together, and I took pride in him as a scholar. In addition to being a world-class Austrian pianist, Scholz was a Mozart scholar. In company with his brother Robert, also a pianist, Heinz Scholz edited a much-used Ur-text edition of the Mozart piano sonatas. The Mozarteum was the conservatory of the International Mozart Foundation, and the building housed a library and archives in which, among other materials, hundreds of Wolfgang Amadeus Mozart's letters and original musical scores were available for scholarly study. Heinz Scholz was a respected Mozart specialist. He was later a recipient of the famed Mozart Medallion and elected a trustee of the International Mozart Foundation.

During my time of study at the Mozarteum I got to see and hear several world-class pianists who came there to teach during the Summer Academy (July-August) or to give a recital. I shall not soon forget the feeling stirred in me as I sat in the building's Grosser Saal, enthralled, marveling over the artistry of Wilhelm Backhaus. Geza Anda came and gave a masterful recital there of the Brahms' Paganini Variations—a technical knockout indeed, and he followed them with Schumann's Symphonic Etudes. I had but one criticism: the tonal qualities of the piano he used did not seem sufficiently brilliant to my ears. Claudio Arrau, the great Chilean pianist, also came to play in 1952, and I went backstage to meet him because upon hearing him I knew I had found the ultimate musician. Arrau was a con-summate artist with a supreme gift for drawing a full tone from each note as he played, and his interpretations always opened the interior dimensions and message of the music he played. After seeing and hearing Arrau play Robert Schumann's Fantasie in C that night, I bought a copy of it and began committing it to memory, eager to add that grand creation to my growing reper-toire. But alas! other business intervened and I did not master its contents sufficiently to risk myself playing it in public.

As for playing in public, Daniel Barenboim excited a rage when he came to Salzburg in July 1952. His playing so stirred the city that his name was on nearly every tongue thereafter. Only nine years old at the time, it was evident to all that he was a Wunderkind and that his phenomenal gifts and abilities had marked him out for an exceptional future in music. And what about me? As I continued to struggle with my studies, I sometimes wondered what kind of future I might have had if my heart had remained committed to music rather than ministry! Young Barenboim returned to Salzburg two years later as a student at the Mozarteum. The rest of his astounding story since those student years is well-known. Mine is less so.

An Additional Task

On Tuesday, May 27, 1952, my off-day, I went to Salzburg for my lesson, as usual. When I returned to Saalfelden that night there was a note for me on the writing desk in my room. The note was from Edward Tefft, a white friend who was a clerk in the camp headquarters office. Chaplain Barnett had placed the note on my desk so that I would see it before the next day. The note was a request from Tefft to take his place on Thursday morning and do the weekly Troop Information and Education Lecture. He mentioned that the lecture needed to be only twenty minutes in length, and he stated the scope it should cover: "Just a resume of unity, strength, and freedom, and how we as a nation are attaining and keeping it—nothing technical." I sought Tefft during breakfast at the mess hall the next morning and talked further about his request. With needed understanding and a full day within which to ready myself for the lecture to the battalion, I agreed to take his place.

On Thursday morning I gave the lecture, using the theme "Unity, Strength, and Freedom," drawn from what Tefft had suggested in his note. "We are Americans," I began, "and as soldiers of our land are both protectors and possessors of our past, present, and future. Who sees us sees our nation; a nation sufficiently varied, sufficiently common, sufficiently loved. There is no real American who must be impressed with the fact of the greatness of America or the value of our heritage. He already knows that. He loves that. He teaches that. But in this century, amidst the constant interplay of reactionary forces intent upon the utter dissolution of our heritage, it is most wise to restate and qualify the ideals which are of first importance for our survival: they are three—unity, strength, and freedom." I finished the speech within the allotted twenty minutes.

I was hardly prepared for the roar of applause that came as I ended that brief lecture, nor for the firm handshake and approving comments that Captain Ridgeway, my company commander, gave me as his response. Across the rest of that day I received compliments from many other officers and enlisted men. Herbert Ellis, my best friend on the post, was especially pleased about the reception I had been given. Ellis was a corporal in rank and worked at company headquarters as a clerk. We enjoyed each other's presence and usually sat together at meals in the mess hall. A graduate of Shaw University, and a teacher by profession, Ellis was also a lover of serious music, especially Verdi's operas. I always informed him about recitals and concerts to take place in Salzburg, and he encouraged me as I continued my studies there. Disappointed like me in being drafted for military service, Ellis was eager to complete his time and return to his teaching, his fiancee Vermelle, and to the life and future he desired. I liked his mind and kindred spirit, so his compliments meant more to me than those offered by others in camp.

One week after my lecture I was surprised again by Captain Ridgeway. He summoned me to his office and informed me that it was his wish that I assume full responsibility for the command conference hour lectures. As he talked on, some unspoken questions gathered in my mind. One of those questions was resolved only when I learned that Tefft would soon be returning "State-side" and thus had to be replaced as weekly lecturer. Another question had to do with my readiness for such an assignment. The company commander had already mapped a plan to get me ready. He announced that I was being given leave to go and receive training for the new task at the European

Command Troop Information and Education School located at Dachau, Germany. The study period was for two weeks, and I was to leave the second week of June. Chaplain Barnett had already been told of the Commander's plan.

I went to the school at Dachau. I completed the training period there along with one hundred and twenty one other military personnel. Our class included majors, captains, lieutenants, sergeants, corporals, and one or two others in my lower rank of private first class. We received studies to acquaint us more fully with information about NATO, the Mutual Security Program, Communist propaganda, the United Nations organization, our nation's relationship with its allies, and so much more. With others, I qualified as a command conference leader and received a Certificate of Proficiency. But to my surprise I received more. I was selected as the top student within the group and was valedictorian for the graduation ceremony on June 20. I later learned that the EuCom TI & E School sent a letter to Captain Ridgeway commending me for the Superior rating I received as a student there. I also learned that, in being cleared to handle secret and top secret information as a military lecturer, a file had been compiled about me. Raymond S. Jackson told me that government agents had come and asked him strategic questions about my background, memberships, work relationships, and lifestyle. At the time they met with him he thought it was all in connection with the possibility of gaining a discharge for me!

My memories of the stay at Dachau include a visit I made to the memorial sites on the grounds of the former concentration camp located there. I cringed as I viewed pictures of victims emaciated by hunger while imprisoned under the racist Nazi regime. I saddened as I saw the hanging tree; the wooden curved table on which Jewish prisoners were strapped, face-down, for deadly floggings; the blood ditch, the crematory, the graves of ashes—and so many more evidences of the devilish history which took place there. As I stood at the guest register book in front of the crematory, I vowed a vow as I wrote my name on one of its pages. I vowed, "I hereby pledge myself to the utmost defense of the personal freedom of those for whose protection I am currently engaged." Standing there in a place where the blood of Nazi victims still cries out from the ground to be avenged, I felt what I vowed. Although valuing the primacy of human life, I have never been a conscientious objector, but standing there in that place of previous torture, if there had been any residue of an unqualified pacifism left in me, the visit to Dachau destroyed it.

Back from the study time at Dachau, I wrote letters to Gwendolyn, my parents, and Pastor Jackson. I wanted to inform them that I had applied anew for a discharge under new provisions announced recently by the Department of the Army. I explained the new provisions and confessed my hope that the new process would be fruitful. As I did so, however, I was aware that I was in no way anxious about the outcome of applying again for a discharge. Knowing that my term of service was almost over might have had something to do with this. In addition, I was enjoying my excursion again into the music I loved—and the increased sense of leadership I felt with a regular speaking schedule again. After sending the letters, I dismissed the new appeal for discharge from my mind and went on with my regular work, my weekly lecture assignment, my writing, and my piano studies.

After an absence of three weeks from my teacher, I returned to Salzburg for a lesson on Tuesday, July 1. The city was under siege from a heat wave that day and I felt great discomfort as I walked from the train station to get through the tourist-crowded streets in time for my lesson. As I made my way and turned up Schwarzstrasse where the Mozarteum stands, I breathed a sigh of partial relief as I entered the building. As I stepped into Professor Scholz's studio, I blurted out, "What a day! Salzburg is so torrid today!" Scholz looked at me as if in wonder and replied, "But surely you are used to the heat where you are from!" I did not know if he had taken my mild complaint as a criticism of his beloved city, and was offering a mild rebuke, or if he had forgotten that I was a native of cooler Michigan and not accustomed to the hotter southern region of America. Of course I had experienced hot days before, but the heat in Salzburg that day was different because of the extreme humidity in that recessed city. I had known some hellishly hot days while doing basic training in torrid South Carolina the previous summer, but that heat had been much drier than what I was feeling in Salzburg. At any rate, I said nothing further about the heat, allowing that while my Austrian teacher certainly knew much about Mozart and music, he might have more to learn about the different temperature zones and conditions in the United States. After cooling off in the studio, I entered fully into the lesson, which went well.

Things also continued to go well in my regular work and weekly lectures. As they did, I was given a promotion and received Corporal rank on July 29, 1952. The promotion encouraged me. It also meant that a few extra dollars would be available in planning for my family future. Gwendolyn was now a staff member at Detroit's Harper Hospital, having graduated from the Wayne University College of Nursing that January. We were steadily projecting our thought toward our needs following my tour of duty.

There was another soldier at the camp who had a background of serious study in music. His name was Thomas Carey. Carey was a gifted baritone who sang ballads and arias with a full-toned voice and a moving sense of competence. We usually rehearsed together on Saturday afternoons and I accompanied him whenever he sang during a chapel service or on programs at the post service club. I thought it especially interesting that one of the teachers Carey had while a student at the Henry Street Settlement in Brooklyn was Robert Scholz, brother of Heinz Scholz! Carey took a class in harmony from him. When Carey told me this after we met and began to practice, I thought: Small world! Heinz Scholz smiled deeply when I shared this news with him.

The springs of creativity opened wide within me as I gave

myself so fully to music. I began to compose again for the piano and to write pieces for voice and choir. Two of my creations for piano were warmly applauded when I premiered them during a recital at the camp. They were my Prelude in G, and a slightly longer Rhapsody on a Theme in A flat. The rhapsody was in the form of a set of variations. I composed three choral works for worship. One was a well-structured and appealing choral response to be used following the public reading of the Scripture lesson. Its wording came from Revelation 3:20, which had impressed me deeply during my devotional time one morning. I titled the piece "If Thou Wilt Hear." A second choral work, structured for SATB and based on the twenty-third Psalm, was "The Lord Is My Shepherd" and required organ accompaniment. The piece was quite Brahmsian, heavily influenced in its form and flavor from my depth study of that master's soul-stirring German Requiem. The third choral work, also influenced by a psalm text, was an expression of spiritual longing. I titled it "Out of the Depths."

In early September I was eligible to receive some leave-time. I applied and received the time and a rail travel permit and went to Vienna again. The rail travel permit was prepared for military personnel and it was necessary if one sought access to the military duty train that made a regular run between Salzburg and Vienna. Written in three languages (English, Russian, and French), the rail travel permit was also necessary because in going to Vienna the train had to enter separated military zones controlled respectively by three armies of occupation: American, Russian, and French. The travel permit allowed its bearer freedom to move within or through the three zones, the borders of each guarded by soldiers who checked the passengers at the required train stops. The rail travel permit was good for six months, and military personnel were instructed to be in uniform whenever using it. When I boarded the train going to Vienna that September I was in uniform, grateful for some free time and a destination of such promise. Upon reaching the city, I shed my uniform and put on civilian attire for easier movement among the populace.

I spent several days of sight-seeing, shopping, and meeting people. I went to many places of musical importance, deeply stirred by the history associated with them. In my coming and going I met Audre De La Varre, a young white New Yorker studying piano at the Music Academy. I also met and spent time with Samuel Robinson, a West Indian who was a medical student at the University. My path finally crossed that of C. Eduard Ward, a fellow Detroiter whom I had met and known while singing with the DuPre Victorian Choir during my high school years. Ward was in Vienna completing doctoral studies under Professor Walter at the University's *Akademie fur Musik und Darstellende Kunst.* He explained his dissertation project and, with undiluted pride, reported on the expertise he demonstrated during the organ recital he had given on June 3. We rehearsed old scenes from musical life in Detroit, shared hopes for our anticipated futures, and enjoyed some good Austrian dishes at one of his favorite restaurants.

In company with Ward and Robinson I also met and visited with some of the "Porgy and Bess" cast who were doing performances of Gershwin's opera in the city. The cast members had been in Germany and were now in Austria on a State Department-sponsored mission to help Europeans better understand the history of the Negro within American life, using such musical productions as their means. The experience of sharing talk and food with such serious musicians, each one a product and exponent of African American culture, left me exhilarated. The time spent with that musical group, especially with James and Bates, was socially refreshing.

At Year's End

Letters from home during the last three months of 1952 kept me supplied with good news and fed my anticipations about returning to ministry at the Detroit church. I learned by letter in late November that my brother Melvin was back from Japan, honorably discharged, and that he and Helen Jackson from Columbus were headed toward marriage. Another letter, from my mother, encouraged me with news about the trip she, my father, and Grandma Townsend made to Kansas to visit George in his church setting there. They were all pleased about his setting and the progress he was showing in pastoral ministry. Additional news was that in a recent church business meeting Raymond S. Jackson had reminded the congregation of his previously-announced plan to install me as his full-time associate upon my return. My mother commented by letter, "Reverend has everything all cut and dried for you as soon as the Lord brings you back to us." Her statement did what it seemed calculated to do: it sounded a caution, and it prodded more prayer on my part about the service-role I was expected to fill in returning home to Detroit.

On Sunday, December 7, in the afternoon, I was featured in a piano recital at the Alpine Corral Service Club on the post. The recital was well-attended and the program I performed was well-received and applauded. A hill-billy band was featured in the same hall that evening, which allowed "equal time" for camp personnel with that musical interest. The evening audience was also large and actively involved. The full house for my piano recital thrilled and enervated me. I will not in folly attempt my own review, but it is not immodest to report that I was in the mood to perform, and I did so with unfailing memory, clear instincts, and projected feeling. My program included the works of three popular composers: Beethoven (Sonata in C# minor, Op. 27, No. 2 "Moonlight"), Frederick Chopin (Waltz in C# minor, Op. 64, No. 2; Waltz in Ab major, Op. 69, No. 1); "Raindrop" (Prelude), and Ignace Jan Paderewski (Minuet in G, Op. 14, No. 1). As encore pieces, I played two of my own compositions, the Rhapsody on a Theme in Ab major and my Prelude in G, Op. 3. A request came soon afterward for me to give another recital before returning to the States. A news report about the recital was published in the January 2, 1953, issue of *The USFA Sentinel,* the military newspaper among the Salzburg military posts. The article was captioned, "Saalfelden Club Bills Soloist Cpl."

On Monday, January 5, 1953, I was notified to ready myself to leave Saalfelden by the thirteenth in preparation to be returned to the States. By late afternoon of that same Monday I met the soldier who was to replace me as the post chaplain's assistant. It was plainly time to say good-bye to Austria, and there was mingled joy and sadness in my heart as I prepared to do so. The service stay in Austria had been good for me. The tomorrow I faced in my return home was clearly connected in my thoughts with the yesterdays I had experienced in a now-completed 1952. As I stood on the deck of the US Naval Ship Geiger and looked out across the water through which we had to move toward the United States and home, I was confident at last that a meaningful plan had been unfolding in the set of experiences which had been mine through being drafted.

Although I said my good-byes to Austria, I could not yet say farewell to military requests. During the return by ship I was conscripted, with some other musicians, for two Special Services Shows. The first performance was presented one evening after supper in the forward Recreation Area of the ship to a full-house troop audience, and the second performance was on the top deck for the cabin class passengers (officers). The performance for the troops involved us in a variety show; I played piano accompaniment for Cpl. Gilbert White as he gave vocal impersonations of several musical instruments. On the serious side of the performance, I played Claude Debussy's "Claire de Lune," which was warmly received. The perform-ance on top deck for the officers and their wives was also a variety show. Because our performances were all well-conceived, popular, and entertaining, those of us who had worked in the Special Services Shows were exempted from any further duties during the entire return trip home.

Blessed with that freedom, I spent some time pacing the deck, watching the wonder-inducing movement of the waves as we churned our way through the pathless Atlantic. I spent some of the free time conversing with other returnees, all of us both eager and apprehensive about what life would be like after time in the army. As the days of travel shortened, I finally spent time sorting out what I had amassed from the creative flow at work within me during the year abroad. On the trip to Europe I had brought with me three books written by others whose thought blessed my life. I was leaving Europe with my duffel bag containing several full manuscripts of my own. The biographical study on Jackson had grown considerably, as had my research about the African American churches and the National Association of the Church of God. In addition to new musical compositions, I had a thick manuscript filled with meditational writings. I sorted through it all, grateful to God for the gift of creating—and wondering about the future of what I had written.

The year abroad had been a critical but creative time in my life, a time when I was forced to examine the roots of my faith and seek a rationale for my experience there. I had examined the exterior events which were the context for my days and the interior events that resulted from their impact. Was my creative output only a shapely compound that kept me busily engaged and out of harm's way? Or was it rather like the thread that Perseus, in the Greek legend, found and followed and thus escaped the darkness of the cave that held him captive? I did not know the full answer then, but as I used my free time aboard that ship, sorting, thinking, and praying, an inner witness assured me, through the words of Psalm 31, that my times had been, and still were, in God's hands. I thanked God and took courage!

James Earl Massey

5

A CHRONICLE OF CRISES

I was released from military service in February, 1953, and returned to Detroit where my wife, parents, and a welcoming congregation awaited me. Raymond S. Jackson had arranged for me to be supported full-time as his associate minister, so I settled into my given work with gratitude and enthusiasm. I soon found, however, that centering myself in my assignment would call for some diplomacy on my part, especially in relating to some of the local ministers in the congregation. To put it plainly, the actions, statements, and innuendoes of some of the older local ministers seemed to betray their displeasure over not being offered the post I had received. Although younger and less-experienced than some of them, I had officially become one of the church's two principal leaders. I was ready and eager to honor and build on our former relatedness as fellow ministers, but a few of them had not made peace with the fact of my appointment.

I soon found, as well, that I needed both diplomacy and discernment in relating to a few of the many members of the congregation of the Detroit Church of God. The congregation was in crisis, with a major and open disagreement between the pastor and some of the more vocal leaders in the church. My wife had not mentioned anything about this in her letters to me during my absence, nor had Jackson, my mother, or anyone else. I did notice a statement my mother made in some of the last letters I received from her just before my return: "When you get back, be your own man." She offered no further comment as to why. I understood her counsel as I sat in a church business meeting shortly after returning.

The open disagreement between Raymond S. Jackson and some of the more vocal members evidenced itself in a voiced complaint that Jackson's church program was demanding too much time in meetings at the church building, to the neglect of family time and home life. Jackson's method of dealing with those who voiced that complaint, as well as some other points of difference, was to rebuke them openly before the gathered congregation. Some members viewed Jackson's action as a prerogative of his pastoral authority, but some others viewed it as an obvious lack of concern for individuals and their desire to have their personal schedules. In dealing with some persons who saw things differently that he, Jackson sometimes resorted to censure and attempts to embarrass them publicly; he sometimes verbally equated their will to voice their opinion with being defiant rather than exercising their right to be heard.

Personal relations were breaking down between pastor and people, and this showed itself not only in church business meetings but also during some worship occasions. It was unpleasant to hear the pastor engage in verbal fighting while preaching. Again and again I heard sermons that betrayed a defensiveness and evident anger, sermons influenced, I thought, by an urge to sanctify or justify anger by allying it with Scripture. I had always known of Jackson's penchant for authoritative preaching, but listening to him deal in intended intimidation and coercion as he preached made me painfully uneasy; as I listened, I was disappointed that Jackson seemed so angered in the situation that his preaching, once authoritative, had become authoritarian. With the shift in the spirit of his preaching, there was a shift in the response of the listening church.

Since I was now allied with Jackson as his full-time associate (and one of the first within black congregations in the Church of God), some members watched to see whether and to what extent I would attempt to defend him, while some others watched to see if and how I would voice an opinion about the church matters under dispute. I decided to follow the caution of James the Elder—"quick to listen, slow to speak" (1:19). Having only recently returned to the Detroit scene, I deemed it the better part of wisdom to share my words only with Raymond S. Jackson. When I did so, however, I met a staunch refusal on his part to engage in any give-and-take on policy matters or in church programming. His penchant for being in control was so deeply rooted in his make-up that he thought any "give" on his part would be viewed as weakness. He could not see himself yielding on any point to those who differed from him in the dispute. Jackson never asked me to defend him; he rather stressed his intent to bring his detractors, the "unruly element" as he called them, under control. Meanwhile, the spirit of freedom that is germane to congregational health had been dampened. Jackson's authoritarian approach was not working to energize or motivate a sufficient number of members to give him the satisfaction of seeing his method validated. I sensed that my best service to him and to the church was to handle my assignment prayerfully and faithfully without making any direct verbal reference to the prevailing currents of complaints. Jackson and I conferred regularly. I kept him advised about the condition of the sick or shut-in whom I had visited. Periodically, I was asked to deliver the Sunday sermon.

My pulpit work on those Sundays when I preached followed the expositional method of delivery. I would treat a text or section of Scripture, giving due attention to the meaning and import of its truth and teaching for our lives, but avoiding any direct reference to current problems within the church. This turned to my disfavor among some who expected me to defend Pastor Jackson. Some of his most vocal supporters interpreted my lack of direct involvement in the on-going dispute as a sly attempt to undermine Jackson's position as senior pastor. Some were so persuaded by this notion that they began sifting every sermon I delivered for statements that might seem to support their claim.

I was surprised to be called into question in a meeting one Monday evening. It happened in Jackson's presence and by a group of nine persons, four of them older local ministers. The questioners read from a list statements from three sermons I had delivered while Jackson had been away from the church during a rest period. The statements were being read as evidences of my supposed disagreement with Jackson's stated concerns for the church. The fact that these sermons had all been preached in Jackson's absence seemed to fire the zeal of those gathered to expose me as disloyal. I had tried to preach to the needs of people, and now, as a result of dealing strictly with scriptural texts and their import, I was being placed "on the spot" by those who had misinterpreted and were misrepresenting my real concern.

The nine accusers had asked Jackson to call the meeting and request that I be present. One of the nine questioned a statement I had made while preaching from 1 Corinthians 12, from the section that treats spiritual gifts. According to this person's notes, I had said: "Every Christian has his proper gift from God. Find your gift and follow its function. Not every Christian can effectively do the same kind of work, nor will every Christian find freedom or pleasure in services urged upon them by someone else." I had indeed said that, and I explained the statement as an application of the textual passage from which I had preached. During the meeting, however, I learned why that person took exception to my statement. While I was away in Austria, the church had continued to send teachers each week to do Sunday School work at Maybury Sanatorium in Northville, Michigan. At some point during the course of the year, the number of volunteer teachers had dwindled, and the need for teachers became so acute that Jackson had commandeered persons to keep that weekly program going. If Jackson "drafted" someone to serve and they declined for personal reasons, that person was rebuked during some public assembly as uncooperative, selfish, and "not in agreement with the church program." The person who took exception to what I had preached about spiritual gifts thought I was openly opposing

Jackson's draft actions to supply teachers for that church activity at the sanatorium.

Two other members of that group of nine raised other questions. I tried to answer all their questions with reason and readiness. After listening to all who wished to speak, Jackson spoke up in my defense. He was careful to assure the nine that he appreciated their loyalty, and he sought to assure me that he understood that I intended no disagreement between us. He was quite forward in suggesting to the nine that my statements should be understood in keeping with the scriptural passages on which my sermons were based, and that I should be given the benefit of any doubt in light of my long absence from the church. It seemed clear to me that Jackson did not doubt my loyalty to him as church leader. But despite what I had said in explanation, and what Jackson had said in my defense, it was extremely difficult to preach with ease thereafter to those nine persons, since I knew that every statement of mine would be scrutinized, marked as exhibit items to prove something on my part adversarial to the church program. News about that meeting with me somehow "leaked out." This did not help the church situation, but deepened the wrangling. An already muddled affair became more acutely problematic.

Across the years of congregational life at the Church of God of Detroit, the pastor had held near-unhampered powers. The pastor had been the strong guide and director. To be sure, the business affairs of the church had demanded democratic procedures, with divided powers and privileges for the proper handling of church work, but pastoral authority was always held as final appeal in questions or concerns of a spiritual nature. The members of the church were accustomed to this order and gave due regard to it. In addition to recognized pastoral powers, the pastor of the Church of God of Detroit had always been a leader at the comparative height of his ministry and was well-respected across the wider church, old enough and experienced enough to bring wisdom to bear upon decisions and judgments and actions. If seen as original in planning, creative in work, and an able spokesperson in teaching and applying essential doctrines, local leaders and preachers in the church would attach themselves to that leader, eager to "sit under" him and, at a time the pastor considered proper, move out into their own ministry with that leader's blessing. Given such factors, the stronger the leader, the more divided their followers can become when that leader becomes a figure of controversy. The leader who can offer people a great challenge can sometimes become the cause of an extended crisis among them.

When Raymond S. Jackson became pastor of the Church of God of Detroit in 1943, he inherited the task of restoring harmony in the church and between the church and former members who had scattered from it in difference and defiance to locate in other congregations across the city. Jackson had been chosen as pastor because of his status and influence, which were still growing, and his proven abilities in dealing with church disputes. His strong preaching was another factor in his being chosen, and all of these factors were of importance to the pulpit committee—chaired by Collins Townsend, my grandfather—when Jackson became pastor. He entered into the congregation's life promoting togetherness, and he led in reconciling previously estranged members. But in 1953, ten years later, Jackson had himself become a figure of friction and dispute, largely due to one of his strengths: a determinative will which was being experienced by others as unyielding, inflexibly stubborn even in matters where a democratic approach might normally be expected—as in church programming.

I did my best to serve Jackson and the church without direct reference to the dispute over programming. The group of nine continued to hold my non-involvement suspect. Many members gave themselves to prayer, waiting on God to act within the dispute and on the disputants. Given the openness of the dispute, there was hardly any member of the church who did not know that things were not going well within the congregation's life. I was deeply distressed when I realized that I had stepped back into the congregation's life at a time of storm, and that the previously strong relationship between pastor and people was no longer warm and winsome, but sadly on the wane.

Whenever I preached during that period of dispute, I sought to trace and treat the spiritual life. As for that emphasis, I wanted to offer an interpretation of essential Christian experience, and I wanted to do so in a fresh way, using no familiar clichés or stereotyped phrases, so that the message could be heard at a new level. I considered this a wise and warranted approach to pulpit work, but I did not anticipate the disapproving response I experienced from some who wanted me to defend Jackson while preaching. A few found my expositional method unfamiliar at first, accustomed as they were to the proof-texting approach honored in their upbringing.

I had changed while away in military service. I had started along a fresh line in sermon planning. I was no longer content to use a collection of biblical texts all related to a chosen theme, I now wanted to treat a single text or textual section, and mine it, and it alone, for its riches. I had been exploring the Scriptures while away, intent on a comprehensive understanding of what the Bible teaches, and I wanted to treat those teachings in an appealing way. I did not want my preaching to sound combative, as if dealing always with controversy, a method and approach with which I was indeed familiar as I grew up in the church. I wanted rather to present truth in such a way as to cast a vision, attract interest, inspire, and engage the hearer's life. And I wanted to do this using freshly minted statements and engaging illustrations, so that the listening people would be encouraged to think about what they were hearing.

Another circumstance stirred some to complain to Jackson about me as I served the church. I began wearing clerical garb on occasion. This choice on my part, especially during hospital visits and sometimes for preaching services, brought me into disfavor with some who judged it as a non-Church of God practice. Having to visit the hospital sometimes at other than visiting hours, my use of the clerical collar always identified me readily for gaining entrance, especially at hospitals strict in their policy regarding visiting hours. My use of the rabat and clerical collar was based on personal and practical reasons. There had been a few times when my youth seemed so prominent as I went to do my hospital visitation that I was asked to show my credentials as a minister. I did, again and again, and finally decided to solve the identity problem by using the universally recognized clerical garb. That settled it.

Most of the members of the church accepted my use of the clerical collar as a sign of my seriousness as a leader, but some of the local ministers in the congregation interpreted it as evidence of a stirring within me for what would be novel and new, a claim for attention, as if I were making a bid to be considered different. Some even took my action as a bold attempt to show how separate Jackson and I were in our pastoral customs, that I was trying to drive a wedge between him and the church! Choices are personal matters, they call for mature thought, and the reasons behind our choices are often misunderstood or devalued by others until life makes plain to them in their experience what it brought to bear upon our's.

When I first began using clerical garb, Jackson made no comment about it at all. If he was surprised that I was sometimes thus attired, he never hinted that he was. The Roman collar was not really a rarity among Church of God ministers in Michigan at that time. Rev. John T. Smith, a pastor in Flint and Saginaw, had regularly worn clerical garb across his years of ministry. So had Clifton M. Morgan, pastor in Pittsburgh, and a former military chaplain. Jackson voiced neither comment nor objection to me about clerical garb. In fact, some years later, Jackson confessed to me that he had desired to wear clerical garb when he first entered the ministry, but the church tradition into which he had entered did not let him feel comfortable doing so at that time, so he had not followed his desire. When he told me this, I ventured a question: "If I purchased a collar for you, would you wear it now?" Jackson laughed, perhaps surprised at my direct thrust. After a brief reflexive pause, he spoke up with punch, "Yes, I would!" Shortly afterward, during an anniversary occasion planned in his honor, I presented Jackson with a rabat and several clerical collars as an anniversary gift. He wore it publicly the very next Sunday and continued the practice across the rest of his ministry.

Jackson's conflict with some of the officers of the church precipitated a crisis in my life. When it seemed clear to me that, in order to maintain control he favored using intimidation rather than dealing with evident differences by talking through the tension points in a reasoned way, I knew that I could not in good conscience agree with his methods. Jackson and I talked about this at great length one afternoon, at which time we had to disagree, despite my concern to be loyal to him as his associate. I was seeing a darker and authoritarian side to Jackson's personality that was making the conflict within the congregation he pastored steadily deepen.

I felt pulled in two directions. I was indebted to Raymond S. Jackson for his help in mentoring me for ministry, and for trusting me as his full-time associate. But at the same time I could see what the problem really was, and I offered a suggestion to Jackson about how I thought the problem could be solved. I became a voice for the culture of forgiving love that he was neglecting in his fear of losing authority. As I saw it, my hero in ministry was failing his test of fire. He was mired in a frustrated leadership position that his attitude and methods only helped to compound. As I saw it, there was no quelling the tumult in the church except through an open hearing of the different views voiced by others about the church programming, for one thing, and even making an honestly humble apology for having been so defensive as a leader. Jackson did not accept this suggestion, and making it did not help my standing with him. Jackson rather decided to test his standing among the membership of the church by asking that a vote of confidence be taken. He decided that he should not be present for the vote, and asked that it be taken in July when he would be away during his regular vacation time. During a special business meeting that July the vote on the pastor was taken by secret ballot, with the chairman of the associated auxiliaries of the church presiding. To the surprise of many, there was a majority vote against Jackson continuing as pastoral leader.

The vote surprised and displeased Jackson and left his staunch supporters deeply offended. Preaching to the congregation was difficult that next Sunday. Although I talked with Jackson by telephone during his vacation and knew of his displeasure over the negative vote, it was only after he returned from vacation that I felt the fire of his anger over how things had turned out. In a private meeting between the two of us, I suggested that while negative feelings had been high among many for so long, and that the vote had gone against him, it might yet prove helpful to take the humble route and show the congregation his love. I tried to convince him that the congregation could change its mind and request that he stay on. But still angered, Jackson insisted that the people did not want him any longer, and promised that he would not set foot in the church to preach to them again. I tried again to dissuade him from that response, but Jackson refused to be comforted or to change his mind. Shortly after one of our private meetings, Jackson sent the following letter to the congregation:

Aug. 26, 1953

TO THE CHURCH OF GOD
2011 W. HANCOCK STREET

Greetings in the Name of Jesus our Lord. Having labored here as your Pastor for over ten years, I can say with my conscience clear before God, that I have done all within my power, yes, and beyond the call of duty, to fulfill every obligation which has devolved upon me to be true to my God and the souls of men. The fruits of my hard labor through the grace of God and the cooperation of the vast majority of the church speak for themselves, without too much elaboration on my part.

I regret to say that circumstances over which I had no control, consequently for which I was not responsible, have caused many whom I feel should have stood loyally by me until God and time could have adjusted matters, to adopt a resentful attitude which is making my load heavy indeed to bear.

Truly I have exhausted myself in explanations, reasons, and in attempts to show you that I was prompted by no other motive but the earnest desire to have a Church in which God could dwell and through which he could work to make a name for himself here in our city. If any mistakes have been made by me, God is my witness they were only mistakes of the mind, and not any wrong motive of the heart. However, if any one feels otherwise I ask you again to please pardon me for the same.

I have been informed that some have said you were only tolerating wife and me until the first of the year, then you plan to vote us out. I have been a Pastor in the Reformation for over thirty-three years and the termination of my labor with the churches I have served heretofore has been with love, dignity, and honor. Therefore, having no desire to suffer such a tragic end to our relationship here I consequently tender my resignation as pastor of this church to take effect at the discretion of the congregation.

Lovingly Yours,
Rev. Raymond S. Jackson & Wife

Some of the members who wanted Jackson to remain as pastor advised me to try and get him to come back to the church. They had heard him promise not to set foot in the church's pulpit again, but they did want him to reconsider and serve out the time remaining as pastor before his resignation took effect. I failed in every attempt to persuade Jackson to return to the church. I believe that had he done so, he could have softened enough to begin cementing relations sufficiently to change the climate that was against him. But the vote to accept his resignation was for him a sadly surprising and disheartening fact to which Jackson reacted with rancor. His refusal to serve out the period of time remaining to him closed the door to possible reconciliation between pastor and people. When I saw that the separation was final, I stopped trying to persuade him to return to the church. Meanwhile, with the leadership of the church left in my hands, some of Jackson's offended supporters suggested that my presence at the church stood in the way of any reconciliation, and that I should resign and remove myself from the scene. They were unaware of my attempts to get Jackson to return to the church and, unfortunately, they were convinced that I had failed to support him properly. It was not long before a false report was spreading in Detroit and elsewhere that Jackson had resigned as pastor of the Church of God of Detroit because I had undermined him.

The Detroit-Jackson-Massey Controversy

Jackson's refusal to return to the church left the leadership of the church in my hands. Since I had served as his associate by his appointment, during a special business meeting after his resignation became effective I did the honorable thing and submitted my resignation as well. In making my statement, I called attention to my indebtedness to Jackson, by whose appointment I had served them. I added, however, that, although resigning as associate pastor, I would remain a member of the congregation because Detroit was my home. Unfortunately, some of those who heard that statement declared that I was making a bid to receive a call from the church on my own. That was not what I was doing. Interestingly, I was at the time pondering and praying about a call I had received from the 12th and Lane Street Church of God in Topeka, Kansas, to become pastor there. Patrick Heard, the previous pastor there, had left to become pastor in Columbus, Ohio. Gwendolyn and I had visited the church and I had conducted a revival there in September, 1953. The church had voted to have me as pastor and was awaiting my response.

117

Given the circumstances of Jackson's resignation, and despite my resignation, the congregation voted its request that I remain with the church as interim-pastor until final disposition about pastoral oversight could be made. After a painful soul-searching and prayer, it became clear to me that I should stay and serve the Detroit church as requested and not go to the church in Topeka. My wife felt drawn to the Topeka church, but she finally agreed that remaining in Detroit appeared to be the wisest choice. Being interim pastor could not only benefit the Church of God of Detroit but could also allow time and opportunity to clear my name. That was the thinking behind my decision to remain in Detroit, and it appeared to me as wisdom at the time.

Not everyone so viewed my decision. Several of Jackson's staunch supporters saw it as confirming their suspicion that I had undermined him, and to my utter surprise and deep disappointment, Jackson began voicing the same accusation against me. Given that complaint, and his publicly voiced agreement with it, about twelve families left the Church of God of Detroit and began worshipping separately. Jackson later became their pastor. On October 22, 1953, the City Pastors Organization, composed of Black pastors of Church of God congregations in the Detroit area, held a special called meeting, chaired by Dr. Cecil M. Washington, to discuss this development and its implications for relations between the churches. Additional meetings followed as new developments took place and as complaints were made to the Michigan State Advisory Board of the Church of God and other adjudicatory groups. The complaint by Jackson and his followers to the Michigan Advisory Board that I had undermined him was answered in the negative in November 1953 by a letter from the Church of God of Detroit, with the signatures of six officers acting at the request of the church. The letter read as follows:

November 8, 1953

Reverend Jay E. Butler, Chairman
Michigan State Advisory Board of the Church of God

Dear Rev. Butler:

With reference to the charge made by Reverend Raymond S. Jackson that Reverend James E. Massey undermined him to gain control of this church, we the undersigned leaders within the congregation firmly declare that the charge is not true. There is no evidence to support such charge. The charge is being made because the congregation chose Reverend Massey to succeed Reverend Jackson as pastor here after the latter mentioned resigned from the pastoral office here some weeks ago. Reverend Jackson's resigning was a move of his own choosing; the church had not requested it. The church's acceptance of the resignation was not an action spurred on by Reverend Massey; it was a move taken by the church after much discussion, prayer, and fasting. Some weeks before Reverend Jackson submitted his resignation several meetings were held for the clarifying of many matters which the church was desiring to know more about. Most of the meetings failed to accomplish their intended purpose and thus caused trouble to result within the congregation. When the dissatisfaction continued indefinitely, Reverend Jackson decided to resign. Reverend James Massey made the statement that should the congregation accept the resignation of Reverend Jackson he would likewise resign, inasmuch as he was the assistant pastor through being appointed by Rev. Jackson. After Reverend Jackson's resignation was acted upon, Reverend Massey did as he had promised. The church later requested Reverend Massey to reconsider the needs of the church and accept the position of temporary pastor. After much consideration Reverend Massey accepted the position.

119

Again we affirm that there is no truth in the charge that Reverend Massey undermined Reverend Jackson to gain control of the pastorate here.

A separate sheet is attached bearing the names of the officers who have signed this letter in support of Reverend James Massey's innocence in the face of the stated charge. These officers have signed for the entire congregation.

With news about the controversy steadily spreading within the Movement's churches across the country, our worship services were regularly visited by other Church of God persons seeking more information about what had really happened, and seeking insight into how what had happened was affecting the congregation. Some visitors saw the controversy as basically a struggle between youth and age, viewing me as an impatient and egotistical young minister or Jackson as an older minister who was jealous of a rising young leader. I learned about conversations in which some eagerly argued for the promise that younger leadership seemed to hold, viewing the older leaders—or those elder leaders with whom they had had the closest dealings—as persons lacking the creative thought and vitality that new demands were making upon church life. I also learned about conversations in which some persons staunchly defended older ministers and decried what they assessed as flaws and distortions in both the preaching and personalities of younger leaders. It was plain to all that the controversy in which I was involved was not a healthy one. That was not only plain to me, it was also painful to me, extremely painful.

The largest part of the pain was in being falsely accused by Raymond S. Jackson. I had at no time ever sought to undermine his person or position. I was unconsolably grieved when I learned that the voiced suspicion of the nine who had earlier accused me was now his voiced claim against me. Another part of the pain I felt was my lack of standing as compared to his positioning in both the state and Movement circles. Jackson was widely known and respected, while I was a comparative newcomer whom he had endorsed. Thus, with his claim against me, I felt victimized, actually disinherited. I felt disadvantaged in Michigan because Jackson was chairman of the state Ministers and Gospel Workers Association, a black organization; he was also chairman of the General Ministerial Assembly of the National Association of the Church of God (West Middlesex, Pennsylvania). As I looked at the situation I was tempted to lament, wondering who would ever believe me or care enough to want the full story behind the controversy.

To be sure, the majority of the members in the Church of God of Detroit knew the full background and details of that story, and knowing this gave me some comfort; but I wished and longed and prayed that the truth could be known by all and not just our congregation.

After I had served a few months as interim pastor, the Church of God of Detroit formally voted to call me as senior pastor. Given their trust, I accepted their call. Several younger members of the Church of God of Detroit volunteered to be sharers in prayer with me. All were from families with parents long associated with the Church of God Movement, and nearly all of the volunteers were from families long associated with that local congregation. Most of us had grown up together. The suggestion to become prayer partners was an act of friendship, but I viewed it also as an act of concern for me as the new leader. We covenanted to pray together and we met weekly in one of our homes, usually on a Friday night, looking forward to the Sunday services.

There were thirteen in our prayer group when we began. Three in the group were children of Daniel F. Oden: Eva (Oden) Walker, Norman Oden, and Rosemary (Oden) Bell, and their companioning spouses were, respectively, Elmer Walker, Ruth Blackburn Oden, and Paul Bell. The other seven in our partnership were Clarence L. Hudson and his wife Valverie (Taylor), Louise Crosswhite Terry, my brother Melvin and his wife Helen (Jackson), Gwendolyn, and me.

We were a homogeneous prayer group and many factors

contributed to our oneness of mind and spirit. We treasured our common church heritage and our long association with our congregation's people, traditions, and foibles. We all viewed church life with seriousness and we each had a hunger for God. We never used our time together for petty matters, but concentrated our concern toward understanding the will of God for our lives. We prayed with openness to God and to each other, mindful of the intimacy of sharing our souls in this way. We were mutual burden bearers. There were times when we sat or knelt in silence, contemplating what had been shared in some scripture reading. There were times of prophetic insight based on some reading, and we glorified God as specific guidance for life came, just as by the process reported in Acts 13—"the Holy Spirit said"—doubtless speaking a fresh word to and through one within the group, to help us deal meaningfully with the issues of life. It was important to us all that we engage in prayer because we knew that through honesty, openness, a sustained questing, and mutual agreement, we would experience God. Praying together helped us all to experience answers to specific requests, but it also kept us spiritually alert and guaranteed needed sobriety and insight for living. Those prayer sessions blessed us with emotional relief as well. They helped to renew my strength as I sought to lead the congregation and deal with the happenings, both good and ill, that my leadership was generating.

Some other younger couples decided to form home prayer groups after learning about our group. They were also longtime friends. I met with those prayer groups on occasion, especially when invited. The house prayer groups became a problem when some older and more suspicious members questioned their operation. They voiced the question during one of our church business meetings, asking why the newer prayer groups among us had not been required to report like the church's other auxiliaries and fellowship groups had done. My answer was that those prayer groups were private, not church-sponsored, and that while they involved church members, they did not involve church monies like the other area prayer groups whose leaders were accountable to the church because they had the benefit of church funding.

I read somewhere about a statement Ben Hogan, the legendary golfer, once made. It was to the effect that when we see someone swinging a golf club for the first time on the teeing mound, we can be sure that they are doing everything wrong. There are indeed some obvious parallels between the art of golfing and the art of pastoring, among which are these: the importance of envisioning in order to project well, a capacity for introspection, and the need for discipline to coordinate forethought and action appropriately for the best effect.

Like a first-time golfer, I did not do everything right as a new pastor, but I never chose to do anything as pastor that I knew to be wrong or unwise. By wisdom's standards, despite the best intentions on my part, I displeased some persons during my first months with them, and even provoked the ire of a few. Perhaps I projected some desired change too soon, or did not coordinate appropriately with them in timing some action for the best results. In hindsight I can point to two actions on my part in which this might well have been the case. The first action was breaking with a local church ban against the use of the wedding ring. The second action was an expressed openness on my part to leaders and believers from other church communions, especially sharing with them in their services, and even receiving from them as equal sharers in grace.

The non-use among us of finger adornments was one of several ascetic customs that some of our pastors and churches promoted as exemplary of the self-denial and modesty associated with Christian holiness. Honoring a strict asceticism, there was a ban even against married couples displaying a wedding band. Shortly after I became pastor, Gwendolyn and I broke with this custom. Before doing so, however, I talked to the Board of Deacons and Deaconesses to inform them about what my wife and I had decided to do. I then spent time listening to the cautions and fears they raised with respect to the congregation's response. I then spoke to the assembled congregation during a mid-week service to announce what we had decided and to explain why we had chosen to break with that longstanding ban.

I began by stating that again and again the non-use of a wedding ring had caused my wife and me unnecessary embarrassment in our contacts with the world beyond the church. The first embarrassing occasion took place immediately following our wedding. I was on leave from the army when we married, and Gwendolyn left Detroit with me when I returned to Fort Jackson in Columbia, South Carolina, where I was stationed. She was to spend a few days there with me. I knew that space in the guest house on the post would not be available for a few days, so I had secured temporary lodging at a boarding house in the city. The boarding house was managed by a woman who was a member of one of the churches I visited while in basic training at Fort Jackson.

When Gwendolyn and I arrived at the boarding house, Mrs. Bailey guided us to our quarters. As she handed me the key, she paused, parted her lips as if to speak, but as if hesitant to say something, she waited a moment longer. We also paused. Then she spoke up, putting a question as kindly as she could manage: "I'm sorry, but I must ask you this … since you both know how soldier towns are—Are you really married?" She caught her breath and waited.

I told her that we were indeed husband and wife, and to assure her I was then reaching into my pocket to draw out the signed and folded marriage license from my wallet. Fortunately, I had brought that document along "just in case," knowing that neither of us had any visible means to indicate our married state, such as a wedding ring on the finger. Mrs. Bailey smiled as she examined the license. "Thank you. I had to be sure, since neither of you have on a wedding ring!" Gwendolyn and I closed the door of our room behind us, grateful that I had followed my mind and brought our signed license with us, but we were feeling humiliated too. From that moment of embarrassment we began to think about the problem of the no-finger-adornment custom of our church and what we would do about it for ourselves.

While I was on overseas army duty, Gwendolyn graduated from Wayne State University School of Nursing and began working as a nurse at Harper Hospital. An elderly patient she attended learned in conversation with her that Gwendolyn was married. Upon learning that I was in army service in Austria, and seeing no wedding band on my wife's ring finger, the woman wrongly assumed that Gwendolyn had dispensed with wearing a ring because she was being an unfaithful wife during my absence. The lady decided to turn her wonderment to words. One afternoon she called Gwendolyn to her bedside and began to offer her some "motherly advice." Gwendolyn felt utterly humiliated. That experience of humiliation went deeper into my wife's psyche than the embarrassment we suffered at Mrs. Bailey's boarding house. Gwendolyn felt doubly embarrassed because she sensed how silly and impractical it would sound to try to explain to that woman our local church custom against wearing finger jewelry. Immediately after that experience at the hospital, Gwendolyn started wearing a wedding band while on the job and out in public. I concurred with her that as a married woman a wedding band belonged on her hand.

The assembled congregants listened with rapt attention as I set forth in brief form a history of the wedding band custom from ancient times. I then stated that my wife and I had made our decision, and that we took full responsibility for a choice that we hoped they would respect. I did not entertain any comments from the floor about my statement. After some days apart, during which much discussion no doubt took place, the majority of the members reacted favorably toward our decision. Interestingly, not long after that week, Gwendolyn and I noticed that two of the women leaders whom we knew had voiced the loudest caution against permitting members to put on the wedding ring appeared at church with wedding bands on their fingers!

My wife and I broke with that longstanding custom for

personal reasons and I granted our members freedom to use the wedding band if they so desired. But those actions brought me into disfavor with some who were intent on preserving the old order, fearing that the dike of propriety would break open to admit a bounding sea of worldly adornment. Those who disagreed with me viewed the change I allowed as still another indication that I was bent on being different and completely changing things in the church's life.

The change I permitted along this line also drew criticism from several neighboring pastors, and it was the subject of a long and heated discussion during one of the meetings of our district pastors. Henry Smith, pastor of the Palmerston Avenue Church in River Rouge, helped to restore sanity to the dispute that ensued when he rose and reminded the ministers that, according to Jesus' parable (Luke 15), when the prodigal son returned home to his waiting father, the father not only outfitted that son with a clean robe and new sandals, but also placed a ring on his finger!

Strangely enough, my lifting the ban against wearing the wedding ring served to strengthen several homes in which there had been friction between wives who belonged to the church and their husbands who did not belong, husbands who disagreed with that one or some other misunderstood or even untenable custom held and advocated by our church group. I was glad to see several husbands finally commit themselves to Christ and the fellowship when they saw that the church was no longer a wedge between them and their wives. Interestingly, the number of men in the church increased significantly after I became pastor, and some of them admitted that the church's ban against a wife's use of the wedding band had been a problem for them. My critics saw that increase of men in our midst from another angle of vision. They insisted that those men, most of whom had not come into the church during Jackson's ministry there, were now in the church because I had "lowered the standard." I finally reasoned that some of my critics might never be convinced of my integrity, and that they might never view my intentions as honest and honorable. However, I kept trying to meet them half-way, eager to connect and praying that it would happen soon.

My openness to leaders and believers from other church communions became a problem for some members when they learned that I had been a visitor on several occasions at Bethesda Missionary Temple, a large church with a Pentecostal orientation. I had first attended at the urging of Louise Crosswhite Terry, a member of our church, a partner in our prayer group, and the daughter of Joseph and Emma Crosswhite, pastors in Ohio. I had listened on occasion to the daily radio broadcast from Bethesda and had appreciated the preaching of Pastor Myrtle D. Beall and her son James D. Beall, who alternated with his mother in speaking. My first visit to the Temple took place when Gwendolyn and I went with Louise Terry to a Thursday afternoon prayer service there. Mindful of the criticisms leveled against me during those days and my need to remain steady, she suggested that it would strengthen my spirit to go and receive from the service at Bethesda Missionary Temple. I went and my spirit was nourished by the word, prayer, and fellowship. Later I attended an in-door campmeeting there. During another visit I preached there, using Romans 4:1-8. I treated the subject "What Did Abraham Find?" Pastor Beall was so impressed by the import of that text that she used it again in a subsequent message on the radio.

The fact of my having attended services at Bethesda Missionary Temple might never have become an occasion for controversy if there had been no report that I had been openly ministered to by the pastors there during a laying on of hands service. It happened during that first Thursday afternoon prayer service Gwendolyn and I attended. During the course of the prayer service, along with several other persons, Gwendolyn and I went forward and knelt at the kneeling rail to receive grace. There were persons attending that service who knew Church of God people, and the news of our openness to have the hands of non-Church of God ministers laid upon us in prayer got back to some in our church. They took exception to our openness; they did not think it conformed to the general rule for a Church of God minister to be that open to receive from another church group.

These were some, if not all, of the matters which became a reason for the call I received one afternoon from Dr. C. M. Washington, pastor of Wisconsin Avenue Church of God. He told me that he was calling on behalf of the Southeastern District Ministers, and that I was being requested to meet with a committee to answer some questions about my preaching and activities as pastor. I did not know who the person or persons were within our church who had voiced complaints to the district ministers about me, and I did not ask. I agreed to meet with the committee. I knew I had done no wrong, and I was mindful of the injunction addressed in 1 Peter 5:5 to younger ministers to "accept the authority of the elders."

Under Interrogation

The committee and I met on February 6, 1954. The members of the committee were W. Dale Frye, president, George K. White, Jay E. Butler, C. M. Washington, vice-president, John T. Smith, Leonard A. Steen, and E. B. Jones. Dr. Washington asked the most questions as I was interrogated, and all but one of the questions were related to Bethesda Missionary Temple. He had made a visit to Bethesda Missionary Temple to secure some of their literature, had read it, and framed his questions to me on the basis of that reading and what had come to his attention as criticisms that my preaching and activities were "pentecostal" in flavor and emphasis.

"Do you believe," he began, "that those who receive the Holy Spirit must evidence this by speaking in tongues?" I readily answered, "No, I do not."

"Do you believe in the laying on of hands?" At that question, I paused before answering. I did not pause because I had to frame my answer but because I was surprised that that question was being asked, given the ancient biblical tradition regarding the practice and the widespread use of the practice in our own Church of God life. I finally answered that I do believe in the laying on of hands. Dr. Washington then narrowed his question to ask whether I believed that spiritual gifts can be conferred by the laying on of hands. At that point I knew I would have to present a more extended answer.

I told how I had seen the practice of laying on of hands observed across all of my life, sometimes allied with prayer for healing, sometimes to prepare someone for a journey that would keep them away from the fellowship for some time, or to prepare someone for a service they were to render on behalf of the church, or to ordain someone to the ministry. I had sometimes seen near-immediate results of healing when hands had been laid on someone. I spoke of my regard for the practice, and that it was associated in my thinking with the graciousness of God, the touch of the hands being emblematic of God's favor. In addition to being psychologically reconfirmed in faith and assurance by such a touch, the laying on of hands can also be a palpable and visible means used by God to announce or certify to someone the reception of some benefit or bestowal, as Paul's words to Timothy (2 Tim. 1:6) clearly indicate.

That is what I replied in answering Dr. Washington's question about whether gifts can be conferred through the laying on of hands. The group did not appear to agree with what I had stated. I wondered whether they held the notion that Paul's apostolic positioning allowed him such powers of bestowal, but that the ministry in these latter days cannot be so used of God. I wondered if this is what they were thinking, but no one commented on what I said, so I was left wondering.

Reference was then made to the report that I had hands laid on me at Bethesda Missionary Temple. Someone asked if they had re-ordained me. I answered "No." I explained that hands were laid upon me during a prayer for strengthening, not to establish an organizational relationship. This explanation did not seem to help, however, because the ministers could not agree with my openness to receive the imposition of the hands of someone whose ministry was not according to "the truth about the church as we teach it." One minister condemned my openness as an indication that I was not adequately indoctrinated. What they considered my lack I understood as my freedom, an expression of my desire to relate to all of the church and receive from it. One of the seven counseled me to stay away from Bethesda and have no further relations with the people there. He then asked if I would promise to do so. Upon hearing that, I knew that I was being pressed to declare who I was and what I could be expected to do. What I heard made me think that my interrogators held a belief that our Movement was absolute and final.

I silently lamented that those in that room had not yet been influenced by what our Movement's theme of unity steadily implies: the need and will to relate with the rest of the church, with all of God's people. Christian unity was a doctrinal theme about which each and all of us periodically preached, and it pained me that we lacked understanding of how that doctrine is to be experienced and exemplified. I knew that the district committee was waiting for me to say, and wanting me to say, that I would not associate with Pentecostals anymore. But wanting to live out what I viewed as the given purpose of our Movement, and to live it out in all the directions where true believers are found, I could not promise that.

While nearly all of the questions Dr. Washington addressed to me related to Bethesda Missionary Temple, there was one other question I was asked by him. "What is the nature and purpose of the late-night prayer groups you attend?" The tone of the question conveyed an air of suspicion, I thought, and I knew that even that question seemed related to someone's fear that our prayer groups were covert clans to nurture others in the beliefs falsely attributed to me. I explained that the groups consisted of members who had volunteered to be prayer partners, and that nothing ill-advised or of a secret nature took place in the meetings.

Our deliberations concluded and I thanked the members of

the district committee for their counsel. I had not wanted to appear stubborn and insubordinate, but with their eyes fastened upon me in evident stares of censure I knew that we were in basic disagreement. A few days later I received a letter in the mail, signed by the seven committee members. Dated February 6, 1954, the day of the meeting, and addressed "To Whom It May Concern," the letter referenced the occasion of meeting with me, and gave the following summary judgment: "... we the undersigned members of the Advisory Board find him out of harmony with the doctrinal teaching and practice of the Church of God (with headquarters at Anderson, Ind.), and by his own confession he does not intend to change his teaching, therefore we must, of necessity, withdraw fellowship from him and all who stand with him, until such time as he sees fit to change his present position."

That decision disappointed me. I was disappointed that I had not been understood, because I thought I possessed an understanding of what was taught by the Church of God (Anderson). And I thought I had rightly voiced some of the implications of our teaching about Christian unity. My disregard for existing group walls had to include our own church group as well as other human groupings we referred to as "denominations." But that became my "crime." How pleased I was, years later, when in 1965, a full decade after I experienced that censure, the General Assembly of the Church of God, meeting in session in Anderson, Indiana, had matured sufficiently in thought and experience to create a Committee on Christian Unity. Even then, however, the recommendation advising this action did not pass with ready ease. Some leaders spoke against the creation of such a committee, fearing that our doctrinal position as a church group would be jeopardized and compromised. It took two days of discussion, with pro and con positions steadily and loudly voiced, before the resolution finally passed with approval. The expressed purpose of the committee was to explore ways by which the Church of God (Anderson, Indiana) could as a group implement our concern for the unity of the church. The older idea of our utter distinctiveness was so entrenched that the margin by which the resolution passed was slight; many who voted against the resolution were reluctant to think of relating in any way with those beyond our group, and some, viewing our group as an absolute entity, saw no need to relate.

The news of the district committee's pronouncement against me spread far and wide. In March, 1954, one month following the date of the letter regarding me, the National Staff Meeting took place in Warren, Ohio. The National Staff Meeting was a mid-year (fiscal) gathering to promote the work of the National Association of the Church of God. Gwendolyn and I went. Dr. Washington was present as one of the announced speakers, and he surprised many when he used his assigned preaching slot to highlight the continuing controversy in Detroit. Interestingly, he did not mention that Jackson had nurtured another congregation—an action that Jackson had earlier condemned—but Dr. Washington did mention me. Citing statements culled from literature he had picked up at Bethesda Missionary Temple, Washington delivered a tirade against Pentecostals. Making assertion after assertion, he ended each thrust with the words, "And this is what they are teaching in Detroit"—the obvious reference being my preaching. The truth is that I had indeed preached about the gifts of the Spirit, using 1 Corinthians 12 as the textual passage, but I had never slanted any of my exposition to honor a Pentecostal emphasis.

It is true that there had been times when people came forward to receive the laying on of hands, but that practice was not new to the Church of God. Dr. Washington's treatment of the practice that night, however, gave the impression that in imposing our hands in Detroit, we were seeking to do something by means of the practice that was radically different than assuring people of the available grace of God. He had disappointed me during the interrogation I underwent in meeting with the district ministers in Detroit, and he disappointed me again while addressing the assemblage in Warren, Ohio. I can still recall the disapproving look I received from some of the leaders, both during the preaching and after the service ended. I also remember the kind words some other leaders spoke to encourage me. Emma Crosswhite, pastor in Washington Court House, Ohio, and wife of Joseph Crosswhite, general manager of the National Association Campground at West Middlesex, Pennsylvania, had not been persuaded by Dr. Washington's tirade against the view that God's grace can be experienced in association with the laying on of hands. After many years of working among the sick and afflicted, she was still being used of God in helping sick people become well by the practice of laying her hands upon them, in alliance with prayer. She understood that healing is a divine deed of grace.

The censure I received from the district ministers caused me to experience some disfavor here and there within the city churches and beyond. Some who were persuaded against me did not know enough about the controversy to assess the rightness or wrongness of my stand, and some others were so persuaded by the fact that I had been charged that they took the charge itself as evidence that I was guilty. Some ministers wrote kind letters to encourage me, advising that I not do anything rash, and telling me that time would be my ally. There were even those who telephoned and shared their own experiences of hurt, eager to let me know of their understanding and to assure me of their prayers. Meanwhile, I continued serving the congregation, grateful for those who were prayerful supporters, open to all who needed my services, and alert to those who acted disagreeably.

A Parting of the Ways

The extent to which some members disagreed with my leadership became acutely evident to me on a Wednesday evening in May. About two hours before the regular mid-week service at the church, Gwendolyn answered the doorbell of the parsonage and was greeted by a sheriff's deputy. The deputy handed her a document addressed to me from the Wayne County Circuit

Court. The document, dated May 17, was a "Bill of Complaint" against me, with an "Order to Show Cause" why I should not be restrained from continuing as pastor. The document listed the Church of God of Detroit as plaintiff, and the names of four church officers were listed as instigating complainants representing the congregation. The Bill of Complaint charged me as guilty of teaching doctrines out of harmony with the doctrinal teachings and practices of the Church of God. Because I had been disfellowshiped by the state ministry, I should be barred from exercising any further pastoral responsibilities in the properties of the church.

I went to the mid-week service and said nothing at all to anyone about the summons I had received. We engaged in group prayer, and I conducted the Bible Study which followed. As the offering was being received before the service ended, a trustee who was one of the complainants listed as representing the church in the Bill of Complaint walked to the front of the group and asked me for permission to speak. I granted it. He proceeded to inform the church that I had been out of order in leading the service we had just had because a court order had been issued against me as pastor. The announcement surprised the gathered group and several members rose up in protest, asking what his statement was all about. He insisted that I knew about the injunction and had violated what the court had ordered. As he tried to explain why he and the others had sought and obtained an injunction against me, the protest became an uproar. I asked the enraged members to calm themselves. I then explained that I had indeed received and read the Bill of Complaint against me, that it had been delivered shortly before the service. I had disregarded it, I stated further, because no congregational action stood behind those whose names were listed as complainants.

I briefly voiced some reminding words about Paul's injunction to the Corinthian believers against submitting church disputes to the jurisdiction of the civil court. On the basis of that injunction, I then asked the members what action they would like to take regarding those persons who had violated the Apostle's clearly stated guidance. By a strong vote of censure, the congregation rebuked the complainants and also removed all four from their elected offices. The following Sunday, during the break period between Sunday School and the morning worship service at 11:00, four ministers, local elders from sister congregations in the city, occupied the four seats in the pulpit area of the sanctuary; they came authorized by the City Pastors Association, they reported, to conduct the service that day because I was no longer the recognized pastor.

Someone came to the choir room, where I was about to pray with the choir before the service, and informed me about what was happening upstairs in the sanctuary. I went to the pulpit area, greeted the ministers, then politely asked them to vacate the pulpit. They refused. By that time, two strong-armed male members had come to stand beside me, and they volunteered to remove the minister who was sitting in the seat I normally used when in the pulpit. I did not let them do so. I left the pulpit, walked down to the front pew, and sat down, leaving the uninvited ministers in the pulpit. Jodie Hollaway came and sat beside me. The intended "take-over" by the ministers was unwarranted and unwise. The ministers were not only guilty of intruding, but they even disregarded Jodie Hollaway, the church's assistant pastor, as the minister the church expected to provide leadership when I was not able to give it.

Shortly after Hollaway took a seat beside me, he asked me, "What would you suggest we do?" I turned to him and replied, "Given this unwarranted interruption of our service, as far as I am concerned, you can stand, offer a prayer, and dismiss the congregation!" He agreed. At 11:00 A.M., just before the choir's processional hymn, Jodie Hollaway walked up to the altar railing, turned around to face the gathered congregation, offered a prayer, and pronounced the benediction. The news had already spread among the people that the ministers came to occupy the pulpit, so after Jodie's announcement of this and the benediction he offered, the majority of the members began leaving the sanctuary. This action took the ministers seated in the pulpit by surprise. Laron H. Cammon, their leader, rose and sought to regain the people's attention, but his plea went unheeded. Then someone associated with the four complainants in their planning immediately rushed to the front of the sanctuary and voiced a second and louder plea for the people to return. I remember hearing the person call out: "Come back! Come back! The injunction was against Reverend Massey as leader, not you!" To which one of the marching members responded, "But the injunction also said, 'and those who stand with him.' We stand with him, not with you!"

The mass departure was steady and long. Jodie Hollaway and I stood together watching it all, wondering what it would finally mean, and wondering as well what would be our next task. Then he and I joined the departing procession. Outside, as the members continued filing out of the church building, I overheard John Arthur Small, one of the choir leaders, cautioning the people to remain quiet and peaceful in leaving. They followed his wise counsel as they walked to their cars. That Sunday marked the time when many of those who left with us lost pride in being related in any way to the Church of God of Detroit.

Dr. S. P. Dunn, pastor of Langley Avenue Church of God in Chicago, heard about the legal injunction filed against me and called me to discuss the problem. He had earlier expressed interest in being invited to help resolve the issues involved in the Detroit-Jackson-Massey controversy. In a letter to me dated May 26, 1954, Dr. Dunn stated:

> Since talking to you and reading that court summon, I have fasted and prayed earnestly over the matter. The Lord has shown me definitely that this matter should not be settled before the civil courts. I am sure this matter can be settled without this great reproach upon the Church everywhere, as it will be if this thing goes to law. When the whole reformation was ready to split

several years ago, over the management of the school at Anderson, I settled the matter with God's word. I also settled the church in Detroit at the beginning of Bro. Jackson's pastorate, so give me a chance now to save all of you, and the work there. I will come at any time. If necessary, I will exchange pulpits for a few weeks or months. Just give me and God a chance and by no means let this matter go to the civil court. See those interested and read this letter to them. Wire or call me as soon as you see or phone other interested parties.

Dr. Dunn closed his letter to me with mention that he had sent the same letter to Raymond S. Jackson. No agreement was reached to involve Dr. Dunn in the court dispute, so we can never know what the outcome would have been if he had been summoned as arbitrator. I do know, however, that Dunn was right in viewing the court case as a "great reproach upon the Church everywhere," because before it was finally settled by adjudication in October, 1956, the court case against me affected the entire body of Church of God ministers in Michigan, white and black, and the ministers and congregations of the National Association of the Church of God. It also occasioned the development in Detroit of a new but full-grown congregation that I served as senior pastor.

News of the court case against me gained space in the May 29, 1954, issue of *The Michigan Chronicle,* a black Detroit weekly, under the caption "Flock Sues to Oust Rev. Massey." The notice seemed worthy because the Church of God of Detroit was one of the city's historic congregations. The June 10th issue of *Jet Magazine* also carried the news; the report appeared as the first item in the religion section of that nationally circulated black weekly, and was captioned "Church Sues to Oust 'False Doctrine' Cleric." I do not know why, but *The Michigan Chronicle* article even mentioned my tenancy of the parsonage and the $150.00 weekly salary I received as pastor.

James Earl Massey

6

THE GROWTH OF
METROPOLITAN
CHURCH

The suit filed against me by the four church officers who wrongly claimed to represent the Church of God of Detroit placed me at the center of a scandal. I was obliged to answer the charges, so I secured legal counsel to represent me.

Given the circumstance of preparing for a court case and waiting to be heard, I was advised not to expect an immediate hearing. Meanwhile, the hundreds who had walked out of the Church of God of Detroit in defiance of the suit against me had stayed in touch with each other and had indicated their continuing trust in me and declared their full support for me. While the four officers who signed the Bill of Complaint against me had claimed to represent the church, they misjudged the real number of persons who trusted my leadership and miscalculated the extent of their own influence—which they discovered was limited. In petitioning the court to restrict not only my services and access to the building but also "all those who stand with him," their mistake was vividly evident, because on that Sunday in May, 1954, 257 adult members walked out of the sanctuary to protest the wrongful suit against them and to show visible support for me as their pastor. Shortly afterward, because of the expected slow process at court and with intent to stay related, those 257 persons, together with their families, covenanted together and became the charter members of what we chose to call "The Metropolitan Church of God."

Our covenant community began meeting in The Danish Brotherhood Hall building located at Forest Avenue and Twelfth Street. The building was known to be available at the time, and it was within convenient reach by public as well as private transportation. Having been advised by counsel that the ensuing court case would likely require not only my response to the charges against me but also a judicial statement from an official ecclesiastical body regarding my status as a minister, the officers and I knew that we would need to prepare ourselves and the people for a long process. There was the need, therefore, to incorporate and plan for the future of our fellowship. Accordingly, we established regular meeting hours and began the task of reorganizing for a fruitful group life and visioning for future development. The work of reorganizing was soon completed because most of those who had been elected to some office while at the Church of God of Detroit were now among the 257 who had covenanted to become a new congregation.

For practical and legal purposes we needed a congregational name. The act of choosing that name took place after a period of fasting and prayer by the church across ten days. We chose a name that would be both representative of our widespread membership, reflective of our primary missional area, and representative of our denominational heritage. Since we were only temporarily located at Danish Brotherhood Hall, we also wanted a congregational name that would not have to be changed when and if we changed our meeting location. In light of this, the name "Metropolitan Church of God." After due discussion, the congregation voted its approval. In a few days, the trustees and I met and framed articles of incorporation, with legally appropriate by-laws. During a congregational business session soon afterward, the church voted to approve the document for enactment and we had the Articles of Incorporation registered. We thus stood legally separated from the Church of God of Detroit.

In covenanting together as a new congregation, I wanted all those who had taken their stand together to examine their reasons for so doing. I wanted each and every member of Metropolitan Church to be serious about Christian ideals and not just displeased about having in effect been dispossessed of the church building from which we had been barred. I wanted to insure that we were a genuine fellowship of alert believers because I knew, as did the experienced officers among us, that we would have to live through a testing period of being criticized as well as dispossessed and disinherited. I cautioned that, as people of God, we would have to meet our opponents with a creative love, that we could be satisfied with no superficial and sub-Christian standards, and that we would be required to show ourselves as Christian in all our attitudes and manners.

Some of our members had already had to deal with some of the criticisms about which I alerted them. One was that "Massey has deceived you!" Another criticism was, "Despite the size of your group, you should be ashamed that you do not worship in a proper church building now!" There were other criticisms. But our members stood tall against critical jibes and they steadily brought their friends and neighbors to worship services and other group meetings at the Danish Brotherhood Hall. The Hall did lack the ecclesiastical atmosphere to which we were accustomed, but what was more important was the sense of oneness and purpose we all shared when together, and the contagion our members experienced even in the small group meetings in homes across the city through the week. Our services and gatherings were full of caring and sharing, the one our pillar of cloud by day and the other our pillar of fire by night. The very newness of our situation, with all of our questions and vulnerability, kept us exposed not only to continued criticisms from those outside our fellowship but open as well to the claiming love and steadying guidance of God through his Spirit. We found ourselves dying daily to the spirit of pride and resurrected each morning with a dream in our hearts. We gathered in peace, mindful of mercies, and deeply grateful for grace.

Given that atmosphere of God's sensed presence among us, our times together involved much that was beyond the ordinary.

The spirit of giving always made the offerings adequate to meet the financial needs. Some who had never tithed before began to do so, joyfully, zestfully. Commitment showed itself in deepened faith, sharing beyond expectation, and zealous deeds of sacrifice. In but a few months together at Danish Hall we received $57,000 in tithes and offerings—and that in 1954, a time of economic pressure for many in Detroit. At the end of that fiscal year, when a new venue opened to us as a possible choice for purchase, the congregation had the necessary down-payment. In addition, several families among us who had been renting across the years purchased homes of their own that year. Having had to leave the parsonage of the Church of God of Detroit, I also purchased a home.

The contagion of the worship services brought a harvest of conversions that year as well. Several spouses who were members had the joy of seeing their husbands commit their lives to Christ and join the church. One of the young men who later became an influential minister and pastor, George Sewell Marshall, was converted during one of the worship services when we were at Danish Brotherhood Hall.

The spirit of prayer was evident in our gatherings and throughout the week. Some people experienced miraculous healings after concerted prayer and fasting by the church. Through prayer, others experienced the correction of some structural physical deficiency that had plagued them for years. In addition, the year our congregation met together at Danish Brotherhood Hall was a time of fruitful outreach. At my request, we began a weekly radio broadcast. We called it "The Metropolitan Bible Hour." It was aired each Sunday evening on WEXL, a local radio station. As it turned out, the program would continue to air across the next eight years, with an appealing format and a responsive listening audience. Sponsored at first by our re-organized Men's Brotherhood, the cost of the weekly program was later placed in the church budget. That weekly broadcast made our congregational witness known both near at hand in Detroit and far and wide across a sixty-mile listening radius. It was through hearing me preach on the "Metropolitan Bible Hour" broadcast that I got to meet several ministers who became strong allies in ministry in the city. The broadcast also attracted to our services, fellowship, and activities many members of other church bodies who sensed a spiritual kinship with us. It was through hearing me preach on the broadcast while he was in Detroit to visit some businessmen that I got to meet Dr. J. C. McPheeters, president of Asbury Theological Seminary. Dr. McPheeters insisted that he wanted to meet me on his next visit, and he did after one of our congregational services and in the company of the businessmen who had first informed him about our program. That introduction led to a visit to Asbury Theological Seminary to preach and deepened into an active fellowship with Dr. McPheeters and his successors, Dr. Frank Bateman Stanger, Dr. David L. Mckenna, and Dr. Maxie D. Dunnam, and that seminary that has continued across my lifetime.

My task at the beginning of our new life together had been to gather and settle the congregation. Given the circumstance of the unsettled court case, we had been left with nothing of the previously held assets. We had nothing at all except ourselves and our faith in God and each other. Our new situation left us without properties and even without status in the minds of some. It was imperative that our members become settled in understanding how things were, why things were as they were, and what our best response must be in the face of it all. This called for strengthening the members in faith and fortitude. We viewed ourselves as pioneers again, and as covenanting partners. We began talking about "the Metropolitan spirit."

"Metropolitan Church of God" was new, in terms of its incorporation, creative spirit, and expectancy, but in actual fact our fellowship was really the latest extension of a spiritual and social grouping that began representing the Church of God in the city of Detroit in the late nineteenth century. Records of the Church of God as found in its national group journal, the *Gospel Trumpet,* show that several persons of Church of God

143

background were meeting in Detroit as early as 1884, but there were no successful efforts to develop an established group life until about 1900 when T. J. Cox (1854-1934), a white minister who entered the ministry in 1886 and worked mostly in Toledo, Ohio, and the Detroit, Michigan, area began meeting with those persons. During those early years of contact, the group met under Cox's leadership in a house on Mack Avenue. Leroy Sheldon, another white minister, periodically preached for them during that period, as well as to some believers who gathered with him for worship in a mission he led in an old saloon building at 418 Baker Street. Some other Church of God believers gathered weekly at a house on Junction Avenue.

Sometime around 1912, Mrs. Christiana Janes, a black preacher, became pastor of the people previously nurtured by Cox and Sheldon. From all indications, that group was the first interracial congregation of the Church of God with black leadership, and the majority of the members were white. Janes led the group in purchasing a lot on the corner of Beniteau and Goethe on Detroit's East Side where they in time erected a two-storied house-store building; Janes and some of the members lived in separate quarters on the building's second floor, and the group held worship services on the first floor. In 1914 a controversy arose among the members, doubtless reflecting to some extent the competitive economic and social scene in the city at that time. The issue was the advantages and disadvantages of interracial congregations in evangelistic outreach. The dispute resulted in separating the black members (who were in the minority) and the white members. The black members who left the Beniteau and Goethe location established themselves as a separate fellowship near the downtown area of the city at 641 Beaubien Street. That dispute became the occasion for the second congregation of the Church of God (Anderson, Indiana) in Detroit, and it was the first majority-black congregation of the Church of God in Detroit. Although the group began meeting for worship and fellowship as a second and separate congregation in 1914, their formal incorporation as a church did not take place until 1925 when, under the experienced leadership of Daniel Felix Oden, a black pastor from Alabama, the name "Church of God of Detroit" was legally registered.

The heritage of the Church of God of Detroit placed it among the first ten black churches organized in the city. It must be listed along with Second Baptist Church of Detroit, which holds the distinction as the oldest black church in Michigan, having been established in 1837; Bethel African Methodist Episcopal Church, the mother A.M.E. church in Michigan, which traces its origins in Detroit back to 1841; St. Matthew's Episcopal Church which started in 1846; and Ebenezer A.M.E. Church which began in 1871 as a mission work under the auspices of Bethel A.M.E. Church. With its heritage of roots in a Church of God witness in Detroit as early as 1884, the Church of God of Detroit was historically linked, like the other mentioned churches, with an early period in Detroit's life. Perhaps it was in part the church's historical position among Detroit's oldest black churches that made the news about its suit against me newsworthy.

Although we were a newly incorporated fellowship, the ties between Metropolitan Church of God and the past to which I have referred were many, strong, and influential. There was, of course, our common and treasured doctrinal heritage, but also the majority of our members were from families long-related to Church of God life. One of our older members, Benjamin Applewhite, our Sunday school treasurer, was a member of the original group that worshipped at the Beniteau and Goethe location under Christiana Janes. When the group divided over the controversy regarding racial togetherness, he was one of the fourteen blacks who covenanted together in 1914 and formed the nucleus of the Church of God of Detroit. In addition to Benjamin Applewhite's active presence in our new congregation there were several members of the family of Daniel F. Oden, that church's first full-time pastor: Hattie (Oden) Hill, Ora (Oden) Parker, Eva (Oden) Walker, and Rosemary (Oden) Bell, four of his daughters, and Norman E. Oden, one of his

145

sons. Hattie was a well-respected local minister; Ora was a popular and effective children's teacher in our Sunday school; Eva and her husband Elmer served on our Board of Deacons and Deaconesses; Rosemary and her husband Paul were two of our youth leaders; and Norman was one of our trustees, the director of athletics for the youth, and scoutmaster for the large Boy Scout troop our church sponsored.

Amanda Townsend, my maternal grandmother, a widow again, was with us. In 1918, just four years after the Church of God of Detroit was founded, she and her husband Collins Townsend, Oden's assistant pastor, had helped to nurture the young congregation for stability and growth, using the living room of their home as a meeting place for group prayer and Bible study. My father was also with us. He was a member of the trustee board when the Church of God of Detroit was incorporated in 1925. There were many others from those early years of church life who were with us as members of the new Metropolitan congregation. The very fact of their presence and support helped many who heard about the charge against me of preaching doctrines contrary to the teachings of the Church of God to take pause and question it all because they knew that such older, knowledgeable, and settled believers, as the "old timers" were, would not endorse someone who was guilty of such. Sally Foster Green also joined us when she returned to Detroit from pastoring a church in the East. She had preached regularly to the pioneering fourteen during the period of 1915-1916, and was instrumental in securing Daniel F. Oden to become their full-time pastor. Sally Foster Green died in Detroit and I officiated at her funeral and delivered the eulogy.

Interestingly, it was the older members with memories of their years of experience in the Church of God of Detroit who seemed less perturbed than many of us about our situation as a congregation being criticized. As I noticed and thought about this, I at first attributed their calm to their grace-seasoned walk with the Lord, but as I continued to think about their composure, I began to understand their serenity from a different perspective. It occurred to me that those older members had been through similar storms before, they were open to the guiding hand of the Lord, and in faith they anticipated a right outcome in the end. Benjamin Applewhite, Fanny Abner Christmas, Fanny Robinson, Sally Foster Green, Catherine Seltzer, Amanda Townsend, my father, and several other older members among us had been there at the Church of God of Detroit when Daniel F. Oden died, leaving the people without his guidance at the very time it seemed needed to complete an unfinished church building. They were there when J. D. Smoot came and led the congregation in completing the upstairs sanctuary of the church building, and soon after resigned under pressure of stinging accusations and criticisms. They were there when Charles A. White suffered the ire of disgruntled officers and resigned under pressure. More recently they had witnessed Raymond Jackson's fury as he battled for footing and advantage. Church disturbances were not new to these believers, so hearing and facing criticisms did not daunt them. I took courage from their presence and deepened in patience as I suffered the abuse of being falsely viewed by some in the Church of God as a supplanter and heretic.

Metropolitan Church of God, as I envisioned its scope and sought to shape its life and direction, was to be an interracial and cross-cultural fellowship. This was the initial character and the original pattern of the Church of God fellowship at its beginnings in Detroit. Our setting in the Detroit metropolitan area not only allowed for an interracial and cross-cultural congregation, it demanded nothing less. Calling attention to the importance of this for our setting, I taught about the New Testament example provided in the Acts account concerning the church at Antioch (chaps. 11, 13), a specific biblical instance of what is possible for a diverse people and what that possibility can bring to pass through vital ministry. I was eager to live, teach, preach, and lead in a way that our members would become such a church, our faith and behavior solidly Christian, our membership multicultural and vitally related, and our

147

leaders and members united in a spiritual democracy. Meanwhile, I was being tested in the crucible of criticism and censure by other Church of God leaders and people, and I knew I had to model for our members the spirit necessary to relate, or seek to do so, even with opposers, actuated by an unselfish love. In the midst of great inward pain, I set myself in prayer and fasting to be that model. At no time did I ever refer to the controversy in any of my preaching.

As the end of the first year of our new congregation was approaching, and as the court case seemed unduly delayed, I was feeling a frustrating tiredness of mind and body. I tried to hide this from the people. Gwendolyn knew what I was undergoing and she tried to help me find periods and means of relaxation. It had been a year of several unproductive and exasperating meetings with ministers, which made me experience disappointment and unrelenting stress. Raymond S. Jackson, a former mentor, was now an opposing critic and accuser. All this, together with the fact that I had been steadily, vigorously, and intensely at work across the year guiding a new congregation had produced an emotional climate that was taxing my nervous system. I was in need of rest.

During April of 1955 an eleven-person committee of ministers had met in Detroit to have a final hearing of the issues involving me and to settle the Detroit-Jackson-Massey Controversy. The meeting was held at the newly finished building of Bethany Church of God. The committee of eleven had five representatives from the Advisory Board of the National Association of the Church of God and five members from the Michigan Ministerial Assembly's State Fellowship Board. The chairperson, W. H. Hunt, was from the national Board of Church Extension and Home Missions, in Anderson, Indiana. That committee of eleven had been constituted to deal with the controversy, following a formal vote passed by the Michigan Ministerial Assembly during its annual meeting in October, 1954.

The committee met across three days. I appeared privately before the committee members to make my statement and answer questions from them. So did Raymond S. Jackson, representatives of the Church of God of Detroit, and representatives of Metropolitan Church. As expected, many questions were put to me, some of them based on minutes and documents submitted to the committee by the other ministerial groups before whom I had appeared and been interrogated. I answered the questions openly, honestly, and forthrightly, hoping that I would at last be heard with openness and understanding rather than listened to for what could be used against me.

After many other questions, I was questioned about my understanding of the church. The view I expressed about the church, and particularly about Christian unity, was too broad for some of the committee members who were still heavily influenced by the "come-out theology" traditional to the Church of God Reformation Movement in its beginnings. I had read, thought, and experienced too much from the streams of theology that had influenced the historical roots of the wider church to be sectarian about our own Movement. As I spoke on, I realized that my openness to embrace denominational differences displeased several members of the committee and I feared that my view of the church would not be judged with fairness. As it turned out, however, I was not censured for my view. The presence of Samuel C. Sharp, with his intellectual honesty, D. F. Marrow, with his biblical astuteness, Robert Fowler, with his practical wisdom, and Emma A. Crosswhite, with her discernment, helped the committee deliberations after they finished hearing me, and they removed the charge against me of my being in doctrinal error.

When the hearings and deliberations ended after three days, the eleven-member committee prepared a document to voice their findings and their decision regarding my status. I was declared doctrinally sound, but because of a perceived proneness to follow my own mind, the committee decided to place me "on probation," presumably because of the previous judgments voiced against me by the local area ministry. I was required to show interest across the next year that I wanted to be in relationship with the Church of God ministry. There was an additional stipulation, issued no doubt on advisement by the five committee members from the state. In order to be in full fellowship again, I was required to show evidence that the articles of incorporation for Metropolitan Church of God be amended to include mention of the Church of God (Anderson, Indiana) as our parent and legally authoritative body. My compliance with these stipulations was to be monitored by the Michigan Ministerial Assembly's Fellowship Board, to which I was expected to report within the year.

I had no objection to the requirement to "show interest to be in relationship" with the Church of God ministry. I had done that by meeting with them when summoned and answering them when questioned, and I continued to attend the area gatherings and regularly scheduled sessions for business. But our officers and I did have a problem with the requirement to amend our articles of incorporation with such wording that our church properties could at the initiative of others again be wrested from our control.

During the Michigan Ministerial Assembly that past October, there had been not only a motion voted to constitute a committee to deal with and settle the Detroit-Jackson-Massey Controversy, but also a motion was voted to merge the black and white ministerial assemblies in the state. A bit of early history will need to be reported here. Ministers of the Church of God in Michigan had originally been one deliberative body, but prevailing societal pressures in Michigan and elsewhere during the pre-World War I period influenced the development of racially separate congregations in the Church of God. By 1934 the black ministers had formed their own Ministers and Gospel Workers Association, a separate deliberative entity parallel in structure to the majority-white Michigan Ministerial Assembly. Although some black leaders still attended both assemblies regularly, there had developed an almost total separation between the two assemblies in matters of programming, business, and ordination procedures. I had been active in the integrated Michigan State Youth Convention during my teenage years and was accustomed to interracial relations, but I found it interesting (and questionable) that it was not until October, 1954, at the time the black assembly was experiencing division over the Detroit-Jackson-Massey controversy, that the black Ministers and Gospel Workers Association—over which Jackson had long presided—sent a resolution to the white assembly asking for action during their annual meeting to merge the two assemblies! Mindful that the black ministers of the Movement were divided because of the controversy in which he and I were central figures, and aware that the majority portion of that division had withdrawn their support for his leadership, Jackson declined to have his name placed in nomination for another term as president of the Ministers and Gospel Workers Association that year. Instead, he favored Emery C. Williams, a Lansing, Michigan, pastor. Williams was voted president, and it was he who signed the black assembly's letter of resolution to the white assembly. But the strong voice urging the merger was Jackson's.

Following procedures agreed upon during the annual meeting by a committee of representatives from both the white and black assemblies, chaired by John W. Batdorf, the merger was completed by December, 1954. As I assessed the results, the black and white ministerial leaders and churches in Michigan not only reunited, but the merger placed Raymond S. Jackson, one of Michigan's favorite sons and a distinguished pioneer, in a more favorable position to counter the support ministers from within Michigan and beyond were showing toward me and the growing congregation of Metropolitan Church of God. I believed at the time that this was the result he envisioned when arguing the case for enacting a merger while the Detroit-Jackson-Massey Controversy was taking place. My view about Jackson's strong role at that time in urging the merger was confirmed years later while reading about it in B. Gale Hetrick's *Laughter Among the Trumpets: A History of the Church of God in Michigan* (1980), where mention about the resolution for a merger named "Raymond Jackson, who strongly supported the action" (p. 172).

All of this was a part of the burden that I felt tiring me during the early months of 1955. Already weary from wrestling-matches with ministers who opposed my stand, sadly disappointed in being falsely accused by my mentoring pastor of undermining him, feeling victimized by legal strategies that had forced me into the arena of a drawn-out court case, busily engaged in guiding the life and growth of a vital new congregation, and undeservedly "on probation" with conditions to satisfy to be restored to full fellowship in the state ministerial assembly, I felt tired indeed. I was at a new place in my experience. I was standing at a new frontier. I was not going to retreat from it, but I knew I needed rest in order to renew my strength and move into it with responsible energy.

A Rest Trip Abroad

One Sunday morning, immediately after the worship service at the Hall, Olivia Smith (chairperson, Pastor's Aid), Clarence Hudson (chairperson, Board of Deacons and Deaconesses), and Osceola Fowler (choir directress) met me as I greeted members and guests up near the pulpit area of the Hall. Olivia Smith drew near and interrupted me with a call to proceed to an area just beyond the waiting line of people. Deacon Hudson and Osceola White joined Smith as she walked over to where I was being summoned. "How would you like to take a trip to Europe?" Smith asked.

The question hit me with such force that I remained dumb for a moment. It utterly surprised me. I gathered my wits, looked intently at the three, and asked, "Europe?" "Yes, Europe," they chimed, "and the Holy Land," Smith added. Osceola Fowler took up the next minute with her statement: "There is a group of Church of God preachers going over in July and we want to know if you would be interested in taking that tour. There are two places left on the group list, and if you would like to take the trip the church will take care of the cost." Smith then softly but persuasively commented, "Brother Pastor, you need the rest!"

The trip was arranged and I went, part of a tour group led by Elmer E. Kardatzke, a well-known pastor of a progressive Church of God congregation in Wichita, Kansas. Arenzia R. Cochran, long-time pastor of Euclid Avenue Church of God in Cleveland, Ohio (and brother of Osceola Fowler), and Marcus H. Morgan, pastor of Englewood Church of God in Chicago, were also members of the group. Kardatzke was an experienced traveler and his leadership style allowed the sixteen members of our tour group to feel an essential freedom despite the rigors of the tour schedule. Although the tour scheduled visits to England, Holland, Germany, Switzerland, Italy, Egypt, Israel, Jordan, Greece, France, Scotland and Ireland, the occasioning event around which the tour was planned was the first International Youth Convention of the Church of God held outside of the Western Hemisphere.

Planned under the auspices of the Board of Christian Education and directed by T. Franklin Miller and Tom A. Smith, the International Youth Convention took place in Fritzlar, Germany, during July 16-20, 1955, using the theme "One Lord, One Faith, One Task." That world convention brought together many young men and women, youth leaders, seasoned pastors and interested workers from Africa, Canada, Denmark, Egypt, England, Greece, India, Ireland, Italy, Japan, the Near East, the United States, the West Indies, and several additional countries in Europe. Among internationals I met during the convention were Carlton Cumberbatch from Trinidad; Daniel Wako from Kenya; Ivy Kahn from Calcutta, India; and Erich Gajewski, Willi Krenz, Botho Maxin, and Helmut Raschpichler, young preachers from Germany. It was while in Germany attending that convention that I first met Samuel George Hines, a young preacher from Jamaica, who was studying in London and was developing a congregation there among international students. The contacts made with those young leaders were mutually enjoyed, and friendships developed between us that deepened and bore fruit across many years.

The trip revitalized me. It was renewing to be in the setting of Europe again. During our tour of Amsterdam, Holland, on the day before leaving for the convention in Germany, I noticed that the billboard at the Concertgebouw listed pianist Clara Haskil as the featured soloist with the orchestra in Mozart's Piano Concerto No. 19, K. 459, that evening, with George Szell as guest conductor. I hurriedly ate and left the hotel in time to purchase a ticket and attend the concert. I went backstage after the event and greeted Ms. Haskil. Mindful of the serious health problems that dogged her daily, I admired not only her limpid clarity, sure musical instinct, and stupendous artistry as a Mozart specialist, but her iron will as well. Attending that concert, experiencing again the "musical heavenlies" to which I was accustomed, gave me a sense of lift that readied me for the next leg of our journey.

My facility with the German language made me valuable to the group as we made our way here and there. Speaking the language gave me an advantage that I enjoyed and I must confess that it was helpful to my emotional health at that time when some back in Michigan were frowning at the mention of my name. I felt especially pleased and privileged when our group went to Essen and Pastor Gerhardt Klabunde invited me to give the sermon at his church there. Early in the service Pastor Klabunde introduced all of the members of our tour group; each member offered a brief statement in English that Klabunde translated into German for his congregation. When Klabunde introduced me, I stood, acknowledging his greeting, but said nothing at the time because he went on to mention that I would be bringing the message later. When the time for the sermon arrived, Klabunde presented me to the congregation and sat down instead of standing beside me to translate. The people understood why when I began to preach in German! Faces across the congregation lit up, and their eager reception of my message on "The Lord's Prayer" gave me renewed strength. I felt myself "on eagle's wings," as the saying goes.

I was greatly encouraged as well during the tour by periodic conversations with A. R. Cochran who seemed quite knowledgeable about the root problem in the "Detroit-Jackson-Massey Controversy." I was especially troubled to learn from Cochran that one of my antagonists stated in a ministers meeting he had attended that the Michigan state ministers would drop all charges against me if I resigned. It was this, Cochran told me, that convinced him that the false doctrine charge was only a ruse to smear my name and make me a victim because I had dared to stand my ground. Cochran also told me that some of my critics had complained that I was "'too young to have that large church."

I wrote near-daily to Gwendolyn and posted each letter right away, which kept her notified about how I was doing and how my health was progressing. Cochran, Morgan, and I closed out each day by comparing and discussing the notes we each made on the happening of that tour day. The three of us could not get over being so surprised by the immensely favorable reception we received both in Europe and the Middle East as persons of color. The courtesies we "high visibility" blacks were offered seemed conspicuous at times, due in part, perhaps, to the interest in American race relations spurred by news of the turn Negro affairs had taken through the vitally active Civil Rights Movement. I remember the trenchant way Marcus H. Morgan reported from his jottings as the three of us discussed this late one night in my room: "The peoples of the nations we have visited have been conspicuous in their preference for showing unusual courtesy and kindness to us brethren of the lineage of Ham. Cataclysmic events are shaking the world and the pendulum of initiative is moving persistently into the hands of the dark-skinned people of the world."

During the one evening that we stopped over in Haifa, Israel, I left the hotel and walked down to the seaport. We were scheduled to visit Nazareth the next day and I wanted to meditate, put aside the tiredness of the day, pray, and ready my head and heart for the trip to the place where, Luke tells us, "[Jesus] had been brought up" (4:16). It was near dark when I left the wharf and headed back up the street to the hotel. The descending darkness seemed alive and vibrant as I slowly paced my way. With my measured steps and "high visibility," I perhaps seemed conspicuous as I entered the lighted outer court of Hotel Zion, and I thought so when I heard a voice call out to me, "Are you looking for something?" I paused, looking around, trying to locate the source of the voice.

"Pardon me, please!" the voice added, as a young man stepped out of the shadows toward me. "I am the bellboy here, and I thought that if you are looking for some particular place I could help you find it." His tone of concern and expression of regard merited a similar response, so I thanked him for his kindness and informed him that I was a registered guest at the hotel for the night. He was a small-figured person but seemed large of heart. "I saw you as you were walking up to the hotel and thought that you had perhaps lost your way and needed some direction which I might give." His openness led to mine, as we sat down in a section of the porch where we could converse in full view of each other. It was not long before we had moved beyond the usual formalities of a first meeting and, at his initiative, into a settled discussion regarding America, first, then Israel. The young man was fluent in English, open, well-informed about America, perceptive in his comments, frank, and willing to answer questions as well as ask them.

As we talked on, I noticed his interest in my interest. The discussion moved into a consideration of the problems of the Negro in America, and I shared with him the important role my religious experience had played in helping me to deal with problems I had personally encountered as a Negro. He followed by mentioning some childhood episodes as a Jew growing up in Cairo, Egypt; he was now twenty-four, and as we talked he seemed to find confidence to share himself more fully. The young man told me that he was working there in Haifa in an effort to find himself. He was on a quest to gain a working understanding of God in his life. He had been seeking help from others. "The orthodoxists in Jerusalem provided no vital help for me. I went there but felt no challenge from what they teach. They feel that they are doing an orthodox and useful job. At least many of their group appear wholehearted in their activities. But I must confess that their policies and the strictness with which they perpetuate those policies do not fully satisfy me. I was raised in orthodox fashion in Cairo, but I have found that I need something more than tradition; I need something connected with tradition, of course, but with a greater offering. I feel that Judaism needs more, something that can influence its course more progressively."

I was as touched by the young man's facility in voicing his views as I was with the open manner in which he did so. He went on to comment that my open manner with him gave him a sense of security to be frank and free in sharing his heart. "Well," I cautiously interjected, "is it your view that what Judaism now needs is a Messiah?" He received the question without seeming disturbed that I raised it, and answered, "Yes, I would say that!"

"Well," I spoke again, "in what area of Jewish life and culture do you feel that the work of a messiah is most needed? What would be the area for a more sure and fruitful messianic leadership?" He did not hesitate in answering: "In religion," he said. "If the hearts of our people can be won, then I believe our major problem will be solved." A fresh consideration of Jesus pressed itself upon my thinking. That Jewish youth had shared his soul with me; through trusting me he had thrust upon me an imperious call to understand his need and respond meaningfully to it. Fresh thought filled my mind about the concern Jesus had voiced for Israel and the way his invitation to fulfillment had been spurned. I thought also about the nation's believing remnant which formed the nucleus of the early church. The direction of the young man's concern led me into an avenue of witness for which I had a word, but I was also aware of the apparent and ancient barrier usually encountered when seeking to witness to Jews about Jesus. I wanted to give a clear and compelling witness. I feared to begin, wanting my expression of the truth I had experienced to portray not only sincerity but the very spirit of Jesus himself. That young man had been helped and yet hindered by his Judaic upbringing: helped in that he was rightly persuaded that "the Lord our God is one Lord," and yet hindered in having heard contradictory claims concerning the Jesus about whom I was about to speak. The problem that pressed me was: how to get beyond the barrier of those contradictory claims. I felt myself vibrating in a prayer to God for help.

I was still trembling with apprehensive urgency when the Jewish youth turned his thought-wrinkled face toward me and said: "I have been to Nazareth, to visit a priest. I have talked here recently with a visiting rabbi from America. To each one I confessed my hunger as I understand it, but neither one helped me. You are here now. Your bearing, your speech, your honesty have challenged me to ask you to say some word that will enable me to see my way and realize God as I so desire. Can you help me?"

The trembling I had been feeling began to subside as I sensed the Spirit of Jesus in our presence. I felt impressed to walk with the young man, and I headed back in the direction of the wharf where I had done my praying that evening. Once there, we found a private spot and there we prayed. It was a holy moment, with evidences of a divine visitation of our spirits. Our time of searching prayer was an experience of reaching God, and being reached by God, and it left its mark upon us both in real and recognizable fashion. Something happened within the young man that my words could never have produced: he experienced the presence of Jesus! The experience outdistanced the ability of his mind to fathom immediately, but he had the understanding that his yearning had been honored, his hunger had been met, and his life had been claimed! As I went to my room that night, my heart was bubbling over with joy, and I found myself humming the lines of the song "I Will Make You Fishers of Men."

The next morning when I was leaving the hotel lobby to

enter the bus for the trip to Nazareth, the young man met me. It was his day off, but he had told me the night before that he would be there to see our tour group take our leave. I protested as he insisted on carrying my bag, but he argued that it was the least he could do. He placed the bag in the bus and turned to take my hand. Facing me with an evident peace of soul that brightened his brow, he said, "Thanks again for last night." I gripped his hand in brotherly fashion with a prayer for his continuance in grace. I later explained to our watching tour group what that word of thanks was all about.

I did not complete the tour as originally planned. Much ground had been covered and much had happened since we left New York on July 6. For one thing, I was becoming travel-weary, but more importantly, Clarence L. Hudson, the broker working on behalf of Metropolitan Church, had been successful in locating a church property for us. On July 22, while in Lucerne, Switzerland, I informed Brother Kardatzke about my plan to leave the tour after visiting Athens and return to Detroit by August 11 rather than the 16th.

Upon my return, I was met at Willow Run Airport by Clarence L. Hudson. He was not only a prominent real estate broker but the chairman of our church's Board of Deacons and Deaconesses. On the way to my house, Hudson surprised me by taking me first to get a brief look at the building that he thought we should secure. The building was on well-known and well-traveled Joy Road, and was conveniently located for those who used public transportation. A much-used branch of the United States Post Office was to the east of the building, and just across Joy Road on the north was the scenic block-sized campus of Sacred Heart Seminary (Roman Catholic). The building itself was a newly vacated Jewish community center, with "Jericho Temple" engraved in the stone overleaf at the top front of the third floor above the street. The facilities pleased me, as they had Hudson and the other church officers who had inspected the building. We all clearly saw the possibilities the building at 2705 Joy Road offered for fellowship and ministry. We soon purchased the building, readied it for our use, and moved there from the Danish Brotherhood Hall.

Efforts at Reconciliation: Phase One

That Fall I sent an application and fee to the Division of Church Service to have my name and our Metropolitan Church listed in the 1956 *Yearbook of the Church of God.* I received a letter back from R. Eugene Sterner, Director of Church Service, informing me that my name had been referred back to our state committee and that its members had not seen fit to ratify my name for listing. I was told that until I could get the ratification of the state committee my name would have to be withheld from being listed in the *Yearbook.* I was further informed that if I could "get things adjusted with your state committee and they notify us not later than November 15th, we can still include you in the new Yearbook." As it turned out, things did not get adjusted by that date. It took much, much longer.

During the second week of April, 1956, I received a letter from J. W. Batdorf, pastor of Jefferson Avenue Church of God in Midland, Michigan, and executive secretary of the Michigan State Fellowship Board. A year had passed since the meeting of the eleven-member committee sent to deal with the Detroit-Jackson-Massey Controversy. The main section of the letter read as follows:

> Since the time of your probation, according to the action of our former committee, is about to end and there seems to be no particular evidence upon which the present committee can base an opinion of your compliance with the terms of the probation, I feel that a statement from you is quite important to your future standing at this time. Although, as I have told you, my attitude toward you has been a very sympathetic one, I am now in a place where I must regard my responsibility to the ministry above my personal

feelings. I am calling a meeting of our State Fellowship Board for next Saturday morning at Mt. Pleasant. I sincerely hope that I may hear from you before that time.

I wrote back on April 17 and thanked Rev. Batdorf for writing and for his personal regard. I went on to report, however, that I was reluctant to believe that I had not given sufficient evidence upon which the state committee could determine my compliance with the terms set by the eleven-member committee the previous year. I mentioned that I had endeavored to be positive and intentional in cooperating with the local pastors and churches across that year, and that we had amended our articles of incorporation to include the General Ministerial Assembly of the Church of God (Anderson, IN.). I then mentioned that I had already informed him of such actions on our part when we had talked during the 1955 state assembly that previous October in Lansing, Michigan. I closed my letter with these two statements: "All that was stipulated in that request of us by that committee has been complied with. My future standing with the ministry was to hinge upon those stated stipulations: to those stipulations I have shown due regard."

Batdorf sent an immediate reply, stating that he had not intended to suggest that we had not complied with the stipulations, but that the state committee could not regard my statements about compliance as evidence of compliance, and that I needed to submit such evidence, namely a personal letter of intent to cooperate with the state ministry and a copy of the amended articles of incorporation. He stated that he thought this action would strengthen my position with the state board.

I was hesitant to write such a letter or to send a copy of our articles of incorporation because my verbal commitment to cooperate had been voiced to the committee several times before and I had also told the members that our articles of incorporation had been amended. I could not understand why that was not enough. My letter to him as committee secretary had been simple, straightforward, and clear about my intention to cooperate as a minister, so I felt no necessity to repeat myself in a separate document. I sent no additional statement to the state committee.

Early in June I was told by letter that the State Fellowship Board had viewed my failure to comply with their request as showing an attitude that was "non-cooperative, independent and unbrotherly." Attached to the letter was a resolution, dated May 19, 1956, which was slated to be submitted to the Michigan Ministerial Assembly regarding my status. The resolution concluded with the words:

> THEREFORE, be it RESOLVED, that we, the Christian Fellowship Board of the Church of God in the state of Michigan, regretfully regard the matter of Rev. James Earl Massey's reinstatement into the fellowship of the ministry of the church as being without justification at the present time; and
>
> Be it further RESOLVED, that a copy of this resolution be sent to Rev. Massey with the information that we will be happy to consider this matter further if and when he may so desire.
>
> Signed,
> CHRISTIAN FELLOWSHIP BOARD
> CHURCH OF GOD, STATE OF MICH.
>
> W. D. Wood /J. W. Batdorf, Executive Secretary
> E. B. Jones /C. E. Dye/R. W. Struthers

I read the resolution carefully, then I read it prayerfully. For the life of me I could not understand why I was viewed as "non-cooperative, independent and unbrotherly." I sat down and typed a letter to Samuel C. Sharp. He had been secretary for the eleven-member committee. I included with the letter a copy of the resolution from the Christian Fellowship Board regarding my status and I explained why I had not sent the state board a written statement of intention. I told Sharp that when I last met with the state board members they were not in agreement about what any written statement on my part should include. C. E. Dye wanted me to submit a statement about my doctrinal beliefs, although the eleven-member committee (of which the state committee was part) had judged me as being doctrinally sound. R. W. Struthers wanted me to write something about my position in the pending court case. E. B. Jones wanted me to submit a written apology for not being submissive to the previous committees before which I had appeared. Only W. D. Wood and John W. Batdorf had asked for a statement of my determination to comply with the findings and recommendations of the eleven-member committee.

Intent to show Sharp that I was not stubborn or obstinate, I also sent with my letter to him a formal Statement of Intention which I thought would satisfy the demand of the larger committee. Sharp wrote back after reading my letter and said that he had sent a copy of my Statement of Intention to Batdorf and that he felt "confident that this communication should make the closing of the controversy mandatory." He also sent me a copy of the letter he sent to Batdorf after hearing from me. In that letter to Batdorf, dated June 20, Sharp wrote:

> As a neighboring pastor of Reverend Massey, I commend him to your Board, and to the limit of my judgment and knowledge, verify his statements as contained in this letter. It is with deep and sincere regret that I have had any part in the proceedings which have been perpetrated upon Reverend Massey, his church, the colored churches in general, and the Church of God in Detroit and the State of Michigan. In my judgment, much damage has been done and no good has been accomplished. It is my hope that this present communication will close the matter and will give us all an opportunity to demonstrate our sincere desire to redeem an ill-advised and vindictive decision which is our corporate responsibility.

I also sent a letter to Batdorf and the state committee. Unfortunately, those communications did not close the matter, because in late August I received a letter from the Fellowship Board informing me that at a meeting its members held during the St. Louis Camp Meeting they had agreed "that the Board would stand by its decision as expressed in the resolution of May 19, 1956." The officers and I finally satisfied the members of the Fellowship Board when we showed our amended articles to them during the annual ministerial assembly held that October in Flint, Michigan. This settled their concern for "evidence of compliance," and the Metropolitan Church congregation and I were reinstated as being in full harmony with the Church of God in Michigan.

It is probable that the State Fellowship Board had been informed about what had happened at the West Middlesex Campmeeting that August to "clear the air" between Raymond S. Jackson and me. During one of the ministers' meetings Horace W. Sheppard, a pastor in Philadelphia, stood before the ministers and solemnly spoke about feeling impressed by the Lord to have a special session to attempt to reconcile Jackson and me. Gladys Broadnax Walker, pastor in Columbus, Ohio, and a former local minister in the Detroit church, immediately stood and voiced her spiritual agreement. There was general agreement among all present.

Jackson and I met with the ministers in special session. He and I had met the day before and talked with specific openness about how we had become separated and how tangled and confused the issue surrounding us had become. We both recognized the need to untangle the knot of our differences and agreed to work at doing so. We talked well into the night. I do not know if Horace Sheppard had seen us together talking, or if news of our conversing had reached him, but his statement to the ministers about their need to meet with the two of us was well-timed. I accepted Sheppard's statement that the Lord had impressed him to call us together to settle our differences and be reconciled.

Mingled caution and anticipation filled the air as Jackson and I took turns answering questions put to us by different ministers. Many questions were asked about statements which had circulated in connection with our names and reported actions which appeared as planned against each other. It was a time for accountability and answers, and we stood to be accountable and give those answers. I was glad to answer that I had not sought to undermine Jackson and was glad to hear Jackson accepting my answer as true. He had reviewed the circumstances surrounding his leadership when he resigned in 1953 as pastor of the Church of God of Detroit and realized his own role in letting things get to that point as they did. After three hours with the ministers, Jackson and I were reconciled and the ministers of the National Association renewed their spirit of sharing and pledged a renewed will to work together.

With the news having circulated that "Jackson and Massey have been reconciled" and that several aspects of the previous controversy were settled, this pleased our state ministry and made my reinstatement easier. Soon after the October, 1956, Michigan Ministerial Assembly I received notice that my name and Metropolitan Church would be placed in the 1957 *Yearbook*. If fairness had prevailed, with more leaders acting with courage, that drawn-out controversy would never have taken so long to settle.

As I thought back on that experience of estrangement and how it had at long last concluded, I was thankful for the trust of a loving and faithful congregation, a dedicated wife, and wise leaders who also had the courage to act. Samuel C. Sharp and Arenzia R. Cochran were two of those leaders. Their wisdom helped them to see that Jackson's regarded rank as an older minister should not be allowed to cloud or erase the problematic picture his own actions created, and their courage inspired them to say so. And because they did say so, their action encouraged me to believe that justice would prevail and that I could have a future in the Church of God. I have never forgotten how they jeopardized their own ministerial standing to speak in my defense at that time when I was being viewed with suspicion and distrust. Their deed of acceptance and advocacy was a deed of moral strength and biblical spirituality.

Earlier that year, on January 15, 1956, the Metropolitan church held a Service of Dedication at our new location at 2705 Joy Road. Despite so much that was still "in the air," it seemed a "fullness of time" for our eager and expectant congregation. The singing of the hymns of praise by our robed choirs, joined by our church orchestra, and the happy voices of our congregational members was of such a joyful and resounding calibre that all heaven seemed to be sharing with us on that day. It was a crowded assembly that attended, with friends and visitors present from many cities and states; the largest out-of-state delegation was from Marcus H. Morgan's congregation in Chicago, Illinois. Among the state and city officials attending was State Treasurer Sanford A. Brown who represented Michigan Governor G. Mennen Williams. Rich compliments and challenges were presented by Judge Nathan Kaufman, Judge George Edwards, and Mr. Lorne Webber, Attorney.

A nostalgic but informative note was struck when Mr. Coit C. Ford, long-time Detroit resident and one of my grade school teachers' spoke. He recalled his sometimes painful dealings with me during those earlier years; he acknowledged that my mischief was common, but added that he recognized something more in me than mischief. When Mr. Ford began to tear a bit as he talked, his continuing and proud sense of tie with one of his former students was evident to all.

The Rev. Arenzia R. Cochran delivered the dedicatory sermon and in it he summarized and intensely elevated the supreme challenge of the day. Among the pastors present at our dedication were: Charles E. Stone, Henry Smith, Jesse L. Caldwell, Daniel F. Marrow, Herbert C. Shankle, Elmer G. Smith, John N. Evans, John F. Lytle, and my brother Melvin M. Massey. Melvin voluntarily prepared an article about that day which was published in the March 1956 issue of *The Home Visitor,* a monthly publication edited by Clifton M. Morgan, pastor of Lincoln Avenue Church of God, Pittsburgh, Pennsylvania. The coverage given the event through that publication enabled many well-wishers across the church to rejoice with our congregation in our development and well-being despite the previous bad press and adverse circumstances; it also informed our detractors about our will to persist and be progressive despite the climate of distrust that still beclouded our name.

Church Life: New Testament Style

Influenced by the account in Acts 2:43-47, I held steadily before our congregation the importance of: (a) spending time together; (b) family prayer and small group gatherings; (c) gladness and generosity of heart; (d) worship occasions; (e) gaining the goodwill of people; and (f) evangelism. Influenced by Acts 6:4, I devoted myself to prayer, study, and the teaching and preaching of the Word. Our congregational life was flavored by daily prayer, with twelve prayer groups across the city which met regularly each week. These prayer groups usually attracted believers from within the community where a house-group met, and this in turn acquainted those who met with us as members of other church bodies with the focus and spirit of our Church of God spirituality.

In the attempt to implement our concern for openness, both to Christians of other church backgrounds and to those of varying racial roots, our congregation had to determine in just what ways we would accent our own church heritage and our predominantly African-American heritage. I was intent to develop a congregation whose members would not be fettered by any denominational or racial prejudices. I wanted us to be a congregation of believers so informed and influenced by the Spirit of Jesus that our group life would speak appealingly and creatively to one and all.

As a majority black fellowship, it was clear that certain racial concerns could not be neglected, that as a segregated minority in American life we must handle problems and involve ourselves in causes related to social change and community betterment. These would remain on our agenda, but would be dealt with always informed by insights from the Christian faith. In connection with this concern, our congregation purchased a life membership in the National Association for the Advancement of Colored People (N.A.A.C.P.), and individual memberships in the N.A.A.C.P. were solicited yearly. During the annual membership drive across the nation, we always announced the event in our weekly church bulletin and the subject was vocally dealt with at announcement time in the worship services by someone appointed to do so.

As a spiritual fellowship, we realized that to be inclusive and appeal to others beyond our black majority our worship services needed to follow a more open pattern than the one traditionally associated with the "folk religion" of Black church life. We decided on a mixed tradition, with the best of tested Protestant hymns, solid classical anthems, distinctive songs from our own Church of God heritage, and a modicum of the "gospel-style" music. In discussing this pattern with some of our leaders and members who favored having more of the gospel-style music, persons who considered it as essentially appealing because of its liveliness, I explained how that style is sometimes problematic when it does not stimulate the worship of God but becomes entertainment, stimulating the people to admire and applaud the soloist, singing group, and instrumentalists. I found that in dealing with such questions I needed to teach our members not only about worship-inspiring music but about the experience of worship itself. Some of what I taught was finally published in my book *The Worshiping Church* (1961, Warner Press), which I appropriately dedicated to Metropolitan Church, "the Congregation to whom I minister in Detroit, Michigan: Friends and Fellows in the Faith." Some of the material in the last chapter of that book first appeared in print in an article I wrote for the *Gospel Trumpet* and titled "Once Again We Come" (June 20, 1959). It was my conviction then, and remains so now, that worship and prayer are the sustaining dynamics of the church. They are the highest and most expressive acts of the believer in relation to God and in response to grace.

The study I wrote on worship was planned as a companion volume to *When Thou Prayest,* my short book on prayer, which had appeared in 1960 (Warner Press). *When Thou Prayest* represents the summary treatment of prayer I shared with our congregation during 1958-1959, and with other churches and retreat groups during that same period. As our congregation was growing, I wanted us to fulfill our course with joy, winsomeness, and spiritual depth, nourished by a strong sense of God's favor and blessed by spiritual creativity. As concerned partners in pilgrimage, I wanted our members to be able to go beyond the stockpile of common prayer phrases when praying. I well remember an occasion when one of our newest members, Baptist by background, offered the following prayer during one of our Midweek Services. Drawing on the traditional racial heritage, he began, "O Lord, we thy humble servants are before you again. O Lord, we have come out to this place with sincere hearts. We have not come for form or fashion or for an outside show to the world." He went on, well-versed in the traditional lines: "We want to thank you that we were privileged to rise from our beds this morning to see the light of day and not the shores of another world. We thank you that our bed was not our cooling board and our sheets were no covering shroud. We were clothed in our right minds and had no disturbing pains." He went on, "We thank you for your care and protection through the night...." The praying person was sincere, and I honored that sincerity. But when he prayed that same prayer at another meeting, and with the same words, timing, and emphasis, I knew that as leader I needed to help him understand prayer in its richer, wider context and learn to pray with greater freedom than a stereotyped expression allowed. I taught our members that prayer is the most serious action and expression of our selfhood because it involves communion with our Creator. The most natural action on our part should be to let our hearts talk when we pray, blessed by a sense of God's caring presence and surrendered to God's wise counsel.

There was a steady influx of other believers into our congregational gatherings at the church, and into our membership, especially when I taught special expository sessions during our Tuesday night Midweek Service during the Fall and Spring. One year I did an expositional study of First Corinthians under the title "The Christian Testimony: Outlines on the First Epistle to the Corinthians." I followed that series with one on Romans, and we had standing room only during that course of study. There was intense excitement among us as we gathered around the open Scriptures and joined our hearts in communal prayer. Our Midweek Service, held on Tuesday night, consisted of study in plenary session and congregational prayer. Sunday provided times for preaching services, while the Tuesday night gathering allowed us to deal with questions and expressed concerns. While I would occasionally offer some sermonic presentation during a Midweek service, that time of gathering was usually restricted to study, sharing, and prayer. I looked forward to every time of gathering, eager to see our members grow in knowledge of the Christian Scriptures, in holiness of life, in openness to relate to all other believers, and in developing an aptness for outreach and evangelism with a cross-cultural and multi-racial focus. As pastoral leader I was intent to see that what had been established would expand properly, be supported properly, and be pastored properly. I was grateful to God for the ministry I had been entrusted to fulfill, and I gave myself wholeheartedly to fulfill it.

In order to assist the spiritual formation of our members and cultivate leadership within our circle, I began to hold periodic retreats for the fellowship and service groups in our church. The first retreat involved the youth fellowship and the church council (which included leaders of all church auxiliaries). We held the retreat in Lapeer, Michigan, on the premises of Detroit Baptist Camp. Some of the sessions included both the church leaders and young people, but some other sessions were conducted separately. That first retreat set the pace and established a desire for more of the same because being together in that way allowed our young people and leaders to exchange experiences, learn from the views and experience of each other, pray in community fashion, and become more tightly knit. My concern was to provide a place and occasion for prayer, reflection, recreation and sharing in depth. The leaders gained increased awareness of the potential within our youth group, and the youth began to sense a greater oneness with the leaders of the church and with me. It was plain to all who attended that first retreat that more occasions on that order would have to be planned, and that the church calendar should include them at stated intervals across the year.

We held that first retreat at Detroit Baptist Camp because the facilities, service, and accommodations there would not be problematic for those unaccustomed to being away from home overnight. After our first retreat there, however, we held only one other at that camp. Fortunately, Clarence L. Hudson, who had attended both of the first retreats, was so impressed by their value and benefits that he decided to find some site closer to Detroit that he might either rent or buy and make available to our church for retreat purposes. It was Hudson, a real estate broker and chairman of our Board of Deacons and Deaconesses, who had located and secured the Danish Brotherhood Hall for our use as a new congregation. He now discovered a listing of some property about forty miles out of Detroit, near Toledo, on Lake Erie, which was available for purchase or lease. Hudson bought the property, and within weeks that property at 4618 Brest Road bore the new name "Erie Acres." The original brick building there featured twelve rooms, two enclosed porches (one front and one back), with a recreation room located in the basement. All the rooms were served by central heating, and all equipment for heating and kitchen use was modern. Deacon Hudson redecorated the house. He and his family used it on select weekends, but he made the entire property available to our church for use in retreats. The property was situated right on the lake, with ample frontage that made the place ideal for boating, bathing, fishing, and meditation. Located only thirty-eight miles from Detroit, Erie Acres was readily accessible, well-suited, and ideal for retreats. Deacon Hudson further developed the eight acres of property, adding cottages and a swimming pool, and he made portions of land available for individual purchase by families in our church. The strategic importance of Erie Acres to our group life was underscored repeatedly across the years. Erie Acres played a major role in the spiritual development and bonding of our members, and in the cultivation of leaders for our Metropolitan Church of God congregation.

Ecumenical Relations

Under my guidance our congregation began to share in the activities sponsored by the Detroit Council of Churches, headed at the time by G. Merrill Lenox, who had been its executive director for 21 years, then by Robert L. Kincheloe, his successor. When I first began attending meetings of the Detroit Pastors' Union, a subsidiary group of the Council, I was surprised to find so few Church of God pastors present. I always expected to see Samuel C. Sharp, pastor of Bethany Church of God, since he was one of the officers, and Richard Maness, his associate pastor. Later, Paul Yutzy began attending after coming to pastor in Detroit. I thought it quite strange that the ministers belonging to our group, with our heritage of concern for unity and related-ness, did not take a more active role in the purpose, work, and fellowship fostered by that organization. The meetings of the Pastors' Union were for me times of stimulation; the speakers who sometimes addressed us usually spurred creativity. Their presentations and example encouraged me to stretch, improve, and extend myself as a minister.

After I had attended over a period of time, someone proposed my name for some responsibility within the Union. I got elected and served successively on several committees and commissions, one of which was the budget committee chaired by Dr. Allen A. Banks, pastor of Second Baptist Church of Detroit. A friendship developed between us that lasted until his untimely death through illness several years later. I was elected vice-chairman of the Union one year, and I had occasion to preach quite often on local radio and television programs sponsored by the Detroit Council of Churches. All such programs were managed on public-service time donated by some particular station for the Council's use. On occasions when a studio choir was not scheduled for a program, our church choir gladly rendered the music when I was scheduled to preach.

It was through Allen A. Banks that I first met Martin Luther King, Jr. A friend of the King family, and as pastor of Second Baptist Church, Banks was a staunch supporter of Martin King's leadership during the Montgomery Bus Boycott, but had earlier had him as guest preacher in the Detroit pulpit while King was a doctoral student at Boston University School of Theology. It was A. A. Banks (and Henry Hitt Crane, pastor of Central Methodist Church) who helped to arrange King's first engagement as a speaker for the Detroit Council of Churches' Noon Lenten Services, and it was during King's visit for those services in 1958 (and two tagged-on engagements at Second Baptist Church of Detroit and Richard Dixon's Trinity Baptist Church of Pontiac, Michigan) that I got to meet and converse with him for the first time. Martin Luther King, Jr., also had relatives in Detroit, as well as some friends and former college classmates whom I knew, like Arthur L. Johnson, executive secretary of the Detroit branch of the N.A.A.C.P., among others Afterward, whenever King came to Detroit, Gwendolyn and I were usually invited to attend the service or function for which he came, and joined him and our mutual friends for an after-service private social gathering at one of their homes. It was while sitting at the table eating that King learned from Gwendolyn that Craigs Beverly, one of his deacons at Dexter Avenue Baptist Church in Montgomery, Alabama, was a first cousin in her family.

I viewed the activities in which I was involved as a member of the Detroit Pastors' Union as essential sharing. I had long learned to dismiss the usual issues of denominational differences when essential sharing was in order. I was intent to make full my pledge, uttered in song across the years in our congregational and camp meeting singing, "We reach our hands in fellowship to every blood-washed one." I did not share in the work and witness of the Detroit Council of Churches merely to represent; I shared because I sensed in depth my ties with the other believers who were a part of its life and orbit. That was the essential upon which and by which I did what I did in, through, and for the Council. While there were those who criticized me, believing that I had lost or scrapped my acquaintance with the teachings and formal structure of the Church of God Reformation Movement, that acquaintance was still my immediate and valued heritage, and in many respects it still influenced the lines of my thought and ministry. But since my army service years when I lacked the support and strength of separate denominational distinctives, I had become accustomed to value spiritual universals over denominational particulars. Aware of more and alive to more, I had learned to relate to God and other believers without direct reference to formal systems, however ancient, historical, meaningful, authoritative, and valid the claims of those systems.

Having felt the stinging ire of my Church of God brethren, I found it easier to relate with other ministers, both white and black, who sought to be open and accepting as I did. Several solid friendships thus developed. Samuel C. Sharp was one of those ministers. So was Jesse Jai McNeil, pastor of Tabernacle Baptist Church. Louis Johnson, pastor of Friendship Baptist Church, was another. James Edward Wadsworth, pastor of St. Mark's Presbyterian Church, was another. Carlyle Fielding Stewart, pastor of People's Community Church, was another, and so was James Edward Jones, pastor of St. John's Presbyterian Church. As it turned out, the proximity of our church locations, plus the comradeship and sense of tie that developed between Stewart, Wadsworth, Jones, and me was so influential that we entered into a partnership that involved our congregations yearly in a Union Good Friday Service from 12:00 Noon to 3:00 PM. Due to its central location and large-sized sanctuary, People's Community Church was our regular gathering place for that yearly service. From our first year together, the Union Service was well-attended, and for hundreds of those who attended it became the favored service among the many Good Friday services held across the city. In addition to Carlyle F. Stewart, James E. Wadsworth, and James E. Jones, Horace White, pastor of Plymouth Congregational Church, preached in one of our first Union Good Friday services. When Nicholas Hood succeeded Horace A. White at that church, he became a regular preacher with us on that day. Later, Jacob C. Oglesby of Greater Christ Baptist Church, Collis O. Stewart of Mt. Pleasant Baptist Church, and the Ebenezer A. M. E. Church with its minister, became sharers in our partnership. Our Union Service was always highlighted by being announced on several of the local Detroit radio programs and it was given notice in the Lenten Season Service flyers produced and distributed by the Metropolitan Detroit Council of Churches. There were many pastors who visited our Union Good Friday Service and encouraged their members to join them in attending it each year. Our annual Union Good Friday Service at People's Community Church was a worship event unequalled elsewhere in the city on that day.

I met James E. Jones after receiving a letter he sent after hearing me preach on "The Metropolitan Bible Hour," the weekly Sunday evening broadcast from our church. The particular Sunday on which he heard me was part of Black History Week. I had preached on "The Negro Spiritual Interprets Jesus." Impressed by a subject in which he had deep interest and about which he had read much, Jones wrote to express his appreciation for how I had treated it; he also expressed a desire to meet with me. We met over lunch one afternoon and discovered that we were kindred souls in our interests, our beliefs, our love for the Lord, and our concern for our respective congregations. Over time Jones and I bonded as blood brothers in head and heart. Our Metropolitan members sensed the oneness between us and claimed James E. Jones and his wife as part of our congregational life, and St. John's claimed Gwendolyn and me as well. In 1960, James and Mildred Jones left St. John's United Presbyterian Church in Detroit to pastor Westminster Presbyterian Church in Los Angeles, but our ties remained strong, and for several years in succession Gwendolyn and I went to Los Angeles to do a preaching mission at their church, and James Jones returned to Detroit to preach for us. The relationships I was blessed to enjoy with these choice friends kept me mindful that the most meaningful and trustworthy ties are Spirit-given, and I have valued these godly friends, as agents of grace in my life.

Efforts at Reconciliation: Phase Two

As 1960 began, Metropolitan took the initiative to deal with the remaining barriers to fellowship with the Church of God of Detroit. I had been reinstated to fellowship in the October 1956 Michigan Ministerial Assembly, and our attorney had secured a summary judgment from the court which had settled and dismissed the unfortunate case against me. Based on that settlement, our congregation had the right to claim interest in the church properties held by the Church of God of Detroit. We chose not to exercise that right. Having purchesed new properties, we were intent to move on, but we were also open to work toward reconciliation when conditions seemed favorable.

The mood for seeking reconciliatin was influenced by a happening in December, 1959. Charles Shackleford, a pastor in Saginaw, had died. The Detroit area pastors went to the funeral, and so did I. Since I planned to drive my car, I invited Raymond S. Jackson to ride to Saginaw with my father and me. Jackson was scheduled to deliver the eulogy. Knowing that we would pass through Pontiac on our way, I called Herbert Shankle, pastor at Southside Church there, and invited him to join us in my car. He agreed and did so. As we returned from the funeral we all complimented Jackson on his handling of the eulogy, and began to reminisce about the former years of Detroit church life in which we had shared so meaningfully. We finally lamented how previous frictions had prevented due appreciation of each other, creating distance and establishing illusions of difference that had hurt the area churches. Having long since talked out our differences and achieved reconciliation, Jackson and I mentioned the need to deal with the "left-over" effects of the controversy, particularly the need on his part and mine to achieve reconciliation with the Church of God of Detroit.

While riding back to Detroit in the car that afternoon, I volunteered to prepare a letter inviting the entire group of churches and leaders in the Detroit area to a unity meeting. I proposed that the meeting be held at Metropolitan Church. The riders suggested a date around which to plan, trusting that those who were to receive my letter would find that date suitable and agree to join us. By the time we got back to Detroit that evening the groundwork had been laid for a needed unity meeting. I informed the officers of our church about the plan and requested their full support. They pledged that support. Under date of January 12, 1960, I prepared and sent the letter of invitation to all pastors and churches we wanted to attend the meeting. The letter sought to make clear that the anticipated meeting was "to explore and eradicate any barriers to the fellowship that we need."

The letter accomplished its immediate purpose. Some leaders were so eager to indicate their agreement that they notified me early by telephone of their intention to be present. On the set day, all of the leaders and churches affected by the "Detroit-Jackson-Massey Controversy" gathered at 2705 Joy Road, all, that is, except the pastor and any official representatives from the Church of God of Detroit. Both that church and pastor had been informed about the meeting and invited to attend, and I had even telephoned the pastor with concern to make the written invitation understood and persuasive. He had given no secure promise at the time to attend. When no official representative reported from the Church of God of Detroit during that meeting on January 19, I was disappointed but not fully unprepared for that to happen. As early as March, 1959, I had submitted a request to that church for our two groups to meet to clear the way for reconciliation. The pastor answered me this way in a letter dated April 4, 1959:

> Recently in a joint board meeting of Trustees and Deacons we considered your request for a meeting of the Joy Road Church of God [sic] and the West Hancock and Vermont Church of God for the purpose of arriving at a more harmonious relationship and Christian fellowship between the two churches.
>
> It was definitely decided that I, the pastor, should write to you to get a clear understanding as to (1) the purpose of the meeting; (2) what will be discussed at the meeting; and (3) we desire no one but ministers, Board of deacons and trustees, and chairmen of organizations of both churches to be present for the purpose of saving our young or new converts from conflicts and problems that they are totally unaware of, if such a meeting is to be carried through.
>
> Yours in the Master's service,
> David J. Jenkins
>
> P.S. I believe it will be wise for both of us if no one is present who is not acquainted with the situation.

Although my reply to Pastor Jenkins' request included the information he sought, the meeting between our two congregations never took place. I learned that some of the Church of God of Detroit officers feared that if such a meeting took place our congregation would press, during the meeting, for a property settlement, and that another legal involvement might result. With consideration of that fear, our officers thought it wise to delay any further action toward reconciliation. By January, 1960, our officers agreed with me that an open meeting in which all of the other concerned churches would share should help off-set that fear, if it still remained. However, the Church of God of Detroit did not agree to be represented at the unity meeting scheduled for our Detroit area churches.

The rest of us met, as planned. Using one of our building's upper rooms, we pastors met in a preliminary meeting before the larger assembly took place with the congregations. As leaders, we first prepared ourselves in prayer and afterward listened and shared with one another. As the two principals during the controversy, Raymond S. Jackson and I both made necessary statements. We assured the area pastors that we had settled our differences and were interested in resolving any conflicts still evidenced among members of our two congregations. We also answered all questions the pastors put to us. As we closed the preliminary meeting, there were overtones of the original "Upper Room" experience. We shook hands with full honesty and warmth, and moved from that first place of gathering down into the main sanctuary of the church building.

The larger gathering in the sanctuary was a welcomed event. It had been years since so many of us had been together in such evident freedom of feeling and depth of concern to relate. A spiritual contagion was present which spread and deepened after the opening period of prayer. Raymond S. Jackson and I gave summary statements. We spoke openly, as individual leaders first, then as representatives for our two congregations, voicing regret for disagreements, misunderstandings, and claiming our share of guilt for the longstanding division between us. After Jackson and I spoke, we urged every-one present to speak as desired, and to settle any and all per-sonal differences that still lingered. The meeting closed in a spirit of acceptance and regard, with many showing tears of joy as a result of the restored togetherness. My mother managed to get to the front of the sanctuary in time to "rescue" me after seeing me shake so many hands and receive so many close embraces, thinking that I might feel exhausted. That unity meet-ing was long overdue, but it had happened, and we all thanked God and took courage.

Ten days later I received a personal letter from David Jenkins in which he assured me of his desire to share in our common church life. He further explained that he had not attended the January 19 unity meeting because of the depth to which the controversy had affected some of the members of his congregation. Jenkins wrote:

Because of currents of ill-will, non-conformity to the Holy Spirit guidance among some, also non-cooperative attitudes and dispositions among some, it is my utmost conviction under careful and keen observation that no full cooperation with the pastor and his program have been realized. In fact, I have observed in some quarters downright disloyalty, therefore no ideal progressive achievement toward full fellowship has been made in this congregation.

He went on to say that he had a "job to begin on the home front," and asked if I was confronted with some members who were similar problems at Metropolitan Church. His closing line was, "In the light of these observations is included my reason for not appearing in person at your meeting on Tuesday, January 19, 1960." I read and re-read that letter to me, then breathed a prayer for David J. Jenkins. I understood what he was up against. I also met with him privately and assured him of my concern.

Two months later, in a mimeographed letter dated March 16, 1960, which he sent to all Detroit area pastors, Jenkins declared his own personal interest in the unity of our churches and appeared to speak on behalf of his congregation as well. The letter read, in part:

Dear Pastor and Co-Worker in the Gospel:

A few months ago the pastors in the City of Detroit caught a vision which included a much-needed emphasis concerning unity and fellowship among the congregations of the Church of God in the entire area of Detroit.

Today much of that vision has already been realized that you have helped to launch.

Inasmuch as I am still a new pastor in this area, moreover, I hesitated to be officially represented at the meeting on January 19th because the real purpose of the meeting was not clearly defined in my own mind at the off-set. Now I have a more definite clarification as to the intent and purpose of the meeting that was called.

To this end I am now making a public pronouncement to all pastors in the City of Detroit, speaking as the "angel" of the church at W. Hancock and Vermont Sts; also speaking on behalf of my entire congregation, that we join with you in this great endeavor of promoting Christian unity and divine fellowship among all the people of the Church of God and the communion of the saints everywhere.

You can be assured that you and your congregation will be received with the utmost respect, confidence, and courtesy. We trust that the same invitation will be extended to us.

May I assure you, again, that old scores and problems that grew out of misunderstanding, unwise moves, and unsound judgment are forever erased and buried as far as we are concerned and we now in the future go on in a united effort of presenting to our respective communities that we love and respect one another as brothers and sisters, and in turn we go out to win precious souls to Jesus Christ and His Church.

Brother Pastor, accept this humble plea from a pastor who desires to help you foster unity and fellowship in your congregation and community, and in turn we humbly invite you into our fellowship to help us foster unity and fellowship in our congregation and community.

I trust that you will feel free to read this official pronouncement to your people at your earliest convenience.

Written by my own hand, March 16, A.D. 1960 in the presence of God Almighty.

Yours in the Master's Service,
David J. Jenkins

After reviewing that statement from Pastor Jenkins and the Church of God of Detroit, I shared it with our congregation during a business meeting. We discussed the letter, and our congregation agreed to send a letter to the church to assure the members that we had no concern to ask for any property settlement. We were now relocated, with new properties, we were steadily growing, and doing well financially. Our letter was to assure the members of the Church of God of Detroit that our concern in all previous attempts at reconciliation had only been to settle the case of our difference and distance as fellow believers. That letter from us to them, dated April 12, 1960, voiced our concern to have the previous friction over legal positions settled and dismissed from our hearts and minds as the case had been dismissed in the courts.

Fortunately, our letter helped to fulfill our intent to be reconciled. A meeting for our two congregations was held at Metropolitan Church. Three officers representing the Church of

God of Detroit spoke for their congregation in asking our forgiveness for what had happened on their part to bring about the division and, as a gesture of restitution, they presented a check to reflect their awareness that we had a rightful share in the assets they held. The check was modest, but our officers and I accepted it as indicative of their goodwill. With all the affected congregations now reconciled, the "Detroit-Jackson-Massey Controversy" ended.

Shortly after reconciliation was achieved, I invited the area congregations to join Metropolitan Church in sponsoring a Cooperative Leadership Training School for the people in the Detroit area. Several leaders and churches accepted the invitation, and our instructors were Samuel C. Sharp, Raymond S. Jackson, David J. Jenkins, Robert Hill, Thomas E. Humphrey, and me. The pooling of our assets allowed us to offer a broadly outlined program of classes and the best instructors. This proved attractive to those intent on advancing their knowledge and readiness to serve. The plan worked well, involving us in a six-week term during the Fall, and we continued the Cooperative Leadership Training School across several years. By 1962, several white congregations joined us. By that time, however, what I originally initiated had become a District-sponsored ministry. Interestingly, it was out of the togetherness that we experienced in our training/learning sessions that a Michigan State Ushers Group was formed.

Evaluating Our Church Development

It was my joy in 1961 to make a detailed evaluation of how our Metropolitan Church of God had developed across the first seven years of our life together. I was especially interested in our vitality, our ministries, our vision and outlook, and our ability to experiment in new ways of outreach. I say it was my joy because I completed most of my evaluation in connection with a visit I made in October, 1961, to The Church of the Saviour in Washington, D.C. Rev. B. Gale Hetrick, executive secretary of the Church of God in Michigan, had been invited to attend a minister's seminar at that church where Gordon Cosby pastored, but because he was unable to attend Hetrick asked me to use his invitation and go. I was asked to report my findings to the Michigan State Assembly at a later time.

I knew about The Church of the Saviour. Sometime earlier I had shared in a prayer retreat sponsored by St. John's Presbyterian Church, where my friend James E. Jones was pastor; the retreat was conducted by a member of The Church of the Saviour, and it was during that retreat that I sensed the current of vital Christianity at work there. Later, Dorothy Quarker, a member of The Church of the Saviour, sought membership in Metropolitan Church of God; her work as administrative assistant to Michigan Congressman Charles C. Diggs, Jr., kept her time divided between Detroit and Washington. The fact of her dual membership permitted me to see and know how the ministries in the Washington congregation affected the lives of its members. The visit to The Church of the Saviour, then, was the result not only of an opportunity but a long-time concern. Gwendolyn accompanied me during the visit.

I was impressed by the sense of commitment which lay at the heart of the group life there. That commitment was primary, the conditioning factor for identity, congregational purpose, and growth. The basic organizational structure of the church was common to most congregations in the free-church tradition, and the teachings of the church were in the historic stream of Christian doctrine and evangelical concern. Membership in the group was open only to those who willingly established their lives in total commitment to the will of God in all aspects of life. This meant being duly informed about that will (learning as believers), ministering to others in the strength of that will (service), and giving Jesus Christ priority at all times (Christocentric). Pastor Cosby put it this way: "To refuse to grapple with this issue of entrance into the Christian Church is not tolerance—it is betrayal of the very Gospel which we so facilely proclaim." Likening the church to a ship, The Church of the Saviour had a motto, "Crew members urgently desired. No passengers." Thus, their emphasis was on "integrity of membership."

The ministers who attended that seminar asked for extended time to discuss this concept further. As the discussion continued, I silently recalled to myself the slogan used by many Church of God congregations somewhere on their stationary—"The Church Where Christian Experience Makes You A Member." I also recalled how the membership at Metropolitan Church had been determined, how our integrity had been tested, and how our involvement in litigation had made us ponder the principles by which our pilgrimage could remain worthy and exemplary.

The church's giving level impressed the visiting ministers. Although the membership of The Church of the Saviour was small by comparison, the commitment of the 68 members to the system of tithing had been so total that they voluntarily carried a church budget in 1959-60 of $60,000. More importantly, however, each member tithed out of a gross income rather than a mere net income. This did not reflect a works-salvation approach, but was an expression of discipleship, one of the many expressions of a consistent behavior of a believer who lives under the Lordship of Christ. Again, I thought about Metropolitan Church of God. Although we were, by and large, a giving congregation, with the majority of members committed to tithing, I knew that there was more development to be encouraged in this area of discipleship disciplines.

The patterning of ministries in and through The Church of the Saviour impressed me greatly. Beginning in 1947 with nine members, the church set itself to the work of fellowship and mission, with small groups organized to serve in specific areas of service and witness. In 1959, the "Mission groups" numbered seven. One of these mission groups sponsored and ran The Potter's House, a coffee shop set in one of Washington's busy spots. In that setting the members gained access to many persons who would perhaps never enter the doors of a church, and there they served as witnesses and interpreters for Christ to any persons who asked to know more about them and Him. A visit to The Potter's House informed me about the aptness of the sponsoring group's planning and the vitality of its witness. There was an interesting turnover of strangers at the tables as they were served, engaged in conversation, and were heard for what they wanted to say. I left The Potter's House convinced, as I had long been, that we are given more opportunities to engage in meaningful evangelism if we meet persons where they are, in the common context of living, rather than if we wait to engage them in the confined setting of a religious service. I felt strengthened and was reassured that my emphasis in Detroit on personal contacts by our members was basic to outreach.

The membership of The Church of the Saviour was not only dedicated, it was diverse in racial composition. Some of the ministers in our seminar, pastors of churches in the South, took note of this inclusiveness, but Pastor Cosby called attention to the church's racial and cultural diversity as merely a natural result of commitment. This also encouraged me as pastor of a growing congregation with a racial mix, and even with members among us of Hebrew background.

After our visit to Washington, Dorothy Quarker wrote a letter to Gwendolyn and me, expressing her delight that we had been able to attend the seminar and meet her pastor there. She added that my way of sharing while there had helped several members to know the spirit of the Detroit church of which she was a part. In her singularly descriptive way, Quarker wrote: "How thrilled I am to learn how much you two meant to my C of S folk! You know how it is—you just have to share those you love with others you love and have the both love each other. They did!" She continued:

> I've not had the chance to talk with Bill Ham, but the word was around the Potter's House last night how deeply impressed he is with one James Earl Massey. Which is only to say, Bill Ham is the least impressionable

person I know of—and I am thrilled that the "charisma" operated. I heard of your prayer on Friday and what it meant to all. Ecumenicity is more real to some for whom it needed to be—because of you two.

Her letter went on to report that Ham had ordered a number of copies of my books *When Thou Prayest* and *The Worshiping Church* for use in teaching sessions for members of The Church of the Saviour. Dorothy Quarker had brought those books to his attention; she was the final typist for my book on worship.

A few months later, in January 1962, the first Conference on Lay-Clergy Ministries for laypersons and pastors of the Church of God was held. We met at the Kellogg Center on the campus of Michigan State University in Lansing. I was one of two featured speakers and, having recently visited The Church of the Saviour, I was asked to give an informative address about what I had found, experienced, and learned there. I did, and spoke on "The Church of the Saviour—An Experiment in Lay Ministries." I also answered questions from the floor when I finished the address. The address I gave was afterward published in *The Michigan Bulletin,* our state paper. I sent a copy of the published address to The Church of the Saviour. About a year later, Elizabeth O'Connor, a member of that church, published her book *Call to Commitment: The Story of the Church of the Saviour,* Washington, D.C. (New York and Evanston: Harper & Row, 1963). I was surprised to open my mail one day and find that I had received a signed copy of her book, with a note from Betty O'Connor expressing gratitude for my call and ministry. Dorothy Quarker had also penned some lines under O'Connor's statement. I viewed her notation as a testimony that she had found a quite equivalent experience and involvement in both our Metropolitan Church of God family and the Washington, D.C. fellowship of The Church of the Saviour. The spiritual help she received in the one church blessed her for her role in the other.

Both churches had their beginnings in grace and had been

sustained by miracle, yet each church was doing something for a mutual member that the other one could not do in just the same way. I took this seriously. It helped to confirm my judgment and concern that every real fellowship must have its own creative edge and atmosphere, and that there is no single pattern by which what is distinctly real in Christianity must be visibly expressed. In assessing the development of Metropolitan Church, I saw that my leadership had taken our members beyond the confining ideas of some leaders of the Church of God Movement and also beyond themselves. I also saw and reminded myself that our church and I must so serve that our members will be able to see and move beyond it and me as well.

It is to be remembered that no local congregation of the church, as an organized group, can fully guarantee itself. The circumstances of any organized life are subject to change. There are conditions to which we humans and our social groupings are exposed and sometimes made subject. Changes in a city can occasion changes in the pattern of a congregation's life and programming. Employment opportunities matter greatly to family support. Children grow up and go away, sometimes to school, sometimes to ruin. Members move away, while some others die. The list of contingencies can be multiplied, but the picture remains the same: a million sweeping changes can threaten the organized result we cherish as "the congregation." The congregation is an organized extension of the church, and as such its future is expected, but because it is an organized entity its future is not guaranteed. The church knows where it is going—Jesus, its founder, promised its future. A congregation only knows where it has been. Aware of this, I wanted so to live and labor that our Lord would protect the path on which we were set and continue to prosper the work of our hands.

Learning from Evangelical Protestantism

As the growth and outreach of Metropolitan Church steadily developed, I wanted my pastoral ministry to be as effective as my calling, gifts, strong intent, and personal resources would make possible. I was eager to complete and build upon my army-interrupted degree program at the University of Detroit, so I decided to transfer to a more directly pastoral ministry degree program offered at Detroit Bible College. My brother Melvin was enrolled there; so was Hattie Hill, daughter of Daniel F. Oden. Both of them at that time were local ministers in our congregation.

The change of schools offered a very different instructive climate, both institutionally and theologically. The University of Detroit was a Jesuit institution, and its Aristotelian-Thomistic orientation had given me a fruitful understanding of scholastic methods, the importance of revelation-aided reason, the relation between nature and grace, and deeper insight into the moral dimension of the human condition. Detroit Bible College, on the other hand, with its moderate dispensational interpretation of the Scriptures and its rootage in Fundamentalism, acquainted me with both a historic movement that had influenced many Protestant churches and a distinctly different theological orientation with which I had to come to grips. Dr. Roy L. Aldrich, who held a Th.D. from Dallas Theological Seminary, was president during my years at D.B.C.

I liked the interdenominational character of D.B.C. I observed and learned much through interacting with students from evangelical sectors in many old-line denominations, and that contact and learning broadened my understanding of the fissures that separate believers. That contact and learning also sharpened my concern to work at bridging gaps between believers. Although we students were from several unrelated church groups, we were all united in an appreciation for evangelical orthodoxy and in our concern to honor the biblical mandate to extend the gospel witness to the four corners of the earth.

Among the focal points of the school's fundamentalist teachings, Detroit Bible College had a theological posture that included: the verbal inspiration of the Scriptures, with the autographs understood as inerrant and completely authoritative in all matters addressed and mentioned; the second coming of Christ as personal in manner, at a premillennial time, and imminent; the primacy of evangelism and the divine mandate to witness about Jesus. There was not much said in class about the church, except that the church was to be understood as "the mystery" which divinely intruded during the interim period between the ascension of Christ and the advent of the promised kingdom of God. Aware that this doctrinal platform differed widely at points from my own church tradition of amillennial-ism, my father cautioned me to remain critical and vigilant as I studied and interacted with faculty and students who were persuaded millenarians and dispensationalists.

I recall occasional references in class to the Modernist-Fundamentalist Controversy of the 1920s, and the way major leaders on the Fundamentalist side of the argument were honored and quoted as heroes of the faith and defenders of the biblical tradition. I applauded the vital interest among fundamentalists for missions and evangelism, but I reacted coldly to the ultranationalism I sensed on the part of many who seemed to lack the insight needed to distinguish between gospel work and national interests. That ultranationalism, allied with dispensationalism, was problematic for me because my ancestors, both on the Native-American side and the African-American side, had suffered unduly at the hands of those whose social conservatism and racist views were rooted in programmatic dispensationalist concerns. I wondered how it could be that those who loved Scripture and sought so avidly to defend biblical faith could miss seeing the demand in Scripture for social justice. But they labeled "social gospel" a product of liberalism, and taught personal salvation in a restrictedly individualistic way that left no room for the dominant ethic of love of neighbor. Among other things, I found the dispensationalist view lacking at the point of a responsible and inclusive biblical anthropology. The more I looked into the phenomenon of Evangelicalism the more I saw the movement as a broad mosaic comprised of clusters and groups in need of closer relations and open dialogue by which to inform and help each other at points of strategic need. I appreciated the obvious strengths of the evangelical movement, but I was not blind to its weaknesses, especially its shortsighted view about how biblical spirituality and social concern relate.

All in all, Detroit Bible College gave me a deepened insight into a major historic movement in American Christianity, a movement responsible for one of the major theological controversies in this land, a movement viewed by some as an essential follow-up to the Protestant Reformation with its claim of an inerrant Bible as the basis for an authoritative faith and its attempt to teach eschatology as a theology of hope for history. Meanwhile, as I studied Scripture, I increasingly viewed the Bible as the record of God's gracious and just dealings with persons and nations, and as God's written agency of self-revelation, the way to salvation, and guidance for faith, hope, and love. Informed as well by the principle accorded priority in Galatians 3:28, I disagreed with the fundamentalist position of denying equality between male and female in the church.

Dr. Charles G. Shaw was a notable mentor. His guidance in historical geography and biblical archaeology gave me a rich feel for the sites and scenes of Scripture. Studying Hebrew under Shaw's tutelage allowed me to enter the world of Hebrew language and life guided by someone who had not only lived with the Hebrew Scriptures but for years had lived in Palestine itself. Classes with Dr. Bartlett Hess, professor of church history, acquainted me with the rich traditions of church life across the centuries, isolating the problems encountered as the faith was spreading and highlighting those whose ministries gave the church needed direction during times of questioning, conflict, and persecution. Dr. John Thiessen taught the practical courses in church ministry and provided strategic pastoral counsel to his students, most of whom were already responsibly placed in a pastorate, as I was. Dr. Roy L. Aldrich, college president, taught biblical theology. His emphasis, understandably, was on "the fundamentals." Rev. David Allen, pastor of an influential church, taught English Bible, and his teaching method involved a ready-to-use memorization of Scripture, a skill my own father had developed. Influenced by their example, I was not only resolved to work out of a ready familiarity with the whole Bible whenever I had to preach or teach, but I also quickened my pace to memorize the entire New Testament. My interest was not in proof-texting but to achieve a comprehensive knowledge of the province that keeps a preaching ministry fresh. Having committed whole scores of music to memory as a pianist, I had confidence that I could do the same with the New Testament texts. I set myself to do so, working with the King James Version. I used methods I had employed earlier in memorizing the notes, structure, and dynamic markings in music scores; those same methods worked just as well in memorizing the chapters and verses in the New Testament. Later, however, armed with a working knowledge of Hebrew, Aramaic, and Greek, I sometimes found it difficult to confine myself to exact quotes from the King James Version because my memory then included nuances from the original languages of Scripture that the English versions do not always offer, nuances that are seldom supplied except in exegetical renderings.

Dr. William BeVier was another teacher of English Bible, and between Allen and BeVier I was instructed in how to study the Bible synthetically to gain the central message of each book; how to study the Bible critically to understand its background, audience, and level of witness; how to study the Bible historically, topically, biographically, rhetorically, and theologically. We studied the Bible deductively and inductively, moving from the simple to the complex and from content to use. All of this blessed my life and provided me with rich resources for my ministry. Detroit Bible College received accreditation within the Association of American Bible Colleges and Institutes during my time of study there, which provided academic security for all of us who were about to graduate with plans to do graduate study elsewhere. Later the college was accredited by the North Central Association of Colleges and Schools.

When I transferred from the University of Detroit with my

two years of liberal arts credit, I had only three years of course work to complete in the biblical and theological subjects to qualify for the Bible-Theology degree. After being admitted into that degree program, I requested an advanced placement Bible knowledge exam, believing that under my father's tutelage and on my own I had amassed a sufficiently wide knowledge of Scripture to pass such a test. Permission was granted for me to take the exam. I took it and passed with a high grade that allowed me to be awarded twelve hours of advanced credit in Bible. This benefit allowed me to register for exegetical courses and related work in the biblical area that first year at D.B.C. I then took eighteen hours a semester, eager to learn, but also eager to put the remaining undergraduate courses finally behind me. Fortunately, most of the classes I needed each year were taught during the morning, which left my afternoons sufficiently free to handle the daily demands of a steadily growing congregation.

In May, 1961, I graduated from Detroit Bible College. Isaac C. Turner, another young Church of God minister, was in the same graduating class. Graduating from Detroit Bible College was a choice of convenience at first, but the succeeding years have shown that choice as a providential one. The symbiotic relationship between me as a black evangelical minister and D.B.C. as an originally fundamentalistic Bible college must at first have seemed rather curious to some others, but time and life have honored that relationship and its effects in many fruitful ways.

The Seminary Scene at Oberlin

Having finally completed my undergraduate studies, I decided to use my vacation time from the church that summer to advance my standing in whatever seminary I would later choose for a divinity degree. Acting on information supplied in a Summer School catalogue from Wheaton College in Illinois, I enrolled there for the 1961 Summer Term. I immersed myself in courses in New Testament Greek. I was so intent to gain an exact knowledge of the language that there was one night during the term when I dreamed in Greek!

In the Fall of 1961 I enrolled at Oberlin Graduate School of Theology, in historic Oberlin, Ohio, a distance of about 150 miles from Detroit. I began in the all-day Monday classes, a program planned with working pastors in mind, allowing me to use my usual Mondays-off creatively. I had learned about the Monday Study Program that Spring while having lunch with James E. Wadsworth and Joseph T. Thomas. While eating in the dining room of the Gotham Hotel, our usual meeting place for lunch, Thomas, pastor of New Calvary Baptist Church, began telling Wadsworth and me about the new joy he was experiencing by being back in seminary again. I asked Thomas where he was studying, and when he told me about the Oberlin program of Monday classes I had the information I needed for planning my life after Detroit Bible College.

Oberlin was within driving distance from Detroit, which meant that I could commute and study without having to give up my pastoral work. After graduating from D.B.C., I drove over to the Oberlin campus and enrolled for the Fall semester of Monday classes. Deep within me was the hope to enter full-time at some point in the future so that I could complete a seminary degree. As it turned out, the church honored that hope and gave me freedom to remain on the Oberlin campus during my final year there. Jodie Hollaway carried the burden of the day-to-day ministry at the church that semester, assisted by Vernon Rayford and Richard McTere, although I was always back in Detroit by Friday night. I continued to chair all the regular meetings of the church council, and I was always present to preach on Sundays and to conduct funerals. I was deeply grateful for the confidence of the church officers and for the cooperative spirit of the members, but these were characteristic of what we had all come to experience and speak about as "the Metropolitan spirit."

The choice of Oberlin Graduate School of Theology was also dictated initially by convenience, with its proximity to Detroit, but I was certainly aware of more than the school's convenient location. There was also its proverbial and enviable record as a place of racial openness since its earliest years. Some of the ministers I knew in Detroit were Oberlin seminary graduates, and I valued the contribution they were making to the churches they served and to the life of the city. Edgar W. Flood was one of those ministers. Flood had been active in Detroit since 1955; he had coordinated settlement extension services for the Detroit Council of Churches and also served as senior minister for a time at Boulevard Congregational Church.

But there was still another appeal that the Oberlin seminary had for me: several leading Church of God preachers, educators, and writers had received their graduate theological educations there: Warren C. Roark, Robert H. Reardon, Eugene W. Newberry, Irene C. (Smith) Caldwell, Louis "Pete" Meyer, Marvin O. Hartman, and Hollis S. Pistole, among others. I knew all these persons, having served with some of them in national committee work for the Church of God. During the years before the Church of God established its own graduate seminary (1950), Oberlin Graduate School of Theology had attracted and educated most of the leading Church of God ministers who sought a seminary education. Thus, in going to Oberlin, I not only had the benefit of a setting that was conveniently close to Detroit, but I was actually continuing a tradition. More importantly, however, Oberlin seminary gave me the depth immersion in biblical and theological studies that I wanted for a creative and effective pulpit and parish ministry.

Robert Kenneth Carr was president at Oberlin College and Roger Hazelton was dean of the college's historic Graduate School of Theology. Both Carr and Hazelton were educators with an impressive background and reputation. Carr was a noted scholar, public advocate, and civil libertarian. His book on *Federal Protection of Civil Rights* (1947) was a landmark study that helped to promote an aggressive federal program through the Justice Department. The Civil Rights Movement of the late 1950s and early 1960s was aided greatly by Carr's research, insights, and recommendations. The report he authored for the book *To Secure These Rights* (1947) as executive secretary of the President's Committee on Civil Rights is sometimes overlooked when studies which contributed to the needed legal and social changes are being listed and discussed. Hazelton was a noted theologian who had recently come to serve at Oberlin, but his warm and cordial way with faculty and students made it readily evident to all that his leadership combined a caring heart and a thoughtful head.

My professors at Oberlin were Walter Marshall Horton, Herbert Gordon May, Thomas S. Kepler, Roger Hazelton, Ruth Lister, George P. Michaelides, J. William Lee, and Robert C. Tannehill. Other professors on the scene at that time were J. Harold Fildey, Richard Wolf, Llewelyn A. Owen, David Jewell, Marlin Butts, and C. Wayman Parsons, but I did not have classes with any of them. Walter Marshall Horton, Fairchild Professor of Theology, was in his last year before retirement when I became a student there, but I was fortunate to have two courses under him before his tenure at Oberlin ended.

Horton was one of the most honored liberals at work in the church, university, and theological scene. I found him to be a scholar who did his work with the whole church in view, eager to help the church recover her ecumenical spirit and task. Horton's contribution to my theological development was considerable. He offered his students a depth introduction to Christian theism and its implications for church and world. Although opposed to authoritarian religious strictures, he did call repeated attention in classes and in his writings to the teaching of the church that ultimate meaning is found in the reality of the incarnate Christ. Horton promoted a realistic theology based upon a fresh encounter with the basic Christian faith. He was politically aware, psychologically oriented, and theologically grounded. He warned us against worshiping human reason, but he was careful to underscore the proper work of the

196

mind. I viewed his position as close to that of evangelicalism in his stress upon God as personal, man as free, and redemption as a real experience for those who open themselves to the influence of the living Christ.

Walter Marshal Horton's classes helped to deepen my appreciation for the continuity and the many forms of the church. He alerted us to the divisive dangers of isolationism and encouraged us to trust the positive values of historic catholicity (oneness). He also helped me to sense more of the depth of the biblical mystery of the future by the way he taught eschatology. This was especially important after my studies at Detroit Bible College where the emphasis on dispensationalism had argued this subject from a differing basis and angle of approach. Horton and I shared a large common ground of understanding. I especially agreed with him that the world and humankind are half-finished, still in process, and that humans need an optimistic outlook regarding redemption as essentially creative. Under Horton's teaching I saw fresh perspectives regarding the relation between psychology and theology, denominational identity and ecumenical demands, revelation and reason, faith and hope, *kairos* and *chronos*. Horton talked much about paradox, about the lack of a neat and self-consistent system in Christian faith regarding God. He stressed the fact that logical inconsistencies are part of human experience, so that their presence in religious matters should not daunt us. Horton gave his students an appreciation for tensions in theology and paradox in theological statements. When he retired, J. Robert Nelson, formerly of Vanderbilt Divinity School, succeeded him as Fairchild Professor. I had completed my systematic theology courses by that time, so I did not get to take any classes with Nelson. He did, however, serve on the committee before whom I defended the thesis I completed for my master's degree.

Dean Roger Hazelton also taught systematic theology. Congregationalist by background, Hazelton had long since moved beyond denominational boundaries by the range of his thought, his associations, and his accomplishments. I was impressed by Hazelton's penchant for well-crafted expressions. He had a devotional attitude along with his erudition, which made his classroom lectures occasions for experiential encounter with God, at least I experienced this as I sat in class. One could not be uninterested in theology as Hazelton treated the subject. He made exacting study seem a work of joy. I sensed from him the joy of study and I wrote my papers for his classes with a joyful discipline. I liked the way he made the artistic and the religious merge, heightening in me a sense of the transcendence that opens to one in life and learning.

Hazelton helped me develop a theological method by which to set forth the findings of faith on both religious and aesthetic levels, a method which I had detected earlier in the preaching and writings of Howard Thurman. Both Thurman and Hazelton knew how to avoid clichés, rather clothing their thought in a stirring expressiveness to bless both head and heart. I watched Hazelton's artistry as he taught in class and I studied it in the writings that he steadily produced. I appreciated the way he always wedded substance with style, message and method, and I was blessed by the spirit that characterized him as a teacher.

I still remember probing Karl Barth's *Church Dogmatics* under Hazelton's guidance. I took the course with interest to assess Barth's treatment of the subject of the historical Jesus. After "doing the reading," as we say, I prepared a paper to contrast Barth's thought about Jesus Christ with Paul Tillich's concept of the "New Being." During the course of that class I studied well, thought deeply, and then wrote carefully. Hazelton was encouraging in his regard for the paper I produced. On the end page of the paper he wrote this comment: "A first-class, thorough job."

I took Old Testament studies under the noted Herbert Gordon May, the Charles Grandison Finney Professor of Old Testament. My first course at Oberlin in 1961 was "The Psalms" with Dr. May. Like Charles Shaw at Detroit Bible College, Dr. May had also lived and worked in Palestine. He was a biblical historian, theologian, archaeologist, linguist, expert cartographer, and had since 1945 been a member of the Standard Bible Committee and one of the chief scholars responsible for the translation and publication of the Revised Standard Version of the Holy Bible (Old Testament section). That was the version May used in his classes, although he sometimes read selected texts from the Old Testament as rendered by J. M. Powis Smith. He commended Smith's literary expressiveness which often unlocked meanings more fully. During my second year at Oberlin we began using *The Oxford Annotated Bible* (1962), a study edition of the RSV with annotations and helps from other scholars who produced the volume under the combined editorship of Herbert G. May and Bruce Manning Metzger, the New Testament specialist at Princeton Theological Seminary. We also used the *Oxford Bible Atlas* which May edited. Before the year ended we had access as well to the newly-published *Interpreter's Dictionary of the Bible* in four volumes, for which May was one of four editors. Herbert Gordon May was very much the scholar and an esteemed writer and lecturer in his field. He always began the first day of the semester course with prayer, an act of devotion that I appreciated, but after that we students had to work as if prayer had no further part in why we were there—or even how we would make it through the rigors of the course demands. Silence fell when May entered the classroom. He would place his folder of papers on the table before him, look out over the assembled class, let his eyes greet all of us (taking the roll, as it were!), and then begin what we needed to note down as if the rest of our lives depended on it.

Since my area of concentration at Oberlin was biblical studies, I had to take an equal amount of coursework in the languages and literature of the two testaments. I therefore took many courses from Dr. May. I learned about his apparent fondness for those who had studied Hebrew and Biblical Aramaic under his guidance. Having had two years of Biblical Hebrew at Detroit Bible College under Dr. Charles Shaw, and New Testament Greek at Wheaton College Graduate School under Dr. Arthur Rupprecht, I only had one additional biblical language to take, Biblical Aramaic, when I went to Oberlin. Palestinian Jewish Aramaic was the major language in use among the Palestinian Hebrews during the Second Temple period that is reflected in the New Testament documents, especially in the Gospels and early portions of the Acts of the Apostles. I took the course in Aramaic from Dr. May and soon learned the relation of that language to Biblical Hebrew. The class did exegetical readings in the Aramaic portion of the Book of Daniel (2:4b through 7:28), working through the section assisted by William B. Stevenson's *Grammar of Palestinian Jewish Aramaic* (1962), with additional helps from works by Franz Rosenthal, Koehler and Baumgartner, and, not least, from Dr. May. I found all of this most helpful not only in understanding the Book of Daniel and other Aramaic portions of the Old Testament, but also in seeking to understand and rightly interpret the stylistic speech of Jesus that was the substructure behind the Greek translation of most, if not all, of the words reported as from him.

Dr. May was naturally reserved in manner, and could seem distant to those who had not been in his classes. I remember another African-American seminarian warning me not to expect anything above a "C" grade from Dr. May, suggesting that he was prejudiced. I found that criticism untrue. Fellow seminarian Carl Harris Marbury, also black, had steadily received "A" grades from Dr. May, and he had been May's student assistant across more than a year when I arrived at Oberlin. While reserved by nature, Dr. May was kind and approachable, but a stickler for solid work on the student's part. He would unselfishly reward that work when it was done earnestly, honestly, and turned in on time.

At the close of one of my courses with Dr. May, I went to his office to retrieve the course paper I had done on "Our Lord's Use of the Psalms." I considered it a good paper, each page saturated with my own blood, as it were. I expected to see the grade of "A" written firmly on the front or back sheet of the paper. But not so! Dr. May had read through the paper with meticulous care and had placed marginal notes on nearly every page. As I sat in his office and read the comments he had written to me, I noticed that he was studying my countenance. I think it was to lighten my feelings a bit when he softly spoke up and warmly commented: "Jim, you have real scholarly ability. I would like to see you go on and do further study." Then, having noticed no apparent anger on my part after scanning his many written comments, some of them quite critical, May added: "You have some rich gifts, and an excellent spirit." As he talked a bit longer, I was grateful for his helpful comments because it was clear to me that Dr. May was sincerely interested in forwarding my studies and career in ministry. I followed his lead, drew closer, and learned more about the scholarly process at its best.

Dr. May and I corresponded after I left Oberlin, and I prize his cards and letters to me. After teaching at Oberlin since 1934, he retired in 1970. Oberlin College honored him by dedicating to him the 1969-1970 Haskell Lectures there. Gwendolyn and I were invited to the dinner planned as part of a week of activities honoring Dr. May, and we went. After the dinner in the dining hall of The Oberlin Inn, a Festschrift honoring Dr. May was introduced and distributed, *Translating and Understanding the Old Testament,* a sizable volume filled with articles by eminent biblical scholars from five countries. When Gwendolyn and I opened our copy of the Festscrift, we found on the frontpiece page a personal handwritten greeting written by Dr. May and addressed to us both.

Several years later, in 1976 when my book *The Sermon in Perspectiv*e was published, Baker Book House sent a copy to Dr. May for him to review. He did review it, and his commendation of the book went far beyond anything I would have expected. I learned about the review through a letter Dr. May wrote to me. We kept in touch until late 1977 when he suffered a tragic and untimely death in an automobile accident in Florida, where he had gone to live after leaving the town of Oberlin.

Dr. Thomas Samuel Kepler was my New Testament professor. Kepler was more than a man of the study, surrounded by learned volumes reflecting many languages learned and areas of knowledge explored. He was a patient teacher and an open-hearted Christian believer. Kepler is remembered by some for the many anthologies he edited, for his aptness as a devotional writer, as a leader of retreats for ministers, and as a master interpreter of classic religious experience. I remember him for these as well, but chiefly for the marks of sainthood that he humbly bore. Thomas S. Kepler blessed my stay at Oberlin by his counsel, encouragement, and teaching. He also encouraged me to write, and often made helpful assessments of materials intended for publication that I shared first with him. Many years later (2001) I would write a Foreword for a new edition of his *An Anthology of Devotional Literature.*

Kepler died in May, 1963, just a few weeks before the semester was to end, and at the very time I was in the middle of preparing a thesis in the New Testament area. I had noticed a few weeks earlier how slow his steps had become and how he moved up and down the stairs in the Quadrangle as if in pain. I thought he was struggling with arthritis or aging, but was saddened to learn, while seated in class waiting for him one day, that he had been taken to the hospital and was terminally ill with cancer. His untimely death affected the timetable for my thesis since he was my major professor. Given the circumstances, I was advised to wait before completing the thesis, and to work with the New Testament scholar who would arrive in the Fall to take Kepler's vacant post. Meanwhile, as the Spring semester neared its end, I was one of three Kepler students chosen to prepare and deliver the final lectures for one of his courses as Kepler lay in the hospital. I gave a scheduled lecture on the thought and contribution of Rudolf Bultmann; Roger Robbenolt and Eugene Swanger did the other two lectures, and Robbenolt computed the class grades. Dr. Robert C. Tannehill arrived in the Fall of 1963 and I finished my New Testament coursework and thesis under his guidance. I wrote on "The

Earthly Jesus in the Epistle to the Hebrews," intent to reflect my understanding of how the author of that unique document sought to do Christology for his generation. I completed all of my coursework just before the Christmas break in the seminary schedule, but since Oberlin still honored the tradition of only one commencement each school year, I graduated from the Graduate School of Theology as a member of the June 1964 class.

As my Oberlin seminary years came to an end and as I was driving back to Detroit after my last exams were done, my heart was filled with gratitude to God. Except for a tonsillectomy early in 1962, my health had held steady across the three years. Despite all the many trips to and from Oberlin, Louis Johnson (my roommate during my first year there) and I had been in no accidents while maneuvering the expressways and narrow-lane roads. Then too, the Metropolitan Church of God congregation had been both patient and gracious throughout the period, allowing me to be away for most of each week during that last year of study. The assisting staff at the church had been diligent, unselfish, and loyal. Interestingly, the congregational life at Metropolitan deepened across that last year, and my pulpit work on Sundays seemed more effective than ever, perhaps in part because my preaching was more informed and my leadership was more strategically focused. I had to thank God because it was only by divine blessing that new life was surging not only within me but within the congregation as a whole.

During my time at Oberlin I still managed to preach twice each Sunday, with the evening service as a live radio broadcast heard throughout the metropolitan Detroit area. As pastor, I received 46 new members into our church fellowship, bringing our membership to 620. I held dedication ceremonies for 33 infants born to families in our church, provided pre-marital counseling and solemnized the marriages of 11 couples; and alas, I delivered the eulogy at 20 funerals honoring church members who died. Driving along I-75, heading home from Oberlin for the last time until commencement, I realized how gracious the Metropolitan Family had been to me and how steadily God had blessed us all. I also realized how much I was going to miss the congregation because I had recently committed myself to serve abroad for a brief period to handle a special educational assignment for the Missionary Board of the Church of God.

An Interruption

Early in December, 1962, I had received a letter from Dr Lester A. Crose, Executive Secretary of the Missionary Board of the Church of God (Anderson, Indiana). The letter asked me to consider accepting an assignment as principal (president) of Jamaica Bible Institute, the Church of God theological college in Kingston, Jamaica, West Indies. Crose made it clear that he was writing on behalf of the Missionary Board, under whose support and governance the college operated.

Aware of my close friendship with Samuel George Hines, a leading pastor in Jamaica, of the several preaching missions I had conducted in Jamaican churches, and of my acquaintance with the major leaders of the Church of God in Jamaica, Crose began the letter:

> You have been close enough to the work in Jamaica to understand the concern on the part of everyone that Jamaica Bible Institute should reopen its doors in 1963, with a program to meet more adequately the needs of training church leadership for the Church of God. You have known perhaps that Brother Kenneth Jones and his family went to Jamaica, and Brother Jones was working with the Executive Committee of Jamaica Bible Institute, as well as with the Executive Council of the Church of God in Jamaica, in the preparation of what has appeared to be a very adequate program for Jamaica Bible Institute.

"However," the letter explained, "very recently due to a physical and emotional collapse of Mrs. Jones, it has been necessary for Brother and Sister Jones to return to the United

States; hence, we are left in a position to find someone who could adequately fill the post of principal of Jamaica Bible Institute. Of course, it is impossible to find someone to be in Jamaica in time to open the school in January 1963, but it is hoped that the school may open in September 1963." Crose then summarized the background out of which the Board had considered me their first choice as replacement for Kenneth Jones. Crose closed the letter with a suggested time for conversation with him about the request.

I shared the letter with Gwendolyn. Given my treasured friendship with Sam Hines, the long-term and fruitful connection with several of the churches in Jamaica, especially in the Kingston area, and in view of the gravity of the request itself, she and I both felt responsible to give the request serious consideration. As the days passed, we both felt the inevitable strain that considering the matter made upon us. The need in Jamaica was clear to us both, but so was the importance of our ministry in Metropolitan Church and the Detroit area. With plans to study full-time at Oberlin Graduate School of Theology during 1963, which meant that I would be absent from the congregation for at least five days each week, I shuddered to think of what resigning from the pastorate immediately after completing my degree work would imply to the people. The congregation and I had been together across a decade, and I treasured our true partnership in pilgrimage. It had been a decade of trust, growth, and effective outreach that had made our collective witness known and valued near and far. I still felt needed as a pastor. I also knew that if I were to accept the assignment offered by the Missionary Board I would need time to prepare myself for such a change and time to prepare the congregation for my withdrawal. I trembled as I prayed. Gwendolyn steadied me by her prayerful and trusting presence as we faced the hard questions.

Interestingly, while Gwendolyn and I were pondering and praying, our decision process was helped by a series of providential happenings. The National Youth Inspirational Convention was scheduled to convene in Detroit just after

Christmas, during the holiday break. Our church was one of the area churches hosting the Convention that year, and we had secured the auditorium facilities of Cass Technical High School for all of the mass gatherings. The mid-year convention had become a large gathering. Hundreds of young people and youth leaders were expected from across the nation. Lester Crose wrote to inform me that he intended to be present for the convention. He came, and during a break in the schedule one afternoon, Crose, Gwendolyn, and I spent some time talking about the scope and details of the offered assignment, the possible impact upon Metropolitan Church if I accepted the assignment, and the problem of the scheduled time to begin work in Jamaica because my study program at Oberlin would stretch across the whole of 1963. The three of us talked at length and in depth.

At one point during our deliberations, I was suddenly conscious of a memory that gave me needed perspective. The three of us were sitting privately in a classroom quite removed from other convention delegates. The memory was of an experience Gwendolyn and I had had while students at Cass Tech during one of the after-school sessions of The Miracle Book Club, of which we were both active members. During the meeting, Gwendolyn and I had done a duet rendering of the song "I'll Go Where He Wants Me to Go." I mentioned this. Gwendolyn remembered and confirmed the happening. That memory was probably triggered because Crose wanted us to undertake the assignment as appointed missionaries of the Board, but the impact of the memory was heightened when Gwendolyn and I realized that she and I had sung that song of mission commitment years earlier in that very same room! She and I thought that realization might be providential, perhaps indicating a direction to us; Crose was impressed by what we had remembered and thought it prophetic. We parted with the understanding that the three of us would continue praying about the matter.

While still wrestling with the question of what I should do,

206

I decided to share the burden of my concern with the church council. I approached the matter from a purely theoretical angle at first, but those leaders and I had been together long enough to know that a practical issue stood behind the discussion we were having. The time for the congregation's annual business meeting was near at hand, which meant that a decision favoring the Missionary Board's request would have to be made soon if my relationship as pastor was to change. An announcement would need to be made so that the church could gear itself for new leadership.

Before any decision was finalized or any announcement needed to be given, a second providential happening suggested itself in a letter I received from Samuel Hines in Jamaica. The letter informed me of his desire to take a study-leave from his pastorate. He wanted me to assist him with information about where in the United States he should do further studies. As I read the letter, my mind raced and my heart pounded. I wondered if he would be interested in coming to a Detroit-area college or university. I telephoned him about this, suggesting several possibilities. Aware that frequent traveling to preach on weekends might be necessary to provide for his family during his studies, and that those trips could be too time-consuming for him to study at his best, I asked if he would consider coming to Metropolitan as associate pastor, full-time, with freedom to arrange his schedule to allow for classes he wanted to take. The thought and proposal interested him. I invited him to come to Detroit, preach for the congregation again, and meet with the church council and me to discuss this possibility. He did so.

On February 23, 1963, the Saturday evening before the Sunday on which Samuel G. Hines was scheduled to preach to the congregation, the church council met with him and me at my request, with members of the Board of Deacons and Deaconesses present. Everyone present had been informed about the purpose of the meeting, and everyone present was also aware that if Samuel Hines accepted the call to serve the church, it would have a direct bearing on how I would answer the Missionary Board. Hines and I had also discussed this at length during our conversation by long-distance telephone. The group discussion was open, detailed, lengthy, frank, and encouraging. I was proud of how the church officers rose to the occasion; they showed a wisdom that assured me of their growth in Christ. I was also pleased by how Hines presented himself and voiced his concerns. When the meeting ended, some firm agreements had been reached on lines of direction regarding the associate pastor's responsibilities, salary, freedom to pursue a study program, and a budget item to pay for part-time assistance, if needed, from a third minister. Hines was at his best as he preached the next morning to a prayerful, listening congregation.

Samuel G. Hines had preached to our congregation several times before, so he was no stranger to our members. We appreciated his manner as well as his messages; he had never stooped to sensationalism or mere novelty when with us, always sensitive to life, Scripture, human needs, and the power of the Cross. I appreciated his friendship as well. Every year since 1958 I had visited and served his congregations in Kingston, Jamaica, as their Summer Mission Preacher, so I knew the effects of his ministry there and was confident that, if he chose to come to Detroit and serve Metropolitan while doing further studies, the congregation would continue to go forward under God's leading.

Samuel and Dalineta Hines decided to come to Metropolitan, and Gwendolyn and I decided to accept a three-year appointment as missionaries to serve Jamaica Bible Institute. During Metropolitan Church's quarterly business meeting on June 25, 1963, the following recommendation was recorded in the Minutes concerning me:

> Recently, our Pastor, in a statement from the pulpit, informed the congregation of his decision to accept an assignment from the Foreign Mission Board in Anderson, Indiana. The assignment is that Reverend Massey and Sister Massey will go to

Jamaica as the Principal of the Jamaica Bible Institute. The Pastor also stated that he would leave the matter of his future relationship to this church to the decision of the congregation.

After careful and concerned discussion with the Pastor, and on the basis of what we are persuaded is the will of God for our Pastor and our Church, the Diaconate recommends that the Pastor's relationship should not be terminated by a resignation, but that he should be granted a leave of absence to cover the period of his assignment in Jamaica, after which he should return to us as our Pastor.

Respectfully submitted,
Clarence Hudson,
Chairman: Board of Deacons

A motion then followed that the recommendation from the Deacon Board be accepted. The motion was seconded and the vote carried with an affirmative standing vote that was unanimous: 106-0. By action of the Church Council a resolution passed to have "a printed copy of the recommendation and the minute of the action taken upon it by the business assembly of the Metropolitan Church of God be placed in the church lounge beneath the picture of Pastor Massey as an evidence of our interest in, devotion to, and esteem for our Pastor and wife during their leave of absence from us."

The Hines Family was expected to arrive in Detroit by early July, which would allow time for settling in and to determine schooling for their children. On Sunday, August 11, 1963, however, I had to inform the congregation that immigration procedures had delayed their arrival. I had to go to Jamaica to prepare for my move and service role there before the Hines family received its expected clearance. I was in Jamaica from August 22 through September 10. I had several meetings with the executive committee of Jamaica Bible Institute and the Mission Staff, examined the Institute buildings, grounds, and equipment, reviewed applications from ministers wanting to gain entrance for study, held interviews with prospective students, approved applications, finalized the curriculum, the roster of faculty members, and fees, visited the leading theological schools in the Kingston area, consulted with Union Theological Seminary leaders on the status of the project for a divinity faculty for the University College of the West Indies, decided on housing for Gwendolyn and me, met often with Samuel and Dalineta ("Vicky") Hines, preached for the Franklin Town Circuit of churches, and preached in the closing service of a Youth Convention. Sharing in that Convention were forty young Americans headed by Alan Egly, Director of the International Youth Fellowship.

I was in Jamaica on August 28 during the March on Washington. I readily recall sitting in the home of Ralph and Helen Little, a missionary couple, listening with them as Martin Luther King, Jr's, voiced refrain boomed out over Ralph's short wave radio, "I have a dream today." I missed being in Washington for that big event but I did not miss the inspiration King's speech gave or the direction it provided. The speech had an immediacy and evident vitality, but it was not composed on the spot. While speaking in Detroit that April, King had used much of that same speech and I was on the committee that planned the "Freedom Walk" down Woodward Avenue to Cobo Hall where he gave the speech. The "Freedom Walk" in Detroit involved an estimated 125,000 marchers. It, too, was phenomenal. Much was happening in America, much that was prophetic, timely, and necessary. Social change was in the air, and some were resisting that change, dead-set against it.

The Hines family still had no visa when I left Jamaica to return to Detroit. Once back in the city I picked up the phone and called the office of Congressman Charles C. Diggs, Jr. Immediate action followed. Within three days Samuel,

Dalineta, and their three children were in Detroit! They were soon settled, and he and I "put our heads together," bent our knees in prayer, and served the congregation. He put his plans for further schooling on hold for a few months while I completed my final semester at Oberlin.

The Massey family in 1943. Rev. George W. Massey, Sr., and Elizabeth Shelton Massey, my parents, are seated. My younger brother, Howard, stands between them. My older brothers, Raymond, George, Jr. (in uniform), and Melvin are standing to my right.

Standing with the counselors (and campers) in 1949 during the National Association's first National Youth Camp, I am in the top row, third from the left. Emery C. Williams, founder and director, stands at the end, second row.

Sharing a light moment with Gwendolyn Inez Kilpatrick at the National Association Campground (West Middlesex, PA) in 1949. I was a campground policeman that year, thus the badge I am sporting.

"Just Married," on August 4, 1951.

Class picture of Detroit Bible College graduates, 1961. I am featured, center right.

A group of local ministers in the Metropolitan congregation in 1963. Seated: Nellie Small, Joneane Anderson, Jodie Hollaway (associate minister), Pearl Cox, George S. Marshall, James Marshall. Standing: Ronald J. Fowler, Ernest Robinson, Richard McTere, Joseph Tumpkin, Charles Dawson, Nathaniel Davis, Marvin O. Robinson, Vernon Rayford.

With Gwendolyn in my study at Metropolitan Church in 1963.

Some of the students at Jamaica School of Theology (Kingston, Jamaica) in the mid 1960s. Kneeling (left to right): Kenneth Smith, Roland McNally, E. Raymond Chin, Derrick Coy. Standing (left to right): are Winston A. Lawson, Wilmer Jackson, Grace Tingling, Winston Jackson, and Derrick Jackson.

Dean Ralph Little smiles as Pastor Roy Galloway receives his Diploma in Ministerial Studies from me during the 1965 graduation ceremony at Jamaica School of Theology.

Berlin, Germany, October 30, 1966. I am carrying the flag of Jamaica during a public "Act of Witness" with other delegates to the World Congress on Evangelism. My Detroit friend Louis Johnson walks to my left, with David B. Clark (with Jamaica placard) and Canon R. O. C. King of the Anglican Church in Jamaica. (Photo courtesy of the Billy Graham Evangelistic Association.)

In Oberlin, Ohio, November 1, 1969, giving a tribute to Howard and Wanda Jones during their twenty-fifth wedding anniversary. Jones was the first African American associate evangelist with the Billy Graham Evangelistic Association. Billy Graham sits to my left, listening intently to the poem I used in closing my tribute. Howard Jones sits to my right, checking out some detail with Louis Johnson.

At the July 1971 banquet given by Metropolitan Church of God to honor my twenty-fifth year in ministry. Gwendolyn and Beulah Johnson are chatting, while Louis Johnson rests before giving the banquet address.

On the Anderson College campus in 1974, sharing a light moment with Samuel G. Hines and Thomas Jason Sawyer. The newly constructed Adam Miller Chapel section of the School of Theology building is in the background.

In Lausanne, Switzerland, in July 1974, during the World Congress on Evangelization. Standing in front of the Palais de Beaulieu, our conference center. With me are (left to right) Charles Tarr, Barry L. Callen, and William E. Reed.

The Metropolitan Church of God congregation assembled in worship on Easter Sunday, 1974. Those on the front pew, center section, robed in white, were new converts about to be baptized during the service. Choir members were assembled along the walls for the group picture.

The Anderson Graduate School of Theology faculty, April 1976.
Dean Barry Callen is seated, center. I am standing, third from right.

December 1976, with members of the Metropolitan Church Board of Trustees after my "Leave Taking" Service to become Speaker for "Christian Brotherhood Hour." Mr. Coit C. Ford, my beloved grade school teacher, was present for that service and obliged me by joining us in this photograph. He is in the second chair on the right. I am standing, center.

THE METROPOLITAN CHURCH OF GOD

UPON RECOMMENDATION OF THE CHURCH COUNCIL,
THE BOARD OF TRUSTEES AND THE DIACONATE
HEREBY CONFERS UPON

DR. JAMES EARL MASSEY

THE HONORARY TITLE

PASTOR AT LARGE

WITH ALL THE PRIVILEGES AND RIGHTS THAT ACCOMPANY MEMBERSHIP IN THE METROPOLITAN CHURCH OF GOD. IN WITNESS WHEREOF, THE SEAL OF THE CHURCH AND THE SIGNATURES OF ITS PASTOR AND REPRESENTATIVE OFFICERS ARE HERETO AFFIXED. GIVEN AT DETROIT, IN THE STATE OF MICHIGAN, THIS
5TH DAY OF DECEMBER, 1976.

Robert O. Dulin, jr.
Pastor

E.D. Anderson
Chairman, Board of Trustees

Clinton Darby
Chairman, The Diaconate

Edgar L. Bell
Church Treasurer

The treasured "diploma" the Metropolitan Church conferred upon me when I left in December 1976.

A photo with Gwendolyn and Dr. Raymond S. Jackson, my revered mentor, during the reception in June 1977 welcoming me as the new Speaker for "Christian Brotherhood Hour."

Gwendolyn and I joined in this 1977 reception photo with Dr. R. Eugene Sterner (left), my predecessor as CBH Speaker, his wife Millie, and Dr. Maurice Berquist and his wife Bernie. Berquist was the newly elected executive director of the Mass Communications Board.

Gwendolyn conversing with the camp director in a refugee camp in Malaysia in 1979, during her service as Coordinator of Relief and Refugee Services for the Church of God (Anderson, IN). Wayne L. Harting, chair of the church's Commission on Social Concerns, stands to her left, loading his camera. (Photo courtesy of the American Embassy, Malaysia).

September 9, 1984. Installation Day as "Dean of the Chapel and Institute Professor of Religion and Society" at Tuskegee Institute. From the left: Carl H. Marbury, myself, President Benjamin F. Payton, Edward L. Foggs and Evans E. Crawford. In the background is the famous Booker T. Washington Memorial Monument sculpted by Charles Keck and erected and unveiled in 1922. Dr. Washington, founder of Tuskegee Institute, is depicted in the heroic act of pulling back the veil of ignorance and superstition to let the light of knowledge shine on the face of a crouching former slave.

On Founder's Day, 1988, I am straightening the hood placed on Dr. Harry V. Richardson, one of my illustrious predecessors in campus ministry at Tuskegee, after president Payton awarded him an honorary Doctor of Literature degree. The award was part of several special events to commemorate the centennial year of campus ministry at Tuskegee.

Addressing the Alabama State Legislature in 1988 during "Tuskegee Day," after some stirring music from the Tuskegee University Concert Choir.

A gathering of Deans. This treasured photo was taken in March, 1990, during my first year as dean of Anderson University School of Theology. I am pictured with the living former deans of the School of Theology: Adam W. Miller (1953-1962), seated without robe; Gene W. Newberry (1962-1974), seated; Barry L. Callen (1974-1983; 1988-1989), left; Jerry C. Grubbs (1983-1988); myself.

Delivering the keynote address during the World Convention of the Church of God, in Weisbaden, Germany, July 19, 1991. Helmut Raschpickler, my translator, is at the podium to my right. Seated immediately behind me is Edward L. Foggs, Executive Secretary of the Executive Council of the Church of God.

The Anderson School of Theology faculty in May 1990.

Enjoying a moment with my long-time friend Dr. Benjamin Hooks, Executive Director of the NAACP, when he came to speak for the Martin Luther King, Jr. Day Service at Anderson University in January 1993. Joining us were my university colleagues Duane Hoak (left), A. Patrick Allen, and Jerry C. Grubbs.

Lecturing in Japan in July 1993 at Hakone Tozannso of YMCA during a Pastors Retreat. Someone else wrote the Japanese characters on the blackboard behind me; I am not fluent in that language.

With Kozo Shimada, a graduate of Anderson University School of Theology, and my host during my lecture trip in Japan, and his wife Rumi.

Signing degrees before my retirement.

James Earl and Gwendolyn Massey in 2000.

A pencil drawing of me, commissioned from Michigan artist Nathan Greene by *Christianity Today* for use with the editorials I wrote while serving as one of that magazine's senior editors. (Drawing used by courtesy of David Neff, Vice President and Editor, *Christianity Today*, Inc.)

With Dr. Edward L. Wheeler, on my right, and Dr. Gregory Gray, in November 2001, who succeeded me, in the deanship at the Tuskegee University Chapel. (Photo courtesy of Frank Graves, Photographer).

7

ON MISSION IN JAMAICA

As the largest of the Caribbean islands and the one closest to the United States, with a large population and boasting the most varied terrain along with beautiful beaches, Jamaica has long been a scene of church mission work and a popular land for tourists. With its independence gained from Britain in 1962, an old island colony had become a new nation, a republic. The Jamaican flag had replaced the familiar British Union Jack. I was in Jamaica on a preaching mission during that summer when the exchange and formal recognition of the transfer of power took place. Even so, while back on the island for a short business trip in 1963, I still noticed some visible evidences of the new nation's continuing relationship with the British Crown. Portraits of Britain's Queen Elizabeth were still hanging prominently in hotels, on walls of restaurants, and in major shops catering to tourists. There was also the presence and regarded functions of Jamaica's Governor-General, the main entrance of whose mansion was immediately visible from my office window in Jamaica School of Theology that was located just across the street at 37 Hope Road.

Tourism was crucial to the new nation's economy and as many as 350,000 tourists visited the island each year. Slavery had been abolished in Jamaica in 1838, but the landscape was dotted with remnants of buildings that once belonged to lucrative estates of slave owners, and a potpourri of racial mixes left no question about the intermingling, forced or otherwise, that had occurred during the slavery period and since abolition. At

212

every turn one makes, there are persons of mixed ancestry, desporting traces that are African, English, East Indian, Chinese, or even Jewish, and usually with an unashamed pride in the fact. Most of the Jamaicans with whom Gwendolyn and I regularly met and worked were highly anglicized in their methods and manners, but there was also a loudly-voiced reverence among many of them for such nationalist heroes as Paul Bogle (1822-1865), the black political and religious leader who organized the 1865 Morant Bay Rebellion in Jamaica, and Marcus Mosiah Garvey (1887-1940), founder and leader of the Universal Negro Improvement Association. Following its independence, Jamaica named Garvey its first national hero. Gwendolyn and I had settled in Jamaica when Garvey's remains were returned there from England where he died. They were reinterred with public honors.

The work of the Church of God in Jamaica had been fruitful from the start of the pioneer ministry there in 1907 of George W. and Nellie Olson, former workers in the Gospel Trumpet Home. Because of the cooperative spirit and zeal of the Jamaican people themselves, the work grew so rapidly that more than one missionary couple was soon needed. With the increase of Church of God congregations in the island, Nellie Olson felt burdened to begin a Bible school to train leaders for local churches. The result was the opening of "Jamaica Bible Institute" in 1926, in the city of Kingston, using the building of the High Holborn Street congregation where George Olson was pastor. There were five students at the beginning, with Nellie Olson as Institute principal and the only teacher. Operating under the auspices and support of the America-based Missionary Board of the Church of God, in collaboration with a Jamaica-based guidance committee, the Institute in time gained the background, notice, and respect needed to establish itself as a viable and valued educational entity. In 1938 the secondary education courses that the Institute had been offering within one of its two study departments were formalized under a high school format and in a new location (Ardenne Road).

The new institutional name was "Ardenne High School." The study department for ministerial training continued under the name "Jamaica Bible Institute." The Institute offered a short-term program in Christian education, a two-year program for gospel workers, and a four—year program for those called to ordained ministry in the church. Throughout those years the administrative leadership and teaching at the Institute continued through missionaries appointed and sent to Jamaica by the Missionary Board of the Church of God in Anderson, Indiana, in the United States.

Evident changes across the years in the Jamaican society, mind-set, and relations with the wider world, particularly the event of Jamaica's national independence in 1962, began to affect the thinking, visioning expectations, and projections of the Jamaican church members. The continuing role, control, and influence of missionaries was brought under strict review, as well as the need to transfer property rights from Board control to the control of the General Assembly in Jamaica, the church's legal entity in its own country. The upgrading of Jamaica Bible Institute was also envisioned, the concern being to meet educational standards currently honored in theological colleges preparing ministerial students to take and pass the London University external Diploma in Theology and/or the Bachelor of Divinity external degree exams. This concern was particularly acute because at that time there was no accreditation program that regulated the work of theological colleges located in the Caribbean area; ministerial students from the area, intent on a certified degree, would either go to England or America for their degrees.

The London external diploma or external degree program could allow able students to complete their work at some chosen school in Jamaica and have their learning validated by registering for, taking, and passing the external degree exam. This was happening in some of the theological colleges sponsored by several church bodies. For instance, there were Anglican (Episcopalian) ministers, Jamaican by birth, who had obtained their intellectual and theological studies in nearby Barbados, at Codrington College, a theological college affiliated to the University of Durham in England. The terms of study were most generous since residence study at Codrington was allowed to count term by term as residence at Durham, whose curriculum and examiners were used. This plan went back to 1875 when William Charles Lake was Dean of Durham. This policy was confined, however, to the British colonies. The same system had been used since 1876 at Fourah Bay College, an Anglican theological college in Sierra Leone.

In contrast to that kind of relationship, some of the local theological schools had recently discussed coming together in an ecumenical plan to form a "United Theological College" based on the Kingston campus of the University of the West Indies. The curriculum would offer a Licentiate in Theology, which would be comparable to the London University Diploma in Theology. This meant that the growing number of young men and women in Jamaica who were interested in ministry, had completed a secondary education, passed the Senior Cambridge exams, and were ready for a university-level background in scripture and theology would no longer have to go abroad to either England or the United States to secure a validated theological diploma or degree.

There had been a voiced concern from major leaders in the Church of God in Jamaica to see Jamaica Bible Institute, our school for ministers, reorganized and its curriculum and teaching staff upgraded to match this level of ministerial training. At an early point in the initial discussions among the other theological colleges, Jamaica Bible Institute was invited to become part of this projected ecumenical venture. The course requirements would be the same for all cooperating schools, while each sponsoring church group would be responsible to instruct its own ministerial students in the distinctive doctrines, polity, and history of its respective denomination. At the time that the initial invitation was made, there was no strong interest among the Church of God leaders in Jamaica in favor of accepting it.

Kenneth E. Jones, the Missionary Board's first choice to undertake the task of reorganizing Jamaica Bible Institute, was aware of that still unanswered invitation. He also knew about the stronger concern among our Jamaican church leaders to upgrade the church's Institute instead of being involved in the cooperative venture. Although I knew about Jones much earlier, both of us having written many articles for the *Gospel Trumpet*, I had occasion to meet him "at close range" during the summer of 1960 when in Jamaica on a preaching mission in Kingston where Samuel G. Hines was pastor. Jones, a white American pastor, was in Jamaica at that time under short-term appointment as mission secretary for the work of the Church of God. Jones came out to the services each night and I had opportunity to visit with him in his office one afternoon. Two years later, under Board appointment, Jones was back in Jamaica to undertake the task of upgrading the Institute and administering its work as its new principal. He arrived with a curricular plan to meet the expressed concerns of the Jamaican leaders, but because of the sudden and serious illness of his wife they returned to America and the implementation of the plans he had developed for the school was delayed.

Jamaica School of Theology

Gwendolyn and I arrived in Kingston, Jamaica, on January 25, 1964, and I began work immediately because the first semester schedule of classes had to begin promptly. In the midst of his monthly newsletter for February 1964, Lester A. Crose, Executive Secretary of the Missionary Board of the Church of God, informed Church of God missionaries around the world about our arrival and assignment in Jamaica. A part of his report read:

Jamaica Bible Institute has been closed for some time, and now the school is opening with a new name: Jamaica School of Theology, and under the leadership of James Massey.... The lack of leadership in the Church of God in Jamaica is so acute that this school must now turn out qualified men of God to take over pastoral responsibilities very soon or a number of congregations will simply die out. Hence the urgency connected with the task before the Masseys.

Jamaica School of Theology opened that January—three days after our arrival by plane—with three academic programs available to interested and qualified students. They were: (1) Certificate in Christian Education; (2) Diploma in Ministerial Studies, requiring four years; and (3) Tutorial studies toward the London University Bachelor of Divinity Degree [External Pass] or the Diploma in Theology [External Pass].

There were thirteen students—a large number by local standards—and each one had been selected with care from a much larger pool of applicants. Some who had applied for admission did not come with the Senior Cambridge Examination (Pass) required for admission to the new diploma programs, nor did they possess a sufficient secondary school background for the new level of courses now being offered. During personal interviews these applicants were informed of their deficiency and advised on how to qualify for reconsideration later. The number of students we admitted could be adequately accommodated in the school's dorm facilities, and the faculty members were able to work more closely with the students. Given the school's more intensified curriculum, this was increasingly appreciated by both faculty and students. The school also administered a part-time work program to assist students with financial needs. A vocational department managed by Ralph Little, an American missionary, was a small furniture factory whose "Master Craft" products were sold commercially. The profits became weekly earnings for the students who worked there.

The year 1964 was very full of work for me. As a missionary, and particularly as principal of the church's theological college, I was expected to accept speaking engagements in the churches, and I was called upon that year, and every year afterward, more often than I could reasonably accept. Most of our pastors knew about the agreement into which I had entered with Samuel G. Hines to preach for and oversee his three congregations in the Franklin Town Circuit of Kingston, so they understood when I declined some invitations based on my need to serve two of those three churches on a given Sunday.

In addition to being an administrator, teacher, overseer for three city churches, and guest speaker at other churches of our communion, I was also favored by invitations to preach for other denominational churches and to represent our school and even speak at academic affairs in the other theological colleges and training colleges for teachers. My work as administrator was not essentially problematic that first year; the curricular programs had been agreed upon by the Board of Governors and prescribed for publication and teachers had been contracted during my preparatory visit to Jamaica in August of 1963. I had taken the programs Kenneth Jones had arranged earlier and updated them during that visit; I had added and adapted only slightly.

My teaching areas involved theological and biblical studies, including New Testament Greek. Some American church leaders who visited us that first year confessed being appalled at the teaching range I had to cover. One teacher-friend criticized my load as unwise and nearly impossible. His thinking was influenced by the setting of American schools where teachers are not scarce and where a teacher is normally responsible for but one field of study, and generally only one small segment of that field. He was not thinking about our particular setting in Jamaica where a new venture was just underway, nor was he mindful that I had come prepared to do all of what he found me busy doing. It was necessary that first year that I personally set the stage and illustrate the standards for what we were seeking to accomplish.

From our time of beginning together, the students and I "hit it off," as we say. Having interviewed them all personally during my visit to Jamaica that previous August, I had had a hand in each one being admitted. Most of the students were to be trained for ministry in churches. The living and dining arrangements on campus promoted a vital communal thinking, and a corporate life of true sharing. We experienced a bonding that first year that gave us all a sense of belonging and pride. I wanted the students to experience not only the educational, spiritual, and social benefits that interacting with me in class made available. I also wanted us all to experience a sense of community that could deepen in us what being members of the church means, and what being ministering servants in the church grants as well as requires. I was their principal and tutor from Monday through Friday, and preacher to some of them on Sunday. As it turned out, the ministerial students began relating to me as a kind of "Father in God," as the Anglicans would term our relationship.

That first class of students in Jamaica School of Theology formed a group that was intellectually alert. They were all pleasant and agreeable schoolmates who took readily to the studies assigned, and they formed friendships that aided their development in both mind and heart. As their principal and one of their teachers, I discerned depths in some that I knew would enable them to do special tasks in the church and world. One of the most gifted within that circle of bright ministerial students was Roosevelt Moses Collins. Collins had come to us from the Catadupa Church of God congregation, and he seemed gifted for a richly informed ministry of preaching and teaching. We were all shocked when he died in an auto accident early one Sunday morning while on his way to preach for a church in his home circuit. His tragic death opened the eyes of our young students to the reality of their mortality and encouraged an even more serious approach to their reason for being in the school.

On Sunday, April 5, 1964, we held a Service of Re-Naming for the school during, the Fiftieth Annual Assembly of the Church of God in Jamaica. Formal recognition was thus made of the institutional name change, from "Jamaica Bible Institute" to "Jamaica School of Theology." The service concluded with the unveiling and hanging of the sign with the school's new name.

In September of 1964 Lester A. Crose visited Jamaica during an extended fact-finding trip he made through Central America and the Caribbean area. During five days in Jamaica, Crose visited with the missionaries, surveyed the field, and visited with the ministerial students at the school. In his last conversation with me before leaving Jamaica, Crose complimented me on the progress that he observed, but then asked me whether I might be overselling higher education to the students because, while interviewing them individually, nearly every student had confessed an interest in further studies after finishing Jamaica School of Theology! Crose seemed surprised at such a love for learning. He feared that their yearning to learn might lure them from the churches that needed them after they graduated. I replied that, given their potential and the learning atmosphere at the school, a heightened awareness in each one of his or her possibilities was to be expected. It is one of the by-products of a meaningful education. After his visit to Jamaica, Crose included in his October newsletter to missionaries a section lauding Jamaica School of Theology as "an exciting venture of upgraded training."

In October, 1964, Gwendolyn and I experienced an emergency situation that threatened to disrupt our stay. Because of complications resulting from an ectopic pregnancy, Gwendolyn had to undergo emergency surgery. There had been no indication of any health problem before that awesome Sunday when I was away from Kingston preaching at one of the country churches. When I returned home late that afternoon and walked through the front door, I found Gwendolyn lying prostrate on the living room floor, wrapped in a blanket and writhing in pain. She hastily told me that she was waiting for a doctor to arrive. Shortly before, when she realized what was happening to her, she had telephoned a church friend, quickly explained her plight, and asked the friend to get in touch right away with a doctor who could visit the house immediately. Then she grabbed a blanket, wrapped herself in it, and got down on the floor to wait for the doctor, hoping that the cold ceramic tiles on the floor would keep her from passing out from such pain before the doctor arrived. I got home just a few minutes before the doctor drove into our driveway. The church friend Gwendolyn called had telephoned Joyce Tate, M.D., a well-known gynecologist. Dr. Tate was at home and had come speedily to our house. She deftly examined Gwendolyn's abdomen, then placed a call to one of the Kingston hospitals and arranged emergency care for her. We did not wait on an ambulance. I bundled Gwendolyn up and hurriedly drove her to the hospital myself. Dr. Tate met us there.

In talking with Gwendolyn after the emergency surgery, she told me that Dr. Tate's manner while examining her at the house had made her feel confident that she was in the right hands. I talked with Dr. Tate afterward to inquire about the expenses. I was surprised when she told me that there would be no charge for what she had done. She added: "You, Sir, are a man of the cloth and have come from abroad to serve our people here. I honor you too much to accept any fee!" In addition to her services as surgeon, Dr. Tate had been assisted by a Dr. Parbusingh, also a gynecologist. Dr. Parbusingh also refused to accept a fee, saying, "Sir, my father was a Presbyterian minister, and in honor of you as a minister I have gladly given my services without a fee." I thanked them heartily, deeply grateful for their uncommon generosity. I also went and thanked Beryl Miller, the friend Gwendolyn had telephoned in distress, because I knew that she and W. T. Miller, her husband, had supplied Dr. Tate with such information about Gwendolyn and me. W. T. Miller was himself a well-known person in government and worked as Trade Administrator for the Jamaica Bureau of Trade and Industries.

Gwendolyn was released from the hospital just before the school had its Christmas break. I decided to take her back to

221

Detroit to spend the rest of her recuperation period there with her mother, stepfather, and older sister Dorothy. She stayed on in Detroit while I went on after Christmas to Pomona, California, to preach December 29-31 for the Southwestern Ministerial Assembly of the Church of God and to participate in the inauguration service honoring DeWayne Bell, the new president of Arlington College. I afterward attended the annual meeting of the Commission of Christian Higher Education of the Church of God held on the campus of Arlington College in Long Beach, California, January 1-4, 1965.

When Gwendolyn and I returned to Jamaica, I soon left again to speak from January 31 through February 7 as convention preacher for the Southern Caribbean Convention of the Church of God held at San Fernando, Trinidad. That meeting involved leaders and representatives from our churches in Trinidad-Tobago, Barbados, Grenada, Curacao, British Guiana, St. Kitts, Nevis, Antigua, Costa Rica, Panama, St. Vincent, and Jamaica. The nature and importance of that meeting for the entire Caribbean area was my reason for attending and serving as I did. I had to miss teaching a few classes while away that time, something I did not like to do. But in connection with my task as speaker there was the need to hold conversations with Carlton Cumberbatch, a Trinidadian, who was president of the West Indies Bible Institute, our sister school, and learn what he and his school's board of trustees were thinking and planning toward the future of theological education in the Caribbean. In his March 1965 newsletter to missionaries, Lester Crose reported about the convention in Trinidad and added: "James Massey did an excellent job of identifying himself with the people of the Southern Caribbean." Evidently those who had been there and communicated afterward with Crose about the meeting and my part in it were pleased.

A 1962 report in *The Christian Ministry* in Latin America and the Caribbean (edited by Wilfred Scopes) listed eight Protestant theological institutions in Jamaica at that time. Included in the order of their founding year, they were: (1)

Calabar Theological College in Kingston, Jamaica (Baptist, dating from 1843); (2) St. Peter's College, Kingston, Jamaica (Anglican, founded in 1892); Union Theological Seminary, Kingston (a 1954 amalgamation of Caenwood College, Methodist, St. Colme's College, Presbyterian, with Congregationalists, Moravians, and Disciples also sharing); (4) Jamaica Bible Institute (Church of God, founded in 1926); (5) West Indies College, Mandeville, Jamaica (Seventh-Day Adventist, founded in 1958); (6) Jamaica Theological Seminary, Kingston, Jamaica (Church Missionary Association, founded in 1959); (7) Jamaica Bible School, Mandeville, Jamaica (started in 1959 by West Indies Mission); and (8) Salvation Army School, Kingston, Jamaica (Salvation Army sponsored, with founding date not listed).

All of the above-named schools were in operation in 1964 when I became principal of what had formerly been called Jamaica Bible Institute. While readying myself for the new assignment, I had done research on the programs, faculty, curricula, and facilities offered by the other schools. In 1964, only Calabar, St. Peter's, Union Seminary, and our Jamaica School of Theology offered the quality tutoring necessary for ministerial students who registered to "sit" for the London University external degree or diploma examinations. The size of our student body in 1964, at thirteen, was also comparable: Jamaica Theological Seminary reported nine students, St. Peter's College ten, and Calabar seventeen. Union Theological Seminary reported an enrollment of fifty students, but that figure represented students drawn from five church groups sharing in the union, which made the average for each church group ten students. Among the eight theological schools, West Indies College and our Jamaica School of Theology led in the presence and employment of West Indian teaching personnel. Among West Indies College theological faculty of eight members, four were Jamaicans. When Jamaica School of Theology opened the semester in 1964, our faculty numbered eleven persons, and seven of them were Jamaicans. Two among the seven—Miss E. M. Claire Gayle and Mrs. Lily Brown—had returned to Jamaica with teaching experience gained by serving in Church of God colleges in America.

As I began my educational assignment in Jamaica, I was aware of the results of several surveys prepared by the International Missionary Council on theological education among the so-called "Younger Churches" and mission territories of the world. The published volumes explored the general and specific background for ministerial training in India, Africa, Madagascar, the Middle East, the Near East, Latin America, and the Caribbean, and provided information on how the churches recruit and train ministers, the types of ministries needed, facilities for training, general attitudes in the countries and areas about ministry patterns and trained leadership, and what the schools were offering to train laypersons for work in the church. The surveys also dealt with the possibilities for inter-church sharing to make the training of ministers more adequate and effective.

Armed with this knowledge, I was interested in what the Church of God leaders in Jamaica were thinking about the formal negotiations then underway between several of the neighboring theological colleges to establish a "United Theological College" in order to support a joint theological program that would be related to the University College of the West Indies located in Kingston. I was also waiting to know how they would respond to the invitation our school had received to be a participant in that proposed ecumenical venture, a venture as I saw it that was an essentially practical one. A Licentiate in Theology was to be offered, based on studies comparable to the London University Diploma in Theology program. Our involvement would mean our cooperative presence as one of the nation's oldest schools. It would mean sharing financially in the ever-escalating costs of theological education. Among other benefits, it would allow a helpful cross-fertilization of theological views in an ecumenical environment. As I saw it, the proposed venture could solve the problem of academic accreditation, enabling graduates to go abroad for advanced degrees without having to validate the quality and level of their previous studies. In addition, the proposal allowed for a synthesis between the academic and the theological disciplines, the sharing of teaching specialties, and more extensive library holdings, all benefits which were not then available at any of the individual theological colleges in just the same way. I also believed that such a cooperative venture could visibly promote Christian unity at the educational level.

As of 1964, the land for this cooperative venture had been obtained and several church bodies had agreed to do their theological education task within such a context. The teaching staff was to reflect each participating church group, and the structured union was to allow for denominational emphases in private classes with students from each participating denomination. How we in the Church of God would respond to the still-unanswered invitation to join in the venture was of crucial concern to me.

Aware that the Church of God in Jamaica had not officially responded to the letter of invitation, in December of 1964 I wrote to the chairperson of the Executive Council of the Church of God in Jamaica and called attention to the need to respond one way or the other. I asked that the proposal from the other schools be placed on the Council's agenda for discussion and I promised to be available for consultation if needed. Our school's Board of Governors had already discussed the proposal and stood ready to commend the merits of sharing in a "United Theological College." The Executive Council finally met to discuss the matter. How saddened I was to have to write not long after to The Reverend John Hoad, Secretary for the Committee on the United Theological College, and share the news that "we are unable to accept the invitation to share with other schools in the suggested plan." The majority of the Council leaders had voted against joining in the venture because they had theological questions about relating this way to other church groups. They feared the possible loss of a Church of God identity and they mentioned "the outstanding matter of our properties here on Hope Road." It was the narrowness and religious prejudice reflected in the negative vote that offended me most. How different and accepting George and Nellie Olson, the pioneer Church of God missionaries from America, had been; they were charter members when the Jamaica Council of Churches began, and she had welcomed without prejudice students from other denominational backgrounds to the Jamaica Bible Institute while principal there.

Given the pressure of ever-escalating costs in running a private theological college, I was convinced that an ecumenical venture in this regard was the most practical way to assure our school's future. I knew that the Jamaican church was not yet able to handle those costs alone, and I knew that the American church would not bear those costs forever. As I entered the next school year, I sensed the continuing opposition of some major Jamaican leaders to cooperative ministry with other church groups and saw no change in the dissenting majority voice against any involvement of our school in the proposed ecumenical venture. It became clear to me that those leaders were not thinking with any practical forward-view. Despite the successes being experienced at Jamaica School of Theology, I finally knew that I would not be open to staying at the school beyond the three-year term to which I had agreed.

In October of 1965, at the mid-point of my three-year term, I wrote to Dr. Crose to tell him that I would terminate my service as a missionary and principal of Jamaica School of Theology at the close of that assignment period. Crose had been informed earlier about the Executive Council's vote against being part of the United Theological College, and understood that this had figured in my decision. He also knew that Metropolitan Church in Detroit had continued to claim me as their Pastor-on-leave. Crose sent the following written reply to me, dated November, 1965:

Of course, the decision which you and Gwen have reached did not come as a complete surprise, but I can truthfully say without any hesitation that we shall be extremely sorry to lose your services to the Church in Jamaica which the two of you together have so unstintingly and faithfully been giving to Jamaica School of Theology. We do appreciate, however, the concern which you have for the Metropolitan Church of God in Detroit, and we can think of no major reason why you should not return to resume pastoral responsibilities there.

In the same letter of reply Crose asked for my suggestions relative to a successor. The letter closed with this statement: "Allow me to express our sincere appreciation for all that you have done and will continue to do for J.S.T., and we will wish to work closely with you during the remaining months you serve in Jamaica to the end that the ministerial training program in Jamaica will continue at a high level."

The mention of "high level" reflected the fact that the new programs had been proceeding well. Earlier, during the summer of 1965, after receiving word from London University, I had shared with Crose the good news that one of our students, Winston Arthur Lawson, had passed the first (the Preliminary Divinity Examination in Greek) of the two exams required for the London Bachelor of Divinity external decree, which meant that he would be eligible to sit for the final examination for the degree in 1967. That summer, Lawson was the only student in Jamaica to pass that exam. Within the first year of the new program our educational experiment in Jamaica had been validated. The faculty and I had worked closely with our students and the students had eagerly applied themselves to their work.

On January 27, 1966, we held the first commencement of Jamaica School of Theology. There were three graduates. Two of them, Lorna Lyseight and Beatrice Patterson, received the school's Certificate in Christian Education, having completed

the two years required for it, and the third graduate, Roy
Galloway, a ministerial student, received the school's Diploma
in Ministerial Studies after four years of study. Galloway had
already done two years at Jamaica Bible Institute when I arrived
to be principal and oversee the upgrading and name-change of
the school. After graduating Galloway was immediately
installed as pastor in one of the churches in the St. Mary's
Parish. The commencement address was delivered by Stanford
A. Webley, Executive Secretary of the Jamaica Council of
Churches. Ralph Little, a fellow missionary from America,
acted in his capacity as school Dean and presented the graduates, and I awarded their respective diplomas. On February 6,
1966, we admitted four new students into the school. Two were
young men admitted to the four-year ministerial studies
program, and the other two were young women admitted to
study for the certificate program in Christian education.

Other Activities

I returned to the United States periodically, but usually
during the break between semesters. I was still an elected member of the Publication Board of the Church of God and I had
permission from the Missionary Board to leave the field and
attend the annual board meeting each May if I so desired.
Actually, my freedom to do so had been arranged by personal
request to the Missionary Board's executive secretary by Steele
C. Smith, Warner Press president at the time. Smith knew that
Lester Crose did not like to set precedents or seem to favor one
missionary over another in granting certain privileges, so after
learning about my appointment to Jamaica, he took it on himself to tell Crose that my presence on the board was essential
and that he wanted me to return for the annual meetings each
May. I learned about this through a letter Steele Smith sent to
me regarding my freedom to stay active on the Publication
Board if I so desired. I did so desire and I therefore left the field
to attend the annual board meeting each May. Smith's letter to
me also reported that the cost of my travel to and from Jamaica

to attend the meetings was far less than that of each of the four board members who lived on the West Coast. The board meetings were always held in Anderson, so whenever I returned there for a Publication Board meeting, Crose and I used the occasion to talk over the work in Jamaica and at the school.

My return visits to the United States were sometimes to handle additional assignments as a speaker. There were several such engagements during 1965. When it was known that I would be at the Publication Board meeting that May, I was invited to preach at Park Place Church of God for several evening services during the same week, and I spoke in the chapel service at Anderson College Graduate School of Theology. While on campus, the Dean of the Anderson College and the Dean of the School of Theology drew me aside to inquire about the possibility of my coming there as campus pastor at some point after fulfilling my assignment in Jamaica. That June I was back in Anderson to give the keynote address for the International Convention of the Church of God. Gwendolyn was with me on that visit.

My writing projects continued during my years in Jamaica. In addition to several short articles and some feature articles in *Vital Christianity* (as well as an article in Spanish for *La Trompeta,* the Latin America edition of *Vital Christianity*), I prepared one of the eight major doctrinal outlines Warner Press published as part of the 1965 literature outreach program in the church. I also made some additions to a biography of Raymond Samuel Jackson, a portrait-style study on which I had worked periodically across several years. The Jackson biography was not published until 1967, two years later, at which time I added fresh information and a few supplemental features.

My research into Jackson's life and career started just after I experienced my call to the ministry as a young member in the Church of God of Detroit, where he was pastor. Close association with him across the years deepened in me a sense of good fortune through our sharing. Across the succeeding years I reflected deeply as I continued my research, and I tempered my admiration with analysis as I kept setting down some details from the larger story of his life. I knew that Raymond Samuel Jackson's ministry in the Church of God had been too meaningful and relevant to be overlooked, so I kept at my research and writing, intent to document aspects of his story for publication some day.

The publication of the Jackson biography was not according to my timetable, however, but his. The manuscript had been put aside when I went to Jamaica, but while there I received a long-distance call from him one afternoon. He inquired about the state of the writing I had been doing on his life. He spoke of wanting to see it in print. From the tenor of his conversation I sensed that Jackson was feeling the need to be affirmed. Recognizing this, I suggested that I would like to send him what I had written, and that if the scope and treatment of details pleased him, he could, if he desired, take the manuscript and rework and revise it as his autobiography. I encouraged Jackson to do this, but he finally demurred and insisted with a now-calm voice that the work should remain mine. It was clear to me that Jackson, now aged and feeling the pinch of time, really needed to be affirmed. He did not ask me to send him the manuscript. I ended our telephone conversation with an assuring promise that what I had been writing about him had not been misplaced, forgotten, nor overlooked. Not long after Jackson's call to me, I took the draft biography from my files, reread it, and wrote to Warner Press to inquire about the possibility of getting it published. The book editor wrote back to inform me that the publishing company's experience of poor returns from biographies and autobiographies had made it necessary to have such works subsidized. He indicated that if the needed subsidy were supplied, Warner Press would gladly handle publication through its commercial service division. I wrote and informed Jackson about this arrangement. He replied by letter, suggesting that the matter could wait until I returned from Jamaica. He knew that I was only on leave from Metropolitan and that I was expected to resume my pastoral role there at the end of 1966.

My ties with Metropolitan Church remained strong across the years that I was on leave from the congregation. In fact, I made some return visits to Detroit at the request of the Trustee Board and at church expense. On those trips, the Trustee Board usually insisted that Gwendolyn should return with me. The visits allowed us to preach to the congregation, handle special items of business with the officers, and meet privately with Samuel and Dalineta Hines.

Having settled the question of whether we would accept another term of service as missionaries, and being convinced that we were still wanted and needed in Detroit, Gwendolyn and I sent the Metropolitan Church of God congregation the following message on October 10, 1965, in time to be read during the annual Metropolitan Week activities:

A STATEMENT OF INTENTION

by Pastor and Mrs. James Earl Massey

My wife Gwendolyn and I are about to complete our second full year of service here in Jamaica as missionaries under appointment. During the course of our stay we have taken time to reflect upon the services we have been rendering, to study responses to our ministry, and to anticipate what will probably follow from the work at which we have been engaged.

We remain grateful that the grace of God was with us as we made the initial adjustment to life in the Tropics. Now that the initial adjustment has passed into a fruitful stay, we are grateful for continued health by which to do our work.

As expected, you--the leaders and members of Metropolitan Church of God, have kept a close contact with us, and have honored your claim upon me as your pastor-on-leave. You have refused to let that designation be a purely technical one. You have

231

acted with high resolve and concern to remain related with us.

In the light of these facts and factors we took time a while back to seek the will of the Lord about our future after our term of service here ends its third year. After a period of prayer (with fasting), it has been made clear to me that we should honor the continuing relations with Metropolitan Church of God and return to you.

This being our considered intention, we have thought it wise to so inform you of it during this time of church celebration. Be assured that we continue to rejoice with you all in the guidance granted to us by God across the years of our rich togetherness.

As we continue with our present work, intent to further shape the program of Jamaica School of Theology and give it increasing stature and stability, we pray also for you at Metropolitan. We trust that God will give our church increasing vision and value and the worthiness to hold and use them always to His honor. Grace and peace be with you.

Pastor James Earl Massey
Mrs. Gwendolyn K. Massey

The United Theological College Venture

The ecumenical development named United Theological College opened in 1966 with The Reverend Dr. Wilfred Scopes, an Englishman, as its president. A graduate of Cambridge University, Dr. Scopes was the secretary of the team that in 1960 made a survey of theological education in Latin America and the Caribbean and recommended the merging of the seminaries to form a United Theological College. Three seminaries had formed the merger: Calabar Theological College (Baptist), St. Peter's College (Anglican), and Caenwood College (Methodist). I was an official representative from our school on

October 19, 1966, when the presidential installation service for Scopes was held in the University Chapel on the campus of the University of the West Indies in Kingston. Dr. Scopes and I enjoyed meeting on several occasions. At his invitation I had earlier delivered the valedictory address to the United Theological College on June 30th during a service held at historic East Queen Street Baptist Church.

I was gravely disappointed that the Church of God leaders in Jamaica did not see the value and promise of working within such an ecumenical venture. That disappointment so affected me that I entered into a period of depression that lasted about three months. I did my work as required, but a heavy blanket seemed wrapped over my head. I felt dark and dead within. I told only Gwendolyn what I was experiencing, unable to explain it fully even to her. Mild relief came at times when I would walk at night, looking up at the stars and praying. It was like the horror of seeing no future for what you are doing. Looking back on that experience some years later, I finally understood it as a sensed omen, because Jamaica School of Theology closed its doors in 1970, four years after I completed my service years there as its principal.

The World Congress on Evangelism: 1966

Early in 1966 1 received a letter from Evangelist Billy Graham and Dr. Carl F. H. Henry, editor of *Christianity Today,* inviting me to be a participant in a World Congress on Evangelism scheduled to convene in Berlin, Germany, from October 26 through November 4 that year. I cleared the matter with Dr. Crose and went. The Congress involved more than one thousand leaders in ten days and nights of depth study, sharing, prayer, and planning. The delegates were from the farthest comers of the world, representing nations from Afghanistan to Zambia, and we converged upon the city of Berlin in a massive demonstration of submission to Christ, faith in God, and concern for the salvation of the world. The Congress was held on the occasion of the tenth anniversary of the theological bi-monthly *Christianity Today*, at that time the largest circulating theological journal in the world. Dr. Henry was our host and the Congress chairman, while Billy Graham served as honorary chairman of this grand gathering.

The Congress on Evangelism was both a celebration event and a commitment occasion. The Congress was the largest ecumenical and evangelical gathering of the church since Pentecost in A.D. 33. Christian leaders were present from every nation of the world except five: Burma, Cuba, Czechoslovakia, Poland, and the Soviet Union. The absence of the church leaders who had been invited from those countries was understood but lamented. During the Congress, learned bishops sat with outstanding lay evangelists. World-famed theologians shared insights and convictions with parish ministers. Skilled evangelists to the masses sat to listen and learn about the various people and means being used by God in the wide areas of the world. Some persons there were from groups that had not previously allowed or respected such interchange and conversation with others who differed from them in persuasion, tradition, or orientation.

Each day of the Congress seemed to carry the delegates to a new high in understanding, confrontation, and challenge. One delegate from Morocco said to me, "I usually go to sleep when I attend an evening service, at least for a few minutes; but not here. There is so much that comes through to me, lifting me. I haven't fallen asleep in any meeting yet." Franco Santonocito, a delegate from Egypt and fellow member of the Church of God, said, "I expected the Congress to be a great Christian gathering. I found it to be a gathering of great Christians with a great God. I expected to hear a display of linguistics and great scholarship. I heard instead a humble exposition of the Word and Counsel of God. I expected to find heated discussions of theological differences. I rather found a warm, unequaled Christian fellowship, and a wonderful unity of mind and purpose. I was afraid to find cultural and racial divisions. I rejoiced to witness the binding force of the love of Christ at work." He added, "I expected to discover new formulas and clichés for evangelism. I found rather that evangelism still is a portrayal and proclamation of Christ through us in the power of the Holy Spirit."

Many persons did not get invited to that World Congress on Evangelism, and some of us who were invited and went continue to live in wonder that we were so summoned. Some Berliners who heard about the Congress expected the crucial issues of the day to be aired there. They were, and a strongly worded declaration about those issues as seen under the piercing light of the gospel was issued as one of the results of our gathering. Aware that such a Congress would undoubtedly discuss racism as an obstacle to evangelism, one Berliner I met at the airport had expected Dr. Martin Luther King, Jr., to be part of our group as we deplaned upon arrival. She questioned me as I passed through customs at Tegel Airport, "Is Dr. Martin Luther King coming?" I replied, "I don't think so." Quite surprised at that, she asked, "Oh! Is he sick or in jail?" I answered, "Not to my knowledge." Then she said, "Well, when you see him, please tell him that hundreds of us pray for him every day." I told her, "I will!" That Berliner had not forgotten King's celebrated visit to Berlin, nor had she missed the obvious fact that evangelism is vitally related to problematic social issues.

It was significant that the 1966 World Congress on Evangelism was held in Berlin. There, under the shadow of political division, and where the zonal frontiers reminded people of two widely different and competing social systems, the conflicts of our times were vividly before us. The wall that then divided the city of Berlin into east and west zones has now been down since 1989, but in 1966 that wall was standing as a stark symbol of conflict and a barrier to freedom. Erected on August 13, 1961, by Communists, it stood to halt the continuing stream of refugees from the Soviet-controlled eastern zone to the free West. The wall was a sign of warring views. The folly of that wall was especially evident at a point adjacent to

Bernauerstrasse. The wall there ran straight across the entrance to the Church of the Atonement, claiming the church within and for the eastern zone. But just above the blocked entrance stood a statue of Christ with his right arm upraised in a gesture of blessing. Near that spot someone had written these words of insight on the wall: *Wir sind doch alle Bruder* ("But we are all still brothers"). Meeting in Berlin helped all of us to recognize anew the divisions between believers as well as nations and the need to reaffirm in spirit and essential action that all humans are family.

As regards the need to affirm our relatedness as a human family, while attending the Congress those of us who were delegates heard many position papers that treated aspects of the Congress theme, which was "One Race, One Gospel, One Task." But as the Congress continued across those ten days, we blacks noticed that no attention had been devoted in any of the position papers to the first part of the theme, "One Race," nor had any papers on that subject been distributed for private reading. We were delegates drawn together from across the world, literally, and we reflected great diversity of languages, backgrounds, nationalities, geographical locations, and color distinctions, and yet no major statement about the oneness of the human race had been given.

We African-American delegates discussed this among ourselves and finally gained audience with Carl F. H. Henry, Congress chair. We questioned the obvious omission. It later came to our attention that some delegates from India, Africa, and South America had also noticed the omission. Dr Henry's response was that that aspect of the theme had been taken for granted. The planning committee therefore had not assigned anyone to treat it. He apologized on behalf of the planning committee, and then asked us if we would be willing to work at developing a summary statement about "One Race" which could be included in the final report to be distributed to the world press as an outcome of the Congress. A number of us agreed to help develop that statement on race, including Jimmy

236

McDonald, Howard 0. Jones, Bob Harrison, Ralph Bell, Louis Johnson, and me. We worked into the late hours of the night, but we managed to finish a draft of a clearly focused statement on race.

In this draft we called attention to the fact that racism hinders efforts to evangelize. We wrote forthrightly about human equality as a biblical principle based upon the oneness of the human family under God as Creator. We stressed the imperative of agape love in our dealings with all humans, and the need to reject racial and national barriers that forbid full fellowship and cooperative ministry in the church. As it turned out, the section we prepared about the worldwide problem of racism was undoubtedly the strongest statement evangelicals had ever made on the subject until that time. Despite our clear statement, we did not offer any distinct strategies for dealing with racism; our concern at that point was not to prod decision about strategy but to give a basic statement that declared our biblical understanding of racism as a social evil, an unjust pattern in society, and a barrier to cooperative evangelism. The full text of the Congress Statement was published after the Congress ended in the book *One Race, One Gospel, One Task,* volume 1, edited by Carl F. H. Henry and Stanley Mooneyham (Minneapolis: World Wide Publications, 1967).

While I was in Berlin for the World Congress on Evangelism, Gwendolyn was back in Jamaica packing some things for shipment back to Detroit. Our term of stay was scheduled to end that December, and much had to be done before leaving our post. At a mid-point during the Congress, with our soon return to Detroit on my mind, I sat in my room at Hotel Europaischer Hof and wrote the following letter to Metropolitan Church:

October 31, 1966

Dear Brethren and Friends:

It is Sunday morning here in Berlin. I have had my breakfast and am now preparing to go out and board one of the buses waiting downstairs to transport the Congress delegates from this hotel to our place of meeting. The next service scheduled is a Reformation Day Service, this being Reformation Day.

I will not attempt to discuss the Congress on Evangelism in this letter. There is too much to say: suffice it to be said at this point that God ordered this World Congress on Evangelism. Over 1,000 leaders are here (together with about 200 or more observers and representatives of the press), and these leaders represent the church across the world, with all areas of the world included. In the midst of study, prayer, discussion, and planning, we are all sensing anew the glory of God and the weight of our collective task to win the world to our Lord. Each day has carried us to new levels of grace and understanding; each day has meant a deepening of our realization of the worth and blessing of each other. There is so much more that I could say, but I will withhold it until a later time.

It is to be regretted that I was not able to send you a more lengthy greeting during the recent celebration of "Metropolitan Week." The man who has been asked to succeed me as president of Jamaica School of Theology was in the Island and I was busy giving orientation about the school and all that is involved in my work as administrator. My time was limited, to say the least. Even now I am actually "snatching" a few minutes to send you a few words, because as I look down from my hotel window I see that our buses have come for us.

Let me close by reaffirming my love for you. I shall see you soon—by the will of God. I remain ever grateful for your partnership with me in the Gospel until now. And I am strongly hopeful that our partnership shall be continued for as long as it can be fruitful. I do not take you for granted, nor my present relationship with you. But I do take seriously the importance of our trust of each other and the vision that stands before us of a united, eager, able people under God. I would trust that we all sense anew the importance of that vision and also see it as pertaining to us.

Peace be with you, indeed, with you all.
Your Pastor-on-leave,
James Earl Massey

My letter reached Detroit in time to be printed in the Worship Bulletin for Sunday, November 6, 1966.

Immediately after my return from Berlin I wrote an article about the Congress for publication in *Vital Christianity*. The article appeared in the journal issue of December 18, 1966. I then finished my preparation to be the Inter-Varsity Christian Fellowship mission preacher at the University of the West Indies during the week of November 17-24.

Leave-Taking

A lot of thought, prayer, and talking were behind the decision Gwendolyn and I made to return to Detroit. There was thought, of course, about the congregation's voiced desire for our return, but there was also prayer concerning the future of the work at which we had been engaged at Jamaica School of Theology. I had prayed to make sure that our return to Detroit after three years of service abroad was not just a sentimental retreat into a treasured past, but the beginning of a new stage and level of growth for effective ministry. I had prayed that my steps would be equal to the next demands for progress, particularly the need to relocate or build because of congregational growth. I had prayed that the changes that we had separately experienced during that term of absence had not made me out of step for where the congregation would be at our return.

Frequent visits back, notwithstanding, I could not presume to trust that all would be essentially the same, for it would not be, and neither was I the same.

I had prayed also with the future of Jamaica School of Theology. Gwendolyn and I had gotten deeply involved in the life of the Jamaican church as well as its theological school. The beginnings of a new thrust in educating ministers had been set in motion. I had prayed that the new thrust would continue to gain strength and maintain its direction. During 1965, our second year, our first full-time Jamaican instructor, Eugenie Campbell, had joined us. A graduate of Anderson College and a trained librarian, Campbell was appointed to teach Christian education. The appointment marked a milestone in Jamaican education, for our school was only the second theological college to employ a full-time Jamaican instructor. All of the other schools used foreign personnel. As my term was about to end in December, 1966, 1 had prayed that George Buck, the newly-appointed principal of the school, and his wife Eva would be equal to the demands I knew would test their wisdom, strength, and resolve.

When Lester A. Crose and I had first talked about the future of Jamaica School of Theology should I not continue beyond my term, he had asked for suggestions about who could succeed me. I advised him that in view of the spirited nationalism in Jamaica, the indigenization of the church, and the imminent transfer of church properties from Board control to Jamaican leadership, it would be wise and prudent to replace me, an American, with a West Indian. I suggested Clifford Payne of Trinidad as a possibility for principal at the school. Familiar as he was with the Caribbean, Crose knew, as I did, that Payne was a graduate of West Indies Bible Institute, that he had earned a London University theological degree, and was a progressive pastor in Port of Spain, Trinidad. Having talked with Payne while visiting Trinidad, I knew of his interest in theological education and I wanted to assist in opening a door of service for him in it. Unfortunately, that was not the direction things took.

Due perhaps in part to the 1961 vote of Jamaica not to join Trinidad and Barbados in a West Indies Federation, the Jamaican church had been affected by the political fallout and rival nationalism, and some of our Jamaican church leaders frowned on the idea of a Trinidadian being principal of the Jamaican school. Interestingly, in 1967 Payne became academic dean of West Indies Bible Institute and served in that capacity until 1974. I cannot say that ethnic frictions were all that stood in the way of his being appointed to serve in Jamaica, but I can suggest that Clifford Payne had the gifts, education, and spirit needed to forward our theological college there. Also, his openness to ecumenical ventures would have been a plus for working cooperatively with neighboring theological colleges. As it turned out, Payne was later given a post in the World Council of Churches office in Geneva, Switzerland.

My successor as principal was George Buck, a white American missionary. As I did before him, Buck gave himself fully to the work of the school, and continued efforts to gain the support of Jamaican leaders for cooperative sharing with United Theological College. He did not gain that support. I had sought to establish the new programs with such strength that the future of the school would be assured under new leadership, preferably West Indian leadership. As it turned out, narrow theological concerns, shortsightedness, and ethnic rivalries among Jamaican leaders precipitated a series of crises. The story of how the fortunes of Jamaica School of Theology deteriorated as the 1960s was ending has well been told by Barry L. Callen in his book *Preparing For Service: A History of Higher Education in the Church of God* (Anderson, Ind: Warner Press, Inc., 1988).

Gwendolyn and I returned home to Detroit just before Christmas, 1966. I was satisfied with the success of the work done in Jamaica. I had done what I went to Jamaica to do, upgrade and lead the church's theological college. In the absence of Samuel G. Hines, I had also served his three congregations as overseer and preacher, ably assisted through the ministry of Ira Walters who handled the day-to-day work at the churches. One month after our return to Detroit, Samuel and Dalenita Hines returned to Jamaica, also satisfied. He had done in America what he had come to do, secure an advanced degree in theology. In addition to achieving his degree, he had served Metropolitan Church of God well as Interim-Pastor, ably assisted in ministry by Jodie Hollaway and Richard McTere. Hines had been a blessing to the Metropolitan "Church Family," as we called ourselves, and the Metropolitan Church Family had been a blessing to him. His pastoral concern, biblical preaching, calm spirit, and magnetic presence were strategic to the stability and continued growth of our congregation. I was present during the commencement ceremony when Hines received his degree from Detroit Bible College, my alma mater.

In 1968, George Buck invited me back to Jamaica to be present and to give the address at the school's second commencement as Jamaica School of Theology. At that time the remaining members of the first class that I taught there graduated and received their diplomas, along with the two young women admitted to the Christian Education certificate program in 1966. My heart pounded with pride and joy as I watched the procession of graduates. I saw them moving not only across the stage, but envisioned them moving out into fruitful ministry, which they did.

After the academic recessional, as the platform party was about to leave the assembly hall, I was stopped by a Jamaican woman who called out to me. After getting my attention, the woman held up a small child and shouted, "Reverend Massey! Reverend Massey, here is your daughter!" I paused, dumbfounded, not knowing what this was about. Her announcement discomfited me because I wondered what George Buck and others around me must be thinking. I must have raised my eyes in a quizzed look because the woman quickly smiled and explained: "Forgive me, Sir, I am Sister ----- from the Jones Town church. This is the child I was carrying in my womb when Sister Massey had her miscarriage here some years ago. My husband and I felt so sorry for the two of you that we wanted to give you one of our children. We had four then, and since I was pregnant with this one, we decided to call this one "the Massey child." That explanation cleared my name and stirred my memory, for the woman had indeed sent that message to us after Gwendolyn miscarried in October, 1964. So that night, after commencement, I was seeing "our daughter" for the first time. I reached down, picked up the little girl, embraced her, and gently set her down again.

As George Buck and others watched and listened, I thanked that mother for her kind gesture of regard, then walked on to the reception area, grateful for the good fortune I had experienced in being received so fully into the hearts of the Jamaican people. While serving in Jamaica across those three signal years, I had indeed lived close to the people.

8

CAMPUS MINISTRY AT ANDERSON COLLEGE (UNIVERSITY)

The plethora of tragic happenings in Detroit and across America during the late 1960s affected me deeply, and quickened my concern to be more effective in the public arena as a moral and spiritual leader. The times demanded relevant spiritual activism and I felt compelled to be more strategically involved. Because of the severe setbacks in our city through mass unemployment, racial frictions, and general unrest, our congregation was active in ministry to the poor, the jobless, and the unchurched. We were maintaining a vital program for spiritual nurture, church growth, and fellowship with other believers, but I was feeling the burden to do more. With America in turmoil, woefully divided over the Vietnam War, and with colleges and universities busy dealing with protesters, my attention was drawn to the multitudes of students rebelling over things as they were, convinced that something sinister was at work in American life, something that needed to be addressed forthrightly. The prevailing climate among socially conscious students was one of ire, disgust, distrust of "the Establishment," and a sense of distance from the mindset of mainstream America. As I watched it all, the importance of moral and spiritual guidance for our social order was highlighted all the more within my spirit. Although busy leading an active and growing congregation, I did not feel that I was at the cutting edge of what needed to be done.

Detroit after 1967 was a very different place than the city I had known and treasured. Automation in the industries had reduced the number of jobs, so joblessness was a perennial problem. This contributed to racial unrest, the breakdown of law and order, and the surge among extremists. We assisted people in the community who were homeless, jobless and hungry. Many were filled with rage, and some were avidly militant. Although our membership at Metropolitan Church of God was predominantly African-American, we were determined that we would not shift ground and become a race-motivated church like nearby Central United Church of Christ, pastored by Albert Cleage, Jr., who espoused black nationalism and renamed his church The Shrine of the Black Madonna. The social issues in the city were complex, to be sure, and the odds against our approach were mounting, but the congregation and I were determined to work at easing racial tensions, allied with the interests of the New Detroit Committee, the Urban League, the N.A.A.C.P., the Detroit Council of Churches, the Detroit Interdenominational Ministers' Alliance, and other peace promoting groups.

Acutely aware of the troubles and social strain in our city, our Detroit Interdenominational Ministers' Alliance sponsored a public service to make our position as Christian leaders known to the entire city. On February 29, 1968, we secured the use of Cobo Hall for the mass service. We issued a call, first by mailings to all churches, synagogues, and religious organizations, and second by all the available media of press, radio, and television, asking men and women of goodwill to meet with us in a service of commitment for a greater togetherness. Although we were the sponsoring organization, the meeting was interracial and interfaith, with the theme "One God, One People, One Destiny." The cost for using Cobo Hall was covered by concerned donors.

As hoped, there was a mass gathering. I was one of four leaders who had been asked to speak. I spoke first, after which Father James J. Sheehan, Director of the Human Relations

Division of the Catholic Archdiocese of Detroit, spoke. Rabbi Leon Fram of Temple Israel followed him, and then Rev. Thomas A. Bailey, Moderator of the United Presbyterian Presbytery of Detroit, spoke. A position paper from our Alliance was read to set forth our stance as moral leaders. A "Call to Commitment" followed and a subsequent conference was announced. We had gathered with an interest to share our concern and agree to work at shaping a climate for togetherness in our city. We had taken a necessary step, aware that the times then upon us demanded acting with dispatch to avoid further social trauma.

Less than two months later came that fateful Thursday evening of April 4, 1968, when the news that Martin Luther King, Jr., had been shot filled the airwaves. Rage, looting, arson, and rioting swamped Detroit and other great cities across the land. On that fateful evening I was busy in the studio of WWJ-TV preparing for a video-taping session with our senior choir for a telecast scheduled for Sunday, April 7. The choir had just finished a presession practice run for the program "Church of the Crossroads," a regular Sunday offering sponsored by the Metropolitan Detroit Council of Churches. Our church was being featured the next Sunday. The choir was taking a break and I was taking a last look at my sermon manuscript when the studio director interrupted me. "Pardon me, Pastor," he whispered, "but there is some news that I just received over the wire service. We have not announced it to the public yet, so you are perhaps the first preacher in Detroit to know this: We have just been told on our teletype that Dr. Martin Luther King, Jr., has just been shot in Memphis. I thought you ought to know this before going on the air!"

The news stunned me. I did not panic, but my pulsebeat increased. I tried to remain calm as I thanked the studio director for informing me. I told him that I would not tell the choir members until after our taping session. I decided that the choir should not be told about the tragedy until our recording session was done, realizing that the singers would be too upset to manage the quality of singing needed for the telecast. Knowing about the tragedy definitely affected the tone of my sermon. Interestingly, my sermon title was "God Still Loves the World," based on John 3:16. I felt sifted as I prayed for composure before the red light went on in the studio. Afterward, when I broke the news to the choir about the shooting, the singers recoiled in shock, horrified over the happening. Everyone was eager to get home, fearful of what might happen on the streets of Detroit once the news filled the city. Their reactions confirmed to me that I was right not to tell them about the shooting before the taping was done.

Later that night I received a call at home from Dr. Robert L. Kincheloe, Executive Director of the Detroit Council of Churches, and Harold Koch, his associate. They called to ask if I would join in a memorial service in King's memory that next day, Friday, during the scheduled Lenten service hour. I agreed that I would, and asked what responsibility I should prepare to handle. Koch suggested that I should prepare a brief address, and that two or three others would be asked to do the same. The other participants would be Dr. Allan Zaun, pastor of Jefferson Avenue Presbyterian Church, Dr. Selwyn Smith, Executive Secretary for the Detroit Association of American Baptists, and someone to represent the Methodists. The plan pleased me.

I wondered why Dr. Joseph H. Jackson, pastor of Chicago's famed Olivet Baptist Church and the selected preacher for the Lenten services that week, had not been named among the speakers for the memorial tribute, so I asked Harold Koch about this. Koch replied, "I asked Dr. Jackson to speak at the service but he declined, and told me that in view of our plans he would be going back home to Chicago." It was widely known that Joseph H. Jackson and Martin Luther King, Jr., were polar opposites where strategies for social change were concerned, and their diversity had deepened in 1961 when King supported the split of the National Baptist Convention, U.S.A., Inc., partly over Jackson's opposition to the strategy of civil disobedience; the split became the Progressive National Baptist

Convention. Despite the known differences between Jackson and King, however, it surprised me that Jackson refused to take part in the planned service of memory honoring the slain civil rights leader.

My tribute to King, prepared late that Thursday night, was the fourth in a line of six tributes delivered to a packed congregation of worshippers in the sanctuary of downtown Detroit's Central Methodist Church that Friday, April 5, at noon. Dr. Allan A. Zaun offered the prayer, Mayor Jerome P. Cavanagh read a Proclamation, and music was rendered by the Osborne High School Choir. In addition to the tributes that Dr. Selwyn Smith and I gave, tributes were also presented by Dr. Joseph H. Williams, of First Institutional Baptist Church in Hamtramck, Dr. Robert L. Kincheloe of the Metropolitan Detroit Council of Churches, Dr. Joseph L. Roberts, District Superintendent of the A.M.E. Church, and Dr. Henry Hitt Crane, Pastor Emeritus of Central Methodist Church.

The week that followed was one of the more traumatic the nation has ever witnessed. Black anger exploded in towns and cities across the land before the calmer day of King's funeral, when the ceremony was given national coverage on television. I did not attend the funeral service in Atlanta. I was in Decatur, Illinois, fulfilling an engagement that week as Lenten Service Speaker for the Decatur Council of Churches. Shortly after arriving I received a call from Gwendolyn who told me that the office of Congressman Diggs had called the house to let me know that if I planned to go to Atlanta arrangements would be made for me to have a seat in Ebenezer Church during the funeral. But I did not go to Atlanta. I reasoned that I could best honor King's memory and our friendship by staying and serving that week in Decatur where racial troubles had mounted.

On the morning of the day of King's funeral I was interviewed on a talk show aired on one of the Decatur news stations. The host asked questions about my relationship with the late Dr. King and sought my reactions to having lost him as leader and friend. He also invited call-in questions. I answered the questions openly but with diplomacy, aware that not everyone understood and appreciated the tactic of non-violent civil disobedience and non-cooperation as a means for social change. I avoided any offending advocacy as I answered the questions put to me. Someone asked why it was that violence occurred so often when King led marches. I explained the concept of non-violent protest as a way to bring to public view some unfair treatment or discriminatory law or social problem, and how a march that is calculated to prod reasonable and public-minded citizens to take action toward solving a problem or to correct an injustice and provide a remedy can also offend persons who resist the changes being sought. The questioner voiced the question with civility and a tone of respectful inquiry, and I answered it sensitively and constructively.

I was surprised when we reached the close of the talk-show time and no one had called in to "blast" my statements about the essential rightness of King's motives and mission as a civil rights leader. Perhaps it was a matter of politeness on the part of any listeners who disagreed, an act of civility at a time when some respect was due because a death had happened.

I sat in my hotel room later that afternoon, watching what was left of the televised public event. As I watched, my mind ran back across the years and I reviewed the times when King had visited Detroit, those times when, after a day of speaking or preaching here and there, he would meet some of his friends for an informal togetherness. Those were the times he had free from news reporters, cameras, crowds, and the public eye. I remembered his levity, the jokes he shared, and his personal warmth. As I sat in my hotel room watching as the world honored our fallen leader, I thought also about that time in April, 1963, five years earlier, when I was part of the planning committee and welcome party that met him at Willow Run Airport when King came to speak at Cobo Hall at the end of a "Freedom Walk" down Woodward Avenue. And I also thought about the time I was asked to fill-in for him when King could not get to Detroit in time to preach during a Lenten service

249

engagement at Central Methodist Church. I thought that afternoon about many things, but especially about what still needed to be done in our nation to bring about a change in the way people think about and act toward those who differ. With King dead, I wondered whether the emphasis on non-violence would survive and I wondered how the emphasis in America on integration would fare.

It was against this background of activities, emotions, relationships, and questions that I had to project my thinking when in late 1968 I received a letter from Robert H. Reardon, president of Anderson College, inviting me to accept a post there as the college's first campus minister and also serve as a full-time faculty member. I knew Dr. Reardon and was quite familiar with the life and history of Anderson College. In 1962 I had served as the college's Religious Emphasis Week speaker and had met most of the administrators and faculty members serving there at the time. In addition, my chairmanship of the Commission on Christian Higher Education of the Church of God had more intimately informed me about the school's operational life through its institutional reports given at annual meetings of the Commission.

Despite all that I knew about Anderson College, and despite my acquaintance with its leaders, many questions clustered in my mind as I pondered Reardon's invitational letter. It had been only two years since Gwendolyn and I had returned from service abroad in Jamaica, and I questioned how our congregation would react to any known consideration on my part concerning another appointment that would separate us again, and so soon. I questioned what outlets Gwendolyn would have for her gifts, training, and expertise in a new setting if we decided to go to Anderson. I wondered whether I should view Reardon's invitation as an indication that it was time for me to cease being pastor in Detroit and move full-time into Christian higher education. I questioned how my calling and experience as a preacher would be enhanced or limited if I went full-time into the academic arena. Still further, being aware that some deep prejudices existed in some churches of the Church of God movement against my being involved in the ecumenical contacts and activities I enjoyed in Detroit and beyond, I wondered how free I could be in that church-controlled college setting to continue that aspect of my ministry if I went to Anderson. I also wondered to what extent working on a college campus might be more confining than my Detroit pastorate had been.

Interestingly, the thrust of these questions impacted my thinking far more than the obvious and no less important question of how I as an African-American man would be received by the majority Caucasian faculty there in the college. My contacts with Robert H. Reardon, Robert A. Nicholson, and other college leaders had been so open and solid that I felt assured I could relate to them with integrity, freedom, and a sense of oneness. One additional question occupied my thinking as I reviewed and pondered Reardon's letter of invitation to me. Given the growth, development, make-up, and ministry of the Metropolitan congregation at that stage in our togetherness, I wondered what would happen to the fellowship and our guiding dream if I left them?

Robert H. Reardon had become president of Anderson College in 1958, following John A. Morrison, the college's first president who served for the school's initial thirty-nine years. In 1961 Reardon had placed before the college board of trustees some strategic plans for the campus, with six specific goals highlighted. The first goal was to exalt the spiritual and train students for responsible Christian citizenship. Another goal was to increase the number of faculty members. In his letter to me, which was the written prelude to subsequent and substantive conversations between us, Reardon spelled out how he thought I could render needed service to assist the college in reaching these two goals in particular. He recalled how I had been accepted by Anderson College students during the 1962 Religious Emphasis Week services, and how my educational background, pastoral experience, and standing in the church

251

seemed, in his view, to mark me out as the person to fill the new post of campus minister. As I thought about it all, the fact that I was, like both Reardon and Eugene Newberry (dean of the college's School of Theology), an "Oberlin Seminary man" who had studied under the same professors there as they, and the knowledge that I was currently doing post-graduate study at the University of Michigan, no doubt factored as well into the invitation for me to join them in that offered capacity and serve as well as a faculty member teaching religious studies.

An interesting story stands connected to my visit to the college in 1962 to speak during Religious Emphasis Week. I remember well the first chapel service in which I was introduced. President Reardon introduced me, using the refrain "the man who has come to speak to us was … has … is presently …" as he gave expected details about my life and work. He soon closed out with the words, "I now present to you, Raymond Massey." As I stood and walked toward the pulpit, there was a mild rumble in the packed auditorium. The students were politely reacting to President Reardon's mistake in naming me Raymond Massey, whom they recognized as the well-known star of stage and screen. Once in the pulpit, I knew that many were wondering how I would react, whether I would let the mistake pass and get on with speaking. So I gave a mild smile, intent to use the mistake to more easily access their waiting attention through a bit of humor. In an unhurried pace, I said: "I observe that your president is much more familiar with the world of the theatre than with the world of the church." The previous mild rumble in the pews became a relieving big laugh throughout the crowd. Reardon accepted my levity with grace, mildly red-faced, but I thereby gained immediate acceptance by the students and was blessed by a sustained hearing from them throughout that week. Some years later, Reardon confided to me that it was what had happened among the students and faculty during my week of preaching at Anderson College in 1962 that inspired him to nurse the hope that I could one day become part of the college's life. In late 1968, using the medium of a letter, President Reardon placed the idea and hope before me for my consideration and action.

I gave the invitation my attention across about a month, discussing with Gwendolyn its implications from many angles of consideration. In addition to much else, there was Gwendolyn's advancing career in nursing to consider. She was then working at Henry Ford Hospital as the Clinical Supervisor of Obstetrics-Gynecology Outpatient Clinics. A move from Detroit would affect her career. Assisted by answers President Reardon and Robert A. Nicholson (college dean) supplied to some of our questions, she and I finally leaned toward accepting the invitation. But, as before when Gwendolyn and I decided to undertake the training of ministers in Jamaica, we finally agreed to test that "leaning" and the reasoning behind it in counsel first with my parents and her parents, and soon afterward we conferred with a few of the most strategically placed officers in our church, knowing that they and the entire congregation would be affected by the choice which was obviously forming within us.

My meeting with our Church Council took place on a Saturday morning and extended into the mid-afternoon. We talked at length about the implications a choice to leave would probably have upon our congregational life and work. The positives and negatives resulting from our absence from the church to serve in Jamaica were reviewed. Interestingly, the discussion took a positive turn when one of the officers noted my reference to the fact that the services requested from me by the college would not involve Sundays, because the college honored student involvement in the local churches in the city.

As it turned out, our officers seized upon that detail. They saw in that the possibility for a continued relationship with me, and suggested that since a ministry on campus did not involve Sundays with students, Metropolitan Church would still want my services as senior pastor if I was willing to return each weekend. The suggestion was made that the college administration should be asked to consent to this arrangement as a church request, so that it would be understood as originating from the congregation. It was further suggested that Jodie Hollaway and Richard McTere could be asked to handle the day-to-day responsibilities through the week, and that the church could budget stipends for their services. I agreed to talk to Hollaway and McTere about this possibility.

When Jodie Hollaway and I talked about the request Reardon put to me, he confessed pride that this had happened. As a graduate of Anderson College and Theological Seminary, Hollaway had a continuing regard for his alma mater and an abiding pride in many who were his teachers, especially Dr. Adam W. Miller. He expressed a willingness to give additional time to church work through the week if I accepted the college post. Richard McTere also agreed to the plan.

As it became clear that I should honor Reardon's invitation and go to serve at Anderson College, the Church Council and I discussed at length the implications of this decision. I agreed to be present each weekend to preach and to continue overseeing the activities of our church, if the congregation so desired. During a special business session, the congregation discussed the new arrangement that the Church Council had sanctioned for presentation to the church; the congregation requested that I continue as senior pastor under the new arrangement. The die was cast.

Thoughtful, dedicated, unselfish church officers helped greatly as I wrestled with that decision process. I had long known and trusted the strategic importance of lay leaders in managing and enhancing our congregation's life and work. Fortunately, Metropolitan Church of God was blessed with several officers of high caliber, and I not only sought their counsel but regularly complimented their helpful services, calling these to the attention of the church they served. While many churches spoke about "lay leadership," we regularly experienced it, which is why Metropolitan Church of God had functioned so well and had grown steadily even while I was away serving in Jamaica.

By agreement with the congregation, I began my service role as campus minister at Anderson College in July, 1969. By agreement with the college administration, I was free on weekends to serve the church in Detroit. After some months of following this schedule, I was surprised by a statement made to me after a Sunday night service by James Hawkins, Jr., chairman of our Brotherhood Organization and a local businessman. "You know, Brother Pastor, some members had reservations about the plan we have been following; but according to my observation, we are hearing you in our pulpit more now than we did when you were here full-time through the week!" As I thought about his comment I had to agree because, whereas earlier I had often hosted guest preachers and had let our local ministers preach to gain needed experience and exposure, my absence from the congregation through the week had made me seek to compensate by preaching myself on most of the Sundays when back in Detroit.

Anderson, Indiana, in 1969

When Gwendolyn and I made a trip to Anderson to locate housing, a college business officer drove us to an apartment complex not far from the campus. Our plan was to locate in an apartment until we knew the city areas well enough to buy a house or build one. The manager of the complex was expecting us and gave us a tour of the facilities. Gwendolyn and I were satisfied with what we saw, and we completed negotiations with the manager to reserve an apartment for us.

About a week after our return to Detroit we received a call from the college business officer who witnessed the negotiations and the agreement. He seemed apologetic as he addressed me, and he confessed being embarrassed to report that the manager had just informed him by phone that she would not be able to carry out her promise to reserve for us an apartment in their complex. He asked her why, and she told him that after our visit some of the white tenants called to object to living beside us, and they threatened to move out if we moved in. In addition, they had called the owner of the complex, and he had called her with a threat to fire her if she admitted us. The college agent, a young man, did not know what to make of this. I explained it as racial bias, something with which we as blacks were quite familiar. The officer was chagrined and stated that, although he had long heard about racial prejudice, he was seeing it for the first time at close range. I asked him to inform President Reardon about the matter. He did.

The news of discrimination against me incensed Robert Reardon, and he swung into action. His anti-segregation stance and his direct-action support of civil rights and racial justice had been publicly demonstrated in the campus setting and in the city of Anderson. Although I located housing in another apartment complex on the city's west side, Reardon mobilized forces from the campus and the Park Place community and in 1970 the City of Anderson passed, as its first ordinance that year, a law banning discrimination in housing! I applauded Reardon's courageous leadership and had my judgment confirmed that I could work well with him.

As for Anderson College itself, in 1969 the school ranked eighth in enrollment among private colleges and universities in Indiana. The student body comprised 1605 students, with 1041 of them listing "Church of God" as their religious preference or congregational background. The next highest number of students by denominational listing were United Methodists (115), Baptists (67), Christian Church (33), and Roman Catholics (27). In all, there were 32 denominations or religious groups represented within the student body, and most were represented by less than 20 students each, while some 222 students did not list any religious preference. The student mix at the time included 78 black and 30 international students.

It was my responsibility to relate to the students and provide guidance in the area of religious concerns. I sought to do this in a patterned fashion: teaching the Bible and Religion courses (required); counseling; advising volunteer religious groups; coordinating religious life activities on campus; providing guidance for pre-theological students; directing Religious Emphasis Week activities; and conducting all College chapel services. I began my work with a concern to enhance the sense of religious community on campus and to bring the Christian dimension and claim into sharper focus in campus life. I was helped in my attempts by several faculty members who shared their time, gifts, contacts, and expertise. There were many other allies, e.g., various deans, resident directors, a counseling psychologist, and several part-time counselors. Some of these persons directed small group experiences. Local pastors were also available to assist when asked, and I did ask for their assistance from time to time.

One of my closest allies in campus ministry was Marie Strong, an esteemed professor in the religious studies department who had served as director of religious life across several years. Under her guidance, Professor Strong had made Christianity-in-Action one of the religious life groups on campus, the largest volunteer group (217 members), and the most popular group doing Christian witness and service on campus and beyond. In addition, the Fellowship of Christian Athletes, Religious Life Council, and Ambassadors for Christ were some of the other active groups in campus religious life. I informed myself about each group, met the leaders, and began working with them all.

The "Anderson Revival": 1970

Because of the confluence of several events in February, 1970, the campus found itself the setting of a contemporary Pentecost experience. Following a spontaneous movement of the Spirit of God on the campus of Asbury College in Wilmore, Kentucky, some Church of God students there experienced the revival and felt impressed to travel to Anderson College and tell how that happening had significantly affected their lives. Those students contacted Charles Tarr, pastor of the South Meridian Church of God congregation in Anderson, and arranged to visit the church and give their testimonies. Tarr was an Asbury College alumnus and had gained a name as an effective evangelist.

The students gave their testimonies on Sunday, February 22, during the morning service at Tarr's church, and a report about their witness spread like fire across the city before the end of that day. The contagion of the students was so fervid that the South Meridian Church members were deeply affected, and many Anderson College students who attended that church returned to campus the next morning fired by a new zeal for the things of God. I was in Detroit that Sunday when the revival was being experienced in Anderson. I was fulfilling an assignment in Detroit as exchange preacher at the Bethany Church of God while Albert Donaldson, Bethany's pastor, was preaching in my place at Metropolitan Church. It was Brotherhood Sunday and it had long been our custom to exchange pulpits on that special day. The exchange only involved our morning service, so I preached in my own pulpit that evening, after which Gwendolyn and I departed the city, rehearsing with some satisfaction the affairs of the day as we drove back to Anderson.

News about the happenings at South Meridian Church met me as I reached my office that Monday morning. John Aukerman, one of our students who had been there, was so deeply affected by the events that he anxiously placed the following letter in my mailbox that morning:

Perhaps you know that 7 students from Asbury College were at South Meridian yesterday. We had about 7 hours of worship and testimony at the church, and several college students are really concerned about bringing revival to the campus. As many as possible are going to meet in Park Place tomorrow at 8 a.m., to pray for revival. We would like your support in this. If at all possible we would like to have some time in chapel to tell the student body what God is doing. Tonight at 7 there will be another service at South Meridian—perhaps you can attend. I know that you've been praying and hoping for revival at

Anderson. It seems as if the Spirit of God is ready to begin. Please help us.

That Tuesday, during our regular campus chapel service in the Park Place Church sanctuary, the air was heavy with anticipation. After the service many students lingered behind and moved forward to the kneeling rails of the sanctuary to pray. Some students were crying, some began confessing sins in their lives, some were voicing expressions of repentance, and still others were openly seeking a closer walk with the Lord. This continued throughout the day and into the early evening.

Given the happenings at church that previous Sunday, Pastor Tarr had announced a special follow-up service at South Meridian Church for that Tuesday evening. Hundreds of students attended, and so did I. Another service was announced for the next night, and with each successive service spiritual interest mounted and the crowds increased. Beginning on February 22, the momentum of the revival increased across another entire month and before it ended on April 12 (after fifty consecutive days of public services averaging over 1000 in attendance), there were focused daily prayers, steady conversions, open confessions, and unnumbered deeds done in restitution.

While some other campuses across the nation were in chaos, Anderson College was experiencing revival. The whole city of Anderson was affected. Prayer meetings were held in the City Hall every day during the noon hour, and the meetings were always well attended. As word of the happenings continued to spread, many requests came from pastors in the area to have students come and share their stories. I gave guidance to witness teams dispatched to those neighboring churches as well as to home congregations of students from nearby states. Assisting me in this task was Sid Guillen, head of the college's foreign language department and himself a dynamic Christian witness.

The news about the revival spread quite swiftly across the region and among many of the nation's colleges. The people of our supporting churches applauded the news, and many of those churches were affected by the happening. The Anderson Revival was a spiritual happening that few would have ever expected to occur at Anderson, and some persons said as much, still questioning whether what was being reported could really be as reported. As one male student, a pre-seminarian, stated to me in an after-chapel prayer gathering during the days of revival, "Mr. Massey, you told us that it could happen, but I didn't believe you! Forgive me for not accepting your word. I just thought that it could never happen here. Thank you for the truth—even though it was too much for us to believe!" The remarkable fact about the deeds of God is that they always elude our scheduling, they always contradict our doubts, they always transcend our expectations, and they serve to expand our faith.

Many of the leaders in the national church agencies located in Anderson were questioned about the news as they traveled on mission. Some agency leaders had attended the revival and prayer services and had a first-hand experience of the phenomenon. They gave informed reports as they went about. Dr. Charles V. Weber, Executive Secretary of the Executive Council of the Church of God, attended a service while in town and left the service with his spirit lifted in praise. In a March 6, 1970, announcement sent out from his office to the church at large, Weber commented about the revival:

> The Asbury Revival has spread to Anderson College and churches in Anderson. It is characterized by services with no preaching, just witnessing, and no organization—it is a spiritual happening. It is not confined to church buildings. Noonday services are happening in the City Hall auditorium. It is predominated by youth—college and high school youth, but many adults are getting help. In the South Meridian Church as many as 1200 have crowded every part of the building with people getting saved in Sunday school rooms

or wherever a group meets for prayer. It seems the Spirit is much at work and we rejoice. I thought you would want to rejoice with us.

My service post as the college's campus minister granted me an advantageous position from which to view the revival phenomenon in clear perspective. Hundreds of Anderson College students were vitally affected by the revival. I observed the effects of that spiritual happening in the lives of the many students I counseled. I knew from their statements of admission and confession and from their deeds of restitution that something more than mere emotion was at work in their lives. Some students eagerly reported to me their new joy in the Lord; but I was not the only one whom they sought out to report what they were experiencing as a result of God's touch upon them. Some students moved beyond a family-taught religious life into a true commitment to Christ on their own; others found a boldness by which to witness about a faith they had previously been too reticent to mention. Now, under the impress of a personal experience of grace, students began to deal with attitudes, emotions, biases, binding habits, and unworthy behavior.

With so many lives touched in a fresh way by forgiving love, an atmosphere of sincere caring pervaded the campus. The spirit of confession, forgiveness, and restitution guaranteed a climate for acceptance and trust. Students who had previously been rebellious in dress and behavior patterns felt accepted. Some who had argued for campus unrest and sought to harass the college administration confessed and forsook their scheming. The "Anderson Revival," as it was called, shaped new attitudes and actions. With these as some of the effects of the revival, especially with publicized campus unrest elsewhere across the nation, there was indeed strong reason for us to rejoice.

Given the fact that I was a black presence within a majority-white campus administrative team, I especially remember the visit of one student who came to talk with me about what he eventually disclosed as his racial bias. The young man sat in the

261

chair across from me with some reluctance at first and stated that the matter on his mind was so personal that he feared mentioning it. I spoke to ease his worry and invite his trust. He began to talk about what the revival had meant in his life. After further words about his gratitude to God for reaching him, he finally reached the point of concern that he confessed was so sensitive. "It should be plain to you where I am from," he suggested, calling attention to his regional drawl. "I'm from Mississippi," he continued, "and that's part of my problem!" He paused at that point and took a deep breath to bolster himself for his next lines. "I'm here to see you because—because I have some questions to ask you about all of this." By "all of this," I was to discover, he meant the implications of the revival in relation to the racial separatism he had been taught to favor and espouse.

I listened as he told me about his boyhood and how he had been trained at home and in church to function without respect for black people. Black people had been beyond the boundaries of his personal and moral concern all during his previous eighteen years of life. But now, feeling the constraints of Christian love as experienced during the revival, that young man had been prodded to reassess that previous training. He had done so before coming to see me, and now knew that he was willing and ready to follow the Spirit and forms of Christian love.

But this new openness had made him aware of another problem about which he desired some advice. He had come to me, he confessed, because his new sense of self and his decision to follow the dictates of Christian love appeared to be a kind of judgment upon all his past, his parents—who were confessedly Christian, and his church. I will not forget the troubled look in his face as he asked me this question: "Mr. Massey, what am I to think about my parents and the church that taught me?" I felt for him, because he was paying the supreme price for knowing truth—he was struggling to hold himself and his loved ones in proper perspective while under the scrutiny of a gripping truth and a new point of reference for himself as a child of God.

Something deep was at work within us both as I sought to interpret his situation to him. We talked with sensitive concern for some time. Afterward, he confessed that his mind was greatly eased.

It is important to report that some days later, after one of the revival services, which were still continuing nightly, that same student saw my wife standing alone as she waited for me to finish assisting someone at the altar, and he used the occasion to introduce himself to her. According to her report to me, he eagerly told her about the help he had gained through talking with me, and joyfully acknowledged that he had escaped the pull of his segregationist past. I rejoiced at the news, my confidence rewarded, aware yet again that the Christian love ethic remains a reasonable ground of hope that we humans can escape the hostilities of our environments and experience each other in the freedom guaranteed by the Spirit of Jesus.

The "Anderson Revival" was in its third week when I received a request from Harold L. Phillips, editor of *Vital Christianity*, to share for publication any report I might be formulating about the spiritual happening. Dr. W. Dale Oldham, a member of the Board of Directors of Warner Press, had attended some of the services and had prepared a statement honoring the revival. Phillips thought that Oldham's statement could be paired together with one I might write to focus attention on the positive aspects of the revival and thus confirm the news being heard throughout the churches. As Phillips expected, I had been making an assessment and so I prepared a report that I shared with him for publication. Dr. Oldham's piece appeared in the April 5, 1970, issue of *Vital Christianity*, dubbed "The Asbury Revival," and my report appeared in the April 19 issue, titled "Reflections on the Revival."

Across many years I had appreciated Harold L. Phillips both as a person and an accomplished leader in the church. Since 1948, when he welcomed and published my first article in the *Gospel Trumpet*, Phillips had shown an openness and regard that encouraged my efforts as a writer; he had even cor-

263

responded with me during my army service years to keep me abreast of publications and happenings in the church. His steadiness during the period of the "Detroit-Jackson-Massey Controversy" had especially impressed me, and I was grateful for the courage he showed in refusing to reject articles from me during that time of my disfavor among some. It was Phillips himself who told me about Raymond S. Jackson's visit to his editorial office at the Gospel Trumpet Company during the 1955 Anderson Camp Meeting to request that all articles from me should be rejected because of the disagreement between the two of us. Elected in 1938, and serving through 1953, Jackson had just ended a long term as member on the Publication Board—its first black member, and his standing in the Movement was respected. But after hearing Jackson out, Phillips courageously refused to honor Jackson's request.

Thus it was that my access to our church publications was never denied and my input as a writer was not denied to the church. Phillips wrote to congratulate me after my name was cleared the next year, and I wrote to thank him for his continued acceptance during that awesome period of pressure. Interestingly, by Phillips's appointment I became a contributing editor for the *Gospel Trumpet* in 1961 and was elected during the General Assembly that year to serve on the Publication Board. I was still serving in both capacities in 1969 when I became campus minister at Anderson College. In writing an article about the Anderson Revival, I was thus responding to Editor-in-Chief Phillips as one of his contributing editors; so was Dr. Oldham, who held a similar assignment during that same period.

A shorter version of my assessment of the Anderson Revival was published earlier than the April copy as a first page article in the March, 1970, issue of *Anderson College News*. I concluded my report in the college paper with these words:

Summed up, the Revival at Anderson has been a phenomenon of integrity. It has provided occasions of felt exposure to the presence of God. It has granted a renewal of life and the deepening of concern to public witness about the meaning of Christ. The Revival has enabled many to establish worthy convictions and higher loyalties. The Revival has allowed us all to sense community as God willed it. The Revival at Anderson has been a worthy experience with God. It has been shaping new [persons] for our time—and God knows that we need them.

Later in 1970, a fuller account of the Asbury College campus revival and its spread to and impact on Anderson College and other campuses was published in Robert E. Coleman's (editor) *One Divine Moment: The Asbury Revival* (Fleming H. Revell Co., 1970). Two years later, when Charles R. Tarr had left the pastorate at South Meridian Church to serve as Director of Witness Evangelism for the Board of Church Extension and Home Missions of the Church of God, he published a more extensive report and assessment of the Anderson Revival in his book *A New Wind Blowing* (Warner Press, 1972). Tarr's book was widely used in Lay Witness Mission training.

Celebrations and Kudos

During its 1970 Commencement, Anderson College did something that pleased many within the Church of God movement, especially many African Americans. The College conferred an honorary doctoral degree upon Raymond S. Jackson. Anderson College had similarly honored Sethard P. Dunn in 1934. Dunn's outstanding pastoral ministry in Chicago had made his name a prominent one among Church of God leaders and churches, but so had his charter membership on the college's board of trustees since 1925 and his active support and promotion of the college across the years. The college had similarly honored Harry B. Mitchell in 1961. In addition to his long-term pastorate in Gary, Indiana, Mitchell had worked

265

ardently across the church in promoting Christian education and the development of church leaders.

There are instances aplenty among colleges and universities when persons of merit have for cause been honored by them, and sometimes persons who have only shown promise have been "crowned" with an honorary doctorate at an early point in their career, thus to highlight them in or for some specific service or to gain for them needed recognition. African Americans applauded the recognition Jackson received because he was a leader of merit. As venerable pastor, church builder, mentor to many of the Movement's leading black pastors, and effective chairman of the General Assembly of the National Association of the Church of God across many years, Raymond S. Jackson's record of ministry had been unquestionably outstanding; he was in the front rank of a host of older servants of the church. His gifts and disciplines had, like the Apostle Paul, perhaps "worked harder than them all" (1 Cor. 15:10), and with quality results. But many of his admirers lamented that the honor came so late in his life. He was seventy-eight years old and had been in retirement since 1967, having shouldered duties in his last pastorate well past the usual retirement age.

There were those who thought and said that my being at Anderson College had helped to condition the environment for the honor Jackson received. Whether that was so or not, it was a recognition that many of us knew he deserved. Across the years some persons had "lobbied" the college leaders to honor Raymond S. Jackson in that way. While some admirers believed that Jackson was being overlooked, some others viewed the delay as a denial, thinking that his outspokenness against race prejudice had placed him in disfavor among some Movement churches whose support the college did not wish to lose. During the June, 1970, Commencement, we all rejoiced as President Reardon courageously and appropriately cited Raymond S. Jackson for his exemplary ministry and conferred upon him the honorary degree of Doctor of Divinity (*honoris causa*).

As Dr. Jackson's host, I was standing beside him as many well-wishers, both white and black, greeted him during the reception in his honor after the ceremony of conferral. As he and I left together, walking to where he would spend the night, he shared his heart with me. Using the endearing term to which I had grown accustomed across our years together, he said, "Son, I want to thank you for what transpired here tonight." He continued, "I say this because I know it would never have happened without you." While it was true that my recently published biography of his life, *Raymond S. Jackson: A Portrait,* had been used in preparing the citation read in his honor during the degree ceremony, I refused to take credit for the college's action in his honor. I was glad to tell Jackson that there had been no reluctance on the part of President Reardon and the honorary degree committee members when his name was put forward for consideration. Jackson spoke approvingly about my new ministry at Anderson College, and about his regard for the new generation of leaders there who were my comrades in daily work.

I was blessed at year's end with additional statements of approval. One was from a student, Steve Birch, who wrote a message on a Christmas card he sent to me:

> Christ gave to us the spirit of giving outwardly to our fellow man. In this spirit I extend to you my friendship and my prayers. I feel God has called you to this campus. I felt this way when I first heard you at the "68" International Convention. I now thank God that you are here. I have heard you in Theology 451 and I feel you have given me invaluable aids to be a more effective Christian and a more capable minister. May God's richest blessings be with you and family.

In Christian love,
/s/ Steve Birch

Another special note card from among many others was this one from President Reardon:

> I cannot let this year pass without a word of commendation for the splendid way you have taken hold of your new assignment. The load has been too heavy—but you have carried it with humor and good grace. Many good things are happening on campus because of you and I am very grateful. Hope you and your dear Gwen have the best year ever.

Robert H. Reardon

In July 1971, during our annual "Metropolitan Week Observance," Metropolitan Church honored me on the occasion of my twenty-fifth year in ministry. This yearly observance was always a well-planned, well-attended, and memorable church celebration, but the happenings of this year were especially encouraging. The week concluded with a Friday night banquet during which I was honored both for my pastoral role in founding and guiding the church and for my twenty-five years in ministry. Dr. Louis Johnson, pastor of the historic Friendship Baptist Church, and my Oberlin seminary roommate, was the guest speaker.

In addition to the special address that Louis Johnson delivered, there was a second and surprising highlight of the evening. A letter was read, addressed to me from Dr. Howard Thurman. Without my prior knowledge in order that it would be a surprise, Mabel Wilson, our church office secretary, had informed Thurman about the upcoming celebration and he had responded in a timely and encouraging letter. Thurman knew Mabel because she had been a member of The Church for the Fellowship of All Peoples in San Francisco during his pastorate in that city and while her husband was stationed at the naval base in the Bay Area. Dated June 28, 1971, Thurman wrote:

To James Massey, my friend:

I am profoundly pleased to send this authentic word of appreciation and felicitation for and of the fact that this marks the 25th year of your Ordination as a minister of the Church. During this period of celebration, you will hear many things said about you and will receive many congratulations; but there will be no word from anyone who stands in relation to you as I do. Under ordinary circumstances our paths would not have crossed and there would have been no moment of encounter to mark our kinship. But such is the mystery of Grace that our paths have crossed, and to the delight of our spirits it is as if we had been companions of the Way from the beginning. You have a neatness of mind that is only matched by your neatness in dress. There is a neatness of mind that is stark, austere, antiseptic, and boring. Yours, however, is a neatness that is paradoxically exuberant, lush, creative. You could belong to any period in any age in any faith, but it happens that you belong to this period, this age, and to your particular religious faith. It is this timeless dimension of mind which I am characterizing by the word "neatness" that is a part of the content of my thanksgiving to God that your life has touched mine and mine has touched yours.

On this occasion, therefore, I salute you as a blood brother of the mind AND of the spirit. If it had been my portion to have had a son and, as a part of the discreetness of life I had been privileged to custom-make him, he would be a young man like you. I say no more; no more is necessary to say.

May God secure you in all levels of your needings and grant to you in full measure all that is needful for your peace in the years left for your fulfillings.

/s/ Howard Thurman

At the bottom of the letter, and to the left side of his signature, was a second tell-tale sign of an authentic letter from Howard Thurman—his hand-drawn pen and ink sketch of a penguin! This memento from that celebration has meant much to me across the mounting service-filled years.

In 1971, as a result of my involvement in campus ministry, and through the influence of my friend William Pannell, a fellow Detroiter, I was invited by Dr. John Alexander to become a member of the Corporation of InterVarsity Christian Fellowship. The Corporation welcomed me, its first black member. In addition to reports of my involvement in the Anderson Revival, President Alexander and the Corporation members had learned of my earlier ministry to students at the University College of the West Indies while serving in Jamaica. Pannell was, at that time, an associate with Tom Skinner in the Tom Skinner Crusades, and had worked with Skinner and others to advise InterVarsity on how to integrate the organization for greater effectiveness among black students and in historically black campus settings. Paul Gibson, a black Harvard graduate, had been added to the staff in 1968, and I viewed that choice as indication that the organization meant to conduct its business as an open fellowship. I gladly worked to promote its aims. It was through my connection with InterVarsity that I got to meet and work with Paul Gibson, David Howard, Paul Little, and Keith and Gladys Hunt, among others. I had long appreciated the organization's emphasis on thoughtful evangelism and a discipleship committed to scriptural principles.

Later that year, in December 1971, I led our congregation in a relocation move to newly purchased church facilities at 13400 Schaefer Highway, near the corner of the block that intersects Grand River Avenue. Because of the continued growth of our membership, Metropolitan Church had outgrown our fabled facilities at 2705 Joy Road. With our building hemmed-in on our right by a well-used branch of the United States Post Office, and on our left by a business establishment, there was no space or opportunity to expand our property line there. As we considered our options, our members followed a recommendation from our church council to relocate.

Aided by Edgar L. Bell, treasurer of our trustee board and an experienced broker, we learned about the pending availability of another church complex that appeared to possess the space and features we desired and needed. The trustees and I visited the site and were initially pleased that the sanctuary, offices, classroom section, fellowship area, dining hall, parking lot, and location of the complex could meet our concerns. After fruitful negotiations for purchase and access were completed, we felt free to place our Joy Road building on the market. Providentially, there was an immediate sale.

There were expressions of deep emotion among us as our congregation held a final service in our beloved "Jericho Temple." It had been a place of spiritual visitation, a locus of divine happenings that were openly and corporately witnessed. The building we vacated after that final service had been the scene of joyful gatherings, fruitful planning, spirited worship, anointed preaching, steady conversions, many immediate healings, and rich fellowship.

I have long treasured the memory of a certain communion service in that sanctuary because of a special happening that accented anew to us the promise of Jesus that "where two or three are gathered in my name, I am there among them" (Matt. 18:20). The happening also made vivid what is possible to faith when the "remembrance" of Jesus is the focus during the Lord's Supper (1 Cor. 11:25). As for the happening, it was an immediate healing of an afflicted member who was present with us again after a long absence due to a debilitating case of rheumatoid arthritis. After undergoing extensive tests, all of which confirmed her doctor's original diagnosis of rheumatoid arthritis, Carolyn V. Reynolds had been carried twice each week to his office, across nearly four months, to receive injections. She could hobble along but could not bend her knees, which remained pained and swollen. Carefully monitoring her situation, the doctor advised giving her system a sixty-days rest before administering additional injections.

When I saw that she was present during the communion service that first Sunday in April, 1960, and mindful of her plight, I summoned an usher and asked him to have two nurses assist her to the communion table to receive the elements. As Carolyn Reynolds hobbled to the table, an assisting nurse on each side, I spoke the words of institution to her: "This is my body that is broken for you," as Jodie Hollaway offered the bread, and "This cup is the new covenant in my blood," as I offered her the cup. As she accepted the cup and raised it to her lips, something unexpected happened. As she described it later, her body felt so shaken that it took all the effort she could muster to place the cup back on the table instead of throwing it down. Her hips and knees no longer felt swollen; her joints felt loosened, and the previous pain was gone. We saw her run from the table, hands raised high in praise to God for what she was experiencing in her body. Carolyn returned to her doctor that next week. He examined her anew, marveling at the evident change in her knees. He had the same tests administered as before, but the conclusion was that every trace of the rheumatoid arthritis was gone. The doctor told her that the divine power she believed in must have taken over. She answered with a smile, "Yes, it did!" Carolyn V. Reynolds later married Louis Reed of Washington, D.C., and moved there, where she and her husband were active in the historic Third Street Church of God pastored by Samuel G. Hines. Her previous condition never returned. As Carolyn "remembered the Lord" during that communion service in April, 1960, Jesus showed himself alive to her by a gracious and lasting healing. Her confirmed story of healing was but one among the many we heard and witnessed at 2705 Joy Road.

But alas, we had held funeral services in that beloved sanctuary, having lost to death beloved members whose witness and support had given steadiness to our congregation, and whose experience and loyalty had been helpful in our given task of nurturing a new generation of our members in "the faith which was once for all delivered to the saints" (Jude 3). We knew we were a blessed people. Along with much for which to be thankful, we were sure that there was even more to which we could look forward. We held our first service in the new church sanctuary on Schaefer Highway in December, 1971, and we celebrated the move in a deeply moving worship service in February, 1972.

Asbury Theological Seminary

In May, 1971, just a little over a year after our campus experience of revival in Anderson, I received a letter from Dr. Frank Bateman Stanger, President of Asbury Theological Seminary, inviting me to serve as one of the speakers for The Francis Asbury Convocation, an event planned in observance of the Bicentennial of Britisher Francis Asbury's arrival on the American continent in 1771. Asbury had been a primary minister in shaping the Methodist Church in the New World, and in shaping the frontier of the new republic as well. Both Asbury College and Asbury Theological Seminary were named in his honor. The Convocation was announced for October 26-28, 1971. I wrote back, agreeing to be one of the speakers, pleased to join with others in a commemoration that was really planned to help us renew our zeal to spread the message of Scriptural holiness and help reform the church for a fruitful mission in the world.

Gwendolyn accompanied me on that trip to Wilmore, Kentucky. As one of the speakers I was allied in the three-day program with President Stanger, Bishop William R. Cannon (bishop of the Raleigh Area of the United Methodist Church), Dr. Kenneth W. Copeland (bishop of the Houston Area of the United Methodist Church), Dr. Ira Gallaway (district superintendent of the Fort Worth, Texas, district of the United Methodist Church), Dr. Paul S. Rees (vice-president and editor for World Vision, Inc.), Dr. Roy Short (bishop of the Louisville Area of the United Methodist Church), and Dr. Timothy Smith (professor of history at Johns Hopkins University and pastor of the College Church of Eastern Nazarene College). My convocation address, "Sharers in Holiness," was well received and was later published in a special convocation edition of the seminary's theological journal, *The Asbury Seminarian* (January 1972).

I had been to Asbury Theological Seminary before, the first time in 1963 to speak in the chapel. I was invited because some taped messages of my Sunday morning sermons and from the Sunday evening radio broadcast had been brought to the attention of the seminary's president and several of the professors. The person who brought those materials to their attention was Marvin O. Valade, a Detroit Christian businessman who owned a brickmaking company and who after listening to our broadcast had visited and worshiped at Metropolitan. Marvin Valade was a Methodist who honored the historic message of Christian holiness. Upon hearing our broadcast each Sunday evening on "The Metropolitan Bible Hour" (radio station WEXL), direct from our church, he recorded the services from time to time.

During one of his trips to Wilmore, Kentucky, to visit his children who lived there, Valade had introduced the tapes to Dr. Delbert R. Rose, an Asbury professor of theology whose teaching chair the Valade Family had funded. After listening to the tapes, Professor Rose used one as a devotional piece during a mid-week prayer service of the seminary faculty. Meanwhile, Dr. Julian C. McPheeters, the seminary president, visited our church one Sunday morning while in Detroit as Marvin Valade's guest. The hearing of those tapes, and President McPheeters' personal experience of our Detroit church services during several other visits resulted in my being invited to Asbury Theological Seminary to preach in April, 1963, and several times afterward. The invitation in 1971 to take part in the Francis Asbury Bicentennial was based on a mutual interest the Asbury leaders and I shared in Christian holiness and it allowed to deepen a relationship that had developed between President McPheeters, his successor Frank Bateman Stanger, Delbert R. Rose, and me.

A few months following that Asbury Bicentennial

Convocation I received a telephone call at my Anderson campus office from President Stanger. I was surprised when he informed me that the Asbury Theological Seminary Board of Trustees had voted unanimously, and that the faculty had concurred, to have the school's honorary Doctor of Divinity degree conferred upon me during the 1972 commencement. "In thus honoring you," he stated, "we sincerely believe that we are giving glory to God for your life and work." I confessed my surprise and managed some words to express my gratitude. Stanger informed me about the date for commencement, and I agreed to be present for the ceremony scheduled that May.

At the appointed time, Gwendolyn and I went to Wilmore, Kentucky, for the commencement, accompanied in the car by John and Dolores Small. John and Dolores had come to Anderson to drive us to Asbury because I was just out of bed, still under restrictions against driving after just undergoing a hernia repair. At my request, several other officers and members of Metropolitan Church joined us there in Wilmore, along with my beloved father and my wife's mother. I wanted those officers, family members and close friends to share that moment with Gwendolyn and me because the honor I received that day would never have come to me had I not been blessed by the loyalty and love of a faithful congregation and supporting family.

In appreciation to Asbury Seminary for the honorary doctorate I received, my first, I dedicated my book *The Hidden Disciplines* (the manuscript of which was then at the press) to Dr. Stanger, the Faculty and Trustees of Asbury Theological Seminary. In 1978, I was elected to the seminary Board of Trustees, a service role that I filled with appreciation, sustained interest, and depth involvement until 1991, when I was honored by being named a "Life Trustee."

The Underwood Fellowship Grant

There are times, the saying goes, when blessings come in pairs. That seemed to be the case for me in early 1972, because shortly after getting the call from Frank Stanger about a

275

proffered honorary degree I received a letter from Dr. Robert Rankin, a member of the Danforth Foundation staff, informing me that I had been appointed an Underwood Fellow for 1972-73.

Given the campus assignment entrusted to me, I had applied to the Danforth Foundation in the Fall of 1971 for a campus ministry study grant, intent, if I could receive it, to enrich my thought and sharpen my programming skills for an enhanced ministry at Anderson College. Across several years the Danforth Foundation had sponsored studies that dealt with significant issues in the relationship between religion and higher education. Given what were being assessed as basic trends in academia with respect to religion on the campus, I was eager to review the dimensions of the campus minister's roles, appraise what was happening or project for what should happen at Anderson College in the areas of spiritual nurture, contemplation of the divine, Christian social action, and the essential role of a faith community in the work of higher education at our private college. I wanted to enhance my leadership in the field and help the college face the challenge of the kind of future that seemed to be emerging.

When I applied for the foundation grant, I was into my third year as campus minister. The period had been a good one as regards campus religious life. More students were regularly attending area churches, and the number of students involved in area church life had increased significantly across the first semester of that third year. Each semester I had met with area pastors and other administrative personnel to assess relations between college religious life and the life and programming in the area churches. These regular discussions with area pastors had been taking place with college administrators before I became the college's campus minister, but my role as campus minister helped those discussions to deepen and college-church relations to become stronger. The revival that the campus and city experienced in 1970 was continuing to show its effects, with volunteer religious organizations on campus working creatively to meet human needs. The continued respect and openness on the part of the majority of students for religious services during the weekly chapel-convocation hours reflected, in my view, a healthiness of student spiritual concern. In addition to these positive results, faculty members informed me regularly about the increased student requests for them to relate classroom work with religious concerns.

My application to the Danforth Foundation for a study grant included a description of my work as campus minister, a statement of the aims and concerns to which I planned to address myself if the requested aid were granted, and the naming of the school where I would study, the place whose resources would assist achievement of the results I projected.

The letter to me from Robert Rankin only informed me that my application had been approved. In a subsequent meeting with him before embarking on my work, I was encouraged by the delight Rankin exhibited as he reviewed two particular items among my aims and concerns: one, I was going west to Berkeley, California, to study across the summer at Pacific School of Religion; and two, that I would be meeting regularly with Howard Thurman for consultation regarding religion, education, and campus ministry. Rankin knew Thurman and held him in high esteem. Rankin had received a good letter from Dr. Thurman in support of my application for the fellowship. I had chosen Berkeley and the Pacific School of Religion not only because of that educational and social context, with that school's considerable resources, but because I would be helped through spending time with Howard Thurman. Thurman was now retired, living in nearby San Francisco, and busy overseeing the work of the Howard Thurman Educational Trust he had founded when he retired from Boston University.

Gwendolyn accompanied me to Berkeley for the summer. Our living arrangements for the entire time were more than adequate; we lived in the comfortable apartment of a seminary couple (of affluent background) spending their summer vacation back on the East Coast. The apartment was close to Pacific School of Religion where my course work took place each morning, Monday through Friday. My afternoons were free for research, writing, or leisure.

I chose my courses at PSR in keeping with the aims and concerns I stated in my application to the Foundation, but also in relation to what I needed toward an earned doctorate later. I was a bit anxious about this, having interrupted my studies at the University of Michigan when I left Detroit to serve at Anderson College. Among several courses I took was one on "Contemporary Theology" taught by Randolph Crump Miller, a visiting professor from Yale Divinity School, and a course taught by Evans E. Crawford on "Blackways of Faith." Crawford's course explicated ways in which ethnicity, culture, and social trauma have influenced African-American religious understandings and concerns. Crawford was on sabbatical leave from Howard University, where he served as Dean of Andrew Rankin Chapel and professor of preaching at the university's divinity school. As part of his sabbatical, Crawford was fulfilling an appointment as Earl Lecturer at Pacific School of Religion that summer. His presence in Berkeley at that time and his position at Howard as dean of the university chapel were for me a fortuitous combination, because our seminal after-class discussions about religion and education and campus ministry proved resourceful and stimulating. Our meetings, together with my weekly visits with Howard Thurman, helped me to "set my sails" more securely as a campus minister.

As a university center, Berkeley provided a unique setting for what I went there to do. It was part of a pleasant region, and Gwendolyn and I rejoiced in our fortune as we sometimes looked out from the back porch of our apartment that offered a grand view of the Bay Area. We were high enough in elevation to watch the sun set over the Golden Gate Bridge, an unforgettable event of beauty and felt awe. Unfortunately, however, after sleeping a few nights in a fog-dampened atmosphere, I suffered my first onset of arthritis and had to be treated at the hospital for the pain that plagued me.

I was busy with study, research, and writing, but

Gwendolyn and I preserved time to be with our friends Curtis and Daisy Barge, who lived in nearby Oakland where he was pastoring. Curtis loaned us one of their cars to use while we were in Berkeley, and he had me preach to his congregation. I did not get to preach for them as often as he requested, partly because of my studies, partly because of visiting other churches, but also because I had to return to Detroit one weekend to give a eulogy. My Aunt Salome, my father's youngest sister, died, and I returned to Detroit to officiate at her funeral and to assist William White ("Uncle Bill"), her husband, in his grief. On another Sunday while in Berkeley Gwendolyn and I went to worship in San Francisco at the Congregational Church downtown. Howard Thurman was scheduled to preach there that morning. He did, following music by a talented foursome of singers whose song seemed to be coming from a mass choir. Thurman preached that day from First Corinthians 13, and dealt with the meaning and implications of love in the context of freedom and a democratic society. Never had I heard the subject of love so meaningfully explained and its implications for a societal order so graphically illustrated, nor had I felt through anyone's preaching the spirit of love more vividly shared.

Once the Underwood Fellowship had been granted, the time away in Berkeley was a seminal period for me. In addition to completing several courses at Pacific School of Religion and being enriched through dialogue with significant thinkers, I managed to complete the manuscript for a book on preaching which was later published as *The Responsible Pulpit*. My research regarding religion and education was fruitful and I gained insights upon which I would draw in planning and executing my work as campus minister, as preacher, and as pastor. I also managed to be of some assistance to Otis F. Brown, a local Church of God pastor, who was studying for the Doctor of Ministry degree at Pacific School of Religion. Brown and I talked through several aspects of the dissertation-project on which he was working. Otis Brown also invited me to preach at his church, but I had committed myself already to preach to

Curtis Barge's congregation on the date he offered.

Back in Anderson in the Fall of 1972, I teamed with Barry L. Callen in preparing a report to President Reardon and the Department of Religious Studies about "Aspirations of Anderson College as a Religious Community." Callen, newly appointed department chair, had succeeded Frederick Shoot, who was named the college's Dean of Instruction. Barry Callen and I were two members of a group of new faculty persons who began the 1969-1970 school year together, although Callen had been on the faculty since 1966 and had just returned from Chicago with his doctorate fresh in hand. Our joint assignment in preparing that report was the first of many projects in which Barry and I would profitably work together across the years. We found common ground and complemented each other well.

Educating New Leaders

I viewed my institutional responsibilities as campus minister and a faculty member in the Department of Religious Studies as a means by which the college: (1) intensified its ministry as a Christian college; (2) further particularized the Christian thrust on campus; (3) provided a more direct and extensive contact between the students and a designated minister of religion; (4) provided direction for religious life and volunteer religious organizations on campus; and (5) provided help for students to develop competency in experiencing and expressing their faith—particularly those students who express interest in becoming ministers and religious leaders.

I looked forward to the weekly chapel services, those times when the campus community gathered to reflect on our common heritage, celebrate our faith, and renew our life under God together. The sense of togetherness was helped by the large number of students who were committed believers and by the presence and leadership of dedicated and vital faculty members. In addition to many special guests, some of them well-known national figures and great church leaders, President Reardon and I were the most regularly scheduled speakers from within our college family. He and I were scheduled to speak at least once each month, and usually with a space of time between our messages. Chapel services were a tradition at Anderson College, and attendance at the services was required because what they represented, occasioned, and sought to provide was at the heart of the college's mission.

For me, addressing the students and faculty during a chapel service was always an experience of challenge and excitement. The challenge was to engage everyone by such promise and contagion that being present would seem a privilege rather than a problem. I determined that I would always be prepared to speak and evidence an interest in the needs and concerns of my hearers. The excitement occurred as I sensed audience interest deepening in what I presented, and when hearers lingered to pray or seek counsel as the chapel service closed. For example, after speaking in chapel during my first semester as campus minister, I received the following letter from a fellow faculty member who had listened attentively to my address:

> Having never had the honor before of sitting under the influence of your ministry, I was very favorably impressed with your chapel appearance this morning. Not only was I pleased as a teacher of speech, but as a person struggling to live up to what I believe is right, it was an uplifting experience to hear you speak. I hope you take this as it is intended, a compliment for the excellent style with which you brought forward the fine things you had for us this morning. As a teacher director, and one-time choir conductor, I like to know when I've reached someone with those things I am trying to do. Today I consider myself "reached" by your sermon. I thank you heartily for this experience. I genuinely look forward to your future ministry among us on the campus. You'll certainly be an influence for good in our community. Again, accept my thanks for all I

experienced in chapel this morning.

Your colleague and friend,
/s/ Robert Smith, Director of Drama

When I became campus minister in 1969, Anderson College was using the Park Place Church sanctuary for chapel-convocations, and the setting, though crowded, was conducive to the religious motive my speaking always sought to engage. Some years later, in 1984, the completion on campus of Reardon Auditorium gave the campus community a new locus for its gatherings and it provided the Anderson community with a much-needed and modern cultural center.

Having to speak in chapel at least once each month, and sometimes more than once, I began to plan my chapel addresses with a sense of continuity, intent to build each time on what I had presented before. This had been most effective in my Detroit pastorate and it proved to be effective on the campus as well. To be sure, given the fact of a required attendance at chapel, there were those students each semester who at first brought textbooks and newspapers to read during that required hour together, but I never let up in my quest to interest them as well, and in time the background noise from rustling papers lessened and respect for the meaning of the hour increased.

My teaching initially involved two curriculum staples of the Religious Studies Department, Bible and Religion 101 and 102, the introductory courses required of all Anderson College students to acquaint them with the Old and New Testaments. Due to my background in music and my research in theology, I was soon asked to teach a course on "Music and Church Worship." I developed and used my own approach to this subject area. The course was offered for credit in both the department of music and in the field of Christian education. Years after taking that course with me, many former students wrote to express their appreciation for the insights they gained from it, especially those who became ministers of music.

Aware that Bible and Religion 101 and 102 were required,

those of us in religious studies sought ways to share the information in the courses with greater appeal. Since several sections of these courses had to be taught each semester to meet the requirements of a growing freshman enrollment, Dr. Gustav Jeeninga visited me one day and with his warm Dutch accent suggested that it might be good strategy on our part to attempt a course together by joining our sections so that we could address them as a teaching team. As we talked further, we agreed that with his concentration in Old Testament and mine in New Testament, supplementing each other's contribution could add appeal, depth, and even delight to the Bible and Religion course for our students. We obtained permission to do this, and because of our inventive approach, focus, and friendship the plan proved so popular that students rushed to find seats in our class. Gustav Jeeninga was a 1947 immigrant from The Netherlands, and after gaining degrees from Anderson College and Northern Baptist Theological Seminary (B.D., Th.D.) had become a specialist in biblical archaeology. He had been teaching at Anderson College since 1960. Serious about scholarship and teaching, Jeeninga and I saw "eye to eye." We enjoyed and complemented each other. We continued the team teaching plan for a second semester, and then during the next two school years. Across these years word about our course spread among new students during registration and Jeeninga and I had the enviable joy of having new students line up to get our signatures to be admitted once our enrollment quota was filled!

I especially enjoyed teaching during the more intensive January Term, newly-instituted on campus. The one-month intensive treatment of a subject area allowed for greater focus and depth learning, which I applauded. The subjects treated during the January Term were not to be those available during the regular semesters, but new courses developed specifically to provide information and deepen learning in new areas of inquiry or to provide additional courses not regularly available in the standard curriculum.

During the first January Term (1971) I developed and taught

a course titled "Christian Disciplines and Resources." I was influenced in that choice by the success of Howard Thurman's pioneering course at Boston University on "Spiritual Disciplines and Resources." Some of the results of his course were published in his book *Disciplines of the Spirit* (Harper & Row, 1963). Out of my preparation and teaching I captured several aspects in my book *The Hidden Disciplines* (Warner Press, 1972), a study in which I discussed four "methods" or acts of discipline by which a commitment to godliness can be strengthened, sustained, and fulfilled: meditation-prayer, fasting, dialogue, and corporate worship. The book was widely used and was later republished in a second edition with the new title *Spiritual Disciplines* (Zondervan, 1985), edited, I must add, by Joseph D. Allison who, years earlier, had been a student in that January Term course I created and taught.

During the January Term in 1972 I taught a four-hour credit course on "Christ and Culture," with concern to introduce students to the process and means for evaluating modern life in relation to Christian values. Because of the need for the students to have some background in history and, hopefully, philosophy and ethics, the course was limited to upper division students or to those who entered by my direct consent as instructor. The next year I offered a course on "Human Nature in the Making." I designed the course to offer an exploration of human life with focus on world pictures of the human being— our origin, nature, needs, accomplishments, and aims. I had a distinct interest in showing how "human" life is shaped under the influence of specific teachings, beliefs, models, and community values. My motive was to show the possibilities for shaping ourselves through full openness to biblical faith as Jesus taught and modeled it. The January Term course I taught in 1974 was titled "Theology and Experience," the purpose being to trace the influence of experience (personal, social, religious, and cultural) upon theological understandings and formulations, and thereby examine our theology against the background of religious, national, and even ethnic concerns. I wanted the students in the course to see the relation between life and beliefs, and to help them move from a knowledgeable and settled faith position in dealing with the demands of life. This course was also restricted to upper division students or those with special permission from me to take it.

Among other courses I prepared and taught during a January Term was one on "Religious Insights in Great Music," which involved illustrated lectures about the religious impulse evidenced in the music created in the Classical and Romantic periods mainly. We examined, and heard, cantatas of J. S. Bach, Haydn's "The Creation," Beethoven's oratorios and late piano sonatas, Schumann's introspective and confessional works, and Liszt's religious creations ("Benediction of God in the Solitude," etc.), among others. This course opened the understanding of many students to the influence of the religious impulse in human creativity. Another course I offered during a January Term (1977) was "The Sinews of Christian Unity." That course allowed me to structure for the students who took it my understanding and thought about one of the major emphases of the Church of God movement and how it can be implemented. Some of that thought was later published in my book *Concerning Christian Unity* (Warner Press, 1979). I wrote the book under assignment from the editor-in-chief of Warner Press to contribute to the Church of God Doctrinal Library planned by the Press in commemoration of the centennial of the Church of God movement in 1980.

I enjoyed teaching religion to undergraduates in the college, teaching homiletics to graduate students in the seminary, and especially teaching a newly-created intensive course during the January Term each year, but I felt most deeply and at the center of things as I taught and related to those who declared themselves pre-ministerial students. These students were on-coming leaders for the church and they formed an eager, apt, essential and responsive group to teach and guide. Early on in my work at Anderson College, President Reardon had discussed with me the importance of having a special seminar for undergraduates who had identified the ministry as their intended vocation. Our discussion resulted in my developing a plan that would allow me to gather with them weekly to deal with the meaning and issues of being a minister. I wanted them to see and understand that calling more clearly and discern their interest and fitness for one or more of its many aspects.

The pre-ministerial students and I began meeting on Wednesdays during the noon hour in what were essentially encounter sessions. During one semester I guided them in research and discussion about "The Language of the Church." The purpose was four-fold: (1) they needed to get a feel for selected Scriptural concepts and major doctrines; (2) they needed to begin exploring how church history has influenced some of our understandings and views about biblical teachings; (3) they needed to see biblical images and meanings in relation to modern notions with which they were more conversant; and (4) I wanted to help them begin to wrestle with ways to pass on the biblical witness in a contemporary setting.

During succeeding semesters we functioned in seminar fashion. For the first seminar I distributed a syllabus to each pre-ministerial student outlining the purpose, procedures, and requirements for the course. I had each student choose a term, phrase, or topic from a sheet I prepared which listed many biblical terms, topics, and phrases. The student was to prepare a brief study on what he or she had chosen, and the study was to be in a form suitable to be duplicated and distributed to the other class members to form a notebook of our collective work. Dates were then assigned for each presentation. We agreed to hear at least two members during each class hour. The rest of the group would be respondents.

I began the round of studies with a presentation on "The Last Judgment." I did this as a model of what the study paper should look like in format and length. The rest of the sessions comprised an introduction to theology and the witness of the church through its Scriptures, as well as occasions for the students to engage in a vigorous interchange with each other and with me. That "Seminar in Church Work," also known as Theology 451/452, was a very popular course that many applauded as they explored the range of church doctrines and the multiple arenas of ministry. That course helped many students to clarify their thinking about the ministry. It allowed some who had occasions to preach or otherwise serve to probe their feelings with some understanding. Early on, it encouraged them to surrender to the process and disciplines of ministerial formation. That course also served the pre-ministerial students well by helping them integrate their learning so that they could enter seminary more alert and personally enriched from weekly dialogue with each other and with me.

It was a joy to meet in a session each week with pre-ministerial students and relate to many of them at close range in private counsel across their college and seminary years. Many who took that course and went on to seminary later distinguished themselves by their work: Joseph D. Allison, John Aukerman, Paul Daniels, Craig Frank, Steve Birch, James Christoff, Brian Barlow, and Richard Willowby, to name a few. Allison pastored for several years and became editor of Francis Asbury Press, a division of Zondervan Publishing House, before moving on to an editorship at Jordan Publishing, now a division of Evangel Publishing House. It was Allison who negotiated the republication of some of my books that had gone out of print, books he had read and known as a student. Years later, Allison honored me by dedicating one of his books, *The Devotional Resource Guide* (Thomas Nelson, 1986), to me, for which I remain deeply grateful. Richard Willowby also became an editor and worked for many years in the Warner Press editorial department as managing editor for *Vital Christianity*. John Aukerman became a pastor, took advanced degrees, then returned to Anderson some years later to teach Christian education in the School of Theology. It was Aukerman who, as a student writer for the *Andersonian,* the campus student paper, had involved himself so intimately in religious activities while I was campus minister. The list of those who stayed in touch with me after studying Theology 451/452 is long, and with appreciation to God I have treasured their regard and friendship.

Many of the pre-ministerial students who were part of my seminar were involved in what the administration had recently developed and announced as a "seven-year track" of studies, a sequential program that would move them progressively through their undergraduate college courses and into three years of seminary study, all on the same campus. The concern behind this emphasis was to strengthen each student's resolve to commit to a long-term study process, on the one hand, and to boost and ensure the seminary enrollment, on the other. The Church of God movement needed more well-equipped ministers, as did many denominations at that time, and the seminary needed more students to ensure an efficiency in its operation. In view of the first concern, the need for more ministers, the School of Theology had instituted some new degree programs. Under the fresh leadership of Dr. Barry L. Callen, a new Master of Ministry degree was being offered, requiring only 45 hours of course work, a degree program that appealed to persons who for various reasons might not be able to stay and complete a three-year program for the standard Master of Divinity degree. The development of the college's Graduate School of Theology since 1950 had been aggressive and successful, with accreditation gained in 1965, but across the years the operational costs had mounted faster than a limited graduate student enrollment or a meager endowment could efficiently manage. This problem had pressed the college to explore alternatives in programming for theological education. The "seven-year track" program was one such attempt to ensure fiscal stability at the School of Theology, and a shorter Master's degree (45 credit hours) was another.

Another explored alternative was for the School of Theology to enter into a cooperative relationship with one or more sister seminaries, such as Christian Theological Seminary in nearby Indianapolis, Indiana, Asbury Theological Seminary in Wilmore, Kentucky, or a proposed ecumenical seminary enterprise under discussion to be based in Indianapolis and assisted by foundation funding. Relating in either of these ways would involve the School of Theology, and its parent college, in interdenominational cooperation. The news that the college administration was engaged in such discussions occasioned negative reactions from across the Church of God movement, and a debate ensued in the 1972 General Assembly which encouraged a vote that killed any possibility of "compromising" the School of Theology by formally relating to any other. The complexity of the issue and the conflict it occasioned in 1972 stirred the Church leadership to develop strategies to increase support for both the School of Theology and its students. As Barry L. Callen reported, twenty years later in his book *Guide of Soul and Mind: The Story of Anderson University,* "Never had such attention and support come to the School of Theology from the Church of God. Although the process had generated considerable controversy, the campus goal of being willing to risk nontraditional innovation to find more productive and viable ways to educate ministers had brought excellent results. The general outcome, in fact, created the programmatic and financial framework in which the School of Theology has operated from then until the present day" (Anderson University and Warner Press, Inc., 1992, p. 289).

I was not present during that volatile debate on the floor of the General Assembly in 1972 about the future of the School of Theology. I was in Berkeley, California, on study leave fulfilling the terms of my Underwood Fellowship from the Danforth Foundation. After the possibility of our joining in the proposed ecumenical enterprise with some other seminaries was defeated by the Assembly's vote, Dean Newberry of the seminary immediately called me to report the news. After filling me in on the Assembly discussion, he asked with concern, "Jim, I hope you are not too disappointed by all this!" I told him that I was, because I saw no good reason for not cooperating. I had been informed about the possible federation, and I had been asked to

289

teach in the new setting if we became a partner in it. I thought
again of how the Church of God in Jamaica earlier had removed
the footing I laid for the future of Jamaica School of Theology
by refusing to link arms and join resources to be part of the
United Theological College. I felt terribly disappointed when
Jamaica School of Theology closed its doors. Fortunately,
thanks to aggressive, responsible leadership and a resourceful
church, the eventual outcome at Anderson School of Theology
was not the same.

There were times when I was quite aware that a high esti-
mate had been placed upon my role and services as campus
minister. As a black person serving in that pioneer task, I interpreted the confidence of the administration in me as an added
strength to get on with the job. I felt prepared for the assignment. I was at home in my work, at peace with its multiple
demands, and I was inspired by the promise the assignment
held. I felt at the cutting edge of what needed to be done—
engage a new generation for life on God's terms! Although a
minority figure within a white majority culture, I did not fight a
daily battle with race consciousness. I never felt I had to prove
anything. I had a calling. I had a cause. I had a challenging
assignment. I had a sense of direction. I had a worthy heritage.
I was working in tandem with valued friends. I had only to
serve. So I did.

My chapel addresses and teaching contacts occasioned
many personal conferences and counseling sessions with
students. I was seldom alone in my office during the hours posted
for counsel. Students sought me out, and did not hesitate to talk
in earnest. As a rule, my office door was usually kept open
unless a student wanted to talk privately with me. My secretary
controlled the traffic. Upon leaving the office to reach a classroom or to attend some meeting, I was usually stopped in the
hallway, on the stairs, or on a walkway, which made it a bit
embarrassing when I arrived late at the destination where I was
expected. To be sure, there were students who came to college
needing to find themselves. There were many of us on campus

who could assist them in that process and help them to achieve that end. I helped many, but I also felt at a loss when I failed to reach those who were not ready.

There were times when I took it upon myself to prod some student into action to avoid wasting the opportunity that college offered for a meaningful future. For example, my first year as campus pastor was the year freshman Al Miles arrived on campus. I met him in a Bible 101 class. Miles was a proud athlete, with a "I-know-I-am-privileged" attitude that made him act as if class requirements did not apply in his case. He would come to class at the very last minute, slide into his seat, and slouch to take a nap, his hat pulled down over his face! I saw too much being wasted on his part that first week, so I proceeded to tell him so. I knew that his coach was not aware of his class demeanor.

I timed my approach, measured my words with care, and spoke my concern with force: "Mr. Miles"—I always addressed a student formally with a Mr. or Ms.—"It has been apparent to me that you are using my class as a place and time for rest rather than learning. If that is your choice, then please heed my words. If you do not begin to apply yourself academically, you will end up ruining your opportunity to make something of yourself. I do not know how pressed your practice schedule makes you feel, but if you continue sleeping in class, you could very well end up sleeping your future away!" I spoke with sternness because I cared about the young man. Al Miles heeded my admonition. He "woke up," took off his hat, stirred himself to action, graduated from Anderson College, and completed a seminary degree to become a minister with a specialization in hospital ministry. Miles later became coordinator of the hospital ministry department at The Queen's Medical Center in Honolulu, Hawaii. He also authored several books, one of which was *Domestic Violence: What Every Pastor Needs to Know* (Augsburg Fortress, 2000).

There were times when it was readily apparent to me that some student was having trouble with life, with the college

291

setting, or even with me. In order to show my openness as a person and my availability as teacher and counselor, I always went to the door of the classroom after the first class session of the semester, intent personally to greet each student present for the course. My concern was to help me associate a face with a name, and to help each student associate my handshake with my concerned presence. During the first year after Decker Hall was completed, I had a class scheduled there. During the first class session I noticed one student who seemed disinterested in the orientation details I was giving regarding the course. As I talked on, I could not help noticing that his eyes were turned toward the window. In fact, it became quite obvious to me that being in that room at that time and for that subject was not something he desired.

I greeted the new students as they left the classroom that day, as was my custom. I noticed that the student who had shown disinterest during the session was watching my manner as I shook hands with the others. When his turn came, I welcomed him to the college and invited him to come and visit me in my office at his leisure. He gave a non-committal reply. Even so, he showed up at my office door a week later, asking if I was in. The secretary informed him that I was. I overheard her suggest that since he had not made an appointment to see me it would be more convenient for my schedule if he would do so for a later time. Having heard his voice, I paused from my work, opened my door and walked to her desk with some letters I had just signed, acting surprised to see him there. I really was surprised to see him! The secretary deferred to me, and I suggested that I could share some time with him then. As the young man walked into the office, I invited him to sit but he chose to stand, stating that he would not stay long. He didn't. He had taken care of some other business in a nearby office, he said, and had just stopped by to say that I had made some very interesting statements during our recent class sessions. He was referring to some quotes I had made from Howard Thurman in a lecture I gave about religion. I thanked the student for coming and for his comments, and I invited him to return when he had more time to visit.

The student's next visit was by schedule, and he was on time. He sat down that time, but soon got up to look at the books lining my library shelves. He asked me what a particular book was about and whether I had read it. I assured him that I had read the book in question, and that I was familiar with the author's subject and point of view. As we talked on, I noticed that he pulled from the shelf *Jesus and the Disinherited,* a book by Howard Thurman. Turning to the back panel of the dust jacket and noticing Thurman's black portrait as author, the student asked me, "and what is this book about?" I gave a brief description of its contents and message. He seemed intrigued and asked if he could borrow it to read. Although reluctant to loan the book, in the interest of openness I decided to do so that one time.

My trust was rewarded. The student read the book and we discussed its contents when we met the next time. He borrowed other books of mine by Howard Thurman; he read them and we discussed them. As we met across that semester, my helpfulness appealed to his trust and his trust was rewarded. He finally found a bridge by which he could move from a troubled past of bad choices into the future he desired despite having dropped out of other colleges before. Anderson College had admitted him "on probation," but within the next year he improved his grades sufficiently to begin a major in the pre-med curriculum. The student graduated, went to medical school, and became a successful practicing physician. Howard Thurman used to say that human need sensitizes us for giving or receiving, and an honest deed that serves a need becomes a meeting place for two lives. That is what happened when student Thomas Hignell and I met during a Bible 101 class. During his later career as a successful medical doctor he stayed in touch with me, characteristically solicitous about my health and general well being.

Interestingly, Thomas Hignell was one of the medical doctors who attended Howard Thurman during his final illness.

Having heard me voice some of Thurman's insights during my class lectures on religion, and having read and discussed several of Thurman's books with me, Hignell had developed a "taste" for the deep thought of my mentor. After medical school he was doing his residency at the very hospital in San Francisco to which Thurman was admitted for care during his terminal illness. Assigned to the intensive care unit, young Hignell was surprised when, checking on one of the patients, he noticed that the man's wristband read "Thurman, Howard." The sight of that name jolted Hignell's memory. He promptly asked, "Are you *the* Howard Thurman?" The answer came back, "Yes," but it was groggily spoken. It had been but a short time since Thurman's operation and the young doctor thought Thurman was not sufficiently awake, so a little later he asked a second question: "Are you the Thurman who wrote *Jesus and the Disinherited*?" Again the answer was "Yes!" Thinking that it was all too good to be true—that he was attending someone whose thought and teachings had greatly blessed his life, Hignell quickly asked a third question: "Do you know a Dr. James Earl Massey in Indiana?" The answer again, and a bit stronger, was "Yes, I do!" At that point Hignell's feelings were so full that he had to sit down! He sat in silence until he had calmed sufficiently to resume his work.

When Howard Thurman was released and went home, Dr. Thomas Hignell went to the house on several evenings to sit with him and give Mrs. Thurman some hours of relief and rest time. He did this until Thurman died. Honest deeds do become meeting places for two lives, and sometimes more than two. There is a grand destiny in good deeds, God-directed deeds. As Shakespeare put it, "There is a divinity that shapes our ends." Hignell has never ceased to marvel about his experience with the dying Howard Thurman.

Occasionally I had to minister to a student whose parent, sibling, roommate, or even a spouse had died. In most cases I assisted the family pastor who officiated during the funeral and burial of the deceased in their hometown. There were times when the campus lost a student or faculty member in an accident or by an unrelieved illness and I was involved in a memorial service for them on campus in addition to a formal funeral in the home congregation. I remember well my first memorial service as campus minister. James L. Snyder, a senior in the seminary, was accidentally shot and killed in December, 1972, while out hunting pheasants with his brothers. Snyder was only twenty-five years old, but had been active in his church and as youth camp coordinator. Two teenagers who were carrying rifles were hunting a stray dog who had bitten a child in the area recently, saw a dog similar in description to the one being sought, and fired in Jim's direction, unaware that he and his brothers were resting themselves along a fence row on the other side of a clump of trees and brush lining the property. Jim Snyder was scheduled to graduate with his Master of Divinity degree in June, 1973, but a fatal accident intervened, preventing that result. We held a memorial service in his honor at the seminary on the day after I joined with his pastor, James W. Bradley, for his funeral and burial from the West Washington Street Church in Indianapolis, where he had been serving as youth associate. I focused my remarks on comforting Jim's parents and brothers, but particularly Brenda, Jim's widow, who was a student at the college and soon to be the mother of his unborn child.

I was not unfamiliar with tragic happenings. I had ministered many times in crisis occasions in the complex urban setting of Detroit, and would have to do so many times more. In November, just one month before James Snyder died, I was back in Detroit to officiate at the funeral of James E. Hawkins, Jr., a charter member of Metropolitan Church, who was shot after being robbed in the store he owned and managed. Hawkins was president of our Men's Organization and a popular leader in Men of the Church of God in Michigan. One year later, in November, 1973, I was at Metropolitan Church to comfort the family and funeralize Joseph Myrick, another charter member and trustee, after he was robbed and shot in the store he owned and managed. Then in January, 1975, I had to assist a grieving wife when George W. Sykes, another trustee and successful businessman, was robbed and killed while going to his parked car from a bank. Sykes was converted and became a member of the church under my preaching.

As I continued an active relationship with both the Anderson College campus community and Metropolitan Church of God in Detroit, there were those who wondered and asked how it was possible to handle the two assignments without breaking under the load or failing in one or the other. That question required a multiple answer. A part of the answer had to do with what we African Americans refer to as "a reasonable portion of health and strength"; another part of the answer was public demand; another part had to do with the maturity of the leadership in the Detroit church; still another part of the answer had to do with how two related careers can serve each other. Years after serving as campus minister at Anderson College while senior pastor in Detroit, I came across a term in an educational journal that was borrowed to apply to the benefits of carrying two careers simultaneously. That term, borrowed from a comment of John Ruskin (1819-1900), was "balance." As Ruskin put it, "In all perfectly beautiful objects, there is found the opposition of one part to another, and a reciprocal balance." In my case, that balance had to do with how the practical service of pastoring bequeathed insights that fed my teaching, while the research undertaken for teaching generated information essential for practical service. I was not living in two different worlds as I served concurrently in the two different settings; the disciplines of each one blessed my duties in both. I moved between both areas exhilarated, not exhausted. My experience and example helped some others to broaden not only their idea of scholarship, but also broaden their understanding of how scholarship and service can relate in a minister's life.

The Second World Congress on Evangelism

I received from Dr. Donald E. Hoke an invitation to take part in the International Congress on World Evangelization scheduled to convene in Lausanne, Switzerland, from July 16-25, 1974. The concern behind the invitation was to bring together for a second time evangelical leaders of Protestant churches from every country of the world. The stated goal of the Congress was "to inspire and assist churches and Christians in commitment to new strategies that will result in completing Christ's great commission of world evangelization in this century." The Congress was planned and hosted by the Billy Graham Evangelistic Association. I had been a participant in the first such congress that the BGEA sponsored in 1966 in Berlin, Germany; this time, I was invited to be an observer. I decided to go.

When I informed Dr. William E. Reed, Executive Secretary of the Church of God, about the invitation, he informed me that he was also invited. Reed suggested that since I was Chair of our Movement's Committee on Christian Unity I could represent the Church of God at the Congress. He also stated that part of the Committee's unused budget could be used to apply against my expenses as our representative. We soon learned of other Church of God leaders who had been invited to attend the Congress either as participant or observer. Having heard about my invitation to take part, Editor Harold L. Phillips asked me to represent *Vital Christianity* during the Congress and he gave me press credentials to gain access to the Congress pressroom and receive press notices from which I could write an informed report about the event for the church.

I went. The International Congress on World Evangelization was held at the spacious Palais de Beaulieu overlooking Lake Geneva in Lausanne, Switzerland. The chosen theme was "Let the Earth Hear His Voice." The meeting involved participants (2,473) and observers (1,300) from 150 countries. The first such Congress, held in 1966 in Berlin, was smaller (1,000 delegates) and mainly a time of theological study about evangelism, while the larger gathering at Lausanne was essentially a planning Congress to explore ways to evangelize. Although no plans had been laid by the Sponsoring Committee to develop a new worldwide organization of evangelicals, the scope of the agenda for world evangelization stirred many participants to believe that some kind of organization seemed to be necessary to implement the vision. Some participants were wary of this voiced option, fearful lest another organization be created in seeming opposition to the World Council of Churches. As it turned out, a majority consensus (as voiced through a questionnaire response) favored forming a functional fellowship to assist cooperative work to achieve world evangelization.

The year 1974 was strategic for the International Congress on World Evangelization. That year had been designated as World Population Year and a World Population Conference convened in Hungary. It was clearly a time of increased concern over the implications of a growing world population. The Congress delegates did not deal with the ethical issue of whether world population should be restricted, nor did they deal with the resource issue of how to supply food for the mounting millions, but they did face the implications of a rate of population growth that exceeded the present rate of Christian evangelization. In 1974 the world population stood at 3.9 billion people, and it was increasing by 76 million per year. The projection was that by the year 2000 there would be 7 billion people living on earth. The Congress delegates sought to deal with the problem of matching world needs with plans for ministry personnel and resources.

The Congress participants were aware of the internal polarizations and divisive structures among the churches and the need for Christians to present a visible oneness as evangelists on mission. There also was the sensed need for social openness and forwardness in dealing with the use of wealth and resources. The final document from the Congress was "The Lausanne Covenant," a theological statement that many delegates signed in personal commitment. Among the major articles in that document was a strongly voiced section about the importance of social action as a part of the gospel and that it is not an avoidable option in evangelizing the world.

In addition to the development and publication of "The Lausanne Covenant," a Congress Continuation Committee was established by vote of the delegates, so that there would be a vehicle for follow-up, continued planning, and essential interchange across succeeding years. That Continuation Committee is better known as The Lausanne Committee for World Evangelization, co-chaired by Bishop Jack Dain (Australia) and Leighton Ford (United States). The members chosen to serve on that Committee were announced near the close of the Congress and it was only after that announcement that I discovered that I had been elected as one of its members. I consented to serve and continued on the Committee across the next ten years. The Church of God leaders at the Congress rejoiced over my appointment to the Continuation Committee.

Among other Church of God leaders who were either participants, observers, or guests during the Congress were: Barry L. Callen, William E. Reed, Mr. and Mrs. Streeter Stuart, Charles Tarr (all from the United States); Elijah F. Akhahenda (from British East Africa); Willi Krenz (Switzerland); Rev. and Mrs. Cleve Grant (Jamaica); Franco Santonocito (Italy); Mr. and Mrs. Fouad Accad, Philippe Accad, and Adel Masri (Lebanon); Ms. Farouri Hadia (Algeria); Ms. A. Boody (United Arab Emerates); and Enrique R. Cepeda (Mexico). A group photograph of some of us appeared later in the October 6, 1974, issue of *Vital Christianity* along with the article that I prepared about the Congress.

During a free day while in Lausanne, I took some time to shop. Being in Europe again, I was eager to locate books not yet available in English translation and to secure new editions of piano music scores. I found a music store that had in stock the first volume of a new edition of Beethoven piano sonatas edited by Claudio Arrau, my favorite pianist. I knew that Arrau had been working on that edition for C. F. Peters Publishers since 1969 and that it had been released in Europe in 1973. I rejoiced over my find and purchased it, glad to see Beethoven's work in an Urtext edition with additional features of Arrau's

299

interpretive suggestions, recommended fingerings, and metronome settings, things he knew to perfection from his years of performing Beethoven's sonatas. I could hardly wait to get back to my piano, aware that the new edition had suggestions to solve problems of hand movement, assure clear articulation, security of tone, and help reduce tension when performing these sonatas.

Later that afternoon, I took a train ride to Geneva, intent to visit the headquarters of the World Council of Churches. While in the library there I met and conversed with Professor James Cone of New York City, who was on sabbatical leave from his chair in systematic theology at Union Theological Seminary. Thanks to help from Archie Le Mone, Youth Coordinator of the World Council of Churches, Cone was doing research in Geneva and other places in Europe that year. Some of that research appeared the next year in his book *God of the Oppressed* (Seabury Press, 1975).

While returning on the train to Lausanne, I was thinking about the invitation I received the day before from David Hubbard, a fellow delegate at the Congress and President of Fuller Theological Seminary, to give the Mary Claire Gautschi Lectures at his school in Pasadena, California, in 1975. Hubbard suggested that I lecture about preaching. While on that train ride, I began projecting plans for that lecture series. There were several points along the way where Mont Blanc could be seen in the distance. With that beautiful mountain peak looming so clearly before my eyes, I noticed that every time the train's position shifted I gained a new vantage point from which to view that peak in a fresh and different way. That experience of shifting perspectives so influenced me at the time that I decided then and there to lecture at Fuller on "The Sermon in Perspective." When time for the lectureship arrived in the Fall quarter of 1975, I gave that series as I had planned it during that train ride. I treated the subject of the sermon from five different angles of view: the sermon as communication; the sermon as commentary; the sermon as counsel; the sermon as creation;

and the sermon as charisma. The full text of the lectures was published the next year as *The Sermon in Perspective: A Study of Communication and Charisma* (co-published by Baker Book House and Warner Press, 1976).

A New Door Opens

Near the end of July, 1975, I received a letter from Phil M. Fair, Executive Director of the Radio and Television Commission of the Church of God, informing me that I was one of five persons named by select leaders from across the church as a possible successor to R. Eugene Sterner at his retirement on July 1, 1977, as Speaker on "Christian Brotherhood Hour." The letter voiced the concern of the Commission to hold exploratory discussions with me if I were willing to be considered for the post. A list of criteria for Speaker and a position description were enclosed for my study. I was told that because of the "necessary time schedule and procedural requirements," the Radio and Television Commission needed to nominate Sterner's successor by November, 1975. The name of the Speaker-elect would then go to the Executive Council through its Board of Directors for action in its February, 1976, meeting. Final ratification by the General Assembly of the Church of God would take place in June, 1976. The new Speaker would overlap with Dr. Sterner from January to June 1977, and assume all duties on July 1, 1977. If interested, I was asked to prepare and record on tape four sermons, each one about twelve minutes long. One sermon was to be topical, a second expository, a third exegetical, and a fourth to deal with a social issue or personal development. I was asked to submit the taped sermons by August 15, 1975.

My first reaction to Phil Fair's letter was surprise. My second reaction was an unreadiness to consider any change in service role. Campus ministry still exhilarated me, and pastoral ministry in Detroit still challenged me. While some of my ministerial colleagues working on campuses elsewhere had "thrown in the towel," plagued by burn-out, disgusted at a lack of student

301

interest, tired at having to experiment endlessly to attract students, or tired of how their denominational bodies related to their work, my experience at Anderson College had been different. My campus ministry work was expanding and rewarding. I did not feel any need to change.

I stated as much in my letter to Phil Fair. I also told him that the stated method of selecting the next CBH Speaker struck me as being competitive, a method that I could not favor because it was foreign to the pattern of guidance I had known across my years as a minister. I told him that it was my custom to react prayerfully only to a firm request made to me by a church or committee already settled on its choice. I further explained that I had never candidated for any post and that the preparation of audition tapes would place me in the position of candidating, so I could not in good conscience submit to that method. I then asked that my name be removed from the Commission's list.

My initial response did not end the matter. I received telephone calls from Gordon K. Powell, Commission chair, and James L. Edwards, Commission member and spokesperson for the search committee, among others. As a result, I decided to enter into exploratory conversations about the radio ministry.

After weighing the issues, engaging in prayer, and times of counseling with my wife, Samuel G. Hines and Edward L. Foggs, on December 2, 1975, I wrote and accepted the call from the Radio and Television Commission, issued in November, to become Speaker on the Christian Brotherhood Hour when R. Eugene Sterner retired. In my letter of acceptance I added, "It only remains to be said that I appreciate the confidence of the Commission members and will, if ratified by the General Assembly, do my utmost to serve responsibly and creatively."

I simultaneously notified Dr. Reardon of my decision. He knew about the Commission's action to secure my services, and we had discussed options in case I chose to accept its call. In my letter to Reardon I explained, "This decision has not been made in haste nor with ease. The strings of my heart now vibrate in a music of sorrow, knowing as I do that certain honored services must be left to other hands and certain working relationships broken in due time." I admitted being consoled "in knowing that no immediate withdrawal [from the College] is demanded—and that some openness to teach remains a strong concern on both your part and mine."

I received many letters of congratulations and support as the news spread about the Commission's selection of me to become the next radio minister for the Church of God. According to a letter Marcus H. Morgan sent to me, the Board of Directors of the Executive Council "gave its unanimous endorsement to your selection." Early in 1976, Donald A. Noffsinger, President of Warner Press, wrote to express his pleasure that the Executive Council had endorsed my appointment, and he suggested that my being ratified by the General Assembly in June was "99.9% certain." I was ratified that June, but only after a lengthy period of interrogation by some members of the General Assembly. The interrogation I underwent related mainly to my doctrinal beliefs, and the questions were not unexpected. Once the news spread that I was the Radio and Television Commission's choice to succeed Dr. Sterner as CBH Speaker, the Commission office received some letters from pastors who questioned my doctrinal soundness. Some pastors wrote letters to Harold L. Phillips, Editor-in-Chief of *Vital Christianity* at Warner Press, to voice their questions about me, and representatives of at least two state assemblies sent letters to W. E. Reed at the Executive Council office to request that time be allotted during the Assembly for them to question me from the floor before the scheduled vote. I was informed about these complaints quite early and sought to address them in "A Personal Statement" printed and mailed in early May to Assembly members, along with a biographical sketch.

When Gwendolyn first learned about the letters received that questioned my doctrinal soundness, she asked me, "Do you really want to be involved in all this?" I answered her, "Well, I realize that I don't need to be involved in this hassle, but if I remove my name at this stage, there will remain unanswered questions about me in the public arena, so I must endure this even if the Assembly members do not ratify me to be Speaker!"

On the afternoon of June 15, Assembly Chair Arlo Newell recognized Dr. W. E. Reed to present the agenda item of selecting the Christian Brotherhood Hour Speaker to succeed R. Eugene Sterner on July 1, 1977. I was seated on the platform with members of the Radio and Television Commission. Dr. Reed stated that the standard procedure had been followed in presenting the name of the one being submitted for ratification by the General Assembly, and then he invited Gordon Powell, Commission Chair, to present the Commission's recommendation to the Assembly. Powell spoke to the issue of the Commission's action, cited some details regarding my qualifications and service-roles, and then referred to the mailing Assembly members had received in early May regarding me. He then invited me to make a personal statement.

Using a condensed copy of the statement mailed earlier, I spoke as clearly as I could regarding my doctrinal views concerning "millennialism" and "the Charismatic Movement," the two controversial issues raised in the letters sent to the Executive Council, the Radio and Television Commission, and Warner Press. Having seen copies of those letters, I knew who the questioners were, I knew the settings in which they served, and I was sensitive to the concerns they voiced. I also knew that some of the letters were from persons who had reservations about me because they did not know me, while some were from those who knew enough to differ with me over my ecumenical openness. Some dissenting letters might well have written because my name was remembered in connection with the well-publicized "Detroit-Jackson-Massey Controversy."

The question regarding my doctrinal position with respect to millennialism had been raised before, in 1974 after a sermon I preached during the International Convention at Anderson that year. In connection with the Convention theme, the sermon title was "All Things Made New." Among several scriptures the program committee listed as possible texts for that subject was

Revelation 21:5, and I used that text as the basis for my sermon. Influenced by a fresh study of the Greek text of that verse—and a depth study of all the passages from Isaiah reflected in Rev. 21:4-5, I declared that the promise in the verse includes a new earth that will match the new (resurrected) bodies of believers. I explained the new earth as a renewed earth because the Greek adjective John used for "new," *kainos,* was used to express both continuity and contrast at the same time; continuity with the basic substance of a thing while contrastingly different in quality from an earlier form of it. My voicing of that view about our expected future in a "renewed earth, a place substantially real, a place with a past but which has been made qualitatively new," did not set well with some who heard me. They immediately classified my view as millennialistic. Some of those hearers wrote to me after that Convention, and I responded to their queries. In fact, I shared with them a three-page, single-spaced working document to trace for them the total exegetical process by which my textual conclusions were reached. One irenic and informed person who sustained a written interchange of views with me on the Revelation passage and related texts such as 2 Peter 3:10-13, was Everett I. Carver, a teacher at Gulf Coast Bible College. We exchanged letters across several months following that Convention. Along with one of his last letters to me on the subject, Carver shared some pages from a manuscript on eschatology he was preparing for publication. I did not satisfy every writer who questioned my exegesis, but I did attempt to acquaint each one with my process of seeking to understand what the Scriptures say and mean.

Remembering the questioners I had answered after that Convention sermon in 1974, I was surprised that no questions about eschatology were among the many questions put to me when I finished my preliminary statement to the Assembly. The questioners at that Assembly seemed more concerned to know where I stood with respect to the Charismatic Movement and "speaking in tongues." I recall being pointedly asked if I had ever spoken in a language that could not be identified as an historical language. I immediately and honestly replied that I have never in my life spoken in a language that is not historical. Given the struggle some of our churches were having in areas where the charismatic emphasis was rife, and given the fact that I had been accused years earlier, falsely, of leaning in that direction, I expected such questions. Another questioner asked if I believed that in the realm of the Church of God there is a place for "tongues." I replied that I was not wise enough to know which gifts should continue and which should cease. I was not feeling edgy or trying to be curt as I answered him; that response was my honest reply.

Lillie S. McCutcheon asked a more pertinent question as she stood before the Assembly. She asked if I could assure the Assembly that, in a radio ministry, I would be positive in voicing the Church of God doctrinal stance as an amillennial and non-tongues speaking group? I answered that if ratified to serve as Speaker I would proclaim the Word of God on the air, but would not be partisan in preaching. I went on to explain that fighting other groups on the air could jeopardize our privilege to receive public service time that some stations provide.

There were many who stood and spoke in favor of ratifying me to become Speaker. Harold L. Phillips was one of them. He mentioned my years of writing for Warner Press and stated that he had never received any letter challenging anything published with my name. Phillips then asked the Assembly members to search their hearts because something other than a supposed doctrinal difference might be motivating the debate. Phillips was counseling against a racist response, and we knew it. Addie Wyatt also spoke to this issue; she appealed to my years at the college as a teacher, stating that none of the complaints being voiced against me had been raised about my teaching there. As longtime friends, Addie and her husband, Claude, knew my life, my spirit, and my teachings. I had preached many times at their church in Chicago. Samuel G. Hines stood and spoke about my years of unquestioned service in Jamaica and his years as interim pastor at Metropolitan Church in Detroit during my absence; he insisted that there was no basis for any of the fears or concerns being expressed from the Assembly floor.

I had been on my feet answering questions for more than two hours when Maurice Berquist stood to speak in favor of ratifying me. Berquist confessed his belief that the Holy Spirit had guided the Radio and Television Commission in choosing me, and his faith that the Holy Spirit would lead in the voting. He then moved the question. Henry Cole seconded the motion. Chairman Newell informed the Assembly that the motion Berquist made required closure to the debate, was not debatable, and would require a two-thirds majority vote. The vote was expressed by rising (which brought a relief to all), and was carried. The ratification vote regarding the Christian Brotherhood Hour Speaker followed by secret ballot. There was no immediate notice of the tally. Later that evening I learned that of the more than 900 persons registered for the Assembly session that afternoon, 725 voted in my favor, and 242 in opposition.

Later that evening Harold Phillips stopped at our home to congratulate me. In the course of talking, he advised that some who voted against me might well change their mind as they see and hear what I do as radio minister. He told me about the narrow margin of votes that made him Charles E. Brown's successor as Editor-in-Chief at Warner Press in 1951. Aware of how he had since gained many friends and influenced many persons, I thanked him for his advice, his support, his friendship, and took courage.

Leave-Taking

Ratified during the June, 1976, General Assembly session to become CBH-Speaker in July, 1977, I followed a pre-arranged plan regarding campus ministry at Anderson College and the pastorate at Metropolitan Church. I decided to resign from both. I announced to Metropolitan Church that I intended to close out my ministry there by December, 1976, and I informed President Reardon that I would resign as campus minister effective June, 1977.

The congregation was characteristically thoughtful and gracious in planning and executing the several occasions related to my leave-taking. The women of the church held a reception for Gwendolyn the last week in November, the church sponsored a banquet for the two of us on December 3, and on Sunday, December 5, I delivered my final sermon as pastor to the congregation as we celebrated Homecoming Sunday. The farewell banquet, held at one of Detroit's choicest hotels, included the presence of my closest minister friends in the city. Samuel G. Hines came from his pastorate of Third Street Church of God in Washington, D.C., and gave the banquet address. Borrowing an expression from Martin Buber, he paid tribute to me as a leader whose work had involved "Walking the Narrow Ridge." He also told how, during his first visit to Metropolitan Church in 1956, he was delightfully surprised by our congregation's racial and cultural mix, which he confessed was a witness to unity that he had not expected to find in such rich measure. He applauded my new assignment, then applauded the congregation for following my lead across the years, and then advised the members to "guard the narrow ridge" along which they had been led, mindful that "the traffic there is slower and not nearly as crowded." It was a tribute to end all tributes, a word that only he was so well qualified to offer to this friend and our mutual church family. My friend Dr. Nicholas Hood, President Pro Tem of The Detroit Common Council, presented a Testimonial Citation on behalf of the Council honoring my years of public service in the city.

On December 5, Homecoming Sunday, my farewell sermon was "Leave-Taking," based on the story told in 1 Kings 11:21b-22 about Hadad's departure from a favored place and favored people. In closing I paid tribute to the members as "the choicest among God's people," and to the officers whose support had been crucial to our pilgrimage and progress as a congregation. Before the day closed I was honored by words, gifts, and the bestowed honorary title "Pastor at Large." My heart was "strangely warmed" again. I was mindful of that congregation's love and loyalty across twenty-four years. As I took my leave from them, our membership stood at 746, and I anticipated their continued progress under Robert O. Dulin, Jr., newly elected to succeed me as senior pastor. At my invitation, and by congregational vote, Dulin had moved from Anderson in 1974 to serve Metropolitan Church full-time as an associate pastor, with special responsibilities for youth and family ministries.

In April, 1977, I spoke in chapel for the last time as the campus minister of Anderson College. I used again the subject "Leave-Taking," and also the same text (1 Kings 11:21b-22), but I reworked the address by highlighting the college context and student body on that occasion. I closed my address with black poet Paul Laurence Dunbar's "Encouraged":

> Because you have loved me I have much achieved,
> Had you despised me then I must have failed,
> But since I knew you trusted and believed,
> I could not disappoint you and so prevailed.

A spontaneous applause began and quickly spread as the chapel audience stood to their feet. The considered sentiment greatly encouraged me. The student body president, accompanied by W. Sherill Fox, director of public relations and coordinator of chapel programming, walked to the podium and presented a plaque from the students citing me as "an exceptional man and friend." The prolonged applause that followed provided me a grand moment to remember. That service marked some of my last services as campus minister, but I had already agreed to continue in a limited teaching role at the college and seminary while serving as CBH Speaker. Donald Collins, former minister of outreach at Park Place Church adjacent to the Anderson campus, succeeded me as campus minister.

RADIO MINISTER: "CHRISTIAN BROTHERHOOD HOUR"

Since I had preached each week on radio across eight years during my Detroit pastorate, having to speak for our denomination's "Christian Brotherhood Hour" broadcast each week was not an entirely new phase of ministry. The CBH-Speaker role did, however, admit me to a wider arena of service and hearers across the English-speaking world.

In 1977 CBH had been on the air for thirty years. Started in January, 1947, the result of a dream in the hearts of Dr. W. Dale Oldham (first speaker) and Richard Lee Meischke (announcer), the weekly broadcast that began on nineteen radio stations in the United States was being heard across the entire English-speaking world in 1977 on nearly 400 stations. Once a "National Radio Project" sponsored by Men of the Church of God, CBH had long since moved from being under the management of the Board of Church Extension and Home Missions to that of the Radio and Television Commission of the Church of God. In 1977 the Radio and Television Commission had received full agency status that made it the Mass Communications Board of the Church of God. Moving from a commission status to a board level provided a new organizational structure that was demanded by developments in the field of communications and was required to handle the anticipated programming in mass communications for our sponsoring church.

I began ministry as the new CBH-Speaker within this newly developed structure, and I was allied in daily work with Dr. Maurice "Berk" Berquist, the newly elected Executive Secretary-Treasurer for the organization. Both Berquist and I came to our new posts from a pastorate, mine in Detroit, his in Daytona, Florida. A popular preacher and seasoned leader, Berquist and I knew each other from across many years. Respecting each other's gifts, we launched into our respective tasks with a sense of comradeship and the will to venture.

Shortly after taking office, while on my way to the recording studio to tape some messages, a statement someone made to me after a preaching service more than twenty years earlier suddenly and unexpectedly flashed across the screen of my mind. In 1955, during the trip abroad that the Detroit congregation gave me, I had preached in Birkenhead, England, at John Larmour's church. My sermon was about "The Unsearchable Riches of Christ," from Ephesians 3:8, and my treatment had impressed one of the worshippers who afterward shook my hand and told me so. The lady greeted me warmly, lingered for a moment, and with a gleam in her eyes and a prophetic thrust to her words, she said, "The world will hear from you!" Those six words filled my memory as I drove to the recording studio that afternoon, and they deeply stirred me. The stirring was not pride; it was a sensitizing realization that helped me know that I must not only be specific but also universal while preaching in the wider arena now opened to me. As I contemplated this, I felt strangely isolated, solitary, but I also felt focused. Those remembered words from that worshipper in Birkenhead, England, helped to focus my attention beyond my particular church heritage, cultural setting, and group expectations, and they readied me for the wider world my preaching now had to address.

There were many satisfactions as I planned and handled my task as international radio preacher. Some of the happenings during the election process I endured had been distasteful, but even those happenings had helped to highlight for me the

311

sovereignty of God in it all. Being aware of this made my satisfaction in work all the more manifest. I felt a higher will at work enabling me. I was encouraged that the logic of life was showing itself in an appointed opportunity. I felt ready, fully open to the demands of the post. I thought about what W.E.B. DuBois once said. Some persons are fortunate in being "born with sail set and seas charted." They walk "unhesitatingly and surely to [their] life work." That was how I felt, and the satisfaction that life had readied me for what I was doing steadily buoyed me as the days and months came and went.

I needed that sense of being buoyed as I began the CBH ministry because I was still feeling the pressure of bereavement following the death of my younger brother, Howard, in June, 1976, the year before. Two weeks before the 1976 General Assembly ratification vote on me, I was in Detroit, at Veteran's Hospital, with Howard when he underwent an operation. Despite all attempts at corrective treatment, however, his condition steadily worsened. His failing condition was steadily in my thoughts and prayers as I stood on the floor during that Assembly, answering questions raised by my interrogators. Shortly after the votes were tallied I raced back to Detroit and was at the hospital with Howard on the afternoon that he died.

Howard and I had talked at length a few days before he was hospitalized. During that visit, he surprised me when he placed in my hands a diary in which he had been charting his reactions to what was happening in his body. Howard knew that death was in his immediate future. On that final hospital visit with Howard, I sickened as I watched him slip into a coma before dying. God embracingly received my brother's spirit, but my bereavement after his death lingered across more than a year. In July, 1977, the heavy shadow of loss still blanketed my spirit, and there were days when I was in tears. Howard was the first in our immediate family circle to die, and his was arguably the ablest mind among the Massey boys.

Working as I was at the national level of our church structure, and as spokesperson for the church on its international radio broadcast, I held a post which by its responsibilities and demands sometimes made me a "marginal figure," a problem known by those whose work keeps them from being as involved in as many settings and activities as expected or requested. I was no longer responsible to be present on weekends at our Detroit church, so other leaders and groups expected my weekends to be free when they called upon me. There were the many invitations to appear at state and regional gatherings, and invitations from friends to preach at their churches or share in special observances in their honor. There were many invitations to be a camp meeting speaker. I accepted a sufficient number of the invitations, but I knew that I did not need to honor every invitation I received. I knew that I should husband my strength and sustain my health. Gwendolyn and I wisely chose to keep some weekends free for ourselves. Having chosen Park Place Church of God in Anderson, Indiana, as our home congregation, we were in worship there when in Anderson on a free Sunday. Again and again we were blessed by the stirring music and substantive preaching we always expected at Park Place Church.

There were occasions when special interest groups sought my time and backing. And alas, there were times when my bi-cultural upbringing and approach made me appear suspect when I was not in agreeement regarding some issue involving race. There were occasions and settings when my being black seemed to set me in a place apart, causing discomfort for some others, despite the fact that I fully belonged where I was. But I wanted to be in relation to all, giving myself and my services as CBH-Speaker wisely, strategically, and with fairness. I worked steadily against being a marginal figure, intent to meet the responsibilities and demands of my work, fully aware that I could not accept every offered invitation or satisfy every request. While carrying out my stated task, I sought to serve where I felt needed, and I refused to "window dress" at places where I thought my presence would be "used" to some end I could not honor.

My travels within the church as CBH-Speaker opened to me, in an even wider way than ever before, the worlds of thought and attitude of many congregations within our church group. I noticed that here and there among us as a holiness people were leaders on a quest for respectability and social recognition. I detected here and there among us a fear of associating with others, especially Pentecostals and Charismatics, who in certain ways differ from us. As I traveled, doing my work, I tried to help our leaders and congregations realize our group potential. I especially voiced afresh and modeled the meaning and implications of our doctrinal tenets, particularly the doctrine of Christian unity. In the midst of it all, I saw how important my experiences of life beyond our Church of God movement had been in readying me to work effectively within, for, and through our movement. Meanwhile, I encouraged myself as I related to two worlds: the world I saw in the church I served, and the world I saw in the Word of God. I looked to this latter reality to anchor my hope, feed my life, and inform the preaching I felt commissioned to do.

Interestingly, I was sometimes the guest speaker in churches whose members were surprised to discover, by my presence, that the new CBH-Speaker was a black man. My voice on radio had not betrayed my color. I remember a certain man's comment, after hearing me preach at his church. He said that I did not preach like any black preacher he had ever heard! His tone was one of lament. I reasoned that he had missed the wider contacts and experiences that would have acquainted him with the incredibly diverse world of black culture. In hearing me, he had expected to hear a "black voice," which, in the popular mind, is associated sometimes with an aggressive, brash, frenetic, chipped-English; sometimes with vocal agility used with explosive energy; sometimes with revolutionary fervor, felicitous outbursts, and volatile spontaneity; sometimes with flamboyant rhetoric; sometimes with the calculated manner of an entertainer; and sometimes, but not usually, with a mild-mannered, straight-forward realism that honors truth above style. Again and again during my travels and in teaching classes I have tried to acquaint non-blacks with the fact that black preaching is not monolithic—that there is no total uniformity among black preachers in the matter of approach, abilities, or accent of voice.

There was an afternoon when William Casey, an Anderson College student, met with me to receive some assistance with a research paper for one of his classes. A day or two before coming he informed his teacher that he had asked me to assist him. According to Casey's report, the teacher seemed surprised that I had agreed to be of assistance, asking, "How is it that you know him? Dr. Massey is so different from the rest of you"—presumably a reference, Casey thought, to other blacks on campus and in the City of Anderson. "He even talks differently than any of you!" Casey told me that he had informed the teacher that we did indeed know each other, that I knew his mother, that I habitually use clear and correct English, and, further, that class differences did not influence the way I relate to people. That teacher did not know much about African Americans, millions of whom have a natural feel for the beauty and cadences of the English language, and make a careful use of it. That teacher left Anderson College after a very short stint; his contract was not renewed. Hindered by class-consciousness and stereotyped thinking, he was not prepared to teach and relate cross-cultural-ly, a demand to which the college had formally committed itself under President Robert Reardon's administration.

A Friction Event

While it can be said that my voice did not always reveal my color, some critics viewed some of my actions while CBH-Speaker as a betrayal of our church heritage. One such action was my appearance in late 1977 as an invited guest on the well-known PTL Club.

Jim Bakker, program host, was gracious during my appearance on his show, and I enjoyed being interviewed by him. Most of the interview centered on the subject of divine guidance, and

I spoke personally about that reality by relating two stories from my life—the details surrounding my birth and my experience of being called to the ministry.

I received many good letters after that program aired. The letter writers applauded my appearance and voiced appreciation for the exposure received through the well-known television ministry of PTL. But there was also a barrage of protest letters from Church of God leaders in Ohio and the South. They protested that I had done the Church of God Movement a disservice by appearing on a program avowedly "Charismatic" in persuasion and promotion. I was told in some letters that I should have used the occasion of the interview to denounce Pentecostalism and the Charismatic emphasis.

Dr. Lillie McCutcheon, pastor in Newton Falls, Ohio, wrote the most detailed letter of protest. Her letter to me even included a barbed statement letting me know that she was not protesting alone but was speaking for others, many others. She stated that I should be prepared to account for my action and even demanded that I cease being so open in relating to others who differed from us doctrinally because I now represented an agency of the Church of God. My openness was an evident point of friction to her. I had discussed the invitation with the CBH Board of Directors and they had agreed that I should go and be interviewed on PTL, so in appearing on Jim Bakker's program I was not violating the terms of my role and the trip was not viewed by them as placing our agency in jeopardy. I answered Dr. McCutcheon's letter and sent a copy of my reply to those whose names appeared at the bottom of her's to me. My answer was that religious segregation among Christians is as heinous and dangerous to the common life of the church as racial segregation is to the common concerns of a stated democracy. It was my view that spiritual snobbery has a barbarous impact upon the life of the church, and that any concern to live and work independently of other Christians is a selfish attitude that forces a dividing wedge between believers. Furthermore, it was my right to act independently as a Christian leader in cases of conscience, and my conscience refused to accept or acquiesce to a segregating of believers.

It was the subsequent appearance on PTL of Mrs. Frances Gardner Hunter, however, that deepened the friction my appearance on that program had occasioned. Mrs. Hunter, a Church of God minister herself, had been involved in charismatic meetings and experiences that had led to dissention in some local churches where she had spoken. During her January 1978 appearance on PTL, she made some statements during the interview which some Church of God viewers thought grossly misrepresented some aspects of belief and life in congregations of the Church of God (Anderson, Indiana). Although Mrs. Hunter intended to compliment me when she lauded my earlier appearance on PTL, describing me as a "Spirit-filled, heavily anointed man of God," she misrepresented me by stating that I was a long-time advocate of charismatic activities. She also made some other misleading statements regarding the Church of God.

Letters about her interview poured into our CBH office and other of our general church offices lamenting "the harm" her misrepresentations might cause the church, the broadcast, and me. One of our pastors who saw the telecast interview was so displeased by Mrs. Hunter's statements that he wrote to Jim Bakker to ask that the Executive Secretary of the Executive Council of the Church of God be given a fifteen-minute segment of air time on his program to put aspects of the record straight. In due course, I got involved in the interchange through a telephone call I received from Riley E. Kaufman, a program director at PTL. A few days after he and I talked on the phone he sent me the following letter, dated February 17, 1978:

> It was a rare pleasure to talk with you on the phone yesterday. I must voice my appreciation for the true spirit of Christ you have manifested in the matter under discussion. I am also glad for what you said about your love for Jim Bakker and the PTL ministry.

It is neither true nor fair to assume that guests on PTL must share the same views as Jim Bakker on the charismatic renewal. Your recent guest appearance on PTL was greatly blessed of God and there was no necessity to discuss Bible truths other than those on which you and Jim Bakker agreed. We sincerely apologize for the concern that was caused for your office and your denomination through the representations made by Mrs. Frances Hunter when she was a guest on PTL. I am sorry for the phone calls and letters you have had to answer from those who wondered why they would hear from a national TV program instead of from your office if you and the Church of God had changed your position on the application of glossalalia in the church today.

During our years of radio-missionary ministry in the Far East, it was my privilege to serve as liaison officer between the Far East Broadcasting Company and gospel broadcasts being released through their facilities in Asia. One of these fine broadcasts was the Christian Brotherhood Hour in the days when Dr. Dale Oldham was speaker.

You and your people have a tremendous ministry and we here at PTL wish you only God's very best in all future days as Jesus tarries. I trust the incident we have had occasion to discuss will in no way diminish the fellowship and rapport PTL has enjoyed in the past with you personally and with the Church of God.

Most cordially yours,
Riley E. Kaufman, Director
PTL Pastor Follow-up

In time, the furor ceased, but some critics never forgot that it was my active openness to other believers, even those with whom I differed, that partly occasioned it.

Program Matters

With a thirty-year history behind the broadcast, a basic format for the program had been developed after much experimentation. I did not seek to alter that format in any major way. In time, however, I did initiate two changes. I had more classic hymns added to the musical portion of the program and I lengthened the time of the sermon. We still utilized spiritual ballads, many of them reflecting the mood of the times and the prevailing style of music honored and used in many churches, but I preferred more solid hymns that were more in keeping with my preaching style, believing that those hymns might better serve the truth I sought to voice in my preaching. I made a judgment call in thinking that using more classic hymns would be appreciated. Fortunately, mail responses confirmed that judgment as being a correct one at that time.

The radio message itself was the heart of the program, as I saw and planned it, the primary agency for shaping an experience of hearing and response. I soon went beyond the nine-and-a-half minute limit set years earlier by Dr. Oldham with his subject-oriented approach. My exposition of some biblical text or passage sometimes lasted fifteen minutes. I was intent on giving a more direct and prolonged use of Scripture in preaching, so I planned the program with this in mind.

Reactions to this change varied. Some members of the Board of Directors suggested that my sermons should be shorter. I did not want to appear inflexible, so I shortened a few sermons. But when many listeners wrote and asked to hear more from me, the directors took notice that the CBH message was viewed by many as indeed the heart of the program. Those letters asking that more time be allotted to the sermon made me feel vindicated as I prepared more expositional messages and delivered them.

At first I did all of the preaching, and understandably so. The listeners needed to get to know me as the regular speaker. I did, however, want my predecessors to be heard now and again on the broadcast, so I reserved the special season programs for them. Both Dr. Dale Oldham, the founding Speaker, and Dr. Gene Sterner, his successor, obliged me (and their expectant admirers) by delivering messages on those special occasions. I invited both men to preach on the program at least twice each year, and both agreed and did so. I wanted to keep the CBH audience aware of our togetherness and I wanted the wider sponsoring church to sense our basic alliance as its spokespersons. This sharing of the "CBH Pulpit," as I referred to it, strengthened my ties both with my esteemed predecessors in that post and with those who had been their supporters.

To illustrate the importance of the sharing I encouraged and received from my predecessors, a listener writing from Manitoba, Canada, sent the following response to our programming:

> Count me among those who have been listening to C.B.H. down through the years, with its changing speakers and all. I well remember when Dr. Oldham was readying his listeners for a change of voice to be heard on C.B.H. Some of us wondered within ourselves, "can anyone ever be found to take Dr. Oldham's place?"—and as it turned out, without diminishing one iota from Dr. Oldham's wonderful ministry, Dr. Sterner began his long term ministry at the microphone, and his familiar soft-spoken voice gave us wonderful truths to ponder and live by, and now we are once more listening to an "unfamiliar" voice that is Sunday after Sunday becoming more beloved and familiar. Dr. Massey is giving us the glorious truths of God's Word that we love, in such a plain way; thank God.

There were many such letters, and the Board of Directors took note of them—and took pride in those responses.

Two years into my term in the Speaker's post, Dr. Oldham drew me aside one afternoon while he was in Anderson and stated that he had something he wanted to confess. He told me that during the ratification process in 1976 he had not voted for me to be CBH-Speaker. He paused, then stated that it had nothing to do with race. "I did not vote for you because I feared that you would preach over people's heads. I was wrong, and I want you to know that I have been enjoying your radio ministry. I am sometimes in places where the broadcast is not heard, but I listen to you as often as I can."

I had wondered in 1976 why I heard nothing from Dr. Oldham after the Mass Communications Board announced its choice of me to succeed Dr. Sterner on the broadcast. Dr. Sterner had written immediately to compliment me and he pledged me his support. I had expected some word from Dr. Oldham during that time, but had received none. His son, Doug, a member of the Christian Brothers Quartet which was frequently heard on the CBH broadcast, had offered his compliments. Doug even reminisced a bit about that much-publicized time when I was at the center of controversy. He knew about that time because he was then serving in Michigan. While complimenting me, Doug Oldham also commended the way I had disported myself during that time in the mid-1950s when, to use his words, "they tried their best to stomp the life out of you!"

Not hearing anything from Dr. Oldham in 1976, I wondered if his remembrance of the "Detroit-Jackson-Massey Controversy" had made him view me as a risk. I wondered if he had suggested another person to be Speaker and was displeased that the search committee went in a different direction. I wondered whether, as founder of the broadcast, Dr. Oldham feared that the listening public's interest and support would be jeopardized by the appointment of a black speaker. I did not know what to think about Dr. Oldham's silence, but out of respect for him I withheld any judgment. After the General Assembly ratified me, one of the first letters I wrote as CBH-Speaker was one inviting him to return as one of my guests during my first year in office. In addition, my first sermon as

Speaker paid tribute to his ministry and that of Dr. Sterner. The subject was "A Place in the Procession," based on the setting and wording in John 4:38, "Others have labored, and you have entered into their labor."

Having at last heard something personal from Dr. Oldham concerning my role, I accepted his statement and thanked him for the encouraging comment. As we parted that afternoon, I believed that my yearly invitations to return and preach on CBH had helped him to realize my esteem for him, and to realize as well that my concern was only to further and enhance the radio ministry. I also thought that he had no doubt learned that the number of stations, listeners, and support had increased, and not diminished, during my term as Speaker!

Many reasons can be cited for the popularity CBH was enjoying at the time. First and foremost, the program was substantive and appealing. Mixed musical styles allowed for variety, the featured musicians were widely known and enjoyed (Bill and Gloria Gaither among them), the preaching was biblical and practically focused, and the announcers were professional and warm. During my first year as Speaker, the program producer and announcer was still J. Richard Lee (the business name of Richard L. Meischke). In January, 1978, Mort Crim became the new program announcer. Crim, forty-one at the time, had been in broadcasting for twenty-six years. Since August of 1977 he had been based in Chicago, the chief news reporter and correspondent at WBBM, a CBS radio and television network affiliate. Crim's duties at the Chicago station involved him as co-anchor on the six o'clock evening news, co-host of a mid-day talk show, and correspondent for the ten o'clock evening news. Mort Crim's knowledge, gifts, and skills made our radio program even more appealing and helped expand our outreach.

As part of my sermon planning for the broadcast year, I projected an expositional series of sermons each Fall, based on some selected Bible book. I had followed this custom while in the pastorate and decided to implement it as a broadcast preacher.

The intent was to present a major statement from Scripture in sequential fashion to deepen faith and grant direction for understanding and living life on God's terms. Although I was convinced about the importance of expositional preaching as I began my first year on CBH, I did not begin an expositional series on the broadcast until my second year on the air as Speaker. I thought it wise to accustom my hearers to my style through isolated topics before subjecting them to an extended series. In addition, I needed to use my first months to chart the course I could aptly use in sharing the biblical message in a long-term fashion. After charting that course I shared my plan with the Mass Communications board members during our annual meeting in 1977. In actuality, what I laid out before them was a five-year plan which included my choice of biblical books to be treated on the air: 1977, sermons based on texts in Genesis; 1978, sermons based on texts in the Acts of the Apostles; 1979, sermons based on texts in Hebrews; 1980, sermons based on texts in Romans; 1981, sermons based on the Book of Revelation. Those sermons were projected for the fall season, and the rest of the year was to be used for spot sermons, situational messages, emphases related to the Christian Year, and at least two to four spots for guest preachers—notably Dr. Dale Oldham and Dr. R. Eugene Sterner.

I began and followed the five-year plan I laid out. The results and comments from the field were gratifying. Lacking the time on the air that is usually available during a "live" service in a sanctuary, I worked for condensation and focus in shaping the expositional sermons I delivered each fall. I worked steadily to ensure a perennial tie-in between biblical truth and contemporary concerns, using biblical books that I knew could spark interest, sustain interest, and give pointed help.

The series based on Genesis was the first expositional series and I drew all of the materials for those sermons from Genesis 49. The unannounced caption for the series was "The Sons of Jacob and the Children of God." There was no announcement that a series was forthcoming. Each sermon stood alone, but

323

those who listened weekly began to see that all the sermons were based on that single chapter and treated one of the sons of Jacob. I began in that way in order to test the audience response to a series, and the receptive response confirmed my intention to preach a planned series each fall.

Public request for selected sermons always encouraged me, and those requests remained steady across my years as Speaker. A CBH sermon was always part of each issue of *Vital Christianity;* this was a courtesy and tradition dating back to the earliest years of the broadcast when Dr. W. Dale Oldham was the Speaker. The CBH sermon was viewed as a means of Christian outreach, so it was requested from the Speaker for inclusion in the church's journal, and the CBH speaker was listed as one of the journal's contributing editors. Thus it was that many of my CBH sermons appeared in *Vital Christianity,* while many others were made available in mimeograph print to those who requested them through the CBH office. A full manuscript was always available to the duplication process and to *Vital Christianity* because I always prepared and worked from a written text when recording a sermon for the broadcast.

Writing out a sermon was not new to me. That was my disciplined way since my beginning years in the pastorate. It was my way to plan for order and movement, on the one hand, and to guard against lack of content and memory slip, on the other. Writing out the sermon was also helpful in timing my pulpit work, and it afforded me the benefit of controlled speech. This was my customary preparation to preach in the "live" setting of a gathered congregation, and it proved essential in preparing to preach on radio. These are indeed different mediums, to be sure, but it is possible so to plan and deliver a written sermon that even a recorded program can convey a spontaneity and impact normally expected only in a live audience context. For me, the written sermon was especially crucial when preaching on the radio because timing the layout of the message is crucial to the time allotted. Across many years, in both live settings and before the radio microphone, I have dis-

covered that intimacy between speaker and listener can be experienced, even guaranteed, if the content, style, tone, and appeal
are aptly planned, projected, and blessed by the anointing presence of God.

I can honestly report that, although I worked always from a
prepared script, I usually felt a spontaneity while recording my
sermons for radio. The microphone in front of me represented
unnamed, unnumbered, and unseen listeners for whom I had
planned and prayed, but the presence of the recording engineer
sitting before me on the other side of the windowed wall
between us kept me with the sense of a "live" occasion in
process. The whole involvement stirred me considerably
and kept my system tuned with a sense of aliveness and
spontaneity, eager always to present the message with clarity,
conviction, and appealing application.

Honoring a request from Dr. Arlo F. Newell, editor of *Vital
Christianity* and editor in chief of Warner Press publications, I
gathered selected sermons from the terms of my predecessors
and my own which then were used to form a book Warner Press
published in 1980 as *The Christian Brotherhood Hour Pulpit.*
Lest the work Newell requested of me seem self-serving (since
some of my sermons were included in the volume), I suggested
to Newell that Maurice Berquist should be asked to edit the
collection. He agreed and Berquist did so. Using eight sermons
each from Oldham, Sterner, and me, Berquist edited the volume
and wrote an introduction for the book. One of my CBH
sermons used in the book, *Something of Value,* had earlier
claimed the attention of James W. Cox, editor of *Pulpit Digest,*
as he was planning an issue of that journal, and he wrote for my
permission to include that sermon in the September-October
1978 issue. Cox later used that sermon again, with permission,
in Volume II of his edited series on *The Twentieth Century
Pulpit* (Abingdon Press, 1981). In a biographical note to
introduce the sermon in his book, James Cox, himself a noted
historian and teacher of preaching at Southern Baptist
Theological Seminary, commended that sermon as "characterized

by evangelical warmth, theological insight, and exegetical thoroughness. . .couched in graphic language in an easily understood style." These are the qualities I always sought in preparing a sermon to be preached. I make no claim that I always succeeded in my quest, but I do claim to have diligently pursued these results.

It was our office custom to send a special Christmas gift each year to persons listed as our special contributors, those who had given $250 dollars or more to the program across the year. Early in 1980 I decided on something special that I myself would prepare for them. I had already written several books that were sent as give-aways, so I did not want to write another book for our contributors. I decided to produce for them a cassette record of my piano playing. I chose a set of chorale preludes from the vast output of Johann Sebastian Bach. Although using a modern Baldwin grand piano while recording the pieces, I even managed at points to simulate harpsichord sonorities for a few of those preludes. I was looking both within and upwards as I made that recording, sharing my soul as I played. When I completed the recording session I taped an introductory statement to call attention to the religious sentiment out of which Bach shaped his musical creations. Preparing and sending that Christmas gift to friends and supporters of our broadcast gave me great pleasure indeed!

The tapes from my CBH years are a humbling part of the record of my ministry. I say "humbling" because the sermons on those tapes are period pieces, occasional messages, each one linked with specific times and concerns, and inevitably flavored by human limitations. Preaching has never been a simple activity for me, and it has never been a merely calculated action on my part. After probing Scripture in relation to some human need, I always sought for simplicity in shaping my utterance. There was some calculation as I did this, to be sure, but it was planning for a proper choice of words, an apt sentence style, essential sequence, and an appealing application of the message. Like every other speaker, I have been dependent upon words, knowing, however, that words properly chosen and rightly handled can be effective agents when blessed by God's Spirit. The choice of every subject I developed and the way I chose to treat that subject was influenced by a strict concern to speak the Word of God to human need. In reality, hearers experience a speaker's message on two levels: at one level understanding is gained, while at a deeper level realization occurs. I preached each message with concern to be understood, trusting God to bless the hearer with realization, an inward seeing, out of which decision and action take place.

Whatever peaks and valleys appear in the taped record of my preaching on Christian Brotherhood Hour, every sermon I delivered was my own, and not borrowed from someone else. Each one was a statement from my soul, a witness of my faith, a public record of my findings and personal reflections from my pilgrimage in grace. In each sermon I tried to say what needed to be said and to say it in the interest of human good, say it on the authority of revealed Scripture truth, and say it to the glory of God.

I was amazed again and again by the "coincidental" (nay, providential) connection in timing between some of my sermon themes and public events. During the Lenten season of 1978, for instance, I preached a sermon about the forgiven thief being admitted into Paradise along with Jesus. During that same week a major television network aired a widely-viewed movie about life after death. As another instance, for the Lenten season of 1979 I projected, prepared, and taped a sermon on "God and Our Errors," a sermon based on the prayer of Jesus to God, "Father, forgive them; for they know not what they do" (Luke 23:34). During the week after that sermon was aired the news broke about a massive mechanical failure that caused a nuclear accident at the Three Mile Island nuclear plant near Harrisburg, Pennsylvania. It was the worst nuclear accident in the history of the country. In addition to that was the current showing of the movie "The China Syndrome," a film about a fictional (but possible) nuclear mishap. The message is still relevant: We humans need more than our own freedom and presumed wisdom in living our lives, because we are mistake-prone, with sinning the greatest and gravest human mistake because, in addition to displeasing God, it also produces results we cannot foresee.

I have listed these instances not to suggest any prescience on my part in preparing sermons, but rather to accent my openness to God for needed guidance as I worked at ministering to people by national and international radio.

One Friday afternoon, while busy reading mail that had gathered during my vacation, a young seminary student stopped in to see me. He wanted to inform me about a glad happening in his family. While driving home one Saturday afternoon that July, his wife and mother-in-law in the car with him, he happened to catch our CBH broadcast for that week, with its sermon on John 3:16, "God Wants You Saved!" The student told me that the three of them stopped talking in order to hear the message, and that when they reached home his mother-in-law said to him, "I accepted salvation while riding along in the car today, while the sermon was being preached." Then she added, "I had wanted to be saved for a long time, but in hearing the message about it today, the desire deepened and I accepted salvation. The preacher made it so clear and plain." That news gladdened me and I felt greatly strengthened. I thanked the student for coming and had prayer with him. Interestingly, he also told me that it was the first time his mother-in-law had heard our radio program.

I maintained my ties with ecumenical and academic settings during my years as CBH-Speaker. I wanted to do so, needed to do so, and was permitted to do so. After my first year with the broadcast I felt free to teach an occasional undergraduate or seminary class on the Anderson campus located just across the street from my office at the Mass Communications Board. After that first year I also felt free to honor invitations to be a commencement speaker or to do some named lectureship. I honored two long-standing commitments for which I had already prepared, in 1977, my first year as Speaker, when I went to Asbury Theological Seminary to give the Freitas Lectures and to Gordon-Conwell Theological Seminary to lecture there. I returned to Asbury in 1980 to give a commencement address.

The year 1980 turned out to be a rather busy one. That year I not only returned to Asbury as commencment speaker, I was also Rall Lecturer at Garrett-Evangelical Theological Seminary, published *Concerning Christian Unity* (Warner Press), one of eight books released in the Church of God Doctrinal Library series to commemorate the centennial of the Church of God Reformation Movement, and edited and published the *CBH Study Bible* (Nashville: Thomas Nelson Co), which was an edition of the King James Version, with special articles and study helps prepared by a team of biblical scholars I chose for the project. My book *Designing the Sermon* (Abingdon Press, 1980) was released in 1980, and I went as a delegate to the World Congress on Evangelization held in Pattaya, Thailand, that year. *Designing the Sermon* was a textbook on preaching that I was asked to write for "The Abingdon Preacher's Library," a new series of volumes to meet the demand of the times for new resources which could, in the words of William D. Thompson, general editor for the series, "serve the practicing preacher whose background in homiletics is spotty or out-of-date, or whose preaching needs strengthening in some specific area."

In 1981 I went to Southern Baptist Theological Seminary to give the Mullins Lectures on Preaching. My gracious host was James W. Cox, head of the preaching department there. While at Southern I met, among others, Timothy George, a brilliant young professor of church history who had newly-received his Harvard doctorate. Professor George happily informed me that my voice was a familiar and treasured one to him because he listened regularly to CBH. He thanked me for my sermons, kindly describing them as "evangelical morsels upon which [he had] fed each week as a heart-hungry doctoral student at

Harvard Divinity School." Our paths crossed often in later years, and I was privileged to be a program participant in the installation service when Dr. George became founding dean of Beeson Divinity School at Samford University in Birmingham, Alabama. In 1982, during my last year with CBH, I went to Eastern Baptist Theological Seminary in Philadelphia and delivered the Swartley Lectures.

I enjoyed ministering as a broadcaster, and I felt at home in that service role, but my fondness for teaching and lecturing made me know that I could not remain only in broadcasting. I knew this when I accepted the broadcast assignment, which is why I never severed my ties with the academic world. Also, my commitment to further the cause of Christian unity kept me open and eager for a continuing ecumenical outreach as well.

On Mission in Australia

In 1978 Gwendolyn and I were in Australia during part of July and nearly all of August. We were not vacationing there and I was not on assignment for CBH. I was there by invitation of the Uniting Churches in Australia to conduct a preaching mission in some of their congregations and to assess the progress of a church union effort between the Congregational Union of Australia, The Methodist Church of Australia, and The Presbyterian Church of Australia. Since 1957 these three church bodies had shared in the work of the Joint Commission on Church Union (of the World Council of Churches) and in June, 1977, they were united in a formal service as "The Uniting Church in Australia," the third largest church body in Australia but the first indigenous church formed there. The new grouping consisted of 1,700,000 members in 1,000 parishes, with about 2,400 ordained clergy serving them. I was approached in 1976 and asked to be present at that inaugural service in June, 1977, as one of the speakers, but I could not accept the invitation because I had just been ratified as CBH-Speaker-Elect, with my term to begin on July 1, 1977. The inviting group respected my problem, but asked if I would be willing to come in 1978 to assess the progress of their union. I agreed to come if my new schedule of work would allow it. By November of 1977 it seemed clear that I would be able to go to Australia in 1978 and serve as requested.

Gwendolyn and I left the United States on July 26 and returned on August 24. Our host, with whom I corresponded during the planning, was Dr. Gloster Udy, senior minister at the Parramatta Regional Mission in Sydney. I held preaching-teaching missions in the two states of Queensland and New South Wales, with daily services first in Brisbane (July 29-August 4), then in Sydney (the Parramatta section, the oldest part of the city) from August 6-11, and finally in Canberra (Australia's capital city) from August 12-20. Our host in Brisbane was The Rev. Rex Smith; in Sydney, Dr. Gloster G. Udy; in Canberra, The Rev. Harry S. Westcott. Morning sessions in each place allowed me to interact with pastors and their wives in Bible study, and before preaching in the evening mass meetings in each place I conducted an hour of Bible study for laypersons.

The meeting in Canberra began on a rather humorous note. When I arrived at Pastor Westcott's church he told me that the layperson in charge of church publicity had had a problem preparing the flyers to advertise the services. He had worked diligently with my photo in his darkroom trying to "get it right" for the printed flyer, but "it wouldn't come right!" He reported this to Pastor Westcott and lamented, "I'm sorry, but our flyers will not have a picture of the preacher from America. I don't know what went wrong, but I just can't get his picture to brighten up. It keeps coming out dark!" Pastor Westcott began laughing when he heard that, and told the young cameraman, "The picture should come out dark because the speaker is not only American, he's a Black American!"

I met and interacted with many Australian youth during a special Youth Rally at which I spoke, and I had the pleasure of meeting the Mayor of Parramatta and some of the local politicians at a reception for me while in Australia's "cradle city." A memento from that occasion is a book the Mayor presented to me titled *The Cradle City of Australia: A History of Parramatta 1788-1961,* written by James Jervis (1978).

The meetings were all well-publicized and well-attended. The mission received wide coverage through radio and the daily press. The wide reception I received allowed leaders and members of the Church of God in Australia to benefit from my publicized identification as our church's world-wide broadcast Speaker. In 1978 there were three congregations of the Church of God (Anderson, Indiana, USA) in Australia, and Dr. Gloster Udy set apart some time for me to meet with their leaders. He graciously hosted several of them at a dinner, at which time Gwendolyn and I shared food and fellowship with our three American missionary couples there: Jack and Bonnie Dunn, leaders of the Canley Heights Church; Andrew and Rebecca New, leaders of the Surfer's Paradise Church; and Kenneth and Sue Jo Good, who were with the Australian Bible Training School, over which Kenneth was director. I also met Lloyd Chilver, an ordained Australian minister working full-time for the Association of the Church of God and editor and printer of the group's bi-monthly paper called the *Gospel Trumpet.*

Shortly before leaving the United States for Australia I received a letter from The Rt. Rev. A. Jack Dain, Anglican Bishop of Sydney, whom I knew from our membership on the Lausanne Committee on World Evangelization. I had recently corresponded with Leighton Ford, a mutual friend and fellow member of the Lausanne Committee, regarding my acceptance of reappointment to the Committee, and in my reply I mentioned to him my schedule of activities for the year. Leighton Ford wrote to let Dain know that I would be in Australia during the summer, so the Bishop sent me the following letter:

29th March 1978

My Dear James:

Leighton has shared with me your mutual correspondence of February of this year, mentioning your preaching missions in Australia in August. I note that these are being organized by the Uniting Churches in Australia, and I am delighted to hear that you are coming to Parramatta and I do hope that it will be possible for us to meet and have lunch together. I am writing to Dr. Gloster Udy expressing hope that it might be possible for us to have a lunch-time kept free for this purpose and if there is any way in which I can personally help please do not hesitate to let me know.

We are moving into top gear for our preparations for the 1979 Graham Crusade here in Sydney in which I am glad to say all the major Churches are co-operating, some of course to a greater extent than others. May God bless you richly in your continuing ministry.

Yours very sincerely,
/s/ A. J. Dain

As a result of his kind invitation, plus the good planning of my host, Bishop Dain and I did meet for lunch. We reminisced about previous meetings, discussed my impressions about ministering to Australians, and ended our time together in a spirit of prayer for the rest of my time in Australia and for the plans being made for the anticipated Graham Crusade there in 1979.

In November, 1977, several months before my trip to Australia was publicized, a letter came to me from Alfred S. Jorgensen, Field Secretary for the Australasian Division of the Seventh-Day Adventist Church, located in Sydney. Jorgensen had sent me a copy of a review of my book *The Sermon in Perspective* that he had written for the *Australasian Record* (November 28, 1977). His letter reported:

My Dear Doctor Massey:

I was recently requested by the editor of one of our Australian church papers to review your recent book, *The Sermon In Perspective.* I am enclosing for you a copy of my review. Let me add to what I wrote in the review that I greatly appreciated your book and I only hope that I may have the privilege some day of possibly having a few moments fellowship with you.

With my Christian greetings,
Yours in the service of our common Lord,
/s/ Alfred S. Jorgensen

I wrote and thanked Dr. Jorgensen for his kind letter and for the appreciative review. After appropriate thanks, I added:

How interesting that your letter should reach me as my plans are being finalized for a trip to Australia! As it now stands, I am committed to a preaching mission (3 weeks) there from July 30 through August 20, 1978. I will be a guest of the Uniting Churches of Australia, preaching one week in Brisbane (Sunday, July 30th, through Friday), then in Parramatta for the second week, then in Canberra for the third week. Perhaps we can meet together after all. I would be delighted to make your acquaintance and have an extended talk with you. Let us pray to that end.

Dr. Jorgensen and I did meet, and the meeting took place during an ecumenical gathering of church leaders from several denominational groups across Sydney. Gloster Udy hosted the meeting. I felt especially blessed by the open reception I experienced on the part of so many Christian leaders that day; and the fact that many of them at such great distance were familiar with my major writings made me all the more eager to keep the wider church always in view in my writing as well as speaking.

During the major meeting I had with clergy of the Uniting Churches in Australia, held on a university campus, I shared my impressions of the progress of their union—three weeks of ministry in two of their states and several of their churches had helped to inform me—and I encouraged them in their togetherness. The 1971 "Basis for Union" paper had been reasonable and relevant and, although about forty percent of the Presbyterians and about nineteen percent of the Congregationalists had not chosen to enter the Uniting Church in 1977, I applauded those who did. My travels among the churches and my talks with their leaders made me sense their will for a life together, and I believed that they would continue to work at equal representation on committees and to reduce areas of friction from procedural differences. I restated the meaning and function of ministry, intent to help the clergy focus anew on what life and order in the church were originally about, and what these should be about in their time and place. I later learned that Dr. Philip Potter, General Secretary of the World Council of Churches, also dealt with the commitment to unity theme the year before when he was speaker for their inaugural union service.

The mission month in Australia was taxing, but I returned home in full strength and with a sense of having been divinely guided. As I plunged into the tasks that awaited me, the mail I received daily from friends in Australia strengthened me. The following portion of what Dr. Gloster S. Udy wrote was representative of many other letters:

Dear Brother Massey:

What a great privilege it was for us to have you in our midst in Parramatta as well as available to the other Churches you served so significantly in Brisbane and Canberra. I can only speak in terms of real appreciation from our people: there have been many references to your ministry and the very wonderful choice of topics has cropped up again and again.

Thank you also for the delight and joy which was ours in having your gracious wife with you. We did appreciate your willingness to be involved in a variety of activities and already people are talking about your return.... I imagine that once you know your schedule for 1981 that if we could have an idea of times when you may be available that this would be greatly appreciated by us as we make preliminary arrangements for another visit.

More than anything else I would like to express gratitude to you for the way in which right across our different groups here in Parramatta you were so wonderfully received. If you don't mind I would like to put in a request for three years time and that is that perhaps you might take the exposition of Romans 8 again. That can really stand repeating.

With best wishes to you and your good wife,

Yours fraternally,
/s/ Gloster S. Udy

Despite the warm invitation, which was repeated, I did not get to return to Australia in 1981.

Other Activities

Shortly after our Australia mission Gwendolyn was asked to become Coordinator of Refugee and Relief Services for the Church of God. Our recent trip and its results, however, had nothing to do with that request.

As the decade of the 1970s closed, Church of God congregations were seeking to respond to some of the special needs in the wider world, one of which was disaster relief. Our churches responded with gifts of support for victims of the earthquake in Guatemala, for example, where we had a sizable church membership. We also sent help to Lebanon, another area of our concern, where a civil war was raging. In addition to contributing to a disaster fund, our congregations in America also began supporting a sponsorship and relocation program for refugees. Gwendolyn accepted responsibility for coordinating these activities for the Church of God and worked in partnership with other church bodies engaged in these services, particularly the Church World Service Immigration and Refugee Program Committee of which she was a member. An article in the November 4, 1979, issue of *Vital Christianity,* captioned "Massey Administers Refugee Program," highlighted and explained her role and task.

Involvement in relief and rehabilitation work was not new to my wife. There was in her background the experience of many years as a senior public health nurse in Detroit, and since our move to Anderson in 1969 she had served on several boards related to health and public relief: the Center for Mental Health, the Madison County Welfare Board (vice-president), the YWCA, and the United Way. As coordinator for Refugee and Relief Services for the Church of God, this work involved Gwendolyn in contacts with leaders and congregations across the nation and with displaced persons from abroad. Her responsibilities were structured within the Missionary Board of the Church of God, which meant much committee work and frequent trips both within and beyond our national borders. Given the scope of her work, and mine, there were some weekends when she and I had to take flights going in very separate directions from each other.

Although busily engaged in the arena of church life, I did not lack or neglect opportunities to serve in the public arena. My life in Anderson was not all educational while teaching at the college and it was not all religious while I was CBH-Speaker. I was still active on the Anderson Civil Service Merit Commission to which I was elected in 1976, serving first as its secretary before becoming its president in 1978. The Anderson Civil Service Merit Commission was established in May of 1975 to work with the police department of the City to insure that police business (testing, evaluating, promoting, and demoting) would be handled without political bias. There were clear rules and regulations by which this objective was to be carried out, and our handling of that process was monitored by the Indiana University School of Public and Environmental Affairs. At the time, there were 147 sworn police officers in the city's employ. Political favoritism had been exercised before the creation of our Commission, with periodic disorder and low morale among the officers and between officers and appointed leaders. Our work as commissioners helped to restore respect, a smoother functioning within the staff, higher morale, and better relations between the police and the public.

The Commission consisted of five members. Two were appointed by the Mayor, two by the police department, and the fifth person was chosen by the four others. The regulations stipulated that the five members were to be different as to profession, business, and occupation: one was to be professional in medicine, dentistry, or law; one was to hold a degree in teaching; one was to hold a degree in theology; one was to be from the field of business or management; and one was to be a labor union representative. I "came on board" from the teaching field, and was the fifth member chosen by the other four: William Anderson, M.D., Father M.A. McClure, William C. Vilcsek, and Michael Oleksy. There were inevitable changes on the Commission through expiring terms or when a member resigned for personal reasons. Some who became commissioners after the terms of our charter members expired were Gordon Brattain, Leo Moss, William Coffey, The Rev. Dr. Nathan Harter, and Charles Henderson.

Both the police and the public benefited from our Commission work because better morale among police led to better public service and better relations with the public. Our monthly meetings were open to the public and our decisions were publicized in the newspapers. Minutes from the public meetings were on record with the Safety Board, the Police Department, and the Mayor's Office. Our Commission operated with concern for honesty, fairness, credibility, integrity, and the public good. There were times when we made an unpopular decision, and as Commission president I felt the heat. Having followed our guidelines, however, I never felt threatened or embarrassed when our decisions were questioned by someone from the police department or the public square. During my tenure as a member and as its president, the Anderson Civil Service Merit Commission dealt with facts as well as persons, and "merit" was the operative factor when any decision had to be made.

1980: The Church of God Centennial Year

In June, 1980, when the Church of God Centennial was being observed in Anderson during the yearly International Convention, I was not present for the occasion. I was in Pattaya, Thailand, a delegate at another World Congress on Evangelization being held there. Conversations there with delegates from Europe, some of them from countries behind the Iron Curtain, helped me to appreciate the opportunity radio afforded us to reach territories that were otherwise "off-limits," especially broadcasting entities such as Trans-World Radio. I also had opportunity to talk at length one afternoon with Dr. Robert H. Schuller, the Garden Grove (California) pastor whose weekly "Hour of Power" telecast had made his a household name. Among other things, we exchanged impressions about Australia, where he had recently been a guest speaker.

Although I was not present for our church's centennial activities in Anderson, I had worked with several others in contributing to that event. Mention has been made already about *The Christian Brotherhood Hour Pulpit,* the *CBH Study Bible* which I edited for release that year, and my book *Concerning Christian Unity,* which was one in an eight-volume Church of God Doctrinal Library series that Warner Press released for the centennial.

Later that year, in November, I shared in a celebration of the centennial held in Michigan. I was a guest of the Church of God in Michigan, and had been invited back because, as the letter from Gale Hetrick explained, "You are among those who have made a significant contribution to the development of the Church of God in Michigan," and because I, along with Marvin J. Hartman (another Michigan native working at the national level), was part of "Michigan's contribution to national leadership in the Church of God."

In one of his letters to me about the upcoming event in Michigan, Hetrick recalled my involvement in 1968 when the Michigan Assembly built its "Service Center" (the first administrative building among our many state assemblies) and reminded me that I led the Litany of Dedication when the building was dedicated. I was Chairman-elect of the Assembly that year. I was told that the Church's centennial event in Michigan would include a service of rededication, and I was asked to participate and give the prayer of rededication. Gwendolyn and I returned to Michigan for the event. The Prayer of Rededication I prepared and offered was as follows:

> God of our weary years, God of our silent tears,
> Thou who hast blessed us thus far on our way;
> Thou who hast by Thy might, Led us into the light,
> Keep us forever in the path, We pray.
>
> For those who have gone before us, We thank Thee:
> They taught us, we learned, and believed;
> They labored, and we have entered into their labors.
>
> For those who are now with us, We praise Thee:
> They trust and love us; We trust and love them;
> They share themselves, and We are being blessed thereby.
>
> For those who will come after us, We intercede to Thee:
> We ask that they will be wise, resourceful,
> appreciative, and responsible.

We rededicate ourselves now,
That the work they will inherit from us will be strong,
and the path we cut will be clear,
and the example we set will be holy.

This is our concern and our prayer
To Thee, our God and Guide.
And we ask it all, with thanksgiving,
In the strong Name of Jesus Christ.
AMEN, AMEN.

A Mentor Passes

In early April, 1981, during Holy Week, I was in Detroit as guest Bible teacher at Friendship Baptist Church, where my friend Louis Johnson was pastor. I was doing a series of studies from the Letter to the Hebrews. Although when I became CBH-Speaker I restricted my appearance at local churches to weekends, I had made an exception this time because I knew it would be Holy Week, that period in the Church Year I have long favored above all others, and a local church setting was the place I wanted to be during that week.

News reached me on Friday, April 10, before I left for Detroit, that earlier that day Dr. Howard Thurman had died. After reaching Detroit I learned that Mrs. Thurman wanted me to take part in the ceremony of burial. Armed with that information, I asked Louis to release me from my commitment after teaching on Tuesday night so that I could fly to San Francisco on Wednesday to be present for the Memorial service on Thursday, April 16. Fully understanding, Louis graciously released me. Mrs. Thurman and I had conversed by phone during her husband's last days. The week before his death I asked her if she thought it might be of some comfort if I made a trip to see him. She replied that she really did not think so, adding, "unless he comes back this way." Dr. Thurman was in a coma. She also voiced thanks to me for "that young man of yours," meaning Dr. Thomas Hignell, the physician who after attending

Dr. Thurman in the hospital had visited him at the house often, assisting as needed.

It was Dr. Hignell who met me at the airport when I arrived in San Francisco and drove me to the Thurman home. Mrs. Thurman explained that her husband's body would be cremated after the funeral, and she wanted Kelly Miller Smith and me to conduct a private service for the family and selected friends just before the body was released to the cremation process. Smith and I agreed, and we then went over to Fellowship Church where the body of Dr. Thurman was lying in state. There we found Jesse Jackson and several others gathered.

A vast crowd was present for the memorial service on Thursday, and the order of service was replete with tributes and personal reflections from colleagues personal and professional who all spoke at their best. Dr. Thomas Hignell was one of the pallbearers. After the service, as Hignell and the other pallbearers carried the coffin from the church to the hearse, I was still reflecting on the impact of Dr. Thurman's life on mine and the many surprises of grace which had come my way because of his caring presence and friendship across more than thirty years. I thought also about the change and growth that had taken place in Tom Hignell because of his contact with "Dr. T.," first through my books, then providentially in-person during Dr. Thurman's last illness.

Howard Thurman was a constituted spokesman, a man readied by insight and outlook to share himself and his sense of reality with others, a man who could relate with full openness to people because he was fully open to God and life. The memorial service that Thursday highlighted aspects of Dr. Thurman's life, which was expected, but it was during the private service of committal on Friday morning when I felt the "balm of Gilead" blessing my spirit. Those of us who spoke personally to the family did so as family members ourselves, and we experienced an intimacy that only family members know. Paradoxically, my experience of that final service helped me gain a sense of closure, even while my heart was feeling a greater openness. Somehow, even my mentor's death was influencing my life.

Later in 1981, Margo Royer, my secretary, stepped into my office to inform me that someone was waiting on the telephone to speak to me from Washington, D.C. When I picked up the receiver the caller notified me that the call was on behalf of President Ronald Reagan, and that the President had expressed interest in having me consider accepting chairmanship of the U.S. Civil Rights Commission. Although I knew about the vacancy created when Father Theodore Hesburgh left the Commission, I was surprised that my name had been forwarded to the President's attention as a possible replacement. I listened intently as the caller detailed some specifics listed in some report about me, specific things which he suggested made me a preferred candidate. The caller then proceeded to mention some details about the work of a commission member, and how an alert and informed chairman was needed to forward the Commission's tasks.

I had not spoken much during the time on the phone, but the caller continued to talk. After a rather full and even florid statement, the caller finally asked if I had any interest in accepting such an appointment if it were offered. Before I could respond, however, he went on to explain that being chairperson for the Commission would not mean having to give up my work at CBH, and that I would not have to be in Washington every day since there was requisite assistance already provided for the daily management of that office. But one aspect of the caller's report raised the "red flag" as I listened. He knew that I was a registered Democrat and asked if I would be willing to become a Republican in order to satisfy the President's concerns. I knew then that our conversation need go no further. I reasoned that the United States Civil Rights Commission should operate strictly on principle, independent of political interference. I also knew that Father Hesburgh had resigned from the Commission because of interference from politicians. I therefore had no interest in the post being discussed. Not long afterward,

President Reagan appointed and secured approval of Clarence M. (Penny) Pendleton to chair the Commission. Pendleton was a black Republican from California, a leader who had served as Executive Director of the Urban League in San Diego.

Tenured Professor

The year 1981 was an inopportune time for me to make a return trip to Australia. The Mass Communications Board was busy that year preparing to produce a television special, and a great deal of time, attention, and travel was being devoted to that project. In addition to that, in July of 1981 I was into my fifth year as CBH-Speaker and had decided that I would not seek another term. Several colleges and seminaries had invited me to accept a full-time professorship, and I knew what my heart was saying about my future. Anderson College made one of those offers, and I accepted President Reardon's invitation to return there as Professor of New Testament and Preaching in the School of Theology, with tenure. By agreement between the college administration and our Mass Communications Board, I began my seminary duties that September and completed my final CBH year concurrently with my teaching assignment. The search for someone to succeed me as Speaker began immediately after I informed the board that I would not seek another term with CBH.

The local newspapers in Anderson gave generous reporting about my return to the campus. The *Anderson Daily Bulletin* was first with three columns in its July 6, 1981, report, "Radio Speaker Rejoins Theology Staff" (p. 10), and the *Anderson Herald* for July 11, 1981, ran four columns of text under the caption "Massey Returning To Teach at AC" (p. 5). *Vital Christianity* gave a report about my return to campus in the August 23, 1981, issue.

When the news spread that I had decided not to accept another term as Speaker of the Christian Brotherhood Hour, the reactions were mixed, and rumors about the reasons behind my decision were many and muddled. Nearly everywhere I went to preach during that last year I was pressed by interested questioners who wanted to know why I would not be continuing on the broadcast. Most of the whites who raised that question with me talked appreciatively about what my witness on radio had meant to them, and several pastors informed me about how that witness had helped their contacts with leaders of other church groups. Many blacks who raised the question with me would not believe that I was leaving CBH out of pure choice; they asked if I had been made uncomfortable, whether undue circumstances had pressed me into deciding to leave. I told them all, "No!" Despite my clear and honest statement, some persons found it hard to believe that my decision to leave CBH had not been forced in some way.

I had taught part-time on the Anderson campus across my term as Speaker. This had kept me connected with classroom work, and I had continued reading in my teaching field. From 1969-1975 I held the rank of Assistant Professor of Religious Studies. I was promoted to Associate Professor in 1975 and was holding that rank when I left the college to serve CBH. I returned to campus in September, 1981, full-time with the rank of full Professor, with tenure, to fill the New Testament chair Dr. Boyce W. Blackwelder was holding at the time of his death in 1976, and which Dr. Harold L. Phillips had filled after his retirement in 1977 as editor in chief at Warner Press. Blackwelder had occupied the chair of New Testament for fourteen years, succeeding Dr. Louis F. Gough, who resigned to become president of Warner Pacific College. In 1981 I returned to campus to succeed Phillips who was relinquishing the post. I had been notified almost a year earlier that the New Testament chair would need to be filled when Harold Phillips ended his teaching term in June, 1981. Phillips had been there for four years, temporarily handling the New Testament courses because of Blackwelder's unexpected and untimely death. The year before Phillips undertook teaching those courses, Gustav Jeeninga and I had been responsible for them, in addition to our regular class loads. We did not mind it, however, because an emergency situation had to be addressed.

In 1980, Dr. Barry L. Callen, School of Theology dean at the time, wrote to ask if I would consider taking the post. I later met with Dean Callen, President Reardon, and Robert A. Nicholson, dean of the college, at their request. The three administrators jointly highlighted the importance of the seminary's New Testament chair in the educating of ministers, and the three suggested that my gifts and training were what the post required. Our discussion was confidential at that time, so I said nothing to anyone about the meeting. It interested me that all three administrators were in agreement that I was the person to take the New Testament chair, and they stated that they were ready to seal an agreement with me whenever I was ready to make one. At the time of that meeting I was not prepared to do so. I still had another year as Speaker on the Christian Brotherhood Hour. Not long afterward, however, I decided to accept their offer, and I informed the Mass Communications Board about my plan to leave CBH when my term ended in June, 1982. Pleased with my decision, President Reardon asked me to deliver the 1981 commencement address at Anderson College. I did. That Fall, concurrent with my last year at CBH, I began my tenure at Anderson College School of Theology as Professor of New Testament and Preaching.

I spent five years (plus a few months) as Speaker on Christian Brotherhood Hour. As I entered into my new academic assignment while concluding my role as radio minister, I was satisfied that I had given the radio ministry my best. I had served the church in general, I had served many individual congregations in particular, and I had even served a few para-church and inter-church agencies in some specific ways. While Speaker of CBH I had participated in significant ways in several annual conventions of the National Religious Broadcasters. I was elected to membership on the NRB Board of Directors while Dr. Ben Armstrong was the organization's executive director, and I remained an active director during the administration of his successor, Dr. Brandt Gustavson.

In January, 1978, I had addressed a general session during the National Religious Broadcasters thirty-fifth annual convention. On that occasion Brandt Gustavson, who was then NRB president, introduced me. As he did so, however, he made an embarrassing blunder. With so much on his mind as the convention began, and with so much still in the news at that time about the man accused of assassinating Dr. Martin Luther King, Jr., Gustavson slipped during his introduction and presented me as James Earl Ray! He realized his mistake almost immediately because as I strode toward the podium he seemed frozen there. Red-faced, he turned toward me, then exclaimed, "I meant to say, James Earl Massey!" I was smiling as I gave Gustavson my hand, and he softly pleaded, "Oh! I'm so sorry! Sooo...sorry!" Still smiling, I waited for the mild laughter among the delegates to subside and then began addressing them.

Later in 1978 I gave the keynote address at the Midwest Regional meeting of the National Religious Broadcasters in Indianapolis, Indiana. When my term on the CBH broadcast ended four years later, I was still being reminded about how, earlier, I was mistakenly introduced, but those who spoke to me about that also spoke appreciatively about the substance of the addresses I had delivered during several conventions. My term as one of the NRB directors extended two years beyond my service at CBH, and I continued my activities within and for the organization until my term expired.

As I left the CBH broadcast in 1982, I had been faithful to a grand assignment and I knew that I had given a needed witness. When the spring semester closed at the seminary, I went to Boston to take some graduate course work in the summer term at Boston College Graduate School. After a very brief vacation, I then went to fulfill a longstanding request to serve as the summer term's Visiting Professor of Preaching at Princeton Theological Seminary and to preach in the Princeton University Chapel.

Three Deaths

In 1983 three persons died whose leaving left gaping holes in my life. Dr. Raymond S. Jackson, the pastor who mentored and ordained me, died on January 29, 1983. He succumbed to cancer after a long struggle to contain its growth. Jackson was within two months of his ninety-first birthday when he died at his home in Detroit. My mother died on February 12, 1983. She was seventy-nine when her end came, two months short of her eightieth birthday, and only a few days short of Valentine's day which would have marked my parents' sixtieth wedding anniversary. My father died on October 11, 1983, eight months after my mother died, and just two months short of reaching his eighty-seventh year of life.

Under the double weight of bereavement and the entrusted responsibility to plan and officiate at each of the three funerals, I felt terribly diminished. Both Raymond S. Jackson and my mother had been ill for some time, but my father had not shown any obvious physical signs of approaching his end until very late. Each death stirred treasured memories stored deep within my memory bank, and vast stretches of my past opened to my view as I fumblingly dealt with my grief.

It was an almost distressing experience as I periodically visited with Raymond S. Jackson during the last months of his life. I say "almost distressing" because it pained me deeply to see him struggle so long with the problem of his self-image as one who preached about the healing power of God and now was the victim of an unchecked cancerous growth in his body. Jackson wanted so desperately to experience a healing, but it did not happen for him, and this left him deeply troubled. He had several stays in the hospital, and each stay became a longer one until it became evident that hospice care was needed. I drove from Anderson to Detroit several times to visit my esteemed mentor, and we talked to each other out of deep levels of trust and regard. Near the end, Jackson could not talk anymore, and his eyesight failed, but he still appeared sufficiently alert to recognize and distinguish my voice and presence from any others.

I recall our last two-way conversation. Jackson had been released to go home to die in his own bed. I could see that his spirit had flagged, that he was deep in the doldrums and needed to be encouraged. I remember how his eyes were turned toward me as we talked, and I shall never forget the pleading look on his face, as if he was seeking any help I could offer in that situation of unanswered questioning about why God had not seen fit to heal him. I sensed Jackson's appeal for help, so I began talking gently about what his life and ministry had meant to me. His facial gestures softened as I talked on. I made strategic comments about his achievements across the years. He knew that I had earlier charted in writing many of those achievements. I "called the roll," naming some of his more notable sons and daughters in ministry, persons whom he had nurtured and helped, and reminded or informed him about where each one was and how each one was doing. I commented that his ministry had been long, essential, and valuable, and that the effects of his life would continue in and through us.

It was a touching moment when Jackson gathered strength and voiced his thanks for what I was helping him to remember. I wanted to see him accept the end of his earthly days in the spirit of trust and with a solid sense of self-worth. That final visit with my mentor afforded him a time for emotional release and proved to be spiritually renewing for us both.

Not long afterward, I honored the request he had made to me years earlier that I plan his funeral service and also give the eulogy. The memorial service for Raymond S. Jackson was held in the sanctuary of Joseph Campau Avenue Church of God, the last congregation Jackson served as pastor and from which he retired in 1967. Among the many who gave prepared tributes were: Dr. B. Gale Hetrick, Executive Secretary of the Church of God in Michigan; Dr. Lawrence P. Wyatt, Chairman of the General Ministerial Assembly of the National Association of the Church of God; and Dr. T. Franklin Miller, President

Emeritus, Warner Press, Inc., and a longtime friend (both Jackson's and mine). As a tribute to Jackson's years of service on the Publication Board of Warner Press (the first black member), Warner Press donated the programs for the memorial service.

The funeral for my mother followed a few days later. My father's funeral was held eight months later, in October. In keeping with each one's will, I planned both funerals, which were held at Metropolitan Church, and somehow managed to deliver both eulogies.

With the death of Howard Thurman in 1981, and the deaths of Raymond S. Jackson and my father in 1983, I lost three persons who had influenced not only my life but also my preaching in very strategic ways. My father's skill in memorizing and quoting from Scripture had encouraged my ambition to gain a working familiarity with the wide range of biblical truth. Jackson's audacity in voicing the biblical witness illustrated to me the importance of bold speech. Thurman's way of shaping an atmosphere within which Scripture can speak its witness with clarity helped to influence my approach to preaching. In my father's preaching I saw the benefits of discipline, in Jackson's preaching I saw the effects of daring, and in Thurman's preaching I felt the appealing influence of depth.

In thinking about these three mentors, I have often recalled a statement Johannes Brahms the composer is reported to have voiced as he realized the high standard Beethoven had set before him as a creative musician: "You have no idea what it feels like," Brahms confessed, "always hearing such a giant marching along behind one." There are times in the pulpit when I sometimes feel like my three hero-mentors are watching and listening from their vantage point in eternity, not to critique me, but cheering me on as I share my witness. The standard they set is never far from my consciousness.

Tribute to a Leader

My return to Anderson College took place as President Robert Reardon was completing his plans to retire. Reardon was nearing completion of thirty-six years of service on the Anderson College campus, with twenty-five of those years as its president, and he had decided he would not seek another term in that office. Aware that the event of his retirement would be honored in significant ways, I watched to see what was planned. The college's Board of Trustees published a booklet Reardon wrote that was based on a report to them of his personal reflections after years of service to the institution. The booklet was titled *Some Anderson College Reflections: 1947-1983* and it included an attractive color frontispiece of Reardon. A commissioned oil painting of Reardon was completed and hung in Decker Hall, the administration building where the president's office is housed. Then in June 1983, during the college commencement, Reardon gave the address as retiring president, and he was awarded an honorary Doctor of Laws degree. Later, a new and spacious community auditorium on campus was named in his honor.

I appreciated those tributes to President Reardon's leadership, but there was another kind of honor that I wanted to see shown to him as an academic. I therefore planned a collection of essays in his honor, a *festschrift,* as it is termed in academia. I enlisted the writers, secured a publisher, then edited and produced *Educating For Service: Essays Presented to Robert H. Reardon* (Anderson, Ind: Warner Press, 1984). The honorary volume contained a frontispiece of Reardon, his curriculum vitae, a dedicatory letter from me as editor, and thirteen essays from as many scholars, all of whom were longstanding and admiring friends. In the first paragraph of the dedicatory letter addressed to Dr. Reardon, I wrote: "The scholar-churchmen and friends whose writings appear in this volume in your honor join with a far larger host of persons in commending your life and services as you retire from your twenty-five year presidency at Anderson College." In the letter's last paragraph I wrote: "As you enter upon a new phase of your life, be assured that you have left a lasting legacy; but be assured, as well, that you carry with you our trust, unfailing appreciation, prayers, and love."

MINISTRY AT TUSKEGEE UNIVERSITY

In 1982, about the middle of July, while vacationing at the home of my in-laws in Greensboro, Alabama, I decided to drive over to Tuskegee University to see the famed school and campus founded by Booker T. Washington, and where the legendary George Washington Carver had spent so many fruitful years in research and teaching. That was my first visit to the campus, and it was a most meaningful one. It was a very hot day, which made walking the campus a problem, but the deep meaning of the visit sustained my spirit.

Standing inside "The Oaks," Washington's home, Gwendolyn and I were deeply moved as we refreshed our memory about his service as an educator and the esteemed place he gained in history. We also paid our respects to his life as we stood at Washington's grave, before moving on in the heat to see the George Washington Carver Museum. I was also impressed by the stalwart modern-style Tuskegee Chapel located just a few yards from Washington's grave. I walked around it, admiring its unique and impressive architectural design. We did not get to go inside because we found that the doors were locked.

A year later, while taking some graduate courses during a second summer term at Boston College, I called back to Anderson to talk with the faculty secretary and learned that Carl Marbury, a former classmate of mine at Oberlin Graduate School of Theology, had left word for me to call him. Marbury was in Tuscaloosa, Alabama, serving at Stillman College while on leave from his academic deanship at Garrett-Evangelical Theological Seminary in Evanston, Illinois. I called Marbury during a class break. He eagerly informed me that Tuskegee Institute had announced a search for a new chaplain to succeed the retiring incumbent, and that he had submitted my name to the search committee for them to contact. Knowing that I had been visiting Alabama at nearby Greensboro (thirty-eight miles from Tuscaloosa) at the close of each semester, and that he and I had once talked about the possibility of teaching later at an historically black college or university, Marbury wanted me to know about the Tuskegee opening that would soon occur.

One month later I visited the Tuskegee campus again and was interviewed by Provost James Hefner. I was not looking for a new post, nor was I thinking seriously about a job change because I was well at home in my work and setting at Anderson School of Theology. Therefore, when I left Hefner's office, although well-informed about the chaplaincy post soon to be available, I had no deep feeling of desire or anticipation to gain the post. I had only recently turned down several grand invitations to serve elsewhere, three of them from prestigious seminaries at which I had been guest lecturer on occasion. Virginia Union University had offered me a professorship in preaching at its School of Religion and Princeton Theological Seminary had approached me about coming there to teach. I had served there as a visiting professor of preaching during the summer term of 1982. My friend Manfred Brauch, academic dean at Eastern Baptist Theological Seminary in Philadelphia, had offered me a named, endowed chair in biblical theology there. Each offer involved an excellently placed teaching position, but I had not been interested in making a change. One of the offers, the one from Virginia Union University, did, however, make me remember what Gwendolyn and I had agreeingly discussed about the possibility of serving a predominantly black university or seminary at some point before retiring.

In August, 1983, I received a telephone call from Tuskegee,

from a minister who identified himself as Chaplain Andrew Lincoln Johnson. He was calling from The Tuskegee Chapel and was inviting me to campus to preach there in a Sunday service in October, if at all possible. Upon hearing the name "Andrew Lincoln Johnson," my memory was triggered. I asked, "Sir, have you ever served as an army chaplain?" He answered, "Yes, I have." I then asked, "Were you ever stationed in Germany or Austria?" "Yes, Austria," he replied. I then declared, "Sir, I believe I know you!" A time of reminiscence followed, during which I recited the time (1952), place (Salzburg, Camp Roeder), and circumstance of our having met. I told him that I had been a soldier stationed in Austria and had visited the post chapel at Camp Roeder when he was the post chaplain, and that I had driven up from Camp Saalfelden, accompanying Chaplain (Capt.) Weldon H. Barnette, the post chaplain at our camp for whom I worked as chaplain's assistant. The memory of meeting Johnson had remained because the experience had been so stirring. I remembered him as spry, well-groomed, intelligent-looking, and quick-minded, a Major in rank, and an African American. I remembered the hospitality shown to me as one of his two guests that afternoon, and I remembered the manner in which he went about discussing the business for which my chaplain had sought his assistance. The whole experience had impressed me. When I recited all of this during our telephone conversation that August day, thirty-one years after the event, Andrew L. Johnson registered both surprise and joy. He sensed that his invitation to me was being made to someone who held him in esteem. I accepted his invitation, indicated the most convenient date for me to visit the campus, and went to Tuskegee Institute that October to preach.

I felt strangely at home as I stood in that chapel pulpit and preached to the gathered congregants. Dr. Benjamin F. Payton, Tuskegee Institute President, was present during the service. He smiled warmly and complimented me on the message when his turn came to greet me as I stood with Chaplain Johnson at the sanctuary door. He asked if I would have time to come over to his home that afternoon for a visit, stating that he wanted us to have some time in conversation before I left the campus. I answered that I would see him that afternoon. We met after I had had lunch. Dr. Ollie C. Williamson, Dean of the School of Arts and Sciences, and chairperson of the search committee, drove me over to the president's house on campus. Pacing himself well, President Payton outlined his concerns about the kind of successor needed at the famed campus Chapel. He shared his vision for the religious activities needed on the campus. He was very open and personal; he even explained why he, though educated for the ministry at Harvard Divinity School, had instead gone into university administration. I listened with great interest, and found myself feeling tugged upon inwardly as he shared his vision. Having been in the Detroit pastorate for so many years, and having given eight years of service as Anderson College's campus minister, I had some appreciation for what President Payton was seeking to make possible at Tuskegee Institute in and through its Chapel.

President Payton spoke appreciatively about reports he had received from mutual friends about my ministry. Evans E. Crawford, Dean of Andrew Rankin Memorial Chapel at Howard University, was one of those friends; another was Charles Gilchrist Adams, pastor of Hartford Memorial Baptist Church in Detroit. Payton seemed well informed about my Detroit pastorate and service years in campus ministry, and had been informed about my close relationship with Dr. Howard Thurman. He reminisced a bit about having often attended Marsh Chapel at Boston University to hear Thurman preach, commenting about how interesting it had been to him, as a student in Harvard Divinity School at the time, to listen to the famed George A. Buttrick at Harvard's Memorial Church on one Sunday and then go to Marsh Chapel and hear the fabled Dr. Thurman on the next. He also confessed how important Thurman's preaching had been to his personal spiritual quest. As our meeting ended, Dr. Payton and I had shared much more than information about respected preachers, mutual friends, and our own selves; we had sensed a kindredness of mind and heart.

It was not a complete surprise, then, when in February, 1984, President Payton telephoned to inform me that, after having heard and interviewed eight outstanding clergypersons across the previous six months, the search committee responsible for recommending Chaplain Andrew L. Johnson's successor had voted unanimously that I be asked to take the post at his retirement. Payton then stated his own sincere desire that I take it. He mentioned again some of the changes projected for the post, all of which he had voiced during our conversation in his home during my visit back in October. He indicated that if I took the post I would be named "Dean of the Chapel," and that if I wanted to continue teaching, I would bear the title "Institute Professor of Religion and Society." I had shared the basic information earlier with my wife Gwendolyn, so when Dr. Payton asked me if I was interested, I felt full freedom to tell him that I was. I felt that freedom partly because this invitation had that certain "pull" I had not felt in any of the several other invitations I had received. My sense of freedom to express a firm interest in the post was also in relation to my father's recent death. With Daddy having died in October, 1983, and because my mother had preceded him in death in February, eight months earlier, it was not necessary for me to stay as close to Detroit as before. All the family property matters were settled, and since my three remaining brothers were all living elsewhere, I realized that a page was turning in my life and might well be alerting me to entertain the notion of a turn in my career. With so many offers being made to me during that time, Gwendolyn and I had been praying for wisdom to sift them carefully for indications of divine guidance.

Gwendolyn and I had discussed the possibility of a call to Tuskegee after my visit to preach at the Chapel. Given the tenor of the conversation with President Payton, it seemed evident that he was showing an interest in me. Thus, during my telephone conference with him that February morning, all the main elements were in place for me to experience a sensed freedom to tell him that I was interested in the post. As Gwendolyn and I discussed the matter further, the call to serve at Tuskegee seemed timely and providential for another reason: it would allow us to be nearer to her Mother, Rubye, and step-father, Henry Joel Jacobs, who had returned to Greensboro, Alabama, from Detroit in 1978 after both had retired, he from the United States Postal Service and she from public school teaching in the Detroit school system.

Tuskegee was but one hundred and thirty miles from Greensboro. My in-laws were getting farther along in age and this move on our part would place us closer to them for any assistance we might need to render. They had built a new home on a twenty-two acre spread that included the previous plot of land owned by Rubye's father and mother, and where she and her sisters and brothers had grown up. Interestingly, that land was close to the property on which my own mother's father and mother, Zack and Clorie Shelton, had lived with their family during my mother's girlhood in Greensboro. All of these factors, plus the plan we had long held to live in Alabama after my retirement, were in our minds as my wife and I agreed to accept the call from President Payton to become Dean of the Chapel and Institute Professor of Religion and Society at Tuskegee Institute. That April we visited the campus again, this time to go over many matters of detail and planning with President Payton and to make house arrangements for living there. Earlier, I had broken the news to President Robert A. Nicholson of Anderson College (University) that I felt drawn to the challenge Tuskegee Institute presented. Once assured in mind and heart that the move was one we should make, I resigned from my tenured post as Professor of New Testament and Preaching at Anderson School of Theology. Gwendolyn, meanwhile, shared the news of our decision with Dr. Donald Johnson, Executive Director of the Missionary Board of the Church of God, the church agency within which she worked as Coordinator of Relief and Refugee Services for the Church of God. Interestingly, Gwendolyn did not have to resign from her post due to our plans to leave Anderson. Johnson suggested that she could continue her assignment if she so desired, working out of an office to be set up in the Tuskegee area. With this understanding, the major details for our expected move seemed to be in place.

When the news broke that I was leaving Anderson to go to Tuskegee, many ministers across the Church of God voiced their surprise. The tone that seemed evident in some of the questions put to me about my leaving made me aware that some of the black pastors thought I was leaving because of some mistreatment on the Anderson campus. I hastened to inform and assure them that this was not the case. In all my dealings with President Robert A. Nicholson, and with former President Robert H. Reardon, I could not have had a better relationship. Nor had I suffered any in relationships with other faculty members. As late as two full years after my move to the South, my friend Rudolph Smith confided that some white ministers had recently queried him about why I had left "our" school to go and serve another. Samuel George Hines also told me that he was often plied with the same question from white ministers whom he met here and there. I had remained in close touch with both of these friends, and they were in a good position to know how best to answer on my behalf.

Some persons who questioned my move to Tuskegee plainly had no adequate knowledge about the place, while some others hardly understood what a campus ministry involves. How different it was with other persons more knowledgeable about it all. For instance, when Robert H. Reardon learned about my call to Tuskegee, he came to me, and with a gleam of pride in his eyes, he commented, "Now that is a premier institution!" Our subsequent conversation about how I would be missed on the Anderson campus did not blunt his concern to show admiration for where I would be going to serve. Reardon never asked me why I was leaving. He knew that I had always followed an inner guidance. That guidance had brought me to Anderson in 1969, when he invited me to serve as the college's first campus minister; now that guidance was taking me in another direction. I was grateful for his trust.

The stature and historical record of Tuskegee Institute across more than a century were significant. Its many graduates held important posts here and there in both the black world and white America. The campus was a strategic educational center among historically black colleges and universities. In going there I was moving intentionally into a major center of black education and the Black American heritage in a new way. I sensed that it was important for me to do so at just that time. More importantly, Gwendolyn and I felt assured that God was being honored in our going there to serve. The following years strongly confirmed the wisdom and timeliness of our choice.

A few months after I had been at Tuskegee Institute I received an issue of *The Shining Light* magazine with an article in it lauding my move there. Written by Rufus Burrow, Jr., one of my former students at Anderson who had completed his Ph. D. degree at Boston University School of Theology, the article was captioned "Massey Leaves Anderson: The End of An Era." The article was part tribute and part polemic, a tribute to what I had meant to him and other blacks while a professor on campus, but a polemic about the need at Anderson College for more black faculty members. Burrows raised the question about whether my service at Anderson would be honored by a greater inclusion of black teachers now that I was no longer on the scene. He wrote as if, in his opinion, the best evidence that my ministry there had been effective should be an increase in the number of blacks on the faculty and at the administrative level, in both the college and the School of Theology.

I moved to Tuskegee in July, 1984, with less than a week before my service as Dean was to begin. I was introduced to the campus during the chapel service on Sunday, July 15, the weekend during which the Tuskegee National Alumni Association was on campus celebrating its Biennial Convention. That Sunday was a special day for several reasons: one, Harry V. Richardson, former chaplain (1933-48), was being honored by the Alumni Association for that service; two, Frederick D. Patterson, third president (and President Emeritus) of Tuskegee Institute, gave the spoken Tribute to Dr. Richardson, his long-time friend and spiritual counselor; three, Raymond F. Harvey, who had served as associate chaplain with Richardson at the Chapel (1944-45), was the morning preacher; four, it was the last service Andrew Lincoln Johnson had to plan before concluding his chaplaincy there; and five, I was being introduced in the service by President Payton as the new Dean of the Chapel. The printed Chapel Bulletin of the day called attention to the historic importance of that service, and in a comment in the printed statement of welcome to me as the new Dean, Chaplain Johnson suggested, "It is quite possible that the Chapel is entering its finest hour." As I read that comment I felt more acutely the pinch of my new assignment.

Although questioned by many because of my move, and even criticized by some few who accused me of having left the ministry, I was certain that at Tuskegee I was "in the right place at the right time." There was never a moment of doubt on my part about this, but if there had been, the steady stream of approving letters that came from long-time friends would have helped to settle my emotions. So would the encouraging visits and approving comments I steadily received from so many Tuskegee "Old-Timers" as I went about my daily work. The presence and blessing of so many Old-Timers provided a strengthening effect for my work that nothing else could match.

There was so much that made Tuskegee such a unique place. I was quite aware of this when I arrived, and I delighted in the glorious past that gave the place its honored ethos. Far from being a museum preserving aspects of a long-gone era, I found Tuskegee Institute a very live scene. To be sure, the spirits of Washington and Carver still haunted the town and campus, and many disciples who were touched by their legendary presence and work were still there; they had put down their roots locally with a pride out of which they regularly spoke to visitors, new faculty, and to each other. After arriving,

I met many who took great delight in sharing with me their memories, and they did so as a treasured but dwindling company of "insiders." I sensed the historical importance of such times of sharing, and I benefitted greatly from the information, insights, and inspiration I thus gained.

The first Tuskegee Institute graduate I had ever known was Christopher C. Coulter, my wife's aunt. As a member in the Detroit church youth group that she regularly taught and often entertained in her home, I used to hear her talk about the principles of Booker T. Washington and about the many scientific accomplishments of George Washington Carver. Aunt C. C., as we called her, had taught and supervised in Alabama schools before moving to Detroit after marriage, and it was she who gave many of us there a "first-hand view," as it were, of the kind of persons Tuskegee Institute sought to produce and send out into the world. She always spoke with pride about black achievers and the black heritage in which she had been steeped and was eager to pass on. Life in her presence and under her tutelage at the church was for many of us a strong encouragement to be an achiever. C. C. Coulter was overjoyed upon learning that her niece and I had accepted appointment to serve at her beloved Alma Mater. So was Coit Cook Ford, whose teachings during my grade school years at Grant School still fed my aspirations and encouraged my every step.

Among some of the Old-Timers still on the scene in Tuskegee when I arrived was Prentice Herman Polk, the legendary photographer recognized as one of the greatest black photographers in the nation. Polk had been in Tuskegee since 1916, arriving there to prepare himself as an artist, although he finally decided to trade his brush for a camera. Polk was best known for his photographic depictions of rural southern blacks, and for capturing on film so much of the many-sided life of George Washington Carver. Polk died near the end of December, 1984, and was honored with a burial in the Institute Cemetery in a plot not far from the grave of Carver. Polk was the official photographer for Tuskegee Institute until his death.

William P. Mitchell was another of the community stalwarts. He had distinguished himself in the successful fight for voter registration of blacks in Macon County and in the celebrated Gomillion vs. Lightfoot case that changed the course of the civil rights movement in both the county and nation. Mitchell was a Tuskegee Institute graduate and the first black executive director of the City of Tuskegee Housing Authority, which was a first for blacks in the entire southeastern United States. Although Mitchell and his wife were ardent and active members of Washington Chapel A.M.E. Church in Tuskegee, there were many times when they graced the campus Chapel with their presence and warmed my heart by their gracious deeds.

Another legendary figure with whom I was privileged to have many times of sharing was Charles Alfred "Chief" Anderson, first black pilot employed by Tuskegee Institute. He had come to Tuskegee in 1940 from Howard University to teach the first advanced course under the Civilian Pilot Training Program. Anderson was the chief civilian flight instructor for Army Primary Training for aviation cadets in Tuskegee in the 1940s, and was celebrated as the one black leader without whose pioneering work there would have been no 99th pursuit squadron. An oft-told story about Chief Anderson recalls a visit Mrs. Eleanor Roosevelt made to Tuskegee Institute and how she, upon learning that he was an experienced, licensed pilot, asked him to take her on a flight trip over the area—this, to the consternation and opposition of her entourage. He did, and through her symbolic deed of trust in the ability and skills of a black pilot Tuskegee Institute was selected shortly afterward for a test program in training blacks as military pilots. The rest is history. Chief Anderson was very personable, and I felt privileged to be a guest in his home on occasion.

The noted William Levi Dawson, musician, was also still active in the life of the city and region. A legend in his own time, Dawson was a musician's musician, a noted composer, choral arranger and conductor. He had come to Tuskegee at the age of fifteen, and since graduation had so distinguished himself in his field that he was appointed founding director of a school of music at the Institute in 1930 and taught and directed the choir for twenty-six years. Credit went to him for carrying the Tuskegee Choir to national and international fame, and his stature and prowess as a creative musician still kept him actively engaged long after he had retired. I viewed his continuing presence as a special boon, and we were in regular association across the years of my ministry at the school. It was especially heart-warming to look out from the pulpit and see him sitting in his usual pew, arms folded, head lowered in a careful-listener pose as I shared the message of the day. His comments after the service were not only encouraging but often insightful; they sometimes provided grist for the mill of our discussion, which we tried to have each week when we both expected to be in town.

Another person with whom I had regular sharing was Daniel T. Williams, historian and archivist at the Hollis Burke Frissell Library on the campus. Williams was not an old-timer from the standpoint of age, but he was with respect to his knowledge about the school's heritage and historical records. Williams and I became fast friends. After I accepted the call to Tuskegee, one of my first actions was to write to Daniel T. Williams requesting pertinent information about previous chaplains and programming at the Chapel. Aware that the Institute had long been a repository for publications and files about the Negro, and that pertinent information had often been published by its press in *The Negro Yearbook* series (some volumes of which I owned), I was not disappointed in my quest. With the helpful work of Williams, and personal research of my own in sifting available volumes of *The Booker T. Washington Papers* and other books about Tuskegee, I soon gained sufficient perspective to orient myself to the ethos and evolution of the campus. That research was crucial as I planned the service of inauguration the president and I projected; armed with information about previous leadership at the Chapel (full names, birth and death dates, exact years of service, education, and so forth), I could pay tribute to those into whose labors I would be entering. This informed perspective was also foundational for the task I would later undertake in writing a centennial history to commemorate campus ministry at the school. I was greatly assisted to this end by the encouraging and ready assistance of Daniel T. Williams.

A Service of Installation for me was held on Sunday, September 9, 1984, and the wider community joined the campus in welcoming me to the area. Evans E. Crawford, Dean of Andrew Rankin Memorial Chapel at Howard University, gave the address. Sharing the platform as program participants were: Andrew Lincoln Johnson, former Chaplain, Carl Harris Marbury, Academic Dean at Stillman College, and Edward L. Foggs, Associate Executive Secretary of the Church of God, in which religious communion I held ordination. President Payton presided and stated the Charge to me. I responded with a prepared Installation Statement that was distributed in printed form after the service concluded. Among the many guests in attendance were seventy-five members from Metropolitan Church of God, the Detroit church I pastored for twenty-four years, from May 1954 through December 1976. The Detroit group was assisted in the chartered travel arrangements by Wilhelmina Quick, who was my office secretary there across many of those years. John W. V. Smith and his wife Margaret were also there from Anderson, Indiana. John Smith and I enjoyed rich fellowship as fellow professors at Anderson School of Theology. As historian for the Church of God, Smith said he viewed my taking the Chapel deanship as a venture of ecumenical significance and did not want to miss being there to record the occasion. Many names fill the pages of the guest book signed by those who attended the service of installation for me. That book remains one of my most treasured possessions.

An initially disturbing, but finally humorous happening occurred during the installation service. As the university choir was ending one of the musical offerings, President Payton turned to me as I sat beside him on the platform and said, "I believe that man coming down the aisle is heading for this pulpit area." I looked out, scanned the figure, and identified him as The Reverend Leonard Steen, an elderly minister from Detroit who had come on the chartered bus with members from Metropolitan Church. I then suggested that perhaps he was seeking a restroom and was heading for the sanctuary exit that was near the platform. But still watching, Dr. Payton slowly remarked, "No, I believe he is headed up here, intending to say something!" He added, "I've seen this often at my father's church."

It turned out that President Payton had assessed the situation rightly. As the music ended, I watched Reverend Steen slowly walk up the steps and move to the lectern. I was momentarily horrified. The printed program was being disregarded, yet I did not wish to embarrass the aged minister by asking him to step down. After learning from me that I knew Reverend. Steen, Dr. Payton seemed content to let him have a brief word. I sat still, experiencing some dismay, unsure about the outcome of this unscheduled and unexpected speech. Reverend Steen did not talk long. He began with a word about how long he had known me, and how he had watched my growth and progress as a minister. As he continued, I scanned the audience and caught the stares of surprise registered on the faces of my former members from Detroit. It was evident that they were as surprised as I that he had seized that moment and was daring to speak on behalf of all the guests who had come down from Detroit.

Fortunately, his speech was brief, and it ended with two statements that "pleased the multitude," eased my trauma, and assured President Payton of the goodwill out of which the interruption had taken place: "So I decided to come down with the others from Detroit who still love him," Reverend Steen announced. He then added, "I wanted to see where he will be working, and to tell you to treat him right. If you don't treat him right, we will come back and take him back to Detroit where he is loved!" Applause erupted from the gathered congregation. The humorous factor within the story is not that Leonard Steen took it upon himself to represent the group from Detroit, but that, although from Detroit, he held membership in a sister congregation there, not at the Metropolitan Church! In a conversation afterward, Evans Crawford applauded what Leonard Steen had done, admitting that it was the first time within his many years of campus ministry of seeing any Dean of a Chapel honored by a former congregation! Crawford asked, in his inimitable style, "And how old did you say Reverend Steen was?" Eighty-eight years old, I answered. He then declared, "At eighty-eight he didn't have to ask to be on the program. His age gave him the right to stand up there and say what he said!"

My appointment as Dean of the Chapel carried with it the additional post of Institute Professor of Religion and Society. As Institute Professor (later changed to University Professor when the school was renamed Tuskegee University) I was free to set and follow my own teaching course, free to explore and work within any of the fields of inquiry of the campus curricula to which I felt particularly drawn. At the time of my appointment I was the only such professor at Tuskegee, although there were some others who were teaching on an inter-disciplinary scale. I decided to identify myself initially with the interrelationship between philosophy and religion and began with a course for upper classmen on Philosophy of Religion. I later used my teaching freedom to plan and provide classwork in a continuing education series for clergypersons, most of them Baptist pastors working in rural settings in Alabama.

Being Institute Professor gave me considerable latitude and I sought to use it wisely. I discovered, however, that my service as teacher would be limited by the growing demand upon me for service as counselor. I set the hours for counsel at times congenial to class scheduling, and the other deans worked with my scheduling for the teaching I desired to continue doing. The counseling hours were regularly announced in the Chapel Bulletin as Tuesday, Wednesday, and Thursday between 11:00 A.M. and 12 Noon and between 2:00 and 4:00 P.M., with other hours to be requested and arranged through my secretary. Counsel was sought by students, as expected, but also by faculty members, administrators, and staff persons. My time was also inundated occasionally with non-campus persons who "dropped in" during a visit to the city or campus, some of whom I knew, but many I had not known before. Being Dean of the Chapel made my name known to many, and many persons came with varied needs and requests for help.

Teaching at Tuskegee Institute was not essentially different from what it had been at Anderson, except that I now had a wider range within which to explore and teach. With my inter-disciplinary role as a professor, I sought and found many occasions for interaction with those in other disciplines, and the sharing helped me to expand my learning and insights. Teaching at Tuskegee was also different in that I was apt to have far more persons in class who were studying for a professional degree than at Anderson, since Tuskegee Institute had long been the scene of concentrations in engineering, mathematics, and other sciences rather than general studies or the liberal arts. Teaching put me in touch with many students I might have never met in relation to Chapel activities, and I valued the experience of gaining an opening to their lives by means of a class setting.

I restricted myself and did not travel much during my first year at Tuskegee. Some persons wondered if I would be satis-fied with my new setting and arrangements. The fact is that I had anticipated it—and loved it. I focused all my energies for the new venture, and once fully into the new pattern I was quite fulfilled. I felt as if I had made my final vocational move. Interestingly, instead of my new role curtailing my ministry—as some skeptics prophesied, being at the Tuskegee Chapel actually widened my windows of opportunity. I was gladly sur-prised when many of my former students at Anderson School of Theology, now settled into their work in churches and elsewhere, sought me out for counsel; their time in life and places of labor were making demands upon them that they sensed I would understand, so they opened themselves to my interest and assistance. I gave time and heart to each and all of them. In this way I remained available to Church of God persons, just as I stayed related to the state and regional meetings our church communion sponsored. Busy on Sunday mornings, I could not accept all of the many invitations to preach in the pulpits offered to me, but I was grateful for the trust of those who showed interest in my ministry and I never took any expressed kindnesses for granted.

From the start I gave myself with intensity to the campus role. I involved myself with the total campus life and with a pastoral concern as my focus. Out of that focus as campus minister I planned all my work and I sought to relate with aptness. Given the tenor of the times—the erosion of traditional values and the need for ethical and moral clarity and spiritual nurture, my task as Dean was clear and demanding. I began addressing myself to that task in classes, in counseling sessions, in the All-Institute Worship Services, in conversations, in committee meetings, and through cooperative planning and work with campus and community leaders.

The All-University Worship Services

Every Sunday during the school year it was my privilege to guide campus persons and community people in a vital celebration of God in the Tuskegee University Chapel. The service usually lasted for about an hour and ten minutes. It was inspirational to stand at the lectern to voice the Call to Worship and feel the contagion of eager students, faculty members, and townsfolk, all gathered in the spirit of praise to God. Attendance was voluntary, so the congregants gathered in full freedom.

During the organ prelude, the University Choir stood waiting in the chapel foyer, just beneath the "Singing Windows" which feature eleven favorite Negro Spirituals in colorful stained glass, ready—one hundred voices strong—to sing this familiar choral introit:

Cast thy burden upon the Lord, and he shall sustain thee.
He never will suffer the righteous to fall;
He is at thy right hand.
Thy mercy, Lord, is great and far above the heavens;
Let none be made ashamed that wait upon Thee.

I then issued a call for all to stand and join in singing the processional hymn as the choir members began their march into the sanctuary and up into the choirloft. The singing was full-bodied, and the atmosphere was charged with a sensed interest as the singers proceeded up two aisles toward their places in the lofty choir area behind the pulpit. Thus the service began, with "town and gown" together in focused celebration. A Litany of Praise usually followed the processional hymn. The Litany was often a six- to seven-line responsive statement, seldom longer, since several Scripture portions would also be read in the course of the service. The litany allowed a brief interaction between people and worship leader, while the Scriptures were nearly always read for the congregants by lectors.

The Chapel family included many townspeople. Some of them were in retirement after years of service at the University; some others were still employed there. Former students could be expected during the worship, many of them remaining after visiting the school, renewing memories, and rehearsing meanings. Guests from other campuses in the area were often with us in worship. All these, together with current students, faculty, and staff persons, made up the Chapel family for which worship the planning had to take place.

Having lived intimately with books about Tuskegee, particularly those by Tuskegee authors, and especially the works of Booker T. Washington, and having daily contact with many of the "old timers" still active in the community, I knew that a serious concern for spiritual nurture was traditional at the school. That had been the case although the school was not church-sponsored or church-related. One would ordinarily associate a strong chapel tradition with a college or university that needs religious activity to strengthen and extend its institutional life and mission, such as at church-controlled and supported educational institutions. But the chapel tradition and campus ministry at Tuskegee University did not have that background and orientation. The school was a private university, yet a vital chapel tradition had been highlighted on the campus for most of its history. In 1988 the University celebrated the centennial of the services of a full-time clergyperson as resident chaplain at the school, and notice was called anew to the strong religious emphasis that continued there with such strength and financial backing.

A part of the background reason for this strength stood rooted in the educational philosophy of Booker T. Washington, founder and long-time Principal of Tuskegee Institute. Washington initiated regular chapel services at the beginning of the school's life. Soon afterward he appointed an ordained clergyman to oversee planning for the services and to give guidance in campus ministry. Washington's view of the educational enterprise was holistic rather than restrictedly intellectual. His motto was: "Hands, head, and heart together . . . so correlated that one may be made to help the others." The concerned view expressed in those words did not change substantially after Booker T. Washington died in 1915.

Another part of the reason for this religious tradition at Tuskegee was found in the strength of concerns at work across the years in the traditional culture of African Americans. Tuskegee University was an historically black school with a predominantly black student body, and because of this most of its black students had come from homes and communities impacted by strong influences from within the Black Church culture. While it is true that student protest at Tuskegee in the 1960s forced the removal of the compulsory chapel attendance rule, thus allowing every student freedom of choice in the matter of chapel attendance and worship occasions, this change did not make the Chapel or University suffer an identity crisis, nor did it undermine the known educational philosophy by which the school had been guided, namely the need to serve the student's hands, head, and heart. The dropping of the compulsory chapel attendance requirement in 1968 actually removed a point of controversy from campus life and freed the programming to gain focus and strength to serve all those who would voluntarily seek its benefits.

As Dean of the Chapel I was stepping into a stream of religious tradition that was as old as the school itself. I was especially impressed by the extent to which religious concerns had been honored in the Tuskegee educational venture from the time of Booker T. Washington down to my time of ministry there. The succession of appointed chaplains was a most impressive listing: John William Whittaker, Edgar James Penny, George Lake Imes, Harry Van Buren Richardson, Raymond Francis Harvey, Carleton Lafayette Lee, Daniel Webster Wynn, and Andrew Lincoln Johnson, who was my immediate predecessor.

The Chapel programming had long involved a tacitly understood level of agreement about the religious essentials basic for its ministries and effectiveness. I say "tacitly understood level of agreement" because there was no stated creed that we followed, no objective written statement of faith prescribed for "membership" as such. The University was understood as an institution with a Christian orientation, and the message of the Bible was to be objectively understood and interpreted without denominational bias. Practically, this level of agreement allowed the biblical witness about Jesus Christ to be proclaimed and honored, and the presence of a cross at the top of the Chapel building forever marked the place as oriented to the traditional Christian focus regarding Father, Son, and Spirit. Eager to affirm such a focus, I drew upon my long-term contacts with ministers I knew who honored this focus and

371

whose experience in a local church or academic setting gave them sensitivity to serve our worship service with combined warmth and wisdom. I also planned series of sermons in which I could share my own witness in a prolonged and patterned fashion.

My ministry at Tuskegee University began with the need to provide further focus and strength to the chapel life, and to interest more of the students in what was available to meet their ethical, moral, and spiritual needs. Societal changes across the 1970s were not all healthy, and the Tuskegee campus scene was affected by some of those changes. My task was clear, and my interest was keen toward doing my necessary work. Important to it all was the All-University Worship Service, that time of gathering when at the community level there could be teaching, advising, ministry, and worship with religious ends in clear view.

As I have stated, the religious orientation of the Tuskegee Chapel was historically Christian. To be sure, there were other religious orientations and persuasions identifiably active among the students and faculty members, and the University sought to honor their concerns and activities by granting charters for their freedom of operation on the campus. But it was understood that the Tuskegee Chapel represented the official Christian orientation of the school. Those who studied the Chapel building could hardly miss the presence of the large Cross that stood at the top of it, on the roof portion just over the front entrance. Given this distinctive heritage, the services I planned for worship occasions purposely kept the Christian claims and worldview prominent.

Since 1932 the custom had been honored of using a printed Chapel Bulletin during each service of worship in the Chapel. Harry Van Buren Richardson established that custom while chaplain from 1932 to 1948, and continuing it across the decades had allowed a sizable body of volumes to be preserved from the weekly services. Continuing that tradition also exacted early, steady, and weekly planning on the part of the chaplain and Chapel staff. I especially appreciated the tradition of providing a meditational reading within each bulletin. Having regularly done this during my pastorate in Detroit, it was no chore to continue it at the Tuskegee Chapel. Apart from special occasions when some scriptural passage was to be highlighted in print for the service of the day, the back of each Sunday worship bulletin contained a meditation I wrote to help the worshippers focus their faith toward God and their services in the world.

My worship planning team consisted of three persons: Professor Roy Edward Hicks, head of the University's Music Department and director of the University Concert Choir, Mrs. Annette West Cochrane, Organist, and me. After Mrs. Cochrane retired, Ms. Valerie R. Reese was organist. The three of us planned the weekly services. With the school year calendar before us, we did long-term planning, taking into account the special days of the campus and Christian Year, but also the themes with which I would deal in the series I often projected for my pulpit ministry. We were candid in our assessment of previous services and effects from our planning. We benefited from the counsel of each other and from comments and suggestions from members of the Chapel family.

The basic direction of our short-term planning was usually set by Tuesday morning of each week; some variation was allowed when waiting for an invited speaker to report on his or her sermon subject, suggested text, and requested hymn. I sought this information at the earliest time and shared it with Professor Hicks, who then chose the processional hymn and the congregational hymn. All special music for the service was in his hands as well, and was usually something on which the choir had been working. Hicks also selected a Melody for use after the sermon, and the recessional hymn. The "Melody" music would fit the nature and spirit of the sermon theme shared beforehand with me by the invited speaker.

The organist was expected to supply the prelude title, postlude title, and offertory choice by Wednesday morning,

373

after which Mrs. Carolyn Robinson, my office secretary, would prepare typed copy for the Order of Service to be placed in the bulletin. By that time, I would have the names and assignments of the volunteer liturgists, with a confirmation from each one to serve at the expected time. Ushers for the service were secured and rostered by Mr. John P. Krouse, head of Ushers. With all these usual details in place, I finalized the notices about coming activities on campus and at the Chapel. By Wednesday afternoon the typed copy of the worship bulletin was ready for my review, after which the copy was submitted to the University Press to be printed. Proofreading for the printed copy took place on Thursday afternoon, and final copies of the Chapel Bulletin were ready for distribution to worship participants by noon on Friday.

There were two concerns that I wanted honored in the choice of music for the All University Worship Services: the music had to be (1) celebrative and (2) confessional. *The Pilgrim Hymnal* we used made available a large range of hymns and songs from the wider church, and we regularly utilized what was offered in it. But the tradition had also allowed other musical patterns and creations across the school year. Each Sunday one could expect to experience not only two hymns (i.e., as processional with the choir and a congregational hymn) but an anthem, a hymnic arrangement (during the offertory), a stylized Negro Spiritual (sometimes two), perhaps a master-piece from the Classical Era, or a contemporary Sacred Gospel number done in tasteful timeliness. The Melody was sung after the sermon of the day, and came traditionally from the black music corpus; sometimes it was a known Spiritual in which choir and congregation joined to express shared commitment after hearing the preached Word, and sometimes it was a Gospel rendering to carry the sensed meaning of the sermon to an affective climax of impression that music best achieves. The Choir was trained well for handling many musical styles.

The Scripture readings for worship were selected with the Christian Year calendar in mind, but we were not bound to a lectionary for every service. The lectionary was consulted in choosing the weekly readings, but its offerings were never compulsory because our emphases and needs were quite different from those expected in a local church setting. Two readings were traditional for each service, one from the Old Testament and the other from the New. As a general rule, one of the passages to be read would be what the minister planned to use as the basis for the sermon of the day. The practical importance of this needs no defense, but an instance can be shared here. Aware that the campus community was excited about the expected visit of President Ronald W. Reagan to give the 1987 commencement address, on the preceding Sunday I chose 1 Timothy 2:1-6 as the New Testament Lesson for that morning, and it was the textual passage I used for my sermon that day on "God and Our Social Order." The lectionary texts listed for that Sunday did not lend themselves to the focus that the next Sunday's event seemed to suggest as timely.

The pulpit schedule at the University Chapel brought to campus some of the nation's most notable and respected pulpit voices. The sanctuary pulpit was not only prominently placed, jutting out into the sanctuary front like the prow of a ship in the water, but its ministry was seriously promoted and publicly respected. I was glad to preach regularly in a place where the worshippers both respected and expected preaching as part of a service of worship. The pulpit schedule was entirely my responsibility. I was free to preach as much or as little as I deemed appropriate. I chose to begin the Chapel preaching schedule and spoke on those special Sundays when a campus focus was traditional (i.e., Freshman Sunday, Homecoming Sunday, Parents' Sunday, and Seniors' Day, to name a few). This regularity on focus days allowed for a greater sense of continuity as a worshipping community, just as a local church experiences under the regular ministry of its pastor.

My guest list included from twelve to fourteen speakers for the other Sundays of the school year. I preferred a mix of men and women ministers, although I was aware that many students were from church traditions that did not recognize the equality of the sexes where pulpit ministry is concerned. I selected the speakers a year or more in advance, with an appropriate racial and denominational spread reflected in the choices. Some guests were returnees, while others came for the first time. The visit of some pulpit guests allowed us to feature them in a Chapel Forum in the Chapel commons area after the service. This let congregants have dialogue with the speaker about the sermon or other issues of choice.

Once the schedule of speakers had been determined, usually by early June, I prepared for printing a brochure to make the names, service roles, pictures, and dates for speakers for the coming school year available to students, campus personnel, local churches, the news media, and others who expressed interest in having such information. Usually ready by mid-July, the printed brochure was available to be placed in the orientation packet given to in-coming students for the Fall semester. More often than not, I invited persons as Chapel preachers who were acknowledged leaders with prolonged or periodic contact with university students. I wanted speakers who would not be daunted by the awesome pressure sometimes experienced when preaching to persons and groups who comprise settings that could make one feel ill at ease.

When I was scheduled to preach, I liked to visit and hear the choir during one of their times for rehearsal; hearing the music helped me to anticipate the coming Sunday service with increased sensitivity, and it readied me for writing the Morning Prayer I usually prepared for the time of worship. Listening to the choir rehearse the hymns and anthem helped me to think and feel in communal fashion so that I could continue planning my angle of focus in keeping with the whole service our worship team had projected.

I was especially impressed by the strong sense of loyalty the choir members showed in handling their responsibility for the worship music. The members practiced Tuesday through Friday, in the late afternoon for at least one hour, and they sang every Sunday of the school year—all on a volunteer basis. Modest academic credit was gained from serving the Chapel in that way, but there was no financial return from it, nor was there any longer a music major toward which such credit could be applied.

The University Concert Choir did not sing during the summer term, although chapel services were held during that study period. To my great delight, during my second year on the scene several of the choir members who knew they would be taking courses during the summer term voluntarily formed a Summer Ensemble to enrich the Summer Worship services. This practice continued throughout my tenure as Dean. This spirit of voluntary involvement was characteristic at Tuskegee. Student and faculty liturgists for the services were usually volunteers; they signed up in connection with a Sunday of their choice. I coached the liturgists for their readings, and Mr. John P. Krouse, a retired professor at the University, trained and directed the ushers. Many of the students who volunteered to assist in the services were from campus fraternities and sororities or from the R. O. T. C. units. On special campus event Sundays, members of the official University Escorts, who served as campus guides for visiting groups, served as ushers. Mr. Krouse not only directed and scheduled the regular ushers, but also kept attendance records of each service, informed me by notes about special guests among us at the services, and directed the flow of traffic as the worshipers left the Chapel after the Benediction and Recessional Hymn.

During each All University Worship Service hour, our concern was worship. Blessed with a setting in which religious concerns were officially promoted, but in a non-denominational way, and possessing a building of architectural dignity that lent itself so readily to the praise of God, it was a labor of love to plan and guide the services. There was a deep sense of reverence as we gathered and a strong sense of community as we sang, gave praise, offered our prayers, and listened to the accent of the message from the Word. Engaged as we were in a transaction of eternal import to all, it was a distinct privilege for me to plan and guide such times together before God.

In addition to the eager-spirited involvement of students in the regular ministry of the Chapel, I liked the international flavor that was present in nearly every service. Many internationals were identified with the regular services we sponsored. Tuskegee University had long had a tradition of providing educational and training opportunities for students from abroad. The first African student arrived on campus in 1896 and by 1906 several distinct groups of students were present from various countries. In addition to what had been happening for individual students who had come to study, the school began to offer technical assistance to developing countries in institution building and agricultural technology. When I went to Tuskegee in 1984 at least ten percent of the student body was international, representing over forty countries. Recognizing the long-term involvement of the school with international students, President Payton appointed Eugene W. Adams to head a new Office of International Programs. Adams led in administering technical assistance programs in Ghana, Honduras, Senegal, Malawi, Swaziland, Haiti, and Jamaica. Situated in Alabama, Tuskegee University was operating in that part of the South that was the most popular among African nationals; actually, forty-five percent of all African nationals studying in the South in the mid-1980s were at Tuskegee.

As Dean of the Chapel, I was eager to assist these students as they sought to interface their several worlds. I felt especially responsible to give a clear witness about Christian vision and values. I wanted to affect their lives in creative ways, knowing that many would be future leaders back in their own countries, serving in government, industry, technology, education, and science fields. Having lived abroad at two different periods of my life, I knew what it could mean to be part of a caring community. I was determined that the Chapel Family would provide such a setting for all those international students who sought this for themselves. In preaching to a congregation with so many internationals, I felt a strong sense of mission as one who, by my message, was touching so much of the known world. Additional opportunities for contact with international students came in my role as University Professor of Religion and Society, with the regular lectures I did each semester in the School of Veterinary Medicine. Across many years this school had received numerous international students into its professional programs. Dean Walter C. Bowie and Associate Dean Albert W. Dade considered me an ally as they provided teaching occasions during which I could lecture to their students on science and religion and on ethics and professionalism. I remember well the positive impact my teaching had on the medical students one semester when I treated some of the personal and professional implications for them of Albert Schweitzer's celebrated ethic of "Reverence for Life."

I was fifty-four years old when my ministry at Tuskegee Chapel began, almost four times the age of the immense building in which many of my duties would take place. The Tuskegee Chapel was the second such building erected in the history of the Institute; it was erected between 1967-1969 to replace the first chapel that had been dedicated in 1896 and was struck by lightning and burned down in January, 1957. The new chapel building was the proud product of Paul Rudolph, head of Yale University's School of Architecture. Working with initial designs prepared by Louis Edwin Fry and John A. Welch, both from the Institute, Rudolph completed the final plans and succeeded in capturing in his creation the spirit of aspiration and the communal focus so germane to the Tuskegee campus. The structure he devised was modern and daring, with its curved brick walls and upward rising roof lines. The ceiling was a long plane that curved in two directions and gave the appearance of a vast sky punctuated by starry lights. The immensity of it all gave a hint of infinity as one sat or stood under it. The many skylights, parallel to the east and west walls, allowed shafts of light to brighten the asymmetrical sanctuary, and there was an ever-shifting kaleidoscope of lights and shadows on the walls across the procession of the day if one sat long enough to watch. But the focus of the chapel interior was the pulpit. As it jutted out high above the front of the chancel it called the attention of all to the primacy and place of the spoken Word in the setting of worship.

Although the focal activities of the Chapel were understandably religious, it had been traditional also to use the building for other activities that elevate human life. So, in conjunction with several other departments of the University, the Chapel staff helped to plan lecture series, community and campus meetings, concerts, recitals, and outreach projects for which the building was the center. Both on-campus and off-campus organizations were permitted to use the Chapel facilities. The history of activity enshrined in that building connected each and all who used it with a rich and goodly heritage of how the spiritual and the secular can relate in vital tension. It was no empty hulk taking up needed space at the center of the campus. Its doors were forever open and its facilities in constant use. We were blessed with an adequate budget by which to manage the cost of upkeep. The regular offerings each Sunday were usually good, the non-denominational spirit of the place allowing one and all to have a sense of ownership which they valued enough to support.

My deanship at the Chapel not only made me the university minister but also someone to whom the area ministers looked as resident theologian. This was reflected in the additional title my post carried, Institute Professor of Religion and Society. Situated as I was at the center of campus life as a teaching minister, it was my responsibility and privilege to think through and share the implications of Christian faith for the campus and the larger community as well. My work kept me at the frontier between the campus and the community, between the church and the world.

During my second year at Tuskegee I was privileged to join with my friend Carl Harris Marbury (who had by then resigned his deanship at Garrett-Evangelical seminary in Evanston,

Illinois, and was now academic dean at Stillman College in nearby Tuscaloosa) and G. Murray Branch, pastor of Dexter Avenue King Memorial Church in Montgomery, in the development of a continuing education program of studies for local clergy. The program was sponsored by the Lutheran Church of America as part of an outreach ministry among rural ministers in Alabama. The program began in the Spring of 1985 and continued throughout 1986. Once a month ministers from various areas of Alabama gathered for a day-long series of sessions on Saturday. Marbury, Branch or I would lecture, covering an assigned subject for the day, supplemented with two other presentations, one by a resident professor from Trinity Lutheran Seminary of Columbus, Ohio, the parent school out of whose budget the continuing education project was funded. Marbury, Branch, and I were all made adjunct professors of Trinity Lutheran Seminary. The local administrator of the program was Rev. E. Taylor Harmon, a black Lutheran minister who served as full-time executive director of the Alabama Rural Council. I was responsible for the courses in preaching and for some of the New Testament studies. Carl H. Marbury also taught in the New Testament area, while G. Murray Branch was the Old Testament instructor. Branch had taught for years at Interdenominational Theological Center in Atlanta in the the field of Old Testament; after retiring he had become pastor at the Montgomery church Martin Luther King, Jr., had once served.

The program in which the three of us taught was captioned "Life-Long Education For Clergy in Alabama." It was a pilot program in which the Alabama Rural Council, Trinity Lutheran Seminary, and the Institute for Mission in the USA, an organization of the Lutheran Church of America, all shared. The Institute for Mission was directed by Rev. Wayne Stumme, a Trinity Seminary professor. The main concern was to provide a study opportunity for clergy of all denominations and races in Alabama at a time when no accredited Protestant seminary program was available. Within a few years, however, the Trinity

Lutheran Seminary presence was overshadowed by the establishment of a divinity school at Samford University in Birmingham. Fortunately, I was invited by Dr. Timothy George, the dean there, to lecture and preach during their first pastors' school and to take part in the installation service when he was formally inducted into his post. I had met Dr. George in March, 1981, when I went to Southern Baptist Theological Seminary in Louisville to give the E. Y. Mullins Lectures on Preaching. George was an associate professor of church history and historical theology there at the time.

After a very intensive first year at the Chapel at Tuskegee, during which I gave myself with all zeal to my campus task, I began to feel sufficiently anchored to exercise again the freedom I had been granted to accept other assignments I might choose. I was privileged to enter the Staley Lectureship circuit again. In addition, I did the Northcutt Lectures on Preaching at Southwestern Baptist Theological Seminary in February, 1986, and the Freitas Lectures at Asbury Theological Seminary in March, 1986 (my second time to do lectures within that named lectureship, the first time being in 1978). In the Summer of 1987 I returned to Princeton Theological Seminary for a second Visiting Professorship in Preaching (the first having been in 1982). Also in 1987 I accepted an invitation from Kenneth S. Kantzer and George K. Brushaber, two senior editors of *Christianity Today* magazine with whom I had worked before, to become one of the Resource Scholars for the Christianity Today Institute, a discussion-writing group committed to meet, probe issues, and publish views with concern to raise public awareness, promote biblical understandings, and urge committed action as responsible believers. Thus it was that my name joined those of other Christian leaders listed on the magazine masthead page. In 1988 I accepted membership on the board of directors of World Vision, Inc., the well-known Christian relief and development organization that administers care projects around the world.

There was only one additional long-term activity beyond

the campus to which I agreed to commit myself while serving as Dean of the Chapel. It was the Health Careers Enhancement Program for Minorities held yearly at Case Western Reserve University Medical School and funded by the Robert Wood Johnson Foundation. The six-week program of study was designed to expose college-age minorities to the medical field and to help prepare them for entrance into medical school. My involvement in the program did not demand that I be present for all six weeks, but I did have to set aside two days each year to serve as one of the motivational speakers for the students admitted into the program. I was invited into the program by James L. Phillips, M.D., of Case Western Reserve University Medical School, whose work there as associate dean for student affairs and minority programs brought him to Tuskegee University on a recruitment visit in 1988. Phillips and I knew each other from our many years of association as members of the National Association Youth Fellowship that met each August during the annual camp meeting at West Middlesex, Pennsylvania. In addition, during the time we were both high school students, he and I (and his brothers Russell and Maurice and my brother Melvin) had spent several summers working at the National Association campground, he as one of the regular workers and I as helper of my father who as an electrician had been engaged to update the electrical system to accommodate the growing number of cottages being built there.

James L. Phillips was himself a 1958 graduate of Case Western Reserve University Medical School. Since returning to his alma mater as an administrator, he had created some attractive programs that encouraged minority students to pursue medical careers. He invited me to serve as a motivational speaker in the program series. I did, and my involvement continued across several years. The statistical results from the programming were encouraging to follow: for example, of the 110 students admitted to the first health careers program at Case Western in 1988, ten gained entrance into medical school, with four of that ten enrolled at Case Western. By the 1992 summer program, medical-minded minority students from sixty-three colleges and universities were in attendance. Across the years I enjoyed that privileged but awesome responsibility of addressing the many students admitted to this special summer program for minority students.

When I went to Tuskegee in 1984, the school was still under its familiar name "Tuskegee Institute." In June, 1985, a name change was formally made. The school became "Tuskegee University." This was but one among many indications of the extent of progressive change President Payton intended to effect within the life of the school. With the coming of Dr. Payton to Tuskegee in 1981, Tuskegee had begun transforming itself into a more broadly international center of education, research, and development. Before taking the Tuskegee presidency, Payton had served from 1972-1981 at the Ford Foundation as Program Officer for Education and Public Policy, and before that for five years as president at Benedict College. With a doctorate in international development, Payton envisioned a broader ministry for the school. He intended to build on all the best of Tuskegee's rich past under Booker T. Washington, Robert Russa Moton, Frederick Douglas Patterson, and Luther Hilton Foster, his immediate predecessor.

The name change in 1985 was mainly to clarify the school's public image by indicating the true scope of its life and offerings. Since its founding in 1881, the school had modified its name several times. Originally founded as Tuskegee Normal, the school name was changed in 1883 to Tuskegee Normal and Industrial Institute. In 1937 the school became "Tuskegee Institute." Pointing out that "Institute" simply did not mean in the 1980s what it meant several decades earlier, Payton was insistent that the school name should reflect its present development and programming. He did not realize that there was a problem with the school name until he became president in 1981. The problem with the name came to focus when he accompanied Mr. George Bush, then Vice-President, on a tour of seven African nations. When African nationals frequently asked Mr. Bush why he had selected as key educational advisor a man from what they thought was a community college, Bush was having constantly to explain the true nature and work of the school Payton represented. Mr. Bush wisely spoke thereafter of Payton as president of Tuskegee University. Four years later, in response to a vote of the school's board of trustees, and concurrence of the state of Alabama, with a stroke of the pen of Governor George C. Wallace at the state capital, another name change for the school was officially registered, making it thereafter Tuskegee University. That joint action of board trustees and state officials was necessary because since its beginning the school had been partially funded by the state of Alabama.

Four Special Occasions

Among the many public occasions with which I was associated during my time of ministry at the Tuskegee Chapel, there were four of them that stand out as highlights in my memory.

The first highlight occasion that I treasure in my memory took place on Founder's Day, March 23, 1986. After an informative address by Urban League President John Jacob, the University honored him and then conferred upon Governor George C. Wallace an honorary degree in tribute for his long-term assistance across the years. President Payton cited the Governor for being "the little man's Governor," for officially championing programs that had improved the life of all in the State of Alabama, but especially for strengthening the historic and special relation that had been traditional between Tuskegee and the State. Sitting on the platform near him as Governor Wallace read from the speech he prepared for the occasion, I could see tears gathering on his cheeks as he spoke in response to the tribute. Like so many others present that day, I could not help but recall how, not too many years earlier, the same man had allowed himself to pander to the South's basest passions by leading resistance against integrated schooling. How the times had changed! How George C. Wallace had changed! I was startled to hear him say, as tears ran down his face, "This is the highlight of my career." Although the shadow of the past fell across that scene on the Chapel platform, at least in memory, it was a tragedy-chastened man who now spoke, not the man who had earlier sided arrogantly with the restrictive mythology of racial bigotry. Some might have viewed his comment as but another ploy, but I did not; Wallace was not running for another term in office. To see and hear George Wallace that afternoon, one saw clear evidence that blacks had indeed overcome.

The second special public occasion was another Founder's Day, March 20, 1988, when the University honored the now-elderly Harry Van Buren Richardson, Institute Chaplain 1933-1948, and conferred upon him an honorary Doctor of Literature degree. Under Richardson's campus ministry Tuskegee had witnessed some strategic developments, and the effects of many were still in evidence. After sixteen years at the Tuskegee Institute Chapel, he had gone on to renew the life and work of Gammon Theological Seminary as its president, and he finally led in the birth and growth of the federated Interdenominational Theological Center in Atlanta, Georgia, where he served as its president until his retirement in 1968. When I suggested to President Payton that we should honor Richardson in this way, he was surprised that this had not been done earlier. An honorary degree was conferred upon Richardson and two other nationally known leaders present on that occasion. They were Damon J. Keith, Judge, U. S. Court of Appeals, 6th Circuit, Detroit, Michigan, a long-time friend from my ministry years in Detroit, and Howell Heflin, United States Senator from Alabama.

A third highlight occasion was the campus visit of the nation's chief leader, President Ronald Reagan, as the 1987 commencement speaker. In his autobiography, *Up From Slavery,* Booker T. Washington told about one of the dreams that stirred him as he worked to develop his school. He dreamed of building a school so serviceable to the nation that a president of the United States would one day come to see it. That guiding dream was fulfilled on December 16, 1898, eighteen years into his work, when President William McKinley came to speak on campus. That was the first in a series of such visits by several who have served in the nation's highest elected office.

As on that day when President McKinley arrived on campus, so it was on May 10, 1987, Mother's Day, when President Ronald Wilson Reagan visited. A record crowd flooded the town and campus. He was there to deliver the 102nd commencement address and to dedicate the new General Daniel "Chappie" James Center for Aerospace Science and Health Education. The late Daniel "Chappie" James was one of Tuskegee's most distinguished graduates, a born leader and achiever who became America's first black four-star general. The crowd present that day was imposing because of its size and composition. There to greet the President were some of Alabama's foremost citizens and leaders—Governor Guy Hunt, Congressman Bill Nichols, Senator Richard Shelby, and Senator Howell Heflin. They all shared with the President in an earlier ceremony of unveiling the marker for the massive building before entering the complex with him for the commencement occasion.

Once all were inside, the spirit of the occasion was evident. More than five thousand were present, and their voices were in harmonious roar as their singing of the national anthem engulfed the auditorium. I felt a deep sense of privilege and pride as I stepped to the podium and asked God's blessing upon our gathering and purpose. After official welcome statements from Senator Heflin, Congressman Nichols, and Governor Hunt, I led the audience in a Litany of Dedication I had prepared for the occasion. I shall long remember the proud roar of voices mingled in rhythmic response in our cadenced reading:

> With grateful thanks for the blessing of Almighty God and for the help of all who have made possible this new Center for Aerospace Science and Health Education;

We join in this service of dedication ...

To honor the life and service of the late General Daniel "Chappie" James, Jr., exemplary alumnus, ardent patriot, and distinguished soldier who became the first black four-star general in this nation's armed forces;

We dedicate this General Daniel "Chappie" James Center for Aerospace Science and Health Education ...

To memorialize a remarkable black American who by his courage, aggressiveness, vision and commitment brought honor to his Alma Mater, his family, his race, and his nation;

We dedicate this Center ...

With appreciation for his example as one who rightly claimed equality of opportunity, and used his opportunities with unselfish concern to benefit his nation;

We dedicate this Center ...

In recognition of one whose strong trust in God and Country helped him become one of this nation's most respected citizens and highly trusted defenders of its freedom and stability;

We dedicate this Center ...

Blessing and honor and power and glory be unto our God, and may peace be unto all who wisely use the facilities of this Center, from this day forward.

Amen and Amen ...

The University Concert Choir, under Professor-Director Roy Edward Hicks, assisted by the Concert Band under Professor Warren Duncan II, electrified us with their joint rendering of an arranged "America the Beautiful." Despite my own uprush of feeling, I noticed that President Reagan had turned around in his seat, so stirred that he wanted to see the faces and expressions of those singing. I felt such a deep-seated pride in belonging. I fully understood when President Payton, standing at the lectern afterward and before introducing the speaker, proudly commented, "You have just heard the best choir and band in the world!" A strong applause of approval followed. Dr. Payton waited for a moment and then said, "Ladies and gentlemen, the fortieth President of the United States." Another depth applause followed which dwarfed the previous one. It was evident the crowd knew that day to be a very special one indeed. The speech was substantive, and the audience responded with openness and high regard. When President Reagan left the scene he carried with him more than another honorary degree from another historic university; he carried with him the flavor of greatness that marks the place where he had spoken. I was thinking about all this as he finished his speech, received a standing ovation from that vast throng, accepted the conferred degree, greeted Dorothy Watkins James, widow of the deceased general, and took a smiling, waving leave of all. It was an historic day for all of us.

The fourth special public occasion that stands out in my memories of life at Tuskegee took place on Sunday, September 24, 1989, when as part of the planning for the Alabama Reunion Celebration, in which our university shared, we gave a ninetieth birthday celebration on campus to honor William Levi Dawson. The Chapel was filled that day, with more than eighteen hundred persons present for the event.

In addition to the musical renderings, all Dawson arrangements ("Ev'ry Time I Feel the Spirit," "Soon-ah Will Be Done," "Ain'a That Good News," and "Ezekiel Saw the Wheel"), there were excellently prepared tributes. Two of the tributes were from former directors of the Tuskegee Choir, Dr. Relford Patterson, then serving at Howard University's School of Music, and Dr. C. Edward Ward, then serving in Trenton, New

Jersey. Tributes were also given from the professional world of music. Dr. David Johnson represented the Alabama Hall of Fame and William Smith represented the Alabama Symphony Orchestra, which Dawson had conducted in rendering his Negro Folk Symphony. David Johnson had done his dissertation for the Ed. D. degree at the University of Illinois at Urbana-Champaign in 1987 on "The Contributions of William L. Dawson to the School of Music at Tuskegee Institute and to Choral Music." I gave the major tribute, which was an assessment of Dawson's place and stature within the heritage of Tuskegee University, the State of Alabama, the United States, and within the rich musical culture of the world. The University had honored Dawson in 1956 after his retirement with an honorary Doctor of Music degree, and during the May 1989 commencement had given him the Board of Trustees Distinguished Award. But that September, using his ninetieth birthday as our occasion, we were "doing it up" again in his honor.

I shall not soon forget that Sunday morning. There was that point in the service when Roy E. Hicks went to the microphone and asked William L. Dawson to come to the choir area and direct the University Choir in one of his choral creations which was listed to be sung next. Dawson did and the results were contagious—so electrifying, so expressive of his art, so memorable! The group of singers Dawson directed that day was larger than usual. The usual one-hundred-member University Choir was swelled that day by the presence of many additional persons who had sung under Dawson in earlier years; they had returned to campus for that special occasion of tribute, eager to show their continuing regard for him. An awesomeness pervaded the event as their singing under his leadership took place. As that master musician did his work of directing them, we were blessed beyond measure. I was but one among hundreds who sensed that it was a moment of reality we would never experience again, that what we were seeing and hearing and experiencing was truly a once-in-a-lifetime happening!

That celebration was timely. William Levi Dawson died just a few months later, in May 1990. I had remained in touch with him down to a week before he died; I talked with him by telephone as he was being treated in a Montgomery hospital. The family asked me to give the eulogy at his funeral. I did. Using Hebrews 11:27, I addressed the subject "He Endured." Here is the last section of the eulogy as I gave it in the Tuskegee Chapel that day:

On the morning of the day that Dawson's time arrived to meet with Death, the angels who had attended his path across those ninety years met for an early meeting. Aware that his breakthrough was imminent, they wanted to give him a strong welcome to his new home. Knowing that he had "come up out of great tribulation" and still endured in his faith, they wanted him to know their high regard for him.

One angel suggested: "To let him know our pride in his work, we should chant one of his songs, perhaps 'Soon-ah Will Be Done.'" Some others nodded support. But another angel spoke up, "No, Dawson has heard his own work enough; he deserves an even higher compliment as he arrives here. I tell you: we ought to play something he has never heard. We ought to sound a new note, play a new melody, create a new song for him." There was unanimous agreement.

Thus it was that as William Levi Dawson took leave from us here, and approached the Pearly Gates there, his ears perked, his heart pounded, and his steps quickened because, to his glad surprise, he heard a welcoming new note; he heard a new melody; he heard a ravishingly cheerful new song. In the words of John Bunyan, "So he passed over, and all the trumpets sounded for him on the other side." We now thank God that it was so! Amen and Amen.

We afterward laid his mortal frame to rest beside other Tuskegee notables in the University Cemetery adjacent to the Chapel.

The Chapel Centennial Observance

Aware that the centennial point in the Chapel history would be reached in November, 1988, I alerted President Payton about the fact and directed my staff in preparing for an appropriate observance. I supervised the staff members in locating and gathering the many historical materials from the Chapel ministry across the years. After gathering the many files, I studied the documents and catalogued them by a formal plan.

Two major accomplishments resulted from our work. The first was a book I wrote, titled *A Bridge Between: A Centennial History of Campus Ministry at Tuskegee University: 1888-1988*. It was published by Tuskegee University Press. The second result was *The Chapel Collection*, which was a formally catalogued collection of the papers of the Institute chaplains, comprising their correspondence with the school leaders, the campus organizations, guest speakers during each one's tenure, and many of their personal records. *The Chapel Collection* was then turned over to the University Archives. It formed a grand witness to the religious tradition that was the epicenter during the most dynamic periods in the school's long and notable history. It remains as a reminder about landmark times and persons and the creative power of religious motives.

A Bridge Between was completed and published in time for The Chapel centennial celebration service that took place during Homecoming on November 13, 1988. During the regular Chapel hour that Sunday we held a Service of Thanksgiving and Celebration. Evans E. Crawford delivered a memorable address based on 1 Kings 17:8-16, which he titled "Where the Increase Is." At an appropriate point after the address I presented a clothbound copy of the book to President Payton and to each of the three former chaplains who were present: Andrew

Lincoln Johnson, Harry Van Buren Richardson, and Raymond Francis Harvey. I also presented a copy to William Levi Dawson and Roy Edward Hicks, whose guidance in music had helped to shape and sustain the worship tradition we were celebrating. A few weeks after that event I received a letter from the aged Richardson. He thanked me for writing the Chapel story, and, speaking on behalf of his colleagues, suggested that if I had not taken the time to prepare such a work, "so much of what we know would have gone to our graves with us." *A Bridge Between* surveys a small but significant segment of the larger story that is the history of Tuskegee University. It treats the religious tradition at the center of the school's life, and it tells the story of those who had a principle role in shaping, nurturing, guiding, enhancing and perpetuating that tradition.

In his 1904 *Working With the Hands,* one of several books he wrote to tell the progress of the school under his leadership, Booker T. Washington explained how religious concerns were being honored in the total educational enterprise. Among several developments which he listed, Washington proudly reported that since 1888, just seven years after school's beginning in 1881, "a regularly appointed chaplain, an ordained evangelical minister, has been connected with the school, which is non-denominational, but by no means non-religious." My study, done to commemorate a century of religious ministry within the university, called attention to the work of each of the religious leaders appointed to serve the campus community, all of them working under the strength of what Washington once referred to as "the force and inspiration of a religious motive."

Where possible, I depended upon primary documents—and there was a wealth of such materials because of excellent record-keeping across the century. The fullness of data allowed an extensive picture to emerge as I did my research. I was informed by pertinent letters, pamphlets, school reports, newspaper clippings, personal journals, and much more. I also interviewed several of the Tuskegee "Old-Timers" who had known and worked with some of the pioneer chaplains. Among

393

those I interviewed were: Mrs. Bessie Bolden Walcott, who came to campus at the invitation of Booker T. Washington; William Levi Dawson, who had known Washington also, having come to Tuskegee about two years before Washington died. Harold Webb was another interviewee. He had worked on campus after completing his studies there, knowing several of the presidents. My conversations with Harry Van Buren Richardson were most helpful to my research. Richardson had known Robert Russa Moton, Washington's successor. Richardson had known John W. Whittaker, Tuskegee's first chaplain, and George Lake Imes, who had often worked in tandem with him in campus ministry there.

I selected the title *A Bridge Between* to express the purpose of the Chapel building and ministries. As a fixed center on campus, the Chapel had kept a sense of history vividly before one and all, and it continued to symbolize the fixed place of moral and spiritual values in the life of balanced learning. The University Chapel had been a ready bridge between many generations of students and campus personnel. It had helped to connect within many minds and hearts the secular and the sacred, the academy and the church, "town and gown," history and hope, place and purpose. With a deep sense of gratitude for the commitment and service of those into whose labors I had entered as the incumbent spiritual leader at the university, I dedicated the historical study to their memory. On the dedication page of the book I wrote:

> In Tribute to my predecessors, who nourished a generation of former slaves and many generations of their descendants in the spiritual and social meaning of faith, hope and love.

After much strategic planning, many focused activities, and steady praying, it was becoming clearly evident to many, both near and far, that there was "a new wind blowing" within the life of the University Chapel. The entire campus was increasingly aware of that new wind and many were being steadily affected by it. Chapel attendance by students had witnessed a marked increase, and the university administrators and I were glad to see that the downward trend which had plagued Chapel attendance since the campus unrest of the 1960s had been reversed. Student religious groups were multiplying across the campus. Some of those groups were inspired by the charismatic movement operative on many campuses at the time, but all of them were supportive of the known religious tradition and leadership associated with the University Chapel. Having served for some years as a member of the corporation for Inter-Varsity, I desired to see an Inter-Varsity chapter established at Tuskegee. The Rev. Alex Anderson, regional director for the Florida-Alabama-Georgia area, and I worked together on this and a vital chapter of that campus-oriented organization began on our campus. It was encouraging and stimulating to observe the many benefits our students were experiencing through association with the religious groups at work on the Tuskegee University scene.

In addition to watching the lives of students undergo rational, moral, and spiritual change through sound religious teaching, decisive commitment to God, and sustained times of fellowship, I had the added pleasure of providing counsel for several students who acknowledged a call to ministry. From among those intent on being seminary trained for a full-time ministry as ordained clergy, I chose some "Dean's Assistants." Four who so served were Anthony "Tony" Hall, Ruben Dicks, Jeffrey Oglesby, and Wayne Felton. There was another student, Derrick Dean, an honor student in biology and chemistry, who also assisted me. Derrick professed no call to prepare for a full-time ministry, but he was so gifted by nature, grace, and spiritual commitment that I wanted him to work with me in the Chapel programming. He rendered such excellent service during his undergraduate years that, when he graduated in May of 1987, he stayed on at Tuskegee for a Master of Science degree in chemistry. I appointed him as my first "Graduate Chapel Assistant." He later received his Ph. D. degree in chemistry at the University of Illinois at Urbana-Champaign, and I had the pleasure of serving as co-officiant with his pastor, Dr. Claude Shelby, Sr., as Derrick and Toya Walker were joined in marriage at Salem Baptist Church in Champaign, Illinois, in June of 1992.

Among the many who confessed a call to ministry and went on to seminary to prepare themselves for full-time service as ordained clergy, there were: Dennis Thomas who graduated from Asbury Theological Seminary in Kentucky; Ruben Dicks who went to Fuller Theological Seminary in California; James P. Quincey, who distinguished himself as student body president at Tuskegee and completed his theological studies at Harvard Divinity School in Massachusetts; Wayne Felton, aware that I held a graduate degree from Asbury Theological Seminary, decided to receive his education for ministry there; so did Jeffrey Oglesby. Roderick Vanroyal did his seminary work nearby at Beeson Divinity School of Samford University. Charles Houston decided to be a minister within the Church of God (Anderson, Indiana) that had nurtured my life. The Chapel scene was indeed a setting with many evidences of new life and effectiveness. Many of those invited to come and preach there carried with them a positive report as they left. As a result, I had to deal regularly with requests from preachers who unashamedly volunteered themselves, wanting to come and preach in the Tuskegee Chapel pulpit!

As I ministered here and there across the nation I was constantly surprised at the level of interest being shown in knowing more about what was taking place at the Chapel under my leadership. Although grateful for the acknowledged interest, I usually gave a rather informal report, being more concerned about the sermon or lecture assignment pressing upon me. The time came, however, when a more formal report was requested. The exact occasion was in answer to a request from some faculty friends at Southern Baptist Theological Seminary to join them in preparing a special study about worship for the Winter 1988 issue of that seminary faculty's *Review and Expositor* journal. I agreed to do so and prepared my article using the topic they suggested: "Planning for Worship at the Tuskegee Chapel." That journal article constituted the first formal report I had prepared to explain our Chapel worship rationale, service design, and related matters to persons beyond the campus. That issue of the journal appeared just a few weeks after my centennial history of the Tuskegee Chapel ministry was released, and I thus had a nucleus of written materials to which I could point when such information was being sought.

News of my work at Tuskegee Chapel had also come to the attention of the alumni association of William Tyndale College (formerly Detroit Bible College), my alma mater. Knowing that President William Shoemaker had scheduled me as the May 1988 Commencement Speaker, alumni president Dan Lewis and his committee decided to invite me to address the alumni association during the annual banquet that took place the afternoon before the commencement. I agreed to do so and prepared myself to handle the demands of both occasions. During the Commencement program, I was delightfully surprised to be honored as the alumni association's Distinguished Alumnus of 1988.

Given the many positive developments we were experiencing in the multi-phased religious life on campus, I felt encouraged and renewed as we gave ourselves to celebrations and worship. But 1988 was not only our centennial year; it was the year I lost by death my oldest and dearest mentor, Coit Cook Ford, Sr. We had remained close since my grade school days, and had talked by telephone only a few weeks before his death, at the ripe age of ninety-two. At the request of his son, Coit, Jr., and his daughter, Elaine Gregory, I went to Detroit to be present for the funeral and give a memorial tribute. I afterward adapted the contents of that tribute and used it as a meditational reading on the back of one of the Chapel worship bulletins. I sent a copy of that Bulletin to the Ford Family as a memento of the appreciation and regard on my part toward my beloved teacher and friend. Here is what I wrote:

My Most Unforgettable Teacher

In his book *Men I Have Known* (1897), clergyman Frederick W. Farrar reminisced about eminent persons he had known. Robert Browning was one of them, and Farrar quoted Browning's comment to him that so important it is that young people have the blessing of landmarks in their lives, especially the memory of "seeing great men." I thought of his comment a few days ago when one of the landmark persons in my life died. The man was a great teacher—and the adjective is used honestly. He was competent, industrious, and caring. His classroom was a virtual picture gallery, with glossy photographs lining the space between the ceiling and the blackboard along several walls. I shall never forget the drama we all sensed as he supplemented the class lessons with information about those whose pictures hung along the class walls. And with each telling story, our information increased, with a justifiable pride in our people—because the pictures on the walls were of black persons who had become great. But, sensing our need for realism, he would caution us—quoting from Longfellow's "The Ladder of Saint Augustine" for deeper effect:

> The heights by great men reached and kept
> Were not attained by sudden flight;
> But they, while their companions slept,
> Were toiling upward in the night.

Those lines spoken in my grade school years at Ullyses S. Grant School in Ferndale, Michigan, still stir my spirit and prod the diligence to which they point, and the teacher who recited that poem to us exemplified its message in his character, competence, and caring. Small wonder, then, that teaching came to stand out in my mind as the noblest of work.

A few days ago, some former students of that teacher gathered with other friends and members of his family for his funeral service in Detroit. I was one among them. We had been close across many years, sharing letters, telephone calls, and visits from time to time. He died in his ninety third year of life, and we had conversed by phone about a month before his death. His last letter to me will remain a treasure: in it was a list of former students still in touch with him, and a statement beside each name about what that person was doing. Also sent with that letter was a gift picture—a photograph of himself at the time I was his student in grade school! These mementos hold deep meaning for me; they remind me about the central issue of living: to touch other lives meaningfully. Mr. Coit Cook Ford, Sr., did so. He was one of the great men in my life, a giant on my path, a "landmark person" on the landscape of my pilgrimage. The writer of Ecclesiasticus eulogized the heroes of Israel's past, rejoicing that "Some there are who have left a name behind them to be commemorated in story" (44:8). My most unforgettable teacher was a Black American of competence, caring, and contagion; he gave the strength of his life to touch other lives for good. And I thank God that it was so! I am but one of many whose lives will commemorate his story, as he now rests in peace.

Dean Massey

An Interruption

All was going well. I was in gear for "the long haul," eager to deepen the growing impact on campus of the Chapel ministry. I was surprised one morning by a telephone call from

Robert A. Nicholson, President of Anderson University, who was calling to request some time with me "to discuss a matter of considerable importance." Upon discovering that we would both be attending the National Youth Inspirational Convention scheduled to convene in St. Louis, Missouri, just after Christmas, we agreed to meet with each other at that time. As it turned out, Nicholson asked me if I had any interest in taking the deanship at Anderson School of Theology. Dr. Jerry C. Grubbs, who was Dean when I left Anderson to take the chapel deanship at Tuskegee, had been appointed Vice President for Student Life and Human Resources at the university, and Dr. Barry L. Callen, also a former Dean at the seminary, was serving as Acting Dean until a new Dean would be chosen. A search committee was at work on the selection process and (as I was told) many letters from School of Theology alumni and pastors across the church had mentioned my name as a favored possibility for the post. Although I was grateful for such a show of confidence in my ministry, I was so deeply involved in ministry at Tuskegee that I politely informed Nicholson that I was not interested in making any change. I took some time and rehearsed for him what was happening under my leadership through the Tuskegee Chapel ministry. Nicholson listened with deep interest, complimented me, but went on to ask, with his characteristic gentleness, if I would be willing to pray about the matter. Feeling rather sure that I was in the right place at the right time, and thinking that I had made my last career move, I deemed it selfish to appear unwilling to pray about his request, so I told him that I would join him in praying about the need for a new seminary dean. We parted with that as a mutual concern.

I received another phone call from Nicholson in February, 1989. He indicated his desire to come to Alabama to meet and talk with me further about the future of the seminary. I agreed to meet with him that next week. On the appointed day I met Nicholson at the Montgomery Airport and took him to a meeting room I had reserved at The Governor's House, a favored lodging center, and we talked for two hours about the needs of the School of Theology before we concluded with lunch. He voiced his judgment that I was admirably suited to serve the seminary as its dean, and confessed his interest in seeing me meet with the search committee to discuss this possibility. I had prayed about the matter, as I had promised to do; but my praying had been done with an interest in the future of the seminary, not open to any change in my own desired future.

I was so sure that the Tuskegee Chapel was where I needed to be until time to retire. Because of this, I had been confident that the search committee would with timely guidance find the right person to be seminary dean. But now, having listened to Nicholson's insights on the needs of the school, and his assessment of how I could be helpful in seeing that those needs were served, I felt compelled to think more personally about the matter, although it was painful to do so. Holding a post at Tuskegee that, as my wife put it, "had my name on it," enjoying the work immensely, and seeing such fruitful results, especially the large number of persons being called by God to prepare for ministry, I felt pained in pondering any change. Nicholson and I talked further as I drove him back to the airport for his return flight to Indiana. As we parted, Nicholson stated that he would be in fasting and prayer about what we had discussed. I promised that I would do the same. I suggested that I could perhaps know within the next three weeks what I should do about it all.

It took me all of those three weeks that followed to come to terms with what I sensed I should do. It was a hard decision, but after many times of talking with God, with Gwendolyn, and with the deepest levels of myself, I was willing to meet with the search committee to discuss the possibility of becoming Dean of Anderson School of Theology. I so informed Robert Nicholson. I knew that I was one of four persons whose names had come to the top of the committee's list and that the list had been prepared from solicited applications for the post, nominations from across the church, and suggestions from the university trustees, faculty persons, staff members, graduates, and other educators and friends of the school. On an appointed day I went to Anderson to meet with the search committee.

The search committee reached consensus on its chosen nominee in early March, 1989, but the committee members wisely decided to test their agreed judgment by engaging in further prayer, fasting, and patient waiting across another week. With their agreed decision still firmly in place, President Nicholson called to inform me that I was the chosen nominee and my name would be placed before the University's Board of Trustees in May for their confirming vote. The news was both assuring and disturbing. I felt assured in that my willingness to serve as Dean of the School of Theology of the Church of God (Anderson) had been honored by an official call to do so, but I was also disturbed in that a change I had not wanted was now necessary. Gwendolyn and I had planned many years before that we wanted to spend the latter part of our ministry years serving in a predominantly black college or university setting. Once on the scene at Tuskegee, we had seen so many positive developments from our presence and work, all of which had confirmed and steadily encouraged us. It was thus no simple thing to handle the inevitable trauma that attended our preparations to leave Tuskegee. Although I felt assured that our move was in obedience to a higher will, I must nevertheless confess that in leaving the Tuskegee University Chapel scene Gwendolyn and I both "died a little."

Following an affirmative vote from the Anderson University trustees, President Nicholson informed the faculty members of the School of Theology that I had been elected to be their new Dean. He also informed them that I would need to remain at Tuskegee University for the first semester of the 1989-1990 school year, so they knew that I would not be on the scene at Anderson on a full-time basis until late December 1989. Dr. Barry L. Callen agreed to continue his interim service so as to make this timing viable. Nicholson then prepared a letter to announce the Board decision to the pastors and representative laypersons across the Church of God, eager for their supportive ratification of me for the seminary deanship when the church's General Assembly would meet in its regular session in June.

Interestingly, the climate of thought and feeling for that vote during the June 1989 General Assembly differed greatly from the questioning climate during the vote taken on me for "Christian Brotherhood Hour" speaker during the General Assembly of 1976. Benefited this time by the absence of any controversy, I was ratified for the seminary deanship by a 95 percent majority of those who voted. The supportive vote was encouraging, but even that high endorsement level only slightly mitigated the deep pain I felt in parting from the campus, ministry, and circle of associates and friends at Tuskegee.

SEMINARY DEAN AND RETIREMENT

On December 21, 1989, I was back at Anderson University, "on the job" as the new dean of the School of Theology. I had made several trips to Anderson from Tuskegee before that month to locate and purchase a house and to get it ready for our occupancy. The movers reached Anderson on time and Gwendolyn and I moved in with several days to spare before classes were to begin for that second semester of the 1989-1990 school year.

On one of those early trips to the campus I brought along a carton of materials for my homiletics class, intent to store them until my final return. I did not intend to be without those materials when my preaching class began. The truth is: I brought the carton of materials myself, and early, because I did not want to entrust my teaching notes to the sometimes uncertain scheduling of a moving company and I did not want them to get lost among a host of other boxes!

Interestingly, when I arrived on campus with that and other cartons, the first person I saw as I emerged from my car was Dr. Barry L. Callen, the seminary's acting dean at the time. Callen knew I was coming to town, but I was especially fortunate to see him at that particular time and place because when he saw the number of boxes I had brought to deposit in my new office, he characteristically volunteered to give me a hand. I welcomed his help. That was not the first time I had needed and received Barry Callen's help, nor would it be the last.

Barry Callen had led the seminary at three crucial times in the school's history: he was its acting dean in 1973-1974 while Dean Gene Newberry was on sabbatical leave in Kenya, East Africa; he held the deanship from 1974-1983, before becoming vice-president for academic affairs at the University (1983-1990); and in 1989 he was acting dean again. Former dean Jerry C. Grubbs had become vice-president for student life at the University in 1988, succeeding Cleda Anderson, and Callen was chosen to provide interim leadership at the seminary again until a new dean was in place. As that new dean, I was now in residence and he felt relieved. Callen and I knew each other well. We respected each other's scholarship and valued each other as trusted friends. His offer to help me carry cartons of papers from my car to my office on that cold December day was not just out of cordiality; it was characteristic of him as a colleague. Barry L. Callen continued to be helpful during that period of rebuilding and new beginnings.

It was plainly a time for rebuilding in the seminary: faculty morale needed attention, student enrollment needed to be increased, the seminary's image in the church needed to be rebuilt, and the seminary curriculum needed some revisions. These were clear needs, and I regarded them as challenges. Many seminaries were plagued at the time by lagging enrollments, and, in addition, the perceived needs of church life and American society were pressing us all to make the standard seminary curriculum more viable for an effective ministry. The seminary faculty and I knew that we had a formidable task before us: that of building and implementing a teaching/practice program that could meet the needs of the times while bucking a downward enrollment trend that seminaries across the nation were experiencing. There was an open door before me to lead in doing what needed to be done.

As I began my deanship, I had some advantages. I knew the faculty members and they knew me. I knew the university and seminary setting. I was not starting from scratch as scholar, churchman, colleague, or administrator, and I was confident

that I could lead our seminary beyond where it was. In an introductory statement to the faculty members, I said, "You take care
of the students, and I will take care of you." I paused after making that statement because I wanted each faculty person to
reflect on what I had said. Mine was a purposed word because
I wanted to begin our time together with a statement about our
roles. A dean's work is administering, choosing those who
teach, guiding and coordinating the work of those who teach,
assigning them space (and tasks), scheduling their classes,
giving oversight to budgets that support the teaching enterprise,
and matching funds with needs and requests. All these are
administrative tasks, and I knew that they must be handled
with wisdom, a sense of priorities, fairness, and timeliness.
Making things easier for the faculty so that they could do their
work with pleasure as well as dispatch was my stated concern
as their new dean. I was intent to be a primary advocate and
supporter of productive scholarship and to use all possible
means to bring our faculty into contact with students, and those
who were interested in writing into contact with companies
which publish.

I was eager to involve each and all in the process of
handling the communal task entrusted to us by the church. I
knew that we had a good seminary, but I believed that together,
in an understood and agreed mutual involvement, we could
make our seminary even better. I took the deanship with that as
one of my goals, intent at retirement to pass the leadership to
the next administrator at a higher level of development. Shortly
after I began my tenure, the spring 1990 issue of *Signatures,* the
university's quarterly for alumni, friends, faculty, and staff,
carried articles featuring our School of Theology, its concerns,
and my role and priorities as the new dean. A photo of me by
Tony Frederick filled the cover, with a caption underneath the
picture, "The James Massey Era: A Time to Build." The cover
story was captioned, "The Dean Is In."

Although I knew the Anderson University setting, some
new developments on the campus had taken place since 1984

when I left to go to Tuskegee University. For one thing, in 1987 there was an institutional name change: Anderson College was now Anderson University. This change of name reflected the scope and range of the institution's structure and programs, and it underscored the separateness of the seminary with its professional dimension and focus. For another, while the School of Theology was still distinctively Church of God Anderson in its orientation, commitment, and accountability, its student body was decisively more ecumenical in denominational spread. In 1989, only sixty-seven percent of the seminary's student body was Church of God by acknowledgement and orientation. This phenomenon was not being read well nor properly interpreted by some critics in the Church of God.

Digging In

There was much to do, and I knew I would need help in seeking to get it done. By prior request on my part, President Robert Nicholson had arranged for James W. Bradley to be my associate dean. The reasons for my choice of Bradley were many and quite open. Bradley was an experienced pastor before becoming a seminary professor; he had been director of the seminary's Center for Pastoral Studies across several years; he was well-known across the church, and he was an experienced administrator. I admired Bradley's excellent spirit and after praying about the direction I knew I should take as dean, I asked President Nicholson to approach him to ascertain his willingness to serve at my side. Bradley expressed a willingness. This pleased me greatly, and our teamwork began in earnest after I relocated in Anderson.

Administrative work is an unending task and often a thankless service. Being an administrator is not a way to glory, although some eager persons may be tempted to view it as a way to a higher salary. I was aided greatly by James W. Bradley. He was an able leader who understood the importance of the administrative task and he gave himself to his assignment as associate dean with competence, a strong sense of caring, and faithful continuity. Among the several decisions that I had to make in 1989 in preparing to assume the deanship, the choice of James Bradley to be the associate dean was crucial—and God-guided. Our teamwork continued in depth, faithfulness, and mutual respect across my years in the dean's post.

During my first meeting with the seminary faculty, I also shared with them my list of priorities. Having informed myself about the seminary's needs, I had developed the list during my last six months at Tuskegee University and I had discussed the list of priorities with President Nicholson during one of my visits before moving back to Anderson. There were five priorities on the list that I shared with the faculty: (1) to increase the enrollment; (2) to revise the curriculum; (3) to fill faculty vacancies with the best scholars available; (4) to enhance the relationship between the seminary and the church at large; and (5) to model for the rest of the seminary world what seminary education can be at its best.

It was time to begin anew, and the fact of having entered into a new year (1990) and a new decade gave us all a sense of new beginnings. The news soon broke that President Nicholson would retire at the close of that school year. Nicholson had told me of his plan quite early, and the timing of my return to Anderson only gave us six months together on campus before his retirement. We used that time expeditiously.

At mid-year 1990, Anderson University received only its fourth president, James L. Edwards. Edwards was no stranger to the campus. His bachelor's degree was from Anderson University, his seminary degree was from our School of Theology, he had worked in student recruitment for the university for four years, and had been director there for church and alumni relations from 1972-1975. Edwards had visited Metropolitan Church when I was pastor there. Before coming to campus as president he had held a pastorate for fourteen years in Columbus, Ohio, and recently had moved to Anderson to take the presidency of Warner Press. I remember well the discussion I had with the search committee when asked for my input after Edwards' name was placed before them as a possible successor to Nicholson as president of Anderson University.

The search committee members asked my advice on whether they should proceed to seek his candidacy, and if they did, how they should proceed, since they did not want to create a problem for Warner Press, where Edwards had been for only about a year. I advised them, "If his experience and credentials impress you, then issue a draft call, and let his sense of priorities and duty determine the outcome." The search committee did just that, and with his doctorate in educational administration James L. Edwards welcomed the opportunity to serve in a capacity closer to the concerns of his terminal degree. He was elected to the presidency by the Board of Trustees and ratified by the church's General Assembly to begin his tenure in June, 1990. With a new president over the university and a recently installed new dean for its School of Theology, it was indeed a time of new beginnings at Anderson University.

Our School of Theology was not alone in its experience of low enrollment as the decade of the 1980s was coming to a close, but our experience was our problem and we were intent on seeing that problem solved. Our enrollment in 1980 numbered 169, and it rose to 189 three years later, but the headcount in 1989, when I returned to the scene as dean, was 100. Most were part-time students. Female students outnumbered males, the number of minority students had dipped, many of our seminarians were from other church bodies, and the number of persons preparing for service in the Church of God represented only about sixty-seven percent of the total enrollment.

Given the new problems facing seminaries across the nation, and particularly our own, a small committee appointed by President Nicholson and the trustees had been at work studying the future of the School of Theology. The committee was entrusted to recommend what should be done to enhance the life of the seminary and guarantee its development. In connection with such concerns, President Nicholson had secured a matching grant from Lilly Endowment Foundation to fund what became known as the "Seminary Trusteeship Project," which was a study-action plan to help the university's Board of Trustees understand the seminary mission and function, thus to inform and strengthen their role in its governance. The grant proposal listed several activities as goals, together with a timeline to achieve them:

1. The preparation of a history of the School of Theology, to increase awareness of the trustees regarding trends, cycles, major issues, turning points, achievements, etc., since the beginning of the seminary in 1950;

2. Launching a major research effort to determine how the School of Theology relates to the university, the sponsoring church, the broader evangelical community, and to the social and political climate;

3. Development of a seminary "Mission Statement," to define the school's role and purpose in a separate statement from that of the University; Establish dialogue with boards of other schools with a similar structure (university-seminary relation with same board of trustees), giving attention to how committees function, how the seminaries are governed, and what changes have been instituted or are under consideration;

4. Creation of a seminary advisory committee to be a resource for the School of Theology dean, giving more direct alumni and church involvement in planning the curriculum and program of the seminary;

5. Preparation of a document to enhance the relationship between the University and the Church of God, in the nature of a cooperation Working Paper or "Covenant Document";

6. Expand and update the report submitted to the Association of Theological Schools and The North Central Association of Colleges and Schools during the reaccreditation process, and distribute to trustees and other decision-makers; and

7. Regularly include reports and information related to the Seminary and to the "Seminary Trusteeship Project" on the agenda of future meetings of the board.

The award from Lilly was part of a funded program of $791,000 offered for use toward strengthening the governing boards of theological schools, and more than 200 seminaries were invited to compete for the grants. Forty of the requesting schools were successful in their attempt to be participants in the grant, and Anderson School of Theology was one of the forty, receiving $28,525 to fund our project.

One of our first faculty actions was to develop a seminary "Mission Statement." We completed that task in early 1990, and submitted our proposed Statement to the Board of Trustees during a retreat held for them that August in keeping with the Lilly Endowment Grant concerns. The "Mission Statement" was approved by the entire board in May 1991. The text of the Statement was as follows:

The Mission of the School of Theology of Anderson University is: To educate at the graduate professional level both men and women for Christian ministry. To this end, we are committed to be a community of scholars who are church-related, and in whose character and servanthood the following are vitally linked: biblical faith; academic integrity; Christian spirituality; love for persons; and a responsible relation with the created order and all humankind.

There was one particular section of our statement that caused considerable discussion within the Board's Seminary Trustee Committee. It was the wording "a community of scholars." Two members of the committee took exception to that description of the faculty and wanted us to revise it or excise that wording from the statement because it seemed to them too elitist. I explained to the dissenters our rationale for describing ourselves as a community of scholars, and I defended the aptness of the description, but promised to report the concern to our faculty. When I did report what the dissenters advised, the faculty did as I expected: we let our chosen wording remain. The plenary session discussion when the full Board of Trustees met in regular session confirmed our faculty judgment. Our "Statement of Mission" thus became part of all subsequent official publications of the seminary.

We were increasingly pleased as our enrollment picture showed evidence of change for the better. Whereas the enrollment in September 1989 stood at 100 (seventy-three full-time-equivalent based on a registration for twelve hours of credit), and had slipped in September 1990 to a headcount of ninety-four (sixty-seven full-time equivalent), that number had increased to 112 in September 1991 (eighty-one full-time-equivalent enrollment). As the 1993-1994 school year began, our enrollment stood at 119 students, with seventy-eight full-time and forty-one part-time.

Many factors were responsible for the low enrollment picture we worked hard at changing. For one thing, fewer Church of God students were seeking a seminary education, and some of those who were did so at other schools or in places more conveniently reached from where they lived and worked. For another, the importance of a seminary education had never been mandated by the Church of God Movement or factored by enough congregations into the list of requirements to be met by ministers seeking to be a pastor. Both of these circumstances had a long-standing history in the Movement, and they were among the strategic problems listed and treated by Barry L.

Callen in a special paper placed before the Board of Trustees during the Lilly Endowment-funded retreat we held at Brown County Inn in August of 1990.

Our enrollment picture was also affected by the off/on relationship between some of our Movement churches and our university. The history of relations between Anderson University and the churches has been a chequered one, like that between a parent and a growing child, with periods of power struggles between the school's visionary leaders and some of the church's spiritual "watchdogs." From its beginning, Anderson University (then Anderson Bible Training School) was religiously based, but its continuing development and direction positioned the school primarily as a center of education rather than evangelism, while some church leaders wanted to set the school's agenda and mandate that the school's mentality be the same as that of the church.

I was familiar with the "uneasy feeling" some church leaders confessed having when graduate theological education was being discussed and advised, and I had heard some of the protests lodged against this educational process. I knew that the roots of our Movement's life were fed by a stream of radical Protestantism that so emphasizes a heart experience with God that any sponsorship of a head experience is viewed with suspicion and mistrust. Like others, I knew that an over-intellectualizing of the Christian faith is always deadening, but I also knew that thinking reasonably and systematically about the issues and implications of the Christian faith is a must in our postmodern world.

As seminary dean I felt the need to address this matter. It was unavoidable as the faculty and I began revising our curricular offerings and specific degree structures and requirements. I guided the faculty in exploring our concern against the background history of the aims and purposes of evangelical theological education. It would not be ours to solve the longstanding problem of a divided mentality in the Church of God regarding education for ministry, but I did stress the importance

413

and timeliness of seeking to bring the seminary and the churches into agreement on some priorities for ministry, especially the concern for church growth and the concern to identify and inspire new leaders. I also wanted the seminary to continue to develop as the place to which those congregations that desired to do so could look for theological insights regarding our times, our society, our goals as a nation, and our group identity and mission as the Church of God.

With students coming to our seminary from diverse backgrounds, racially and denominationally, we needed to be eager not only to maintain the ethos of our Movement's life, but to share it with them. We were attracting students of merit and we had the grand opportunity to help shape them for spiritual leadership in the church, nation, and world, readying them to lead in crisis times in our pluralistic society, and readying them to model a Christian spirituality and Christian social conscience. As I saw it, we not only needed to prepare competent leaders for churches, but to help our students be received as creative and credible moral voices in a society woefully lacking in integrity and a sense of values. We realized that we could help them best through accenting scholarship, spirituality, and service. We also knew that we would have to provide our students with more opportunities to intern with vital leaders and congregations through a well-managed field education program.

As the faculty and I reviewed and revised our curricular offerings, we were mindful of many things: changes in society, changes in the church, changes in faculty expertise and expectations, and, among other things, changes in backgrounds, types, and ages of seminarians. More older, second-career students had come to study with us, and the average age of our seminarians was up to thirty-four, which was a large shift from the previous decade when the average age was twenty-four and when most seminarians were fresh out of college. The seminary population in the early 1990s was more diverse, student needs were many, and more resourceful funding was demanded through scholarships, not repayable government loans. Our

Church of God students were all informed about the benefits available to them through the Blackwelder Fund provided by the Church of God.

Our task was to design and implement educational programs that were viable and valuable. We concerned ourselves with what we knew as basic and germane to the study and practice of ministry, aware that training for any specialized ministry had to be based on the "fundamentals" (with a small "f"). Our faculty was small by comparison, so we could not employ full-time faculty to teach several specialized ministries, but we could partner with other schools and institutions that had such faculty persons, and we could create internships and supply funding for students interested in such specializations. And we did.

As we did our work, we had to ask ourselves what kind of image our seminary was projecting. We needed to know the shape and spirit of our life at that stage in our forty-year history. We had to ask what kind of leader we were expected to produce. Our faculty agreed that we should seek to prepare persons of devotion and discipline. Each graduate should leave with a disciplined heart and mind, ready to serve people, grappling with contemporary concerns in light of biblical faith, using a thorough-going intellectual integrity and a Spirit-led evangelical fervor. We did not need to re-engineer the seminary to do this; the seminary structure needed no such change. It was rather a matter of revisioning the curriculum, restructuring courses, and honoring new areas of focus.

There were many ideas for improvement as we reviewed and revised the curriculum. The many different ideas and ideals made for some very lively and engaging faculty sessions. While I had my own vision of the direction we should take in serving the new generation of students, I remained open to hear and discuss the suggestions my colleagues offered to me in private and to the entire faculty when in session. I saw the processing of different viewpoints as a healthy experience, and I was a mediating person serving as arbitrator when different ideas and ideals tended to clash. I saw arbitrating as part of my role as dean. Having been a pastor for so many years, I knew how to do that and how to keep a spirit of peace alive in a community of thinkers and activists.

We worked in teams. The members of each department mapped out recommended courses within their province of studies, and the recommendations were distributed to the entire faculty for study, discussion, and action. Several courses were thus revised, basic hours of concentration were amended, and a few new degree concentrations were added to meet the needs of persons seeking specialization in some area of career and ministry concern. With the time already upon us for a new seminary catalog (1991-1993) to appear, that catalog carried only a modest number of changes, but the refined curricular offerings and new degree concentrations were ready to be announced when the 1993-1995 catalog was printed.

There were three degree programs: the Master of Divinity degree, the basic theological and professional degree for persons preparing for Christian ministry; the Master of Religious Education degree for persons seeking professional competence for service in the educational programs of the church; and the Master of Arts degree, an academic rather than a professional degree. The three-year M. Div. degree was restructured to allow three optional concentrations: Master of Divinity: Standard; Master of Divinity: Christian Education; and Master of Divinity: Urban Ministry. The Master of Arts degree was structured to give a concentration in Biblical Studies or in Historical and Intercultural Studies. Those choosing the latter were allowed a choice between three tracks of concentration: track A, Church History; track B, Urban and Multicultural Studies; and track C, Ethnic and Overseas Studies. We also revised the course numbering system. The downside to some concentrations for specialized ministry was that a greater number of required courses inevitably left the seminarian room for fewer electives.

Although it did not receive official approval from our

accrediting bodies in time to be printed in the 1993-1995 catalog, there was an additional degree offering that we began to publicize shortly after that catalog was published. It was a program of studies leading to the Doctor of Ministry degree. This was perhaps the most ambitious innovation at the School of Theology during my deanship there.

Until 1992, when a Master of Business Administration was first offered by the University, the only graduate degree programs on campus were offered by the School of Theology. Prior to the actual beginning of the MBA program, the Board of Trustees approved the plan I submitted to begin offering an in-service, contextual Doctor of Ministry degree program of studies. When I first talked to faculty about the hope expressed across the years for our seminary to initiate a doctoral program, there was a mild laugh. I had acquainted myself with the papers left from previous deans, and I knew some of their dreams. Actually, in promoting our seminary, I knew it would be important to introduce at some point the logic of taking the next degree step as indication of our growth and development as a servant arm of the church. With this in mind, James W. Bradley and I worked in earnest across a year on a plan that we finally submitted for discussion. We refined the plan using research I had conducted while studying the strengths and weaknesses of programs already in existence elsewhere. I had an intimate knowledge about other programs since I was a member of the Commission on Accrediting of the Association of Theological Schools.

I was elected to membership on the ATS Commission on Accrediting in 1991. Our seminary had been accredited since 1965, fifteen years after its beginning, and it was the nineteenth school within the evangelical wing of Protestantism to be accredited at that time. Membership on the Commission on Accrediting kept me in full contact with what was happening at other schools both through their reports to ATS and through visits in which we members were often involved for purposes of reaccreditation or problem solving. All of this had aided my "schooling" regarding degree standards, operational problems, concerns for efficiency, and the awareness of how to proceed in projecting and implementing change and growth.

In addition to experiences from having been on several accreditation visitation teams, sometimes as member and often as chairperson, I was quite familiar with the ATS standards that were applicable to graduate degree programs. Armed with such information, and assisted by Associate Dean Bradley and his research, we developed a D. Min. degree track. I prepared a proposal that President Edwards reviewed, along with A. Patrick Allen, the university's Vice President for Academic Affairs. Allen suggested that we should allow the M.B.A. some time for development before introducing the proposed new doctoral degree program. I saw the two programs as serving different clientele and knew that the proposed doctoral program could well fund itself. President Edwards gave me approval to move forward with the planning, aware that the faculty would voice its concerns. They did, but they agreed to endorse the plan for presentation to the trustees. The Board of Trustees approved the plan in May, 1992, for implementation in the fall of 1993.

I then submitted a formal request to the North Central Association and the Association of Theological Schools' Commission on Accrediting, the two accrediting bodies to which we were accountable, asking them to schedule a focus visit to assess our school's readiness to offer the degree. The focus visit team came to our campus, with representatives from both accrediting bodies as its members. The team examined our operations and resources and afterward submitted a report of approval to the ATS Commission. Shortly afterward, we were in business, as the saying goes. Dr. Bradley and I prepared and distributed a separate brochure about the Doctor of Ministry degree program and almost immediately his office had a long list of applicants wanting to be interviewed for entrance into it. In his Annual Report to the Board of Trustees for 1993-94, President Edwards spoke approvingly about this new development at the seminary:

The primary achievement of the year was the establishment of the degree program, Doctor of Ministry. The program is contextual, requiring persons applying for admission to have a minimum of three years of pastoral ministry experience and come to the program with a covenant of support from the congregation or ministry context where she or he is serving. The program has had the review of a joint visiting committee of the North Central Association and the Association of Theological Schools. Both accrediting bodies have now approved this addition to the degree programs of the School of Theology.

The faculty and I were greatly pleased in having accomplished much of what we set out to do. I was pleased, as well, in being referred to as a "teaching dean," because teaching kept me present at the focal point of what must happen in any first-rate school—learning for life and labor. I taught courses in my capacity as Professor of Preaching and Biblical Studies. Despite the time given to classroom teaching, seminary staff sessions, faculty and committee meetings, plus weekly meetings with other members of the President's Executive Staff, I managed to find time to work with some others beyond our campus who came to see me. Most of them were people who requested some personal time with me because of their professional interest in the field of theology or preaching.

One such person was Richard Gray, an Anderson University graduate studying for a Ph.D. at Fuller Theological Seminary. Gray completed an independent tutorial course that I directed. Brenda Champney was another. She needed advisement on her dissertation project while studying toward the Th.D. degree at Boston University School of Theology. Reginald George Smith, a pastor in Florida, and also an Anderson University alumnus, was doing graduate studies at St. Thomas University in Miami and requested my help as reader of a paper he wrote on Howard Thurman for one of his courses there. Melvin Smith was a

Doctor of Ministry student at Pittsburgh Theological Seminary. I spent some time advising him. Gerald Thomas, a Ph.D. candidate at Southern Baptist Theological Seminary, sought time with me, visited my office, and received my help as a reader of his dissertation on Gardner C. Taylor's preaching. And there were others.

I answered the telephone one afternoon and received a call from Louisville, Kentucky. A young man was on the line who identified himself as Robert Smith, Jr. He informed me that he was a doctoral student at Southern Baptist Theological Seminary. He identified his major field as preaching and reported that he was at work preparing a prospectus about the dissertation he was interested in completing for the Ph. D. degree there. Smith asked to have some time with me, at my convenience, to go over what he had written. We agreed on a time and he drove to Anderson from Louisville.

During the course of our time together, Robert Smith, Jr. showed evidence that he was familiar with my books on preaching. He mentioned having listened to tapes of the Mullins Lectures on Preaching I gave at Southern in 1981, and he confessed a desire to take a course from me in advanced preaching as part of his work for the doctorate. He also wanted me to be on his dissertation committee. His advisor at Southern, whom I knew, had agreed with this plan, so I agreed. In connection with his desire to take a course from me, I asked Smith about the problem of distance and time for driving between Louisville and Anderson. He had computed both and was willing to make the trip. He enrolled in the class for the next semester and met the sessions with regularity and promptness. All this, in addition to pastoring a church in Cincinnati!

Robert Smith, Jr., impressed me by his focus, his stamina, his work ethic, punctuality, persistence, and sense of mission. It seemed evident to me that he had what it would take to become a teacher of preaching. Smith completed his dissertation and his doctorate; he wrote on Helmut Thieleicke's preaching. Smith's aptness for the role he chose for his future was validated by

Southern's choice of him to be one of its professors of preaching. He accepted their call, but later went to Beeson Divinity School to teach there. It was at Beeson Divinity School, on the campus of Samford University in Birmingham, Alabama, that Robert Smith's career flowered. I took great delight in watching his work gain deserved notice.

I was greatly surprised a few years later when Dr. Robert Smith, Jr., and Dr. Timothy George, dean at Beeson Divinity School, called to inform me that they were in the process of jointly writing for and editing for Broadman & Holman Publishers a new book on racial reconciliation and had decided to dedicate the book to me. It was their judgment that the book would minister to many in both the church and world and they wanted to honor me as one whose life commitment has been to promote racial reconciliation. In due course their book appeared as *A Mighty Long Journey: Reflections on Racial Reconciliation* (Broadman & Holman Publishers, 2000). On the dedication page they placed these words:

> For
> James Earl Massey,
> our beloved friend and mentor,
> theologian of reconciliation in
> the service of the church,
> on the occasion of his seventieth birthday.

Some Other Activities

As a part of my office mail one day I received a letter from Harold Myra inviting me to accept an assignment to serve as one of the senior editors for *Christianity Today.* I agreed to do so, having served across several years as a contributing editor and as a resource scholar for the magazine's Institute. I viewed the requested service as another means of ministry. Having written for *Christianity Today* before, I reasoned that perhaps my participation at that level had been appreciated and I was thus invited into the managerial circle where the issues were determined, themes projected, and writers identified, enlisted, and assigned. It was as I thought, with the added responsibility of writing editorials and occasional pieces myself.

One of the first pieces I was asked to write was an appreciative interpretation of Tom Skinner, whose unexpected death stunned so many. Next, I was asked to treat the meaning and impact of Martin Luther King, Jr., which I did. In both instances the interpretative angle was central, and in both cases my work was published largely as I prepared it, with no alteration of my perspective or emphasis. All of what I wrote was fresh. Nothing was recycled from previously published writings, although it can be wisdom to recapture from a previous printing something that needs to be made available to new readership in a new setting. I continued my work as a senior editor for *Christianity Today* across the years I served as dean in Anderson.

I enjoyed the work we did and the collegiality we experienced in our senior editors meetings. It was plain to me that we each honored the enterprise that brought us together and that we appreciated each other as well. George Brushaber, president of Bethel College and Seminary in Minneapolis, was the senior editor and a friend of long standing. He and I had worked together during the 1970s on the editorial board of *Christian Scholar's Review,* a journal published by Christian scholars to encourage communication and understanding between themselves and to promote dialogue with others. Timothy George, dean of Beeson Divinity School and another long time friend, was also one of the senior editors, and so was James I. Packer. Although I had heard much about him and was familiar with many of his writings, it was at a meeting of senior editors that I first met Jim Packer.

Some time earlier, back during the second semester of the 1989-1990 school year, I was surprised one morning in April to receive a letter asking for my involvement in a publishing project of considerable importance to the wider church world. The United Methodist Publishing House, through its Abingdon Press, was about to undertake the production of a new biblical commentary series which would make the best current scholarship in biblical studies, hermeneutics, and homiletics available to clergy and laity who preach or teach in local churches. I was invited by Robert K. Feaster, president and publisher of the United Methodist Publishing House, and Jack A. Keller, Jr., project director, to serve as one of the ten members on the editorial board for *The New Interpreter's Bible,* a twelve-volume set to replace the older *Interpreter's Bible* that had been published during the 1950s.

The editorial board would have the immediate task of determining the best possible format for the new commentary series, shape the guidelines to be followed by scholars chosen to contribute to the series, and identify and contact the scholars desired as contributors. Later, the editorial board members would have to work directly with the contributors to assure the successful preparation and editing of the manuscripts submitted. Given the magnitude of the project, a project director had been selected and assigned to manage the details of coordination and production. The publishing project was expected to include twelve volumes and require eight years for completion. *The New Interpreter's Bible* was to be a new reference work both scholarly and practical, a resource work that would enhance faithful preaching and teaching in local churches, and provide more "handles" for grasping the meaning and significance of Scripture for faith and life than one typically finds in the more critical commentary series.

The editorial board was to be configured in three basic groups: four members were to edit the Old Testament commentaries and related general articles; three members were to edit the New Testament commentaries and general articles associated with those books and their historical period; and three members were to work with all of the chosen commentators to help them "focus" throughout on the preaching and teaching possibilities of the manageable textual units of each biblical book. Given my work in biblical studies and homiletics, I was asked to commit myself to be a contributing writer and a member of the editorial team. I would join Thomas G. Long of Princeton Theological Seminary and Gail R. O'Day of Candler School of Theology in overseeing the homiletical aspects of the projected series. "As a preacher, you are renowned across the church," the letter stated. "As an author and a homiletician, you are highly respected by preachers serving local congregations and by colleagues in the academic community. By virtue of your talents and experience, you would bring to *The New Interpreter's Bible* uncommon sensitivity to the practical needs and concerns that readers in local congregations bring to a critical biblical commentary."

In deciding how to respond to the letter of invitation, I thought about the original *Interpreter's Bible* commentary series, with its twelve volumes published between 1951 and 1957. I thought about the context in which that distinguished series made its entrance and how it was received and used. I had often used the volumes of that series in preparing to preach and teach. I thought about the need to do in the 1990s what our scholar-predecessors did in the 1950s, and about the opportunity the projected publishing venture offered to help the church to be the church. I thought, as well, about the trust and confidence posited in me by those who issued the invitation, and about how pleased Howard Thurman would have been to see me serve as a writer and working editor for the new commentary series planned to supplement and update the older series for which he had been a writer and a consulting editor.

As I continued to think about the letter, it became clear to me that my answer would have to be "Yes." I wrote back, committing myself to serve, adding: "Aware that this commitment will demand much on my part, I readily pledge my best efforts for a project that is worthy, timely and so needed." Thus it was that I joined Leander E. Keck (Convener), Jack A. Keller, Jr. (Project Director), Neil M. Alexander (General Manager, and later President of United Methodist Publishing House), and the distinguished cadre of scholars who comprised the guiding team for *The New Interpreter's Bible* commentary series.

The new commentary was, in the words of Leander E.

Keck, "to be a wholly new work for a largely new situation," because so much had changed in the society, churches, and scholarship during the four decades its predecessor series had been in use. Not least among the many changes which made the new commentary series necessary was the changed climate with respect to inclusiveness—denominational, racial, and gender inclusiveness. For example, when *The Interpreter's Bible* was published in the 1950s, there was only one woman (Louise Pettibone Smith) and only one African American (Howard Thurman) among the one hundred twenty four contributors. The new commentary series corrected that imbalance and lack, among others, while serving its main end of providing a useful resource for an effective use of the Bible in our time.

A few days after Jack A. Keller, Jr., the project director, received my reply, I received a copy of the letter he sent to inform President Nicholson about my having been chosen to be part of the editorial team for the project. "We are gratified to have this outstanding member of your faculty join with us in what promises to be one of the major events in religious publishing in the 1990s." President Nicholson sent his congratulations and encouraged me in the work, and so did President Edwards when he succeeded Nicholson in that office; both leaders understood and applauded my involvement, and both took some pride in that I was doing so as a representative leader from Anderson University. Working on this commentary series exacted much from me, but the attention I gave to that task fed my teaching and preaching. The burden of that multi-year task was always lightened by the understanding, trust, and cooperativeness I experienced as a colleague of the other editorial board members, and also by the understanding and blessing I received first from President Robert A. Nicholson and later from President James L. Edwards.

While working on *The New Interpreter's Bible* aided my teaching and preaching, there was another study project in which I was involved, a project that, together with my service on the Commission on Accrediting of the Association of

Theological Schools, aided my administrative focus. That project was the Fuller Consultation on the Aims and Purposes of Evangelical Theological Education. The project was sponsored by the Institute for the study of American Evangelicals, funded by Lilly Endowment, and directed by Richard Mouw, president of Fuller Theological Seminary. Working on that project gave me a sharpened perspective for viewing many of the issues that our own seminary had to face in promoting theological education in a church group whose focus and history has kept higher education (particularly for its ministry) on the periphery of its life. The understanding I gained through the Consultation about the past of other evangelical bodies was most useful in helping me to guide our own seminary faculty in revisioning and revising our curricular offerings. One of the project results from our Fuller Consultation was the publication of the book *Theological Education in the Evangelical Tradition,* edited by D. G. Hart and R. Albert Mohler, Jr. (Baker Books, 1996).

The 1990-91 school year saw several projections proceeding well and on schedule. As the school year closed, Gwendolyn and I traveled to Wiesbaden, Germany, to attend the 1991 World Conference of the Church of God. There I was the keynote speaker, and also, during the World Forum, led discussions based on a predistributed booklet containing seven papers on the topic of sanctification. The booklet, *Sanctification: Discussion Papers in Preparation for the Fourth International Dialogue on Doctrinal Issues*, was published by the School of Theology in 1989. While at the Conference I was contacted by the delegates from Japan who presented me with an invitation to visit Japan and speak during their general assembly in August of 1993. In follow-up correspondence I agreed to make the trip.

Before leaving on the trip to Germany I knew that 1991 was the bicentennary year of Mozart's death, and that commemorations of that extraordinary composer's life and work would dominate the scene across Europe, and especially in Salzburg, Austria, his birthplace and home city. So after the World

Convention ended in Weisbaden, Gwendolyn and I followed our prearranged plans to go to Salzburg, Austria. Being mindful, too, that Claudio Arrau had died in Austria that June, I wanted to secure any articles and books published in Germany and Austria about him.

Using our Eurailpass tickets purchased before leaving the United States, Gwendolyn and I were entitled to make as many stops en route to Salzburg as we desired, and at no extra cost. So we left Wiesbaden going north first to Bonn, Germany. I wanted to see the capital city and especially to visit the Beethovenhaus. The ninety-five mile trip to Bonn did not take long. The train was on time, the coach was clean and comfortable, and we enjoyed a good meal on the way. Once in Bonn we took a taxi to the elegant and intimate Steigenberger Hotel Venusberg, where we were preregistered for a suite; I wanted the best accomodations throughout our trip because Gwendolyn and I were celebrating our fortieth wedding anniversary.

Gwendolyn was not feeling well on the day that I set out to see the Beethovenhaus, Bonn's pride and joy, so she did not accompany me when I visited the house where Ludwig Beethoven was born in 1770 and lived until 1774. Although my days at the conference in Wiesbaden had been workdays, I felt no exhaustion; the prospects of the leisurely travel and anniversary plans had exhilarated me. During my visit to the many rooms in the Beethovenhaus, I took notice of that master's last fortepiano, several portraits and busts, his glasses, some of the ear trumpets on which he depended for a time, and even a lock of his hair, among other exhibited items. In a museum room I also took notice of a photograph of Claudio Arrau, my keyboard idol, hanging among those of musicians who had been awarded the Beethoven Prize.

The 400-mile trip south to Salzburg, Austria, allowed me time to reflect on the musical heritage to which Mozart and Beethoven contributed so creatively, and to anticipate the concerts we expected to experience in Salzburg across the next week. The Salzburg Festival was in progress and we secured tickets to several musical events. We visited several Mozart museums, but I felt touched by the exhibitions and memorabilia in Wolfgang Amadeus Mozart's birthplace. As we paced the several floors of the house, Gwendolyn and I were part of a long line of visitors the press of whose presence seemed to demand a more hurried walk and look than I thought reasonable.

The International Summer Academy at the Mozarteum was also in progress, and during an evening recital there on Thursday, July 25, I got to hear, among others, Rachel Jordan, a young African American violin student from New Orleans, play Gabriel Faure's Sonata in A major. I was impressed by her talent and interpretive skill and went backstage to greet and compliment her (and her accompanist) after the recital. A Friday, July 26, 1991 evening concert we attended in the Large Festival House featured a Mozart Divertimento (K, 136) and two of his symphonies (No. 40 and 41), played by the Vienna Philharmonic under guest director Riccardo Muti. During the intermission I saw several big name musicians in the milling crowd and identified them to Gwendolyn; Seiji Ozawa was one of them. During the second part of the concert I noticed again the presence and activity of several camera personnel upfront, and whispered to Gwendolyn that the concert was being video-taped. I made a mental note to watch for the release, and purchased the video when it reached the market later that year as a Philips Video Classic.

But it was the opportunity to see *the Mozarteum* again, and to introduce Gwendolyn to that school and setting that gave me the greatest joy. I wanted her to see the place and feel the atmos-phere that helped me to survive that year we were forced by my "serving the nation" to spend apart from each other. I walked the halls of that famous music school again, located favorite spots, and listened with interest and hope for the students I overheard practicing their assigned lessons and memorizing works for recitals.

It had been thirty-nine years since I studied there, and while much had changed, so much remained the same, as befits an historic school. I went to the Mozarteum office, introduced myself to one of the secretaries, and was delighted when the director came to greet me. After a cordial exchange of pleasantries, the director told me that Professor Heinz Scholz, my teacher during 1952, had died in 1988 at 91 years of age. The director gave me the telephone number of his widow and presented me with a copy of a 230-page history book, a chronicle published in 1980 to mark the centennial of the International Mozarteum Foundation (1880-1980). Heinz Scholz was named and pictured at several points in the chronicle, highlighted not only as a professor at the Mozarteum University but as a long-term member of the Foundation. On a copy of the notice the director shared with me about my teacher's death, I took note that Scholz was regarded as the prime scholar among the generations of pianists associated with the Mozarteum. As I left the office, walking back toward Hotel Osterreichischer Hof, where Gwendolyn and I were lodged, I breathed a prayer of thanks to God for the musical teaching and inspiration I received from Heinz Scholz as a special student of his thirty-nine years earlier at the Mozarteum. I finally paused over a cup of coffee in the hotel pastry shop, mindful of what my life had embraced and emitted across the years as a sent preacher rather than a skilled pianist. Blessed by the understanding that I was busy doing what I was really born to do, I suffered no regrets and therefore enjoyed the music-making of others there in Salzburg all the more.

Later that fall, just as the first semester of the 1991-1992 school year began, Gwendolyn had to be hospitalized. The test results from a battery of examinations indicated the presence of a cancerous breast tumor that needed to be removed. We finally understood why she had not felt at her best during the trip to Europe and the weeks after our return. Our spirits moved from the high ground of celebration to the lowland of crisis. The operation took place, with a successful outcome, but only after years of regular and repeated testing did we experience some sense of relief from that very wearying experience.

Bowing Out

As the last year of my five-year term as seminary dean approached, I took a look back across my time and services as the School of Theology dean. I had honored the trust of the church in handling my assignment with care and diligence. I had worked with the faculty in seeking to achieve the goals on which we had agreed. We had experienced some successes. A modest increase had taken place in student enrollment. New curricular programs were in place to meet the needs of the church and specific ministry requests, and a Doctor of Ministry degree program had been established. Strengthened relations between the seminary and the church were vividly in evidence, and a faculty vacancy caused by George Kufeldt's retirement had been filled by Timothy R. Dwyer, a young Church of God scholar of outstanding background and potential.

I had provided leadership to the faculty as a collective body, on the one hand, and worked closely with each faculty member as colleague, on the other, seeking to encourage excellence, provide equipment, aid their productivity, and open doors for publication of their work. I had sought to lead the faculty in modeling our mission before the students and in seeking to convey at every turn what theological education provides and makes possible. A faculty can sometimes be a group of independent thinkers, each member a specialist in his or her field of knowledge and inquiry, with some influence gained therefrom to wield among students. Our faculty members each had an authority from their learning and an attractiveness from their experience which made their presence a potent force in our seminary, but my services as dean were necessary to help the faculty be and disport themselves as a community. I was concerned that no faculty member would dominate students, disappoint students, disgust students by excessive demands, or because of pride-inciting opportunities desert their students.

The range of my work as administrator had been considerably detailed from the first, but the obligations had multiplied across the years. The wider Anderson University scene made its understood institutional demands, and there were the ever-present calls from within the supporting church to serve on committees, attend meetings, preach here and there, and serve as consulting theologian and counselor as needed. As expected, I had remained alert and open, eager to serve. There were times when I had to decline some invitation, but I always sought to be prepared for those services required and expected in all engagements I did accept.

Deans of theological seminaries are like pastors of churches, not only in work, but in that they are in succession, part of a procession of servants. Each term of service must be built on the previous term, and each succeeding leader must appreciate who and what went before if there is to be continuity, stability, and a sense of community. I did not view my deanship in the perspective of a career but a calling, so I had set myself to deal with the needs of the seminary and to achieve the goals germane to its smooth and efficient and continuous operation. As I looked back on what had happened, and was happening, in cooperation with my leadership, I felt satisfied that during my term as dean our School of Theology had moved several steps forward.

I retired as dean of Anderson School of Theology in June, 1995, which was the end of the five-year term to which I had committed myself. In early October, 1993, I sent President Edwards a letter announcing my intention to retire at the end of the 1994-1995 school term. Although I was at home in the administrative post as dean and valued the opportunity I had to serve the seminary and the church, I knew that I did not desire to continue beyond the time to which I had previously committed myself. I thought telling the president at that mid-point would allow him time to project his thinking and prepare for the selection of a new dean. He announced my decision to the trustees in his annual report to them:

Dean James Earl Massey has indicated to me that at the time of his sixty-fifth birthday, he wishes to retire from the deanship. Dr. Massey has served this university, the School of Theology and the church in remarkable, gifted, committed and effective ways. He has extended the reach, reputation, and service of the school to the highest levels of association in the academy of theological education and the wider church. We have agreed that he will complete his leadership with us at the close of the 1994-95 school year. With this decision, I will be bringing to you a recommendation for a special relationship and role I would like to retain with Dr. Massey.

Edwards further stated: "A process for identifying excellent and promising candidates for the deanship will be initiated. After wide consultation, I will bring a recommendation for the deanship before this Board for your confirmation, and subsequent General Assembly ratification."

I was succeeded in the deanship by David L. Sebastian, a graduate of our School of Theology who had earned his doctorate at Fuller Theological Seminary. Sebastian was a prominent younger pastor who had served in Phoenix, Arizona, and at the distinguished Salem Avenue Church of God in Dayton, Ohio. He left the Dayton church pastorate to take the seminary deanship. I did not have to retire when I did. I was experiencing a comparatively healthy life at sixty-five, and free, by University code, to seek or accept appointment for a second term, but I chose not to do so. Retiring at that time seemed the right thing to do, so I did it.

Those who serve or lead will confront a dilemma from time to time, and the dilemma is forever the same: whether to stay put or move on, whether to hold on or let go, and wisdom and courage must prevail in dealing with that dilemma if one is to have peace of soul. While in leadership one can feel needed, and even be needed because the service being rendered is necessary. But even then, wisdom and realism remind us that we should "number [count] our days," as the psalmist advised (Ps. 90:12), and not anxiously seek to guarantee them or ambitiously seek to extend them. I have long viewed that admonition as applicable to the days of some particular service role as well as the days of our life itself. As it is in life, so it is in our labors: we come, and we must go. Both in life and in our labors we are involved inevitably in a procession. Wisdom shows itself when we live with a sense of granted time and when we labor with a sense of when to let some service role go, trusting the sovereignty of God for a right shaping and handling of the future of that to which our time and services have been given.

Unlike the six previous deans of the seminary, David Sebastian was not an academician, but he nevertheless entered into his new role with an adequate background for partnering with the seminary faculty in their servanthood to the churches. Since 1986 he had served as a member of the university's trustee board, and since 1991 as the board chair. It was through Sebastian's involvement with the board's seminary committee that he and I first worked with closeness, although we had known each other at long range.

As David Sebastian succeeded me as seminary dean, I thought it a most interesting parallel that I was being succeeded a second time in a national church post by a senior pastor from the Dayton church. J. David Grubbs had been my successor as *Christian Brotherhood Hour* Speaker. And, interestingly, Sebastian's successor in the same church, Rolland E. Daniels, had been a student in my seminary preaching classes. Among those who took homiletics courses from me, I ranked Daniels, with his gifts, within the top percentile. From the first, Daniels showed considerable giftedness for pulpit work, as did Spencer Spaulding, G. Lee Wallace, Harry R. Kuehl, Claude L. Robold, Jeannette R. Flynn, Edward L. Nelson, David C. Shultz, Andrew David Johnson, David Markle, Kerry B. Robinson, Lori Salierno, and Bartholomew Riggins, among others. I have named these leaders, still impressed by the way they each applied themselves and by how their pulpit ministries became noteworthy. In teaching homiletics I sought to help students go beyond being mindful of their gifts to being mindful as well that a gift is but a capacity that must be cultivated, disciplined, and surrendered to God before it can yield its intended benefits. Thinking about these former students, as well as many others, I rejoice before God for the privilege I had to interact so meaningfully with them during their seminary years, and since.

My retirement was honored by the university through two bestowals. The Board of Trustees voted me "Dean Emeritus and Distinguished Professor at Large" and during the commencement that May I received at the hands of President Edwards the university's honorary Doctor of Letters degree. In the March 16 issue of *The Andersonian,* our university campus newspaper, an article by Glendan Guttenfelder lauded my service years, referring to me as "one of Anderson's most revered professors." During the summer, a festschrift edited by Barry L. Callen was published in my honor. The honorary volume included essays written by twenty scholar-friends, and was titled *Sharing Heaven's Music: The Heart of Christian Preaching* (Abingdon Press, 1995). I was remembered on the occasion of my retirement also by the administration and faculty at Warner Pacific College. During their commencement, which took place one week following Anderson University's, I gave the commencement address and at the hands of President Marshall Christensen received an honorary Doctor of Divinity degree. That August, the National Association of the Church of God, during its annual camp meeting at West Middlesex, Pennsylvania, presented me with a Distinguished Christian Service Award in Leadership, a Distinguished Christian Service Award in Ministry, and a special medallion that named me "National Association Minister-at-Large." That October, after my year of service as their Preacher-in-Residence during their pastoral search, Park Place Church of God named me its "Minister-at-Large" after their new pastor, Edward L. Nelson, began his ministry there. Nelson, one of my former students, had urged that honorary appointment, and the congregation agreed. I was grateful for these gestures of regard from the church for my services within its life. I was sure then, and remain so now, that my friend T. Franklin Miller, chair at the time of the church's Staff-Parish Relations Committee, had more to do with that honorary appointment than he was willing to admit!

Much to my surprise, honors were accorded me from other sectors during the year I retired. Early in January that year I received a telephone call while at home from Dr. Benjamin F. Payton. Mindful of my pending retirement, he invited me to deliver the Annual Founder's Day address at Tuskegee University on Sunday, March 26. I agreed to speak. Gwendolyn and I went to Tuskegee and I delivered an address on "Tuskegee's Enduring Excellence." The reception my wife and I received from the university community, and equally from the descendants of the Booker T. Washington family who were present, gave Gwendolyn and me a sense of "homecoming." The remarks President Payton gave in introducing me on my return to that beloved setting made me know that he viewed the occasion of our being back as such. Tuskegee University honored me on that occasion by President Payton conferring upon me an honorary Doctor of Humanities degree. Later that year, on November 3, I went to Nampa, Idaho, to attend the annual meeting of the Wesleyan Theological Society, meeting at Northwest Nazarene College, where I preached in the closing worship service and was honored by that Society with its "Lifetime Achievement Award."

My Retirement Years

In 1995, as I wrapped up my work as seminary dean, I was looking forward to the time in life left for me. There were both unfinished and projected writing projects to which I needed to give attention. I was still involved in the authorial and editorial teamwork to produce the remaining volumes of *The New Interpreter's Bible* (Abingdon Press) on schedule, and I needed to prepare for several named lectureships to which I had committed myself, in addition to other ecumenical, educational, and church engagements. I was feeling sufficiently healthy and looked forward to days of freedom from formal work assignments. I had no interest in any long-term service roles. I had spent many years in congregational life, missionary work, campus ministry, broadcasting, classroom teaching, and educational administration, all service roles that had been challenging, perennially engaging, and to some extent fruitful. I had faced the fact that at age sixty-five there were more years behind me than before me, but I was still eager to live, learn, and serve, and I was confident that the better or even the best part of my life had not passed. As I looked forward to retirement it was clear to me that, while my healthiest years were in the past, I still knew an energy and a zest for life and a readiness to serve.

At sixty-five, there were sure signs in my body that the aging process had not given me an exemption, but despite the surgical procedures I had undergone across the years, and despite the inevitable stresses which past assignments had brought to bear upon me, I was leaving the seminary at a time when I had not yet experienced those graver physical and mental distresses about which T. S. Eliot wrote lamentably in the "Little Gidding" section of his *Four Quartets,* namely,

> . . . the gifts reserved for age,
> To set a crown upon your lifetime's effort.

Unlike many at sixty-five, I was having no trouble with memory loss or distorted vision, no biological nightmares, no blocked hearing. Age was working in me and on me, to be sure, but standing side-by-side with what physical negatives I had come to know, I could see some positive personal gains at that point in my life. I had a sharpened insight regarding what is truly important. I was imbued with a sense of justice, and a courage that prompted me to seek good for others. I had a wisdom about problem-solving and a deeper appreciation for settled values. At sixty-five I had an adequate knowledge about who I am, a sure faith regarding where I am headed ultimately, and a clear understanding about how to get there. In addition, there was within me a willingness to leave the future to others. As I prepared for the retirement years, I was facing the unknown future with faith-tutored eyes, and I could see more than the degenerative process that is a part of being human; I could see the hand of God outstretched in my direction, pointing the way, beckoning, assuring me, and I firmly believed that that hand will one day receive me (Ps. 31:5; Luke 23:46).

There was much behind my thinking anew about faith, the future, and the problems of mortality, because on Thursday, January 5, 1995, my close and long-time friend Samuel George Hines died. His sudden and unexpected death shocked the church at large. I had just returned to Anderson that afternoon from Pittsburgh, where I had been in a work meeting of the Commission on Accrediting of the Association of Theological Schools. As I walked into my office, Lucille Wheeler, my secretary, handed me the phone. Dalineta Hines, Sam's wife, was on the line. The message she shared shook me. I fell to my knees when our talk ended. I offered a prayer of thanks to God for Sam, a prayer of intercession for Dalineta, and then a prayer for myself as a grieving brother in the Lord. In the course of our talk, Dalineta explained the circumstances surrounding Sam's death and we projected the necessary funeral arrangements. She reminded me of the pact Sam and I had made years earlier, that I should eulogize him if he "went" first and that he would eulogize me if I "went" first. I assured her that I remembered the agreement and would join with the family in Washington, D.C., for the funeral.

Gwendolyn and I went to the funeral, and so did several other Anderson University personnel and church agency leaders. The "homegoing" service in Sam's honor involved persons and greetings from the four corners of the church world, Americans and others, and this was befitting his ministry as a world Christian. I based my eulogy on 1 Thessalonians 4:13-18, preaching on "Asleep in Jesus." After the funeral, Milton Hines, Sam's youngest son, informed me that his father had used that passage for the family devotions on Monday night of the week he died! I managed to complete the sermon without losing my composure, but the assignment caused me to struggle strenuously with emotion. The prayers of many helped me. Before the funeral service began, while standing in the church narthex to instruct the large procession of ministers on the procedure we would be following, I saw President James Edwards in the group. Edwards looked in my direction, sensed my burden, hurriedly scribbled a note and handed it to me. It was a pastoral note that read: "I am praying for you, Jim!" I did what the Apostle Paul did when greeted in an hour of need by beloved believers: I "thanked God and took courage" (Acts 28:15).

I was pleased to see the *Christianity Today* notice about the death of Samuel Hines, and the *Vital Christianity* notice (February 1995). Shortly after his funeral I was one among several who contributed an article honoring his memory to *The Shining Light* (Jan.-Feb. 1995) and I wrote another, "My Friend," for the *Church of God Missions* magazine (March/April 1995) when those two Church of God publications paid special tribute to Hines's ministry. Later, in April 1995, *Vital Christianity* published an entire issue highlighting the reconciliation initiative that was a perennial theme in the preaching and ministry of Samuel G. Hines. The cover of that issue displayed a photograph of Sam, and by request of editor David C. Shultz, I wrote the guest editorial.

My sense of loss when Samuel G. Hines died was not easily managed. Strangely and sadly, as the first month of 1995 had brought a death that affected me deeply, the last month of that year brought a death that affected by wife deeply. Her mother died. But grace prevailed, and new experiences of joyful events helped to ease the pain. One of those experiences was the return visit to Tuskegee, and the honors I received there, just two months later. Another source of strength was my depth involvement with the Park Place Church of God congregation in Anderson, Indiana, serving it as Preacher-in-Residence during their months without a pastor after Donald Johnson retired.

It also was an experience of comfort when I returned again to the Tuskegee campus that September, following my retirement. I was there by invitation to deliver another address. The occasion was the first Booker T. Washington National Symposium and Exhibition, planned in commemoration of the famous speech Booker T. Washington delivered in Atlanta, Georgia, in 1895 during the Cotton States and International Exhibition held there. In commemoration of that event which brought Washington to national and world prominence, Tuskegee University teamed with the Library of Congress in preparing a centennial exhibition and a symposium of scholars who treated the theme, "Booker T. Washington's Atlanta Exposition Address Revisited: A Centennial Exhibition and Reflection." The symposium was an educational forum of scholars known for their research regarding Booker T. Washington, his celebrated speech, his times, and his legacy. The event was the beginning of a three-year project to revisit, reread, reanalyze, and reflect on the many issues Washington's speech addressed, anticipated, and influenced. I addressed the symposium on the topic, "Racial Uplift and Race Relations."

In 1997, two years after leaving the deanship of Anderson School of Theology, I was privileged to experience an unforgettable moment of grace by returning to the Anderson campus for a formal occasion at Dean Sebastian's invitation. That April, I gave the annual Senior Recognition Chapel address. It was the year-end chapel service of the seminary, and it had long been the school's custom to honor the graduating class by inviting the president or dean of some sister seminary to address them on that occasion. In following the custom that year, Dean Sebastian chose me as speaker. I especially appreciated the dean's invitation because, as his immediate predecessor, I had the joy of speaking not only to graduates from the Master of Divinity, Master of Religious Education, and Master of Arts programs, all of whom I knew, but also the first graduates from the Doctor of Ministry degree program that was developed and initiated during my tenure there as dean. It was indeed a moment of grace to see James B. Milner, Larry C. Taylor, and G. Lee Wallace each receive his hood that Friday as a doctor of ministry, the first from Anderson University School of Theology. That day of recognition and hooding was special both for them and me. I was also present for the university's degree-granting commencement ceremony the following day, and I sat with honor among my beloved former colleagues as part of the emeritus faculty.

Although I had decided in 1995 not to accept another full-time service role, I felt it necessary to make an exception when President Payton called me in early 1997 to request a conference with me. The concern he voiced merited my consideration, so we met. He informed me that Dr. Edward L. Wheeler, who succeeded me as Dean of the Chapel when I left Tuskegee, had accepted the presidency of Christian Theological Seminary in Indianapolis, Indiana, and would be leaving campus at the end of the semester. Payton asked if I would be willing to return to Tuskegee and serve The Chapel ministry until another dean was secured. After some inward wrestling, and some reminding counsel from Gwendolyn about the priorities we had agreed upon, I decided to enter campus ministry anew, but for only the next school year.

That 1997-1998 school year at Tuskegee University seemed to end all too quickly. As the second term was nearing its end and the Chapel Dean search committee was still involved in its work, President Payton said to me one afternoon, "Dean Massey, I had hoped that you would stay as long as I am going to stay." I asked him how long he planned to stay. Having just been voted another term as president by his board of trustees, Dr. Payton smiled as he replied, "Another five years!" He understood when I respectfully declined such a lengthy appointment. My pulpit work in The Chapel during the 1997-1998 school year involved a special series of sermons on "Understanding Our Human Journey." The sermons were well received, so well, indeed, that I prepared them for publication as a book, with a few sermons from my previous tenure there as dean. The book was published as *Sundays in the Tuskegee Chapel: Selected Sermons* (Abingdon Press, 2000) and received wide distribution and regard.

Expressing gratitude for my having served the university again, and at a recognized time of need, President Payton asked me to deliver the Summer Commencement address that year. I did, and was surprised afterward when he awarded me the coveted President's Distinguished Service Award and named me "Dean Emeritus of the Tuskegee Chapel." After the academic ceremony, President Payton and I followed custom and stood side by side to greet graduates, faculty members, and family members as they filed by to leave the scene. Dr. James H. M. Henderson, a senior professor and noted biologist, approached, halted, held my hand and congratulated me on the honors I had just received. Then he said, "James Earl, to my knowledge you are the first one who has worked at Tuskegee to receive both a Tuskegee honorary degree and the President's Distinguished Service Award!" I paused, unsure of how I should respond; but he, still holding my hand, immediately smiled and added, "But you are worth it!" I smiled, grateful for that senior professor's regard. He knew that I came out of retirement when I returned there to serve.

Dr Benjamin F. Payton and I enjoyed a close working relationship as administrators, but we developed a close friendship as well. My working relationship at Anderson University with presidents Robert H. Reardon, Robert A. Nicholson, and James L. Edwards was also blessed by the bonds of friendship. My relationship with each Anderson University president was enhanced both by personality factors and by our mutual rootage in a treasured Church of God heritage, while my personal relationship with Benjamin F. Payton was blessed by the historically rich Tuskegee context and our common heritage, experience, and aspirations as African Americans.

The return to Alabama from Indiana gave me more time to write and I could at last make extensive use of the library I had

441

developed across fifty years of ministry. Although I donated several hundred books to the seminary library before leaving Anderson, and gave away many books to interested students, I brought thousands of treasured volumes with me in the return to my wife's home state. All of those volumes are treasured resources, but so is the building that houses them, the place in which I read, pray, write, listen to music, and meet with leaders and former students who seek my counsel or wish to do some study. My library is situated on a back strip of our family land, within a separately fenced area some distance from our house. Because it sits out in a field area of its own, and at its distance from our home, Gwendolyn dubbed the library building "The Outback."

The building has a history. It was formerly a school building located on the grounds of the Hale County High School in Greensboro. Sometimes used as a classroom and later used by the school band as its practice place, the wooden frame building was gained by purchase in 1987 during an auction sale to clear the land for a new brick structure on the campus. After buying the building, I had it moved to our property, a distance of about two miles from its original site. Interestingly, it cost more to move the building than to buy it! Once it was relocated, the old building was restored, and then developed as my library-study, with built-in wall-to-wall and floor-to-ceiling shelving to house my books. The outside schoolroom appearance has been retained, and inside are several sitting areas where reading is done, two desk areas where writing is done, and a word-processing area where both a typewriter and computer are used. The restoration and redevelopment project was handled by J. B. Washington, a local contractor (Tuskegee University graduate), who worked with pride and superb skill in completing his task.

It was in "The Outback" that I prepared the sermons I delivered in the Tuskegee Chapel during the 1997-1998 school year, and there I afterward prepared the manuscript for *Sundays in the Tuskegee Chapel: Selected Sermons,* which Abingdon Press published in 2000. Still earlier, it was there that I completed the manuscript for my book *The Burdensome Joy of Preaching* (Abingdon Press, 1998), which *Preaching Magazine* named the 1998 Book of the Year. The book on preaching was an expanded treatment of the William E. Conger Lectures on Biblical Preaching which I delivered in March, 1995, at Beeson Divinity School at Samford University, in Birmingham, Alabama. The chapters of that book were written with a pen dipped in ink drawn from my veins, as it were, because in them I wrote about preaching from inside the task, explaining it as I have long experienced it—and as many others who have read it confessed to me that they experience it—as a burdensome joy!

It was in "The Outback" that I read, wrote, and edited manuscripts for *The New Interpreter's Bible,* and prepared for speaking assignments. "The Outback" was where I sorted through my personal papers, preparing them for deposit with institutions that formally requested them. There I sat to read, leisurely but with special interest, the first and following issues of a new quarterly magazine for preachers called *The African American Pulpit* (Vol. 1, No. 1, Winter 1997-1998), a magazine founded by Rev. David Farmer, white pastor of University Baptist Church in Baltimore, Maryland, and editor of *Pulpit Digest*. According to Farmer's own reporting, he started the magazine out of inspiration he experienced through hearing two black preachers whom he credits with having influenced his preaching style: Gardner C. Taylor and James Earl Massey. Both Dr. Taylor and I visited and preached at Southern Baptist Theological Seminary when Farmer was a doctoral student there. The quarterly he founded is dedicated solely to the sermons and writings of black preachers, thus its name.

There in "The Outback" I prepared for the second series I gave of the William L. Dawson Lectures at Tuskegee University in March, 1998. Also prepared there were: The Biblical Studies Lectures I presented during the Meeting of U. S. Church Leaders in Washington, D.C., in January, 1999; the keynote address to The Wesleyan Educational Conference at Indiana Wesleyan University in May, 1999; the Gardner C. Taylor

Lectures on Preaching delivered at Duke University Divinity School in October, 1999; the Howard Thurman Centennial Convocation Sermon delivered at Morehouse College in November, 1999; the William L. Self Lectures on Preaching delivered at McAfee School of Theology, Mercer University, in March, 2000; the B. Julian Smith Lectures at Phillips School of Theology of the Interdenominational Theological Center in January, 2001; and, among others, the Staley Lectures delivered at Carson-Newman College in November 2001.

My "Outback" library has been a place of retreat and renewal. Working in it since retirement, I have used my time there regularly and wisely. There I prepared for my classes at Beeson Divinity School, after accepting an adjunct professorship in divinity to teach an intensive course each January. In the "Outback" I prepared the lectures and class discussion outlines used when I met monthly in Birmingham across two years with the Northern District Church of God ministers. The teaching sessions were requested and arranged by Darrell Dawkins, pastor of the Northside Church of God and a practicing pediatrician in that city. There in "The Outback" I prepared baccalaureate and commencement addresses, and I was especially glad to be the baccalaureate speaker at the 1997 commencement weekend at Washington and Jefferson College, where my friend James Phillips, M.D., has long served on the Board of Trustees. I was also honored to be commencement speaker in 1999 at The Evangelical Covenant Church's North Park Theological Seminary, where my friend Everett Jackson was professor of pastoral care; he retired in 2000.

"The Outback" has been for me a place for contemplation, communion with God, and creativity. There I have done my solid reading, depth praying, thinking, and writing; there I have catalogued items from research, counseled with former students and other ministers, answered correspondence, and interceded in prayer for others. There in my beloved "Outback" I have spent time voicing a steady thanks to God for his goodness and guidance and there, for a time, I enjoyed the vigilant company of my dog, Indy, until her untimely death.

Our dog "Indy" came to us unsought and unexpected. She appeared in our yard from "out of nowhere," it seemed. I first noticed her on the morning after a night of heavy rains in our area; she emerged from the doghouse in our rear yard, a haven that had been vacant since our last family dog died. She was sniffing her way across the yard, as if on the scent of something. She might well have been trying to scent her own tracks so as to find the way back from wherever she had come the night before. Alas, the rains had removed the traces she sought! She tried again across the morning, but finally stopped her quest and sat down to rest. I watched the dog's demeanor that morning. She was a mixed breed, with evident elements from a German Shepherd line and those of a Beagle hound. There was a red collar around her neck, a sure sign of being owned. My watching made me notice a larger ring attached to that red collar, which made me suspect that the dog must have been part of a team for hunting. The dog's bearing bespoke some training, and I began to wonder from whence she had come and to whom she belonged.

The dog stayed all day. As evening approached, Gwendolyn and I discussed placing a bit of food at her disposal, not wanting to leave her hungry. We knew it was a gamble, aware that feeding a stray usually becomes an expected attention. But this dog did not disport herself like a stray, so we placed a bowl of milk out on the patio. In time, she came and lapped up the milk. The dog appeared in the yard the following morning, so I called the local veterinarian and reported her presence. I described the dog's features with some detail, giving sufficient information to match with any call he might receive from someone whose pet was missing. The veterinarian told me that no one had reported missing their dog, so I fed the dog a second time, and watched her actions across another day. We also searched the local newspaper for any notice about a missing dog that fit the description of our visitor. Seeing nothing across four days of reading

445

newspapers and hearing nothing from the local vet, we tried befriending the dog. Despite our gestures of regard in supplying some food, the dog was initially reluctant to let us approach her. She seemed not just reticent but also independent. Gwendolyn noticed that apparent trait of independence and amusingly referred to her as "Miss Indy," since she was acting like an independent female!

Within a week I had gained Indy's confidence, and she was, literally, eating out of my hand. Mindful of the collar about her neck, I slowly attached a strap to it, walked her to my car, and drove her to the veterinarian to have her inspected and treated. It had become clear to me that since we had not located her owners, we should continue giving her the responsible care she showed signs of having had before losing her way and finding our yard. The vet applauded our deed. In finding no name or number tag on the dog's collar, he told us we would need to supply her a name in order to register her for treatment. Gwen said, "We call her 'Indy'." Aware that we had just moved to Greensboro from Indiana, the vet said, "Ah yes! after the Indianapolis 500!" We said nothing about what we meant in calling her Indy!

The three of us bonded well, and the dog rather quickly understood herself as "Indy" when we addressed her. Indy, Gwendolyn, and I enjoyed the outdoors together, bounding as we walked the acreage, strolled the country roads, or roamed the woods. Like a strict sentinel, Indy patroled the property line, guarding the territory with jealous care. She stood on guard when we stepped out of the door each morning, alert to how she might be needed. She watched from a safe distance when I operated the riding mower and drew near when I otherwise tended the lawn. She seemed to understand human discourse, sometimes acting as if she had anticipated what we wanted on her part. She also seemed to understand those times of silence when having to sit alone while I worked at my desk in "The Outback."

Indy was our pride and joy across three years. During one of my trips to fulfill an engagement, Indy was injured while guarding our property line. While trying to inform a careless driver that he had left the public road and was on private property, she was the victim of a selfish deed. Gwendolyn telephoned the veterinarian; he came to the house, examined Indy's injury, and carried her to the hospital for treatment. It was a painful word that the vet gave when I returned home and asked about Indy's condition and prognosis. The vet offered us no hope for Indy's recovery; her injury was too severe for him to save her. She died.

Indy came to us "as one unknown," to borrow part of Albert Schweitzer's description of Another Visitor, but it was in Indy's company and by her servant spirit that Gwendolyn and I sensed the love of God in a fresh way. Indy had come to us only a few months after Gwendolyn's mother died, and the ministry of that dog to us helped to ease the pain of our understood bereavement. Intelligent, patient, vigilant, courageous in facing the unfamiliar, and always eager to serve, Indy shared with us a providential love and reminded us about the oneness of all life. When Indy died, "The Outback" and I no longer enjoyed any "dog days." The space on the library floor that she occupied, and the special rug crocheted and placed there for her use, were now vacant. When they learned of our loss, several friends advised me to get another dog. I answered those friends with a mild "Perhaps I will," then added a firm "but not yet!"

Not yet! I have thought long and often about what I call the "not yet!" element in life, particularly about its discrete operation in my own personal pilgrimage. The "not yet!" element is part of our experience of the mystery of life and the stages we undergo in the quest to understand the meaning of our journey. The "Not yet!" element is inevitable in every person's life since our journey involves segments of time, happenings, and stages of growth. There have been those happenings that were within my control, and I determined the timing of them through my choice and action. Some happenings in my life were subject to the will of other persons or contingent circumstances. Still other happenings were because of God's sovereign will and decisive control. I can remember times when I felt ready to preach on some biblical text because I had probed it for its meaning and I felt confident about its implications and about how to apply them to life and living; but I was held back from preaching on that text by an inward and insistent "Not yet!" that I sensed. I later realized that the "Not yet!" allowed a necessary delay, and when I finally preached from that text it was at a time and place where its use was more strategic, impacting, and necessary. It was my task to ready the sermon, which involved my choice and action, but the preaching and the preacher had to be readied by God, who knew the necessity and importance of that delay. As I have come to understand it, the "Not yet!" element at work in our life is part of the discreteness in God's plan to shape us in circumstances, discipline us by containment, enhance us by allowing choice, and lure us forward through anticipation.

I continue to value and depend upon a biblical perspective as I view life, experience its stages, confront its mysteries, order my ways, and make a mark in the fresh concrete of history. I have found the biblical perspective an asset to be prized. As I have looked at myself and thought about the mystery of being alive, standing in awe as a human being facing the world, I have often thought about those words of Frenchman Blaise Pascal (1623-1662) as found in number 205 of his *Pensees:*

> When I consider the short duration of my life, swallowed up in the eternity before and after, the little space which I fill and can even see, engulfed in the immensity of spaces of which I am ignorant and which know me not, I am frightened and am astonished at being here rather than there; for there is no reason why here rather than there, why now rather than then. Who has put me here? By whose order and direction have this place and time been allotted to me?

Pascal knew the answer from biblical faith, which steadied him for a passionate engagement with the world as a thinking self alert to responsibilities, alive to God, and humble before the mysteries of being and time.

In early childhood I too came to know that faith, and across the rest of my life that faith has informed, inspired, steadied, and sustained me. The meaning of that faith has blessed my will to serve and the scope of that faith has bolstered in me the courage to live, ready and eager to relate to persons, institutions, churches, and causes whose place and service in God's ordered universe I respect, and whose enriching fellowship I enjoy.

AFTERWORD

Until I reach my home,
Until I reach my home,
I never 'spect to give the journey over,
Until I reach my home.

The above words from a beloved Negro Spiritual bespeak the need for a settled commitment to fulfill the Christian pilgrimage. As for commitment, I have always been encouraged by Abraham's example. The writer of the Letter to the Hebrews tells us: "By faith Abraham obeyed when he was called to set out for a place that he was to receive as an inheritance; and he set out, not knowing where he was going" (11:8). This does not mean that Abraham lacked direction, but rather that in setting forth at God's call he would experience the new, the different, and the unfamiliar. His pilgrimage to gain Canaan would be a long and sometimes lonely journey into life, a journey with features and fatigue-points which would mark his body, burden his mind, tutor his spirit, and test his resolve. But Abraham set out, open to travel lanes of test, but also prepared to become heir to ascending levels of truth and the living rewards of trust.

The beckonings of God also came to me, inviting me to pilgrimage in the divine will. Like Abraham, I too have been on the way somewhere, not knowing the journey beforehand, but steadied by an assurance that God has been directing my steps. This is the meaning of pilgrimage for us all, and the demands of this unfinished journey keep exacting on our part an open ear, a steady step, and a resolved will. An open ear, a steady step, and a resolved will are the pilgrim's trinity for triumph, and they must remain well in place as we deal with the dust and grit of life's journey.

No human is ever privileged to understand in full the logic of his or her life, and whatever understanding one gains cannot be spoken with fullness. We humans cannot understand our individual paths except when flashes of light from God illumine

450

crucial points along the way. As I view my life, my years hang together bound by a central thread called guidance. My upbringing made me sensitive to this reality, my studies informed my thought about the meaning of this reality, and my experiences of moments of grace deepened my appreciation for this reality.

More than anything else, I have always wanted to be led into meaning, received into God's presence, and to be a servant whose life can help others experience that meaning and sense that presence. It is a sense of meaning and a sense of God's presence that bring a world of difference to our human condition. God is the one to satisfy our quest to know and understand as we journey, and God is the other to satisfy our need for companionship and guidance in the loneliness of our pilgrimage.

I have been steadied by the memory of certain days when a fresh beckoning came to me, and two of the earliest such days still stand out in my mind, as fresh to my consciousness as the present hour. I have told about that grand day, that Sunday when during worship I was beckoned to ministry. But there was also that grand day, the final day of a period of fasting when I heard that same Voice beckon again, promising aspects of meaning that became mine far later as I journeyed. I was still a teenager, a senior in high school. I had walked into a vacant classroom of Cass Technical High School, purposely alone, and seated myself to read in the Scriptures during my lunch hour. As I read, the Voice spoke! In a moment that was intensely real, that room became for me the center of the universe. The clarity of the message excited and exhausted me. As rich meanings gathered in my brain, I sensed the future unfolding. It was a mystic moment, a holy hour! On that day, in that room, in that way, I heard the Word and embraced the future, and ever afterward I would be undaunted by the human categories and constraints of race, region, or religious preferences. Because of received meanings and a sense of God's presence, life for me has been an unfolding drama, a joyful pilgrimage, a sequence of guided steps as I have remained surrendered to the lure of what was held before me. What I experienced then, and in holy moments since then, still lures and holds me now.

God calls us into pilgrimage in his will. The crucial response is to give God our full consent, granting him freedom to guide our lives. With our consent, God will take us from where we are to where we ought to go, shaping and using us by his wiser plan. Abraham did not choose the place from which he started in life, nor do we; but like Abraham, we too must choose the direction we will follow as we live. Abraham wisely trusted God, obeying as beckoned and directed. Following ever onward, he "stayed the course," and succeeding history keeps vindicating and validating his daring deed.

It is my intention to keep saying "Yes!" to God, whose wisdom shows the right way, whose strength helps us move with purpose, and whose direction keeps us assured. Having this, we need nothing more, while lacking this, any life is poor indeed.

> *Until I reach my home,*
> *Until I reach my home,*
> *I never 'spect to give the journey over,*
> *Until I reach my home.*

INDEX

SUBJECTS AND PERSONS

Miller, Adam W., 254
Miller, Beryl, 221
Miller, Randolph Crump, 278
Miller, T. Franklin, 153, 349
Miller, W. T., 221
millennialism, 304-305
Milner, James B., 439
Ministers and Gospel Workers
    Association, 150-151
Missionary Board of the
    Church of God, 204-208,
    213-214, 337
Mitchell, Harry B., 265
Mitchell, William P., 362
Mohler, R. Albert, Jr., 426
Montgomery Bus Boycott, 173
Mooneyham, Stanley, 237
Morehouse College, 48, 443
Morehouse Institute of
    Detroit, 24
Morgan, Clifton M., 113, 166
Morgan, Marcus H., 153, 155-
    156, 303
Morrison, John A., 251
Mouw, Richard, 426
Mozart, Wolfgang Amadeus,
    43, 94, 154, 426-428
Mozarteum, 91-95, 99, 428-429
Mullins Lectures on
    Preaching, 329, 382, 420
Muti, Riccardo, 428
Myra, Harold, 421
Myrick, Joseph, 295-296

National Association for the
    Advancement of Colored
    People, 168, 245
National Association of the
    Church of God, 11, 24, 54,
    67, 104, 121, 132, 137,148,
    165, 266, 434
National Association Youth
    Fellowship (Church of
    God), 383
National Religious
    Broadcasters, 346-347
National Youth Fellowship,
    64, 66
Nazareth, Israel, 155, 158-159
Nelson, Edward L., 433-434
Nelson, J. Robert, 197
New, Andrew and Rebecca, 332
Newberry, Gene W., 195, 252,
    289, 405
Newell, Arlo, 304, 325
Nicholson, Robert A., 251,
    253, 346, 357-358, 399-
    402, 407-409, 425, 441
Noffsinger, Donald A., 303
Nolan, Robert L., 47
North Central Association of
    Colleges and Schools, 418-
    419
North Park Theological
    Seminary, 444
Northwest Nazarene College,
    435
Northcutt Lectures, 382

Signatures, 406

Skinner, Tom, 270, 422

Small, Delores, 275

Small, John Arthur, 136, 275

Smith, Henry, 75, 126

Smith, John T., 113, 128

Smith, John W. V., 364

Smith, Kelly Miller, 342

Smith, Melvin, 419

Smith, Olivia, 152

Smith, Reginald George, 419

Smith, Rex, 331

Smith, Robert, 281-282

Smith, Robert, Jr., 420-421

Smith, Rudolph, 84, 358

Smith, Steele C., 228

Smith, Timothy L., 273

Smith, Tom A., 153

Smoot, J. D., 21, 32, 147

Snyder, James L., 295

South Meridian Church of God, 257-260, 265

Southern Baptist Theological Seminary, 329, 382, 397, 420, 443

Spaulding, Spencer, 433

speaking in tongues, 306

St. Johann, Austria, 89

Stanger, Frank Bateman, 143, 273-275

Steen, Leonard, 75, 79, 128, 365-366

Sterner, R. Eugene, 160, 301-302, 304, 320

Stewart, Carlyle Fielding, 174-175

Still, William Grant, 35

Strong, Marie, 257

Struthers, R. W., 163

Sundays in the Tuskegee Chapel, 440, 442

Swartley Lectures, 330

Sykes, George W., 296

Tannehill, Robert C., 202

Tarr, Charles, 257, 259, 265, 299

Tate, Dr. Joyce, 221

Taylor, Gardner C., 443

Taylor, Larry C., 439

Tefft, Edward, 95-97

Tenth Cavalry, 9-10

Terry, Louise Crosswhite, 122, 127

The Burdensome Joy of Preaching, 442

"The Miracle Book Club," 46, 206

The New Interpreters Bible, 423-424, 435, 443

"The Outback," 5, 442-444

The Potter's House, 185-186

The Responsible Pulpit (1974), 279

The Sermon in Perspective (1976), 201, 301

The Worshiping Church (1961), 168, 187